UNDELIVERED

UNDELIVERED

FROM THE
Great Postal Strike of 1970
to the Manufactured Crisis
OF THE
U.S. Postal Service

PHILIP F. RUBIO

THE UNIVERSITY OF NORTH CAROLINA PRESS

Chapel Hill

Designed by Jamison Cockerham
Set in Arno, Scala Sans, Cupboard, and DIN Next LT
by Tseng Information Systems, Inc.

Cover illustrations: Thomas Germano III, *The Great Postal Strike · 1970* (1995; oil on canvas, 58″ × 66″); title stamp typeface © istockphoto.com/Thomas Pajot.

Manufactured in the United States of America

The University of North Carolina Press has been a member
of the Green Press Initiative since 2003.

LIBRARY OF CONGRESS CATALOGING-IN-PUBLICATION DATA
Names: Rubio, Philip F., author.
Title: Undelivered : from the Great Postal Strike of 1970 to the
manufactured crisis of the U.S. Postal Service / Philip F. Rubio.
Description: Chapel Hill : University of North Carolina Press,
[2020] | Includes bibliographical references and index.
Identifiers: LCCN 2019052213 | ISBN 9781469655451 (cloth) |
ISBN 9781469655468 (paperback : alk. paper) | ISBN 9781469655475 (ebook)
Subjects: LCSH: United States Postal Service—Employees—History. |
National Association of Letter Carriers (U.S.)—History. | American Postal
Workers Union—History. | Postal service—Employees—Labor unions—
United States—History—20th century. | Postal service—Employees—Labor
unions—United States—History—21st century. | Postal Strike, U.S., 1970.
Classification: LCC HE6499 .R84 2020 | DDC 331.892/81383497309047—dc23
LC record available at https://lccn.loc.gov/2019052213

The appendix originally appeared as Thomas Germano, "The 1970 Postal
Strike: An Artist's Interpretation," *Labor's Heritage* 7, no. 4 (1996): 18–19.
Reprinted courtesy of AFL-CIO Collections. RG96-002 Photographic
Negatives, Charles Alexander Collection. George Meany Labor Archives,
Special Collections, University of Maryland Libraries, College Park.

For Paula

CONTENTS

FIGURES

ABBREVIATIONS
USED IN TEXT

AFL-CIO	American Federation of Labor-Congress of Industrial Organizations
AMF	Airport Mail Facility
APWU	American Postal Workers Union (1971–present)
BMC	Bulk Mail Center
CCA	City Carrier Assistant
CLUW	Coalition of Labor Union Women
CSC	Civil Service Commission
CSRS	Civil Service Retirement System
EEOC	Equal Employment Opportunity Commission
EPA	Equal Pay Act
GCSPO	Grand Central Station Post Office
GPO	General Post Office
LIUNA	Laborers International Union of North America
MBPU	Manhattan-Bronx Postal Union (NPU member)
MHA	Mail Handler Assistants
MPLSM	Multi-Position Letter Sorting Machine
NALC	National Association of Letter Carriers (1889–present)
NAPFE	National Alliance of Postal and Federal Employees (1965–present), formerly NAPE (National Alliance of Postal Employees, 1913–1965)
NAPOGSME	National Association of Post Office and General Services Maintenance Employees, 1947, merged into APWU in 1971
NARMC	National Association of Railway Mail Clerks (defunct)
NASDM	National Association of Special Delivery Messengers, merged into APWU in 1971

NASPOE	National Association of Substitute Post Office Employees (defunct)
NDC	Network Distribution Center
NFPOC	National Federation of Post Office Clerks (1899–1961), merged into UFPC in 1961, which merged into APWU in 1971
NFPOMVE	National Federation of Post Office Motor Vehicle Employees, 1939, merged into APWU in 1971
NPMHU	National Postal Mail Handlers Union (1912–present)
NPTA	National Postal Transport Association, merged into UFPC in 1961, which merged into APWU in 1971
NPU	National Postal Union (1960–1971), first called National Postal Clerks Union in 1959, merged into APWU in 1971
NRLCA	National Rural Letter Carriers Association (1903–present)
OCR	Optical Character Reader
P&DC	Processing and Distribution Center
PAEA	Postal Accountability and Enhancement Act, 2006
PRA	Postal Reorganization Act, 1970
PTF	Part Time Flexible
RMS	Railway Mail Service (1864–1977)
TE	Temporary Employee
UFPC	United Federation of Postal Clerks, (1961–1971), merged into APWU in 1971
UNAPOC	United National Association of Post Office Clerks (later Craftsmen), 1899, merged into UFPC in 1961, which merged into APWU in 1971
UPW	United Postal Workers, merged into UFPC in 1961, which merged into APWU in 1971
USPOD	United States Post Office Department (1775–1971)
USPS	United States Postal Service (1971–present)

UNDELIVERED

Introduction

It all started in New York. It was 12:01 A.M. on Wednesday, March 18, 1970, when a handful of letter carriers from the National Association of Letter Carriers (NALC) Branch 36 and two members of the Manhattan-Bronx Postal Union (MBPU) set up a picket line at the Grand Central Station Post Office (GCSPO) on Forty-Fifth Street and Lexington Avenue in the midtown borough of Manhattan in New York City. Less than two hours earlier, hundreds of Branch 36 members had left the Manhattan Center on West Thirty-Fourth Street, where they had just voted to strike until Congress granted them a pay raise. Branch 36 was the largest in the NALC at over 8,000 members from Manhattan and the Bronx.[1] Over at the General Post Office (GPO) on Thirty-Third Street, Branch 36 pickets were getting set at 5:00 A.M. while "officers and delegates [stewards] of MBPU were busily spreading the word of the strike among their members," according to Tom Germano, Branch 36 strike organizer at the GPO, a huge post office with 10,729 employees. "Focus was on Tour II which began with the carriers at 6:00 A.M. and a majority of clerks and mail handlers between 7:00–8:00 A.M."[2] Many of those clerks and mail handlers belonged to the MBPU, which at 26,000 members was by far the largest local in the 80,000-member independent, militant, industrial National Postal Union, and would itself soon vote to strike.[3]

This was a "wildcat strike," meaning it was unauthorized by the nine national postal unions. Those on strike for the next eight days could have been fired, fined, jailed, and had their unions decertified, because it was illegal to strike the federal government. Nonetheless, picket lines were spreading from New York into New Jersey, Massachusetts, Connecticut, Pennsylvania, Ohio, Illinois, Michigan, Wisconsin, Minnesota, Colorado, and California. Over 200,000 postal workers struck 671 post offices in dozens of cities and towns across the nation, including New York City, Albany, Buffalo, Boston, Worcester, Providence, Newark, Jersey City, Bridgeport, Hartford, New Haven, Philadelphia, Pittsburgh, Cleveland, Cincinnati, Toledo, Akron, Chicago, Milwaukee, Detroit, Grand Rapids, Minneapolis-St. Paul, Denver, San Francisco, and Los Angeles.[4] And when it was over no one was fired.

From a handful of pickets in New York City to a nationwide strike, this grassroots labor action was transformational. It effectively forced collective bargaining on the administration of President Richard M. Nixon even before he signed it into law as part of the Postal Reorganization Act (PRA) on August 12, 1970, at the headquarters of the U.S. Post Office Department (USPOD) in Washington, D.C., just a few blocks from the White House. Surrounded by politicians, postal officials, and postal union leaders, Nixon, who had blasted the strikers just five months before, praised the law that created the U.S. Postal Service (USPS) that as a government/corporate hybrid would replace the USPOD on July 1, 1971, and provide a 14 percent wage increase to postal workers. The USPS would collectively bargain with the postal unions without whom, Nixon said, "this reform could not have been accomplished. This is the American system working in a way that we all like to see it work, where we put the country above the party and where we put service to the people above any other interests." Nixon further foresaw "better operation of this department . . . better service . . . [and] better working conditions and better pay over the years for the hundreds of thousands of people who work very proudly for the Post Office Department here in Washington and across the country."[5] The new USPS, "an independent establishment of the executive branch," would be run by a nine-member Board of Governors (BOG), which would appoint a Postmaster General who in turn would appoint a Deputy Postmaster General—both of whom would serve on the BOG. Postal rates and mail classifications would be set by a five-member Postal Rate Commission (PRC, renamed the Postal Regulatory Commission in 2006). The president would appoint both BOG and PRC members.[6]

Forty-one years later, in the middle of 2011 contract negotiations with the NALC, USPS management suddenly "called upon Congress to eliminate the no-layoff provisions in union contracts to facilitate massive downsizing, and also to permit the Postal Service to unilaterally replace federal pension and health benefit programs with the Service's own programs," according to NALC historians M. Brady Mikusko and F. John Miller, writing in their book *Carriers in Common Cause*.[7] But the intimidation tactic did not work. Arbitration had been written into the PRA if contract talks ever were to fail, and this was one of those times. In 2013 a settlement was announced by a panel consisting of a mutually respected arbitrator along with one representative each from the USPS and the NALC.[8] That settlement also came four years into a huge postal financial crisis that to date has crippled the USPS with a $15 billion debt. How did the promise of a reorganized post office with collective bargaining, better working conditions, and improved service—all promised by a conservative, antiunion Republican President Nixon—now four decades later look so uncertain, with massive debt, widespread post office closings, service cutbacks, and a shrinking workforce, and all under a liberal pro-union Democratic President Barack Obama?[9] How was so much lost after so much had been won?

The best place to begin is by asking: how did that strike happen and win what it did, and why does it matter? Using archives, government documents, periodicals, oral history interviews, and key secondary sources, I argue that the 1970 postal wildcat strike was a groundbreaking, successful labor rebellion against the federal government and postal union leadership. Both organized and spontaneous, it was the product of an increasingly diverse workforce exploding after years of frustration and rising expectations. It was a strike that also helps us understand American and global rank-and-file militancy during that time as something rising, not falling—especially in the growing public sector (government). Postal labor was vital to the movement of mail, and postal workers were well-positioned to wildcat by virtue of being so thoroughly unionized yet forbidden by law to strike. Enjoying only partial collective-bargaining rights since 1962 and having to solicit Congress for raises and benefits was a frustrating process. But it also led to pre-strike public demonstrations that served as performative "civic lobbying" and strike dress rehearsal. The stage had already been set for upsurge with ·the 1960s spike in the hiring of blacks, women, veterans, and young people. Black postal workers, having led the long fight for equality in the post office and its unions, would play a key role in the 1970 strike. Further enabling the revolt were (1) rank-and-file union social networks; (2) the death of Jim Crow postal unionism; (3) the emergence of 1960s radical and antiracist postal labor trends; and (4) the failure of Cold War AFL-CIO bureaucratic unionism to dominate a lively postal labor landscape populated from 1962 to 1971 by nine competitive postal unions—three of them independent. The strike—both unique and representative of the times—revived the post office and empowered the postal unions. It provided the labor movement with a model of rank-and-file activism and union democracy. And the strike led to postal reorganization, which improved service and better regulated labor-management conflict. But by mandating financial autonomy along with universal service for this federal agency still under congressional oversight, the PRA also inadvertently paved the way for the 2009 USPS postal financial crisis. The principal cause of that crisis was a 2006 postal reform law that revised the 1970 PRA and included huge annual USPS payments over ten years to the U.S. Treasury for retiree health benefits far into the future.

The postal strike came in a decade of strikes. More than one-third of them were wildcats, "often repudiations of the union leadership, and, implicitly [against] the entire postwar system of industrial relations," as labor historian Cal Winslow puts it, noting a global labor upsurge as well.[10] This largest wildcat strike in American labor history was a protest against low wages and an authoritarian workplace that was not only highly unionized nationwide, but one that also frustrated their desires for representation and negotiation by providing them only partial collective bargaining rights along with the need to lobby Congress for wages and benefits. The strikers were led by New York City postal workers, who were the most organized and set the tone for nationwide acts of postal labor solidarity. It was a "leaderless movement" nationally that also had many leaders locally and regionally. Strikers returned to work after eight days, having made their point that the mail did not move without them and that their jobs deserved better compensation. They were desperate but also confident, and encouraged by what they and others around them had already won. The strike came at a time when unions in the United States were still politically strong despite a slow decline in workers belonging to unions—from 30.4 percent in 1962 to 28.5 percent in 1973. Wildcat strikes were common, especially in New York City, from 1965 to 1981, in what Winslow calls "the long seventies" and "the decade of the rank-and-file." Winslow finds 1970 to be one of the highest strike years in U.S. labor history—5,716 strikes by over 3 million workers. The rank-and-file impulse that drove the postal wildcat strike made it arguably the most successful of all of them.[11]

The 1970 postal wildcat strike also took place against a backdrop of public-sector union organizing and strikes after World War II. "Membership in public sector unions grew tenfold between 1955 and 1975," writes labor historian Joseph McCartin, "topping four million by the early 1970s. Moreover, newly organized workers behaved just as militantly as did auto and steel workers a generation earlier. In 1958 there were a mere 15 public sector strikes recorded in the United States; in 1975 the number hit 478."[12] This narrative is a far cry from popular imaginaries of the American labor movement declining and turning rightward, epitomized by the "hard-hat riot" on May 8, 1970, where angry white construction workers attacked young student anti–Vietnam War demonstrators in lower Manhattan in a riot with racial overtones—less than two months after the end of the nationwide postal strike that began and ended in the same city.[13] That strike resulted in postal workers becoming the only federal employees with full collective-bargaining rights under a reorganized USPS in 1971.

In addition to encouraging labor militancy elsewhere in the federal government, the strike elevated two postal unions—the NALC and the American Postal Workers Union (APWU, a merger of five postal unions)—to prominent roles in the AFL-CIO (American Federation of Labor and Congress of Industrial Organizations). After the strike and postal reorganization, job turnover dropped dramatically as the post office became a well-compensated, desirable career, thanks primarily to the enhancement of union power. The 1970 strike revitalized the postal unions even as they absorbed the strike's grassroots spirit. The strike also led to the passage of the 1970 PRA and the formation of the USPS. Nixon's words in August 1970 predicting postal progress in both service and labor-management relations were in some ways prophetic, as the USPS succeeded overall in providing more efficient universal service as a hybrid government agency/self-supporting corporation using no tax dollars. Labor relations often continued to be antagonistic, however, and automation challenged job security and satisfaction, while postal workers' standard of living improved, as did the diversity of the postal workforce.[14] The PRA itself was a compromise that replaced a government bureaucratic post office with a corporate-government bureaucratic postal service, as sociologist Vern Baxter points out. Its "essential purpose" was "the liberation of postal managers from extensive interagency oversight of daily postal affairs."[15] Understanding the roots of the 2009 USPS financial crisis requires a focus on postal labor and its historical conflicts with government, which entered a new phase with the 1970 strike.

Almost half a century after the strike and reorganization came the first serious challenge to the existence of a public post office in its 240-plus year history. All evidence suggests the 2009 postal financial crisis was politically manufactured but very real. Internet services and the 2008 Great Recession presented challenges to be sure. But the chief cause of the crisis was the 2006 Postal Accountability and Enhancement Act (PAEA), which required the USPS to pay on average $5.6 billion per year for ten years into a Retiree Health Benefits Fund (RHBF). The PAEA is the reason we are today even discussing a "postal financial crisis." The 1970 interest convergence of "POD appointees . . . monopoly sector business, and national political leaders" that created the USPS made it vulnerable decades later to a scenario where political manipulation, USPS managerial semiautonomy, and a corporate (as opposed to service) culture combined to create an unnecessary debt crisis. This in turn has opened the door to a new model that seeks to convert the

USPS from a service-business hybrid where labor is a partner, to a business where labor is powerless.[16]

WRITING ON LABOR AND THE POST OFFICE

This book is part of a small but growing scholarly literature on U.S. postal history that includes the following: Richard Kielbowicz, *News in the Mail*; David Henkin, *The Postal Age*; Richard John, *Spreading the News*; and Wayne E. Fuller, *The American Mail*. These are rich works explaining the rise of the early post office. Discussion of African Americans' struggles at the post office and the changes they brought have been provided by Eric Yellin's *Racism in the Nation's Service*; Paul Nehru Tennassee's *History of the National Alliance of Postal and Federal Employees*; A. L. Glenn's *History of the National Alliance of Postal Employees*; Henry McGee's *The Negro in the Chicago Post Office*; and my own *There's Always Work at the Post Office*. Three accessible recent popular histories of the post office to the present (with differing assessments of the post office's future) are Winifred Gallagher, *How the Post Office Created America*; Devin Leonard, *Neither Snow nor Rain*; and a lesser-known but well-researched book by Christopher Shaw, *Preserving the People's Post Office*. Gallagher and Shaw mention the strike in passing, while Leonard devotes a chapter to the strike that is "top-down" history. Vern Baxter, John Tierney, and Kathleen Conkey discuss the strike in their scholarly studies of labor-management relations in the late twentieth-century post office. By contrast, the two largest postal unions, the NALC and the APWU, have venerated the strike with articles in their respective monthly journals, on their websites and at conventions, as well as in their published institutional histories. M. Brady Mikusko and F. John Miller's *Carriers in a Common Cause* is a history of the NALC, while John Walsh and Garth Mangum's *Labor Struggle in the Post Office* chronicles the postal craft and industrial unions that came together in 1971 to form the APWU. There is brief mention of the strike in Lester F. Miller's history of the National Rural Letter Carriers' Association (NRLCA), which did not participate in the strike. No work to date has been published on the history of the National Postal Mail Handlers Union (NPMHU), and documents available on its website only mention it in passing.[17] The USPS Historian's Office mentions the strike in its comprehensive pamphlet *The United States Postal Service: An American History, 1775–2006*.[18]

Meanwhile, American labor historiography still focuses mainly on the private sector. Far fewer books have centered on public sector workers and their unique potential for organizing around community as well as workplace issues, such as *Public Workers* by Joseph Slater; *Black Workers Remember* by Michael Honey; *Success While Others Fail* by Paul Johnston; *Blackboard Unions* by Marjorie Murphy; *Upheaval in the Quiet Zone* by Leon Fink and Brian Greenberg; *Working-Class New York* by Joshua Freeman; and *Collision Course* by Joseph McCartin—his classic study of the failed 1981 strike by the Professional Air Traffic Controllers Organization (PATCO). *Solidarity Divided* by Bill Fletcher Jr. and Fernando Gapasin considers both public and private sector union activity, as well as struggles within and between labor federations. The decade of the 1970 postal strike was, as labor historian Lane Windham puts it, "far from the 'last days of the working-class,'" as labor historian Jefferson Cowie has suggested. "Rather," she writes in *Knocking on Labor's Door*, "these were the first days of a reshaped and newly-energized American working class."[19] Windham's book challenges the notion of labor's decline in her study of private-sector union organizing that was blocked by "increased employer resistance."[20] On the other hand, Fletcher and Gapasin in *Solidarity Divided* remind us of the role played by "internal union repression" in the overall decline of 1970s reform movements and the need for organizational reforms today to survive "privatization and the systematic elimination of the public sphere."[21]

Why has the 1970 postal strike seen such sparse scholarly treatment, especially given that it was a *national* wildcat strike in a vital communications sector?[22] Tom Germano, in his doctoral dissertation, has provided us with the best account to date of the strike, its background, and its meaning—all from a unique vantage point. Germano was a Branch 36 rank-and-file leader and a GPO strike captain on the first day of the strike. He aptly termed his writing "detached compassion"—seeking an objective way of discussing events and people with whom he was deeply engaged. His work, which greatly influences mine, is a historically informed sociological study focusing on strike activity at its New York City flashpoint and ending in 1983. This book includes background history as well but is more national in scope in chronicling and analyzing the 1970 strike and its aftermath. I also had the benefit of time in being able to extend the study of the strike's rank-and-file activist legacy past 1983 into 2019. That period saw the development of the APWU and NALC into stronger, more democratic, and more socially conscious unions contesting privatization and antiunion initiatives that have challenged what Germano calls the "institutionalized conflict" framework established by the PRA.[23] Another fine discussion of the strike appears in a section of Aaron Brenner's 1996 doctoral dissertation, part of which was later revised into an academic journal article.[24] My 2010 book *There's Always Work at the Post Office* includes a chapter on the strike.[25] But there is little else written by academics on the strike, or for that matter on postal workers and postal unions.[26]

Despite scant media and scholarly references to the strike, participant narratives, combined with accessible archival evidence, make a case for why it was such an important event in labor history. It may not have had the same impact on the labor movement as did the iconic Flint Sit-Down Strike of 1936–37, during which about 2,000 General Motors workers in that Michigan city occupied their plant for 44 days as they fought for control of the work process, won union recognition for the United Automobile Workers, and advanced the cause of industrial unions as a vital part of the American labor movement.[27] Yet the 1970 postal strike, as a grassroots uprising, marked a different kind of labor ascendancy in a different time—when wildcat strikes represented labor revolts against management and union leaders in manufacturing; when public workers were lobbying or striking for representation and workplace rights; and when militant protests were at their height in freedom movements by people of color, the women's movement, and the antiwar movement. Why do we tend to lionize 1930s strikes, ignore postwar labor struggles, and mourn the post-1960s "declension" of the labor movement? New Deal–era organized labor was bold and exciting but certainly not without its contradictions. The American Federation of Labor (AFL), one-quarter of which then either excluded or segregated black workers, in 1937 expelled the rank-and-file-oriented Committee of Industrial Organizations, which in 1938 became the Congress of Industrial Organizations (CIO). During the "Second Red Scare" in the United States, the CIO purged eleven so-called communist unions (about one-third of its membership) between 1949 and 1950 before reuniting with the AFL in 1955 at a time when about one-third of American workers belonged to a union—the high-water mark of unionization in the United States. During these imagined glory days of organized labor—when unionists in fact did make many sacrifices and win many gains—a long battle also had to be waged against Jim Crow unionism while "business unionism" was undermining union democracy. There was also no end to battles with antiunion forces, as the 1947 Taft-Hartley Act and organized union-busting began chiseling away at the 1935 Wagner Act that had empowered unions. As part of a conservative pushback, Taft-Hartley banned "closed shops" (employees must join the union before being hired); allowed states to pass "right-to-work" laws banning "union shops" (employees must join the union after being hired); placed limits on the right to strike; and required union officers to sign affidavits swearing they were not communists. Manufacturing jobs moving south, offshore, or into automation, fed the decline of private sector industrial unions after the 1960s. Public and service sector unions have risen since then, however; people of color and women have been winning leadership roles in trade unions; and rank-and-file uprisings have challenged control of both the workplace and the union hall.[28]

In recent years it has been the NALC and APWU, as well as the AFL-CIO labor federation to which they both belong, who have most prominently referred to the 1970 wildcat as "The Great Postal Strike."[29] What made it "great"? This book explores why it was not just one signature event but rather a lingering legacy with a promise of possibilities. Chapter 1 provides a background for the strike, from the first postal unions after the Civil War and their relationship with the federal government to the early 1960s and partial collective-bargaining rights under Democratic President John F. Kennedy's Executive Order 10988. Chapter 2 looks at the low pay and poor working conditions in the late 1960s and the upsurge of rank-and-file postal worker reform campaigns against what they called "collective begging" of Congress. It also charts the growing postal worker anger at Congress, President Richard Nixon, and their own national union leaders, as militant rank-and-file organizing in New York led up to the March 18, 1970, strike. Chapter 3 chronicles the first five days of the strike, spreading from New York City to postal union branches and locals across the nation, as almost one-third of the workforce walked off the job. Chapter 4 follows the last three days of the strike, from President Nixon's dramatic intervention on March 23, when he sent thousands of troops to New York City to try to move the mail and break the strike. Chapter 5 charts the rocky aftermath of the strike with threats of more strikes, arguments within and among the unions, and the making of the 1970 PRA as a labor-government compromise and interest convergence. Chapter 6 covers the first decade of the USPS. During the 1970s, postal unions made use of collective bargaining rights to win higher pay and increased benefits, while at the same time there were constant conflicts with postal management and within the unions on issues of democracy and militancy. Chapter 7 studies how antagonistic labor-management contract negotiations almost ended with a called strike in the first year of President Ronald Reagan's administration (1981–1989) — a strike averted by an arbitration mechanism built into the PRA. This chapter also charts the effects of automation on the workforce in the late twentieth century. Chapter 8 examines the privatization impulse, the devastation done by the 2006 Postal Accountability and Enhancement Act (PAEA) leading to the 2009 financial crisis of the USPS, and the response by postal unions and the public to crisis-based cutbacks.

Postal Workers and the
Rise of Collective Bargaining

"The reason we went on strike is because we just couldn't live in New York City with the amount of money we made as a postal employee. Everybody had two or three jobs." That was how letter carrier Frank Orapello remembered what sparked the 1970 postal wildcat strike that began in his city and quickly spread across the nation.[1] There had been no postal raises from 1925 to 1943. The five raises won from 1943 to 1953 were because of postal unions successfully lobbying Congress. Republican President Dwight D. Eisenhower vetoed four of five postal pay bills from 1953 to 1961. The 1962 Salary Reform Act signed by President John F. Kennedy declared that postal and other federal employees should earn wages comparable to similar jobs in the private sector. After Kennedy's assassination in November 1963, Democratic President Lyndon B. Johnson, along with Congress, would bitterly disappoint postal workers by ignoring the government's own wage schedules and enact minimal raises that made them slip farther behind. President Nixon would do the same in 1969 and early 1970. An annual starting postal salary by 1970 was $6,176, compared to sanitation workers in New York City making $7,870, police and firefighters ($9,499), and transport workers ($10,000). By 1967 the turnover rate at the post office had reached 26 percent. "The Post Office in the late 1960s was in a crisis," writes labor historian Aaron Brenner, as mail volume increased by one-third in the 1960s while "the cost of handling all that mail doubled. . . . [B]y 1969 its deficit was draining more than $1 billion a year from the national treasury . . . [as] service deteriorated."[2] Working conditions were also appalling, with sociologist Vern Baxter referring to the postwar post office as "an authoritarian bureaucracy that lacked the legitimacy to effectively manage conflict in the workplace." Postal workers looked to their unions to fight for them, but the possibilities were limited by federal law, including a ban on federal employee strikes.[3]

Postal workers had union representation starting at the turn of the century, but not in the way that unions represented workers in the private sector. There were no negotiations with management over three-year contracts — not even a binding formal grievance or arbitration process. In fact, prior to Kennedy's January 17, 1962, Executive Order (EO) 10988, which granted partial collective-bargaining rights to federal labor unions (as long as they did not discriminate or segregate on the basis of race), postal and other federal unions were forced to engage in what they often bitterly referred to as "collective begging." That meant their "bargaining power" consisted of lobbying Congress for wage, benefit, and working condition improvements.[4] That "begging not bargaining" format had also failed to dislodge a long-standing authoritarian workplace atmosphere, which both embarrassed and concerned members of Congress. In the Senate in the early 1960s, words like "despotism" and "Victorian" were commonly used by postal reform supporters to describe postal working conditions.[5] And while Kennedy's EO 10988 was widely considered a progressive remedy, it actually preempted the Rhodes-Johnston bill that was still being debated in congressional committee. That bill, had it been enacted into law, would have provided greater collective bargaining rights to unionized federal employees while containing weaker language on racial segregation and discrimination in unions. Ultimately, EO 10988 would furnish fewer collective bargaining rights to postal unions than they would win in 1970 with the Postal Reorganization Act PRA.[6] Joseph McCartin observes that Rhodes-Johnston would have been a tremendous breakthrough for federal unions in terms of recognizing their right to organize, negotiate on terms of employment with government agencies (even if Congress still held the purse strings on wages), and be able to submit grievances to an impartial board.[7] But McCartin also notes that this bill had no chance of passage in the Eisenhower administration (1953–1961), and that labor unions and their advocates were subsequently dismayed to see his successor President Kennedy (1961–1963) undermine this stronger labor bill with the weaker EO 10988 — apparently fearing the potential bargaining power of federal unions, as had Eisenhower. There was an important unintended consequence of the weaker executive order compared to the proposed legislation. EO 10988 enabled government-employee unions to compete both for national and local recognition at varying levels, based upon secret ballot votes by, in this case, postal workers. While a frustrating half-measure for postal unions, it also represented a major break with long-standing public policy. The way that postal unions even got to this point was by way of a long and rather convoluted process that began during the Civil

War, with the first postal worker associations to protect the rights of those engaged in this ever-expanding universal service.

Both the United States and its post office were born in the American Revolutionary War with Great Britain. The first U.S. postal employees were postmasters, beginning with Benjamin Franklin, the first postmaster general, in 1775.[8] Historian Richard John notes that the early post office was an "agent of change" for the new republic with the 1792 Post Office Act that spurred "a communications revolution" by mandating universal postal service.[9] Along those same lines, historian Jeffrey Brodie has written that in contrast with the eighteenth-century British Post Office with its emphasis on earning revenue for the treasury, "the primary function of the new Post Office in America was to serve as a political and information network for the new nation."[10]

Article I, Section VIII, of the 1789 U.S. Constitution gave Congress the power "to establish Post Offices and post Roads." Congress also passed a series of temporary postal laws starting in 1782 with a federal mail monopoly and concluding with the significant Post Office Act of 1792 that established the USPOD, allowed cheap rates for newspapers, established mail privacy, and authorized Congress to provide new mail routes to serve the whole country. The Post Office Act of 1794 established a permanent post office and announced a new labor category with minimal wages. It proclaimed "that letter carriers shall be employed at such post-offices as the Postmaster General shall direct, for the delivery of letters in the places, respectively, where such post-offices are established; and for the delivery of each such letter, the letter carrier may receive of the person to whom the delivery is made, two cents."[11] By 1828 the post office was the largest employer in the federal government, with almost 30,000 workers. By 1831 it accounted for three-quarters of all federal civilian employees. Their hiring and firing was based on partisan patronage beginning in 1829 with President Andrew Jackson's "spoils system." Most postal employees were postmasters, who outnumbered soldiers. In 1816, there had been 3,341 postmasters, 69.1 percent of the federal workforce, and by 1841, they accounted for 79.2 percent. Richard John points out that by 1840, to move 41 million letters and 39 million newspapers throughout the twenty-six United States required a "sophisticated division of labor" that featured three administrative levels: senior clerks at postal headquarters, postmasters at the mail distribution centers, and postmasters at the branch offices.[12] Eventually post riders and stagecoach drivers would give way to railroad and steamship transportation as the main mover of the nation's mail in the nineteenth century.[13]

Prior to the Civil War, postal patrons had to collect their mail at their local post office. By the early 1860s, as mail volume grew, and types of mail became more diverse and required more processing, postal clerks and postmasters far outnumbered carriers. In the winter of 1862–63, a Cleveland, Ohio, clerk/assistant postmaster named Joseph William Briggs was dismayed at lines backed up around the block—largely of families of soldiers waiting to see if there was mail from a loved one in the U.S. Army or Navy engaged in fighting the Confederate proslavery rebellion. Briggs marked the routes, had clerks sort mail at local grocery stories, and then carriers delivered the mail directly to residences.[14] Coincidentally, postmaster general Montgomery Blair's 1862 *Annual Report* had already proposed to President Abraham Lincoln the inauguration of free city delivery by letter carriers who would be paid their own salary rather than the much smaller postage-due fees, using the example of England to show how service and revenue would increase with regular delivery to homes and businesses. Congress followed up on March 3, 1863, by passing a landmark postal act, signed by Lincoln soon after, to be effective on July 1, 1863, that provided for free city delivery, Monday through Saturday, "as frequent as the public convenience . . . shall require," and other reforms including the establishment of branch post offices and mail collection boxes on the street. Besides Cleveland, that year 449 carriers delivered mail door-to-door in the U.S., including 137 in New York City alone. Blair invited Briggs to postal headquarters in Washington, D.C., the following year to supervise the new letter carrier system, which for the first time provided a salary of up to $800 a year, with the potential for performance-based raises to increase that salary to $1,000 per year. Briggs later even helped design the letter-carrier uniform. The number of participating free-delivery cities was 65 in 1864 with 685 carriers, rising to 104 cities and 2,628 carriers in 1880, and 796 cities and 15,322 carriers in 1900. Most cities saw multiple daily deliveries, especially to businesses. New York City led the nation by 1905 with nine daily deliveries from its main post office.[15]

LABOR AND POLITICS IN THE FIRST POSTAL UNIONS

What was behind the formation of postal unions? It was not just the desire for representation in winning better wages and benefits. According to Vern Baxter, it was in large part a response to "despotic management and political patronage," which also led to the creation of clerk and carrier crafts.[16] Postal workers first started their own unions during the Civil War with letter-carrier associations in New York City in 1863 — the same year that saw the beginning of daily home delivery along with branch post offices and mail collection boxes on the street in forty-nine American cities. Following the Civil War, many postal workers joined the Knights of Labor. It was no accident that the rise of the modern postal unions emerged from the Grand Army of the Republic's (GAR) annual gatherings of Union army veterans, which led to the first of today's major postal unions, the National Association of Letter Carriers (NALC). Union army service was embedded in the formation of this first national postal union to include African Americans as members and officers. The NALC's 1889 founding convention in Milwaukee grew out of the GAR encampment in that city, as NALC organizers who were also GAR members saw this as a practical way of saving expenses for members attending this inaugural meeting. Letter carriers in New York City later tried to bring the NALC into the Knights of Labor, but the latter was already in decline.[17] The GAR's evolution into a powerful political lobby and fraternal order became a model for the NALC and the other postal unions.[18]

NALC branches with low numbers reflect the first fifty-eight branches at their first annual convention in Boston in 1890. These fifty-eight were spread out across the north and west and in most cases were probably dominated by Union army veterans, such as Branch 1 in Detroit; Branch 2 in Milwaukee; Branch 5 in Omaha; Branch 11 in Chicago; Branch 18 in New Bedford; Branch 36 in New York City; Branch 40 in Cleveland; Branch 38 in Newark; and Branch 47 in Denver. Notably, also in many early branches — which included black members — were southern- and border-state branches like Branch 27 in Memphis; Branch 33 in New Orleans; Branch 52 in Jacksonville; Branch 94 in Vicksburg; Branch 217 in Jackson; Branch 14 in Louisville; and Branch 142 in Washington, D.C. With a wave of new member cities the NALC totaled 333 branches by 1892.[19]

Another sea change for both service and postal work came during the Civil War with the explosive growth of railroads, which for the post office meant the fastest, most accessible transportation network yet. It was a technology far advanced over stagecoaches and steamboats, and which had been steadily advancing for the previous two decades. A new postal division was added in 1864: the Railway Mail Service (RMS), where clerks sorted mail as trains were moving, while also picking up and dropping off mail sacks at stations they passed.[20] The RMS, writes Vern Baxter, also became a springboard for the advertising and publishing industries.[21]

Two letter carriers, ca. 1890, loaded down with mail. Free city mail delivery in the United States began in 1863. In 1889 the first national union was formed to represent postal workers: the National Association of Letter Carriers (NALC). Courtesy of NALC.

For African Americans in the South, the railway mail-clerk position was an especially appealing job that allowed them to travel outside the South, where they were less likely to be hired as postal clerks. There was also competition with whites for the best "runs" or railroad routes, with management favoring whites. When the job became less dangerous with the replacement of wooden with steel railroad cars in the early 1900s, more whites displaced blacks from railway clerk jobs.[22] Congress had first barred blacks from moving the mail in an 1802 law governing "Public law and Post-Roads" with a clause that proclaimed that "no other than a free white person shall be employed in carrying the mail of the United States," making whites who violated that law subject to a fifty dollar fine. White officials feared that blacks would be inspired by the Haitian slave revolution and use their position to organize rebellions themselves.[23] African Americans began to make the post office a "niche" job as soon as it became legal for them to work there in March 1865 as the Civil War was ending. Republican Party patronage, especially in the South, propelled mostly black men—and some black women as well—into positions as letter carriers, clerks, laborers, and local postmasters.[24] Some of the first black postal workers were abolitionists and Union army veterans, probably most of them working as postmasters.[25]

With the end of the Civil War came expansion of the post office and postal jobs. European immigrants, military veterans, and African Americans in particular secured appointments to postal "crafts" (occupations) and supervisory positions through Republican Party patronage. Blacks were hired as carriers, clerks, and laborers (mail handlers) in the 1860s and 1870s, especially in the South. They continued to receive those appointments after the 1883 passage of the Civil Service Reform Act (also known as the Pendleton Act) made hiring contingent upon scoring high marks on Civil Service exams. Even with the 1877 fall of Reconstruction, African Americans were still managing to be appointed as postmasters in the South, although they were also subject to harassment, threats, and lynching by white mobs.[26]

In the era before government employee unions, there was strong white opposition to black membership within private-sector unions. When the National Labor Union formed in 1866, white member unions suggested blacks form their own federation. That kind of treatment led to the formation of the Colored National Labor Union in 1869, although both collapsed in the early 1870s. The Knights of Labor, which included postal unions, formed in 1869 and welcomed blacks, women, and integrated unions.[27] In 1874 railway mail clerks formed the Railway Mail Mutual Benefit Association to provide low-cost life insurance as well as to lobby for better wages and working conditions. And postal clerks in Louisville, Kentucky, established the first known clerks' union in 1884, which became the forerunner of the National Federation of Post Office Clerks (NFPOC).[28] It is not known if African Americans were charter members of the NFPOC, but they were included among the first members of a rival clerks' union, the National Association of Post Office Clerks (NAPOC). The NAPOC began with a New York local in 1888 and became a national organization in 1890. Unlike the story of the NALC, the formation of competing clerk unions makes for a complicated read. The Railway Mail Association (RMA), freshly renamed in 1904, then changed its name in 1949 to the National Postal Transport Association (NPTA) and was absorbed into the United Federation of Postal Clerks (UFPC) along with the NFPOC in 1961. The United National Association of Post Office Craftsmen (UNAPOC) was regarded by rivals as a "company union." It merged — first with NAPOC in 1891, then in 1961 with NFPOC and the NPTA. Vern Baxter observes that during this time the federal labor movement was split among three tendencies: conservative groups like NAPOC that avoided management confrontation, "moderate" AFL-oriented trade unions like the NALC, and radical activists who identified with organizations like the Industrial Workers of the World (IWW).[29]

The 1883 Civil Service Reform Act establishing the Civil Service Administration was an improvement over the previous "spoils system" of party patronage established in 1829 by President Andrew Jackson, which had resulted in frequent turnover and thus diminished quality in postal service. Appointments to postal crafts (in addition to other federal government jobs) began to be replaced in 1883 with merit examinations. Those Civil Service applicants scoring high on the exam still faced rejection by the "rule of three" that allowed personnel officers to pick one of three applicants from each batch of applications for a Civil Service position. The "rule of three" (first known as the "rule of four" from 1883 to 1888) was meant to "offer some discretion for the appointing officer," according to historian Paul P. Van Riper.[30] In particular, even African Americans who scored high on the exam often found themselves removed from consideration by white officers.[31]

The Railway Mail Association was originally open to all railway mail employees. But in 1911, a majority of white members voted to amend the union's constitution and exclude blacks under Article III of the constitution. Whites also began driving many blacks from coveted railway mail jobs.[32] Subsequently, a group of African American railway mail clerks met in 1913 in Chattanooga, Tennessee, to form the National Alliance of Postal Employees (NAPE). In 1923 the NAPE welcomed postal employees of all crafts.[33] The

Postal clerks in 1890 big city main post offices hand-sorted and processed thousands of pieces of mail every day before mail processing machines came along. And African Americans, first allowed to work at the post office in 1865, often found more positions there than in the private sector, which typically discriminated against them. The first postal clerk unions were also formed at the turn of the century. Courtesy of the National Postal Museum, Smithsonian Institution.

NAPE had its first chapters in the South, where most African American railway mail service workers lived. Its origins were in a group calling itself the Colored Railway Postal Clerks in Houston — a site of significant black industrial union and civil rights organizing. The NAPE's origins narrative included founders from the nine Southern and four Midwestern delegations comprising what they called the "thirteen original colonies."[34] This was a unique and independent black labor organization led by college-educated intellectuals. Politically to the left of most of the predominantly white organized labor movement, they embodied Progressive-era, middle-class, black uplift ideology.[35] Belonging to the NAPE also gave black activists an opportunity to fight for both civil rights and labor rights.[36] Many NAPE members also belonged to one of the craft unions, especially the NALC, since blacks were more likely to be employed as letter carriers than as clerks in the South.[37] Black postal union activists were often also civil rights activists.[38] The Mississippi NAACP leadership from the 1930s to the 1960s included black postal unionists like attorneys Carsie Hall and Jack Young. Willenham Castilla was an African American NAACP activist who simultaneously belonged to the

Jackson NAPE branch and NALC Branch 217. Castilla recalls that this kind of dual union membership was common for blacks who wanted both craft and civil rights representation, who even exercised some post-Reconstruction power in the South during the early Jim Crow era. Castilla has this to say about Mississippi in particular and the South in general: "There was an unspoken 'gentlemen's agreement' during the early '30s. The whites would work inside [as clerks], blacks would work outside [as carriers] . . . I guess they felt a certain superiority working inside . . . But when times got tough they disregarded that . . . agreement, and the whites were working inside *and* outside."[39]

According to Castilla, even though whites controlled the eastern half of the state, blacks ran the NALC Mississippi Association based in western Mississippi towns like Jackson, Natchez, Vicksburg, and Yazoo City. Black Mississippi postal workers were what he called "the backbone" of the NAACP, in part because "the local [postal officials] couldn't fire them so easily."[40] Jim Crow–segregated union branches and locals in the South were typical of organized labor at the time and represented deference to white southern racism. Black postal unionists fought against separate branches and locals throughout the twentieth century, while at the same time often belonging to them, even with dual membership in the NAPE. While the NFPOC monthly journal did not acknowledge the existence of separate locals until World War II, it is likely they were there from the start.[41] In the NALC, there were probably segregated southern branches from the beginning. But the work of black protestors along with white allies led to the 1919 abolition of segregated branches (called "dual charters"), which had been formally recognized in 1917.[42] Ironically, 1917 had been the same convention where the NALC voted to affiliate with the AFL—ratified by membership referendum in 1918. This was a dramatic turnaround from the 1914 NALC referendum that had overwhelmingly rejected it—likely from government gag order intimidation.[43] After the 1919 vote, black members, mostly from the South, acted as a progressive conscience at those conventions, holding the line against recognizing segregated branches, only to see them reinstated from 1941 to 1962 after a white southern resurgence. Black members actually exerted sizable power in the state NALC organizations from Deep South states like Louisiana, Mississippi, and Florida, and Upper South states like Tennessee and Virginia.[44]

Meanwhile the composition of the postal workforce by craft was changing. Out of 229,435 postal workers in 1892, 111,875 were clerks, about 49 percent, compared to 10,892 letter carriers, a complete turnaround from half a century before when carriers far outnumbered clerks (this clerk total does not include 6,440 RMS clerks). There were now also 67,368 postmasters, or just under 30 percent of the total workforce, having also been surpassed by clerks. The "clerk" category also apparently included "laborers" who by 1944 would be called mail handlers—those who load, unload, and move mail around post office buildings to work areas of "distribution clerks" who over the years have sorted the mail for carriers to deliver. According to Jennifer Lynch, USPS historian, "in the *Official Register*, 'laborer' didn't seem to be broken out until 1907—previously the laborers were 'clerks.'"[45]

Another major postal service reform—rural delivery routes in 1896—resulted in the birth of a union to represent those carriers in 1903: the NRLCA. Its first convention was held in Chicago, Illinois, with twelve state associations representing about 16,000 carriers; many of them were part-time, with main occupations in other work, such as farming. The service itself had been established by Congress after years of lobbying by rural advocacy organizations and individuals associated with the National Grange and Farmers Alliance in the West and the South. Rural Free Delivery (RFD) was first established in Charleston, West Virginia, in 1896, growing to 35,666 rural routes in 1906.[46] The RFD's origins represent an interest convergence between rural advocates and service-minded postmaster general John Wanamaker (1889–1893), referred to by the USPS Office of the Historian in their 2006 history as "one of the most innovative and energetic people ever to lead the Post Office Department," combining "business logic and social philosophy as reasons to give rural dwellers free delivery." The logic of Wanamaker's project kept prevailing even over Postmaster General Albert Burleson's 1914 proposal to convert the Rural Service into a contract service—a privatization measure meant to save money.[47]

Professor of communications Richard Kielbowicz and historians Richard John and David Henkin have reminded us that postal services available today have a history not only in constitutional and congressional mandates but also popular demand, institutional innovation, and private-sector failures in providing those services. For example, household-to-household mail flourished with cheap postage in 1840s America, in which newspapers had been the main item in the mail stream.[48] The early twentieth century saw a growing demand for creating a package service with low costs, uniform rates, and delivery anywhere. Parcel Post began as an act of Congress in 1912 to remedy the void left by private carriers in this field. Four years later, the Postal Savings Bank was launched to meet the needs of those who needed convenience as well as security, especially after the national banking panic of 1907, when many banks went under.[49] During the 1910s, the post office and its workforce were still expanding. By World War I there were a dozen postal employee associations, including those for postmasters and supervisors. Supervisors were allowed into some of the early postal craft associations. Unable to collectively bargain for wages, benefits, or working conditions, associations nonetheless became important lobbying and mutual benefit organizations. Even their right to lobby Congress over terms of work was subject to debate and at times repressed in the early twentieth century.[50]

By removing previous presidential gag orders imposed on postal workers not to petition Congress with their grievances, the 1912 Lloyd–La Follette Act also enabled postal workers to organize and represent workers, although they could still not strike. The Lloyd–La Follette Act was a Progressive-era reaction to protests by railway mail workers against speedup of work after routes were combined and crews were cut.[51] It accompanied two other relevant labor laws passed that year. The first protected the rights of postal workers from being forced to work continuously on a "stop-and-go" basis (the Reilly Eight-in-Ten Hour Act), and the second mandated one day off per week (the Mann Sunday Closing Act). Specifically, the Lloyd–La Follette Act struck down the notorious executive gag orders of Theodore Roosevelt (EO 163 in 1902; and EO 402 in 1906) and Howard Taft (EO 1142 in 1909) that prevented federal employees from speaking out about job conditions or appealing for legislation to improve them. The Lloyd–La Follette Act also gave federal employees the right to form unions to represent them in disputes with management—but denied them the right to strike.[52]

President Woodrow Wilson's administration (1913–1921), if hostile to the interests of postal labor generally, was devastating to those of black postal workers. Wilson, a Southern Democrat, brought into his administration avowed white supremacists like North Carolina newspaper publisher Josephus Daniels (whom Wilson appointed Secretary of the Navy), Secretary of the Treasury William McAddo, and Postmaster General Albert S. Burleson of Texas. On April 11, 1913, with no objection from Wilson during a secret Cabinet meeting, Burleson ordered the separation of blacks from whites in the Washington, D.C., post office.[53] Wilson and Burleson were also responding to white popular demand for a segregated federal service by a group calling itself the National Democratic Fair Play Association that decried integration as "UnDemocratic, UnAmerican, and UnChristian." At a secret 1913 cabinet meeting Postmaster General Burleson announced he was segregating the post office. In 1914 the Civil Service Commission, with Wilson's support, began requiring photographs with civil-service job applications to prevent "impersonation." The real purpose was to exclude African

Postal Workers and the Rise of Collective Bargaining

American applicants, even as blacks were also being purged outright from the post office.[54]

Burleson also saw postal unions as an obstacle to keeping labor costs low, believing that the "postal establishment should be self-supporting . . . to equalize postal revenues and expenditures in so far as it is possible to do so. . . . [T]he controlling purpose of this administration has been to promote efficiency by the complete standardization of the service."[55] That excerpt came from Burleson's 1919 *Annual Report of the Postmaster General* where, among other things, he hailed the postal surplus of about $2.3 million.[56] Burleson's rhetoric embodied two dominant Progressive-era mainstays: labor efficiency and racial segregation. This was the era of "scientific management," whose goal was to increase worker productivity in private industry. In the post office it was applied to letter carriers especially. Burleson favored the repeal of the Lloyd–La Follette Act because it "is construed to permit the affiliation of postal employees with labor organizations which sanction recourse to the strike or boycott to enforce their demands. . . . They are fast becoming a menace to public welfare and should no longer be tolerated or condoned."[57] His antiunion screed was reprinted in the January 1920 issue of the NALC's *Postal Record*, along with a front-page rebuttal by NALC president Edward J. Gainor, who asked rhetorically: "Shall a postal surplus be achieved at the expense of inadequate service or underpaid postal employees?"[58] Gainor defended the right to organize as a "right which at once is an asset to the service and society and will not be lightly relinquished. . . . It is quite plain that, with the record of the past seven years in mind, postal employees cannot afford to trust their welfare to the caprice of chance or rest their hopes alone in paternalistic authority."[59] Gainor's response came during a time when the NALC was growing but was under attack by the USPOD. Confrontations with postal management were standard operating procedure even without collective bargaining rights.[60]

Since its 1828 founding, the Democratic Party had been home to labor unions, while the turn-of-the-century fraternal organizations like the Grand Army of the Republic that gave rise to the NALC were historically Republican. A glance at invited speakers in the first few decades of the twentieth century to NALC and NFPOC conventions, while bipartisan, tilted Democratic, wherein lay the most sympathy by elected officials. The Democratic Party–postal labor union link has been predominant ever since.[61] There existed, however, a tension in the postal unions, along with labor unions in general, over leftist political militancy. If New York City was the national stronghold of the Democratic Party, so it was with the Communist Party (CP) and other left-wing organizations. The first NFPOC historian was probably Karl Baarslag, a former Brooklyn Local 251 member who turned anticommunist witch-hunter in 1945. Local 251 appears to have been an independent left-wing local holdover from the radical 1930s, when a few left and CP-oriented postal unions tried to organize substitute employees.[62]

The 1939 Hatch Act, which restricts the political activities of government employees, was not designed as an exclusively anticommunist law, but it had a chilling effect on all political activity by postal and other federal government workers. Historian Ellen Schrecker has noted the extensive use of the anticommunist clause of that act: "Though primarily designed to curb the Roosevelt administration's electoral activities, the measure also contained provisions for dismissing government workers who belonged to 'any political party or organization which advocates the overthrow of our constitutional form of government in the United States.'"[63]

The early 1950s had seen the rise of the "Progressive Feds" caucus within the NFPOC, in part out of alienation from a national organization that tolerated Jim Crow locals in the South. Some New York City postal clerks involved in left labor activity in the 1930s were part of this important trend, embracing democratic union procedures and rejecting segregated "dual locals" and other forms of discrimination. New York was increasingly becoming the locus of the most militant and antiracist postal labor organizing.[64] New York delegates, in fact, helped lead 200 others out of the NFPOC August 1958 convention in Boston (called the "Boston Tea Party"), protesting the lack of union democracy, tolerance of Jim Crow locals in the South, and union racial discrimination.[65] They regrouped in May 1959 as the National Postal Clerks Union (NPCU) in the nation's capital at their inaugural convention: a union that was about 25 percent black.[66] For taking progressive stands for equality and independent industrial unionism, the NPCU—renamed in 1960 the National Postal Union (NPU)—would be red-baited (accused of being communist) and denounced for practicing "dual unionism" by the NFPOC, the AFL-CIO, and government officials.[67]

EXECUTIVE ORDER 10988 AND PARTIAL COLLECTIVE-BARGAINING RIGHTS

At the time of the 1970 strike, wage and benefit increases for about 739,000 postal workers were at the discretion of Congress and the president. At the time, federal government employees only enjoyed partial collective-

President John F. Kennedy signs Executive Order 10988 on January 17, 1962, which allowed limited collective-bargaining rights for federal employee unions that did not practice racial discrimination. Directly behind him are, from left to right, postmaster general J. Edward Day, an unidentified Austrian labor leader, secretary of labor Arthur J. Goldberg, president of the American Federation of Government Employees James Campbell, and president of the National Alliance of Postal Employees Ashby G. Smith. Courtesy of NALC.

bargaining rights, as provided under EO 10988. This order allowed government employees to vote for which unions they wanted to represent them in negotiations over work rules with their respective agencies in a three-tiered system (exclusive, formal, and informal), from local to regional to national levels. In the U.S. Post Office, postal workers by 1962 belonged to nine unions—seven craft and two industrial (open to all crafts).[68]

With EO 11491, signed in October 1969, President Richard M. Nixon abolished all categories except "exclusive." Originally intended as a progressive modification of EO 10988, and one that was supposed to have been handed down during the Lyndon B. Johnson administration, it effectively stripped national representation status from the two independent industrial unions: the historically black NAPFE (National Alliance of Postal and Federal Employees, which changed its name in 1965 from National Alliance of Postal Employees to reflect its expansion to organizing outside the post office) and the militant NPU.[69] Regardless of which union postal workers chose to represent them, all postal unions still had to lobby Congress for pay raises and benefit increases. By the 1960s they had become accustomed to seeing their annual pay raises averaging less than 2 percent.[70]

Both the NPU and NAPE were on record as opposing segregated union locals and branches from their respective beginnings. The same could not be said of other postal unions. But to represent any postal workers, those unions now had to renounce any vestige of segregation they might have. The first steps toward full collective-bargaining rights for postal workers accompanied the demise of official racism in federal government employee unions. For years, black and white activists inside the NALC had kept up the pressure to abolish segregated branches.[71] The Rhodes-Johnston bill would have granted collective bargaining rights, while EO 10988 did not even contain that term, providing instead "recognition," "discussion," "consultation," and "negotiation." Yet a form of "collective bargaining" was implicit in EO 10988. It was even cited in a ten-page conference memo circulated by the New York City postmaster's office in 1962 to prepare local postal officials for this new process. "Remember," the memo counseled in its final section, "collective bargaining is play acting, it's a poker game, it's horse trading."[72]

What did EO 10988 (also known as "Employee-Management Cooperation in the Federal Service") do? It protected federal workers' right to belong to a union while forbidding federal unions from striking, advocating the "overthrow" of the government, or discriminating based on "race, color, creed, or national origin." It mandated that federal agencies provide an ascending hierarchy of union recognition: "informal," "formal," and "exclusive," all based on preference elections among federal workers. "Informal recognition" required no vote minimum, but only provided for that union's representatives to express its members' views to government agency officials. "Formal recognition" gave a union consultation rights on personnel matters based on winning at least ten percent of the vote. "Exclusive recognition" required a majority vote of any craft and entitled the winning union "to negotiate agreements covering all employees in the unit and . . . be responsible for representing the interests of all such employees without discrimination and without regard to employee organization membership."[73] The "formal" and "informal" statuses at least provided some form of representation to unions that lost the election for "exclusive" representation, and the "exclusive" status could also be won on not just a national but also a regional or a local basis. For example, the NPU lost employee balloting in every region to the UFPC for representing clerks but one—the New York Region, won by its largest local, the MBPU, which represented 26,000 members from all crafts. Industrial postal unions like the NPU and the NAPE could compete to represent any craft, including letter carriers and mail handlers. By denying a "winner take all" formula, it helped elevate two militant industrial unions, the NPU and the NAPE (later NAPFE).[74]

One of the key provisions of EO 10988 too often forgotten was its abolition of discrimination and segregation by federal employee unions.[75] EO 10988 disallowed *any* form of discrimination: "When used in this order, the term 'employee organization' means any lawful association [including] Federal employees and employees of private organizations; but such term *shall not include any organization ... which discriminates with regard to the terms or conditions of membership because of race, color, creed or national origin.*"[76] For its part, Rhodes-Johnston declared that federal unions "shall not include any organization which, by ritualistic practice, constitutional or bylaws prescription, or tacit agreement among its members, or otherwise, *denies membership* because of race, color, religion, national origin."[77] Rhodes-Johnston, while banning federal unions from *excluding* black members, said nothing about *internal* union segregation. While segregation always constituted a form of membership denial, it could have been argued, as many unions did, that those unions did not deny membership to blacks. On the other hand, EO 10988 banned segregated locals outright. For that matter, the Rhodes-Johnston antidiscrimination clause would have applied to no existing postal union, as the last one to bar blacks from membership — the National Postal Transport Association (NPTA), with a "Caucasians only" clause since 1911 — had lifted that ban at its 1958 convention.[78] The abolition of segregated branches and locals in the postal unions set the tone for a decade of struggle parallel to that outside the post office. The new clerks' union, formed in 1961 and called the United Federation of Postal Clerks (UFPC), was made up of the NFPOC (from which the NPU had split in 1958), an old, previously unaffiliated conservative clerks' union called the UNAPOC (United National Association of Post Office Clerks), and the NPTA — the union that had begun as the Railway Mail Association (RMA) that in 1911 banned blacks as members, causing them to form their own union, the NAPE.[79]

Ironically, the most conservative of the postal unions, the NRLCA, was the first union to sign a national exclusive contract with the post office on July 12, 1962, under the provisions of EO 10988.[80] But there is no mention in their official union history of black members or racial policies in the NRLCA, which is to say, no acknowledgement of their segregated past. For example, the constitution of the NRLCA only allowed black members to belong to segregated locals. The NRLCA constitution further stipulated that "only white members are eligible to serve as delegates to conventions or to hold office." A search of back issues of the *National Rural Letter Carrier* turns up no resolutions since 1943 abolishing either provision. But in the February 10, 1962, issue there suddenly appeared a reprint of EO 10988 titled "Policy on Employee-Management Cooperation." The April 7, 1962, issue subsequently ran an article that concluded, without irony: "It has also been emphatically stated that employee organizations have certain obligations which must be met before recognition of any type can be extended. The first is the requirement that the organizations not discriminate because of race, color, religion, or national origin." The NRLCA's constitutional provisions against black delegates and providing for segregated locals were probably dropped soon after EO 10988 was issued, as there is no evidence of movements within that union to overturn those provisions until that point—unlike the anti–Jim Crow efforts within the NALC and NPTA.[81]

POSTAL UNIONIZATION IN THE 1960S

The 1960s saw the rise of impatience among postal workers with USPOD management. Even before EO 10988, postal workers in 1961 had a remarkably high union membership rate of 84 percent. This figure included members in antiunion "right-to-work" states that did not allow "union shops" (workplaces where union dues are deducted from the paychecks of all workers represented by a union).[82] This was also a workforce with relatively high turnover and growing frustration among those who remained, combined with a greater influx of young people, blacks, women, and military veterans. While there may have been demoralization among postal workers, growing labor solidarity was the flip side of the coin.[83] In 1963 the first national labor agreement was signed between the Post Office and its "national exclusive" unions, and it included the automatic dues checkoff, which meant that union officers no longer had to collect dues on the shop floor. But the contract did not include the NAPE or the NPU, two of its biggest unions.[84] Why were postal unions so dispersed?

Failed efforts to merge postal unions had to do with issues of organizational and craft autonomy between the NALC and the UFPC, as well as differences between the craft and industrial unions.[85] There were also differences between the two industrial unions over issues of militancy and who could best represent black workers. The NAPE had a more specific civil-rights union agenda. The NPU considered shop floor militancy as important a practice as lobbying and negotiating—if not more so. If the fight for equality by

Clerks sorting mail in "pigeonhole cases," which required a great deal of "scheme" training and memorization, at the General Post Office, New York City, 1969. Note the adjustable stools that enabled clerks to sit, stand, or prop themselves up while doing this work. Courtesy of NYMAPU Collection, Tamiment/Wagner Archives, NYU.

the NAPE was from a self-consciously nonsegregated black organization, for the NPU it was important but within a perspective of democratic industrial unionism. That latter concept was the main sticking point that prevented its merger with the UFPC in the 1960s that would have created a huge industrial postal union with exclusive representation over most crafts.[86]

But if a nationwide merger between postal unions was a nonstarter, in New York City it was a different story. NALC Branch 36 and the MBPU initiated talks and conducted joint demonstrations for higher pay. They were joined by the local NAPE branch. These were not outlier positions within their respective organizations—far from it. But they were far more active in the theory and practice of a single industrial postal union than in any other city. They held meetings in February of 1961 and proclaimed the desirability of forming "ONE BIG UNION as soon as possible."[87] In 1964, the MBPU, New York's huge NPU branch, and NALC Branch 36 formed the Metropolitan Postal Council. The NAPE remained interested without formally committing to the organization. The three locals held a joint outdoor pay raise demonstration in March of that year at the GPO in Manhattan. This was probably the first time such a protest rally had been held since 1952, when the old NFPOC Local 10 clerks' union had combined with NALC Branch 36.[88] Even wider unity was literally demonstrated in Brooklyn on May 2, 1965, when NPU's *Progressive* monthly approvingly reported that "all Brooklyn postal unions [UFPC, NALC, NAPE and the NPU] . . . combined to hold a joint legislative-grievance rally . . . triggered by the fears of . . . the Joint Conference of [Brooklyn] Postal Employees that we were reaching an impasse on . . . much-needed legislation."[89]

But as promising as local unity efforts were in New York, on the national level they seemed to always lose steam because of union competition. Ironically, a major cause of the failure of postal union merger was that EO 10988, which in 1962 forced unions to integrate and collectively bargain, also allowed them to compete for membership and representation. Limited collective-bargaining rights encouraged postal unions to compete at the same time that some were making proposals for "one big union." The latter was a longtime slogan, often capitalized, that was reminiscent of the IWW from the early twentieth century. The NPU was always merging's biggest proponent, because as much as the NAPE shared its vision of a merger in theory, in practice the NAPE was skeptical of merging with unions for whom equality was not a priority, or which could mean their losing influence.[90] The NAPE continued its criticism of the postal unions and organized labor in general for failing to deal with discrimination and segregation in its ranks, as well as what might be called a "white backlash" against civil rights advocacy and law enforcement.[91]

While the UFPC and NPU alternated between trading charges at each other and negotiating over a possible merger, the animosity simmering between the NAPE and the UFPC finally boiled over when the NAPE picketed the UFPC's Washington, D.C., headquarters from July 30 to August 1, 1963. This came just a month before the March on Washington for Jobs and Freedom, and right in the middle of the UFPC's Legislative Conference (also known as a "Pay Rally"). The NAPE was protesting what they called the UFPC's "opposition to minority group promotions."[92] The NPU may have competed with the NAPE for members and influence, but now it backed the NAPE, which also gave it an opportunity to sting the rival UFPC. The NPU shamed the UFPC's "exclusive recognition" status for clerks in Mississippi and Alabama, pointing out that there were only two black clerks in the whole state of Mississippi, and that the UFPC had fought black promotion in Alabama.[93] NAPE President Ashby Smith in 1963 rebutted the charges of

Postal Workers and the Rise of Collective Bargaining

"reverse racism" by the UFPC: "How false are they who cry that Negroes in the postal service are getting preferential treatment the moment that the historical preferential treatment for whites is breached and a dusky face appears as a level seven [management status]."[94] In 1965 the NAPE became the National Alliance of Postal and Federal Employees (NAPFE), open to all federal employees. They had decided at their 1963 convention that it would help expand their organization to try and win national "exclusive recognition" in other federal agencies. In 1966, along those same lines, the NAPFE's monthly journal discarded the agency-specific name *Postal Alliance* in favor of the union's longtime popular name, the *National Alliance*.[95] Before the 1964 Civil Rights Act established the Equal Employment Opportunity Commission (EEOC) for private-sector workers—until it was amended in 1972 to include government workers—the Civil Service and Post Office had their own Equal Employment Opportunity (EEO) committees, based on President Kennedy's famous "affirmative action" executive order, EO 10925.[96] Many early EEO officials were NAPE members, as it had long trained members to fight racial discrimination in postal hiring, promotion, and work life.[97] Unlike the private sector, blacks at the post office tended not to form caucuses in the predominantly white unions, possibly owing to the existence of the NAPE.[98]

THE 1966 CHICAGO MAIL SHUTDOWN
AND THE KAPPEL COMMISSION

One might say the two-week shutdown of the Chicago post office, which was unable to keep up with a spike in mail volume in October 1966, was an institutional accident waiting to happen. It soon provided an impetus for investigation and change, as President Johnson in early 1967 convened the Kappel Commission (named for its chair, Frederick Kappel, retired chairman of American Telephone and Telegraph Corporation) to provide solutions to prevent future postal gridlock.[99] Airmail had not kept up with the demise of the postal railway system, where mail could be sorted on trains, leaving all the sorting to urban post offices. Yet now a major urban post office and mail distribution center was suddenly flooded with bulk-rate mail. The Chicago post office was short-staffed and experiencing increased worker absenteeism in a repressive work environment, leading to rumors of there being a concerted sick-out. In addition, Chicago's first black postmaster, Henry McGee, had just been hired the month before to displays of hostility and hints of administrative sabotage from outgoing white postal officials.[100] The commission's 1968 report, *Towards Postal Excellence*, concluded that there were problems within the U.S. post office that went beyond one city or one holiday season of bulk mail. If anything, the commission's report of postal dysfunction was too short and too narrow. The first page was blunt: "The United States Post Office faces a crisis. Each year it slips further behind the rest of the economy in service, in efficiency and in meeting its responsibilities as an employer. Each year it operates at a huge financial loss.... Although the Post Office is one of the nation's largest businesses, it is not *run* as a business but as a Cabinet agency of the United States Government.... In what it *does*, however, the Post Office is a business: its customers purchase its services directly, its employees work in a service-industry environment, it is a major communications network, it is a means by which much of the nation's business is conducted."[101]

The commission's critique of the USPOD was scathing. Readers can easily gather the tenor of the report from the table of contents alone. Chapter 1 was dubbed "The Post Office in Crisis" and was broken up into three parts. Part A included three sections: "A Postal Catastrophe: Chicago," "Dissatisfaction with Day-to-Day Mail Service," and "Unresponsiveness to Public Needs." Part B, which discussed "The Circumstances of Postal Employment," contained sections that were titled, in order, "Antiquated Personnel Practices," "Poor Working Conditions," "Limited Career Opportunities," "Inadequate System for Supervision," and "Unproductive Labor-Management Relations." As far as the crucial area of "Postal Finances," the Part C subheadings were also self-explanatory: "The Growing and Unnecessary Debt," "The High Cost of Postal Service," and "The Irrational Postal Rate System."[102] The commission reported that "dirty facilities, crowded and noisy work areas, inadequate locker space and rest rooms and poor lighting, heating and cooling systems are common."[103] They noted that 85 percent of postal workers occupied the five lowest pay grades (the federal government otherwise uses the General Schedule pay system).[104] Chapter 2 was entitled "The Roots of Failure," of which the "principal" failure was "one of management," that is, a crisis of method, not individuals.[105] Chapter 3 provided the commission's proposed reforms with the optimistic title "A National Opportunity."[106]

The commission argued that a broken system hampered the modern post office. One telling example had to do with what the commission called the "traditional practice of allowing the Post Office to run a deficit." "The presence of the tax crutch," it argued, "has meant that the Post Office must stand in line with far more urgent national needs in order to obtain capital." The commission shook its head at the inefficiency of having all postal

Postal Workers and the Rise of Collective Bargaining

revenue have to "pass through the appropriations process," thus diminishing the "service needs of the public."[107] Looking back, Richard Kielbowicz also notes that the 1970 Postal Reorganization Act (PRA) passed just weeks after the postal workers' strike was intended to reform the post office still operating in a "hard copy" world. On the one hand, the Kappel Commission failed to anticipate the future challenge of electronic communications. But at the same time, the commission also determined that a reformed post office should be allowed to innovate.[108] The commission's intent, says Kielbowicz, was to "free" the post office from "political control," allowing "postal officials [to] apply business principles to the management of the enterprise," including innovation, new services, and new technologies.[109]

The post office needed reform, but what kind? Would a reorganized post office be allowed to innovate in competition with the private sector while maintaining its first-class-mail monopoly? A hybrid formation that became the USPS in 1971 was a calculated risk, from the beginning, in trying to combine service and business.[110] Reorganization came about as a result of a strike by thousands of frustrated postal workers whose labor was ultimately responsible for the movement of the mail. Three scholars writing in the early 1980s—Charles Benda, Kathleen Conkey and Joel Fleishman—have all offered critical assessments of the Kappel Commission and its influence on the 1970 PRA, reminding us that there is more to the story. Kathleen Conkey's 1983 *The Postal Precipice: Can the U.S. Postal Service be Saved?* sketches the sequence of events leading to the commission. Postmaster General Lawrence O'Brien took the lead six months after the Chicago mail slowdown with an April 3, 1967, speech to the Magazine Publishers Association, calling for replacement of the post office with a self-sufficient government corporation that would collectively bargain with postal unions.[111] "Five days after O'Brien's speech, President Johnson issued an executive order creating a presidential commission to study postal organization," writes Conkey, quoting from that order that the commission was directed to "determine . . . the feasibility . . . of a transfer . . . to a government corporation, or such other form of organization as the Commission may consider desirable."[112] There have been government corporations since the Tennessee Valley Authority in the 1930s New Deal, but "never before had the idea been applied to an existing agency," Conkey stresses. "Each of the previous corporations was created only because it was decided that a necessary government task could not have been accomplished within the normal government process and because private enterprise would not meet a public need."[113]

O'Brien's cheerleading for a corporate solution did not sit well with "some Congressmen, postal labor union leaders and postal officials," includ-ing former Postmaster General James Edward Day who caustically criticized O'Brien's solution: "The speech has provided ammunition from a surpris-ing source for those who delude themselves by believing that business has [*sic*] monopoly on brains and efficiency and that government employees and managers are lazy incompetents."[114] Conkey argues that "the Commission had set out only to document a case for a postal corporation—not to ana-lyze postal problems. Nor did the Commission see the postal corporation as a final step away from a public mail service. It suggested that 'the possibility remains of private ownership at some future time.'"[115] Kappel himself later testified to a 1969 congressional committee that postal privatization was his personal preference. "Congress," concludes Conkey, "should have had little doubt that to Frederick Kappel, postal excellence meant private ownership of postal operations."[116] Conkey maintains that "Congress . . . was eager to rid itself of the responsibility for postal employees" who "were growing in-creasingly militant in their wage demands" while also opposing corporatiza-tion proposals. When NALC president James Rademacher testified before a July 17, 1969, congressional committee, he noted (as did former Postmas-ter General Day) that Kappel's testimony the month before displayed "an almost naïve faith in the efficacy of paying top executives majestic salaries as a means of curing the Post Office of all its ills," adding that "[the Post Office] is, and always must be, a service to all the American people. It is not a money making scheme; it is not a public utility."[117]

For his part, Fleishman believes that postal unions—as frustrated as they were with congressional lobbying—rejected corporatization "because they feared that severing their bargaining relationship with Congress would substantially reduce their power" and would have jeopardized the civil ser-vice status and pensions of its members. Fleishman adds that AFL-CIO President George Meany, "who represented labor on the commission but attended few of the meetings, dissented from the report's recommendation of an independent establishment" out of concern for the post office losing Cabinet status.[118] Fleishman notes the Kappel Commission's excitement at the potential for savings through "mechanization and productivity in-creases" in exchange for wage and benefit increases, besides the opportunity to take over postal rate-making from Congress.[119] Charles Benda concludes that the PRA became "the somewhat classic bargain that has often taken place between big capital and big labor in the private sector . . . manage-ment exchanges large immediate monetary benefits for the ability to mecha-nize operations and decrease the labor force through natural attrition in the future, unhampered by union opposition."[120] Benda argues that the Kappel Commission virtually ignored alternatives to the government corporation model, devoting only forty out of over two thousand pages of its June 1968 report to those alternatives. Moreover, Benda notes, they were also rubber-stamping a proposal that Postmaster General O'Brien had formulated *two months before* the October 1966 Chicago mail shutdown. O'Brien convened a "small internal task force . . . known as the 'Quadriad,' [that] operated in secrecy to explore alternative methods of increasing managerial control of the post office."[121]

In other words, the Chicago mail breakdown was symptomatic of major problems, but those were not the "last straw" leading to a reform commission and reorganization. It certainly had "public relations value," as Benda puts it—one that upper-level postal managers had floated "for many years prior to the Chicago breakdown."[122] O'Brien's task force provided the blueprint for his April 1967 postal reorganization proposal that the Kappel Commission a year later agreed would be worthwhile. This was a commission, Benda reminds us, that President Johnson formed through executive order "rather than through congressional action," and it consciously excluded members of Congress, postal middle management (who actively opposed reorganization), and the mailing industry.[123] Executive postal managers thought the corporate model would take care of problems they saw in previous "labor relations" (unions lobbying Congress), "fiscal affairs" (mailing industry pursuing subsidies that raised the postal deficit), "congressional action" (setting everything from postal rates to wages and mechanization), and "partisan politics" (postmaster appointments). "The executive managers thus had an interest in a reorganization that would limit the congressional role in determining postal policies and isolate the problems of postal politics from other state affairs," Benda concludes.[124]

THE SUMMER OF 1968: A THREE-WAY BATTLE

At the same time that the Kappel Commission report was being issued in June 1968, a vivid illustration of the three-way battle between Congress, the USPOD, and postal unions unfolded when both the UFPC and the NPU voted to repudiate the "no-strike clause" in their respective constitutions, while the NALC voted to "study" the repudiation of that same clause.[125] And with eerie parallels to similar activity and conflict some forty years later, this also could have been called the "Postal Crisis of 1968." In fact, the words "postal crisis" were part of the title of an editorial published in the *Postal Record* in

August 1968.[126] These were the waning months of the Lyndon Johnson administration, with Congress voting in June a 10 percent income-tax increase to fund the Vietnam War while simultaneously mandating federal workforce reductions.[127]

Threatened with 83,238 postal job vacancies left unfilled "at a time of an increased workload," Postmaster General Watson had a threat of his own: all post offices would be closed on Saturdays, effective July 27, 1968; there would be an indefinite closure of 350 small post offices; Saturday collections would be moved to Sundays; and eventually mail delivery would be cut back to four days in cities and three in rural areas per week, with thousands more post offices closed.[128] While those cuts were averted, their threat should remind us that the Post Office has always been subject to exigencies of federal budgets and the economy. Being a full-fledged government agency did not exempt it from the threat of cutbacks in services. But in 1968, Watson's threat to Congress worked, although some in that body grumbled at what they called "blackmail." Congress could not be seen curtailing the U.S. mail. It voted by huge margins of 47–8 in the Senate on Friday, July 26, and 345–24 in the House on Friday, August 1, to exempt the post office from any job cuts, after which Watson "immediately canceled orders for postal cutbacks that were scheduled to begin on Saturday."[129]

From a labor standpoint, EO 10988 had created both dissatisfaction and rising expectations among postal workers, whereas President Kennedy and others had hoped to provide the minimal amount of labor representation in the government service. Postal workers were growing increasingly restive as well as influenced and inspired by labor and civil rights protests happening around them. As they did in other sectors of labor and civil society, the increasing numbers of young and African American people in the postal workforce would prove pivotal in making this strike happen. Aaron Brenner observes, "In the 1967–1976 period, the average number of workers on strike rose 30 percent and the number of days lost to strikes rose 40 percent compared to the period 1948–1966."[130]

As a publicity boost to Nixon's postal corporatization, in 1969 Postmaster General Winton Blount launched a "citizen's campaign."[131] A look at the national officers of the "Citizens Committee for Postal Reform, Inc." included six vice chairmen and a co-chairman who had served on the Kappel Commission; the co-chairman was former postmaster general Lawrence O'Brien. This full-blown media blitz, backed by major magazine publishers, rolled out on May 24, 1969, three days before Postmaster General Blount announced postal reorganization legislation in conjunction with President

Nixon, emphasizing "true collective bargaining in its best sense," with disputes to be settled not by strikes but "by third-party binding arbitration."[132] From 1962 to 1969, postal workers' lobbying had won significant gains for demands *other* than pay, which still lagged — in spite of the fact that the NALC remained the top-spending lobbyist on Capitol Hill in 1969 at $295,970, with the UFPC in second place.[133]

Rising expectations pushed postal workers to seriously consider the strike option. Anger expressed at NPU, NALC, and UFPC conventions that summer, especially by younger members, was directed at postal management and the failure of Congress to come through with an adequate pay raise.[134] In New York City, leaders of the two largest postal unions offered a study in contrasts: NALC Branch 36 president Gustave "Gus" Johnson and MBPU President Moe Biller. Johnson was described by Tom Germano as a "likeable fellow," but as executive vice-president demonstrated that he was "quite unprepared" to assume the presidency in the summer of 1968 with the sudden death of the formidable and popular president Philip Lepper. Johnson, in Germano's words, also "was no match for the volatile president of the MBPU," Moe Biller.[135] Biller was the son of Eastern European Jewish immigrants living on the Lower East Side. He had left college during the Great Depression in 1937 to join the post office. After two years of military service during World War II, he returned to the post office and union activism, later joining the 1958 NFPOC "Boston Tea Party" convention walkout by future NPU members. The following year, Biller became the first and only president of the MBPU, the NPU's largest local.[136] By March 1969 both Biller and Johnson were warning of a wildcat strike. Neither they nor the rank-and-file postal union members who would soon push both of them to help lead a walkout realized at the time just how explosive that pent-up rank-and-file anger was. The momentum of a movement was gathering.[137]

Rising Expectations and Brewing Conflict

Buried on page seventeen of the *Columbus Dispatch* on April 20, 1969, was a report of the visit to the local NALC "Buckeye" Branch 78 by NALC national president James Rademacher. It was not so much his visit that made the news as what he said publicly that prompted this headline: "Union Head Predicts Mail Carrier Strike: Postal Unrest Blamed." Sometime in the next ninety days, Rademacher had predicted at a Sheraton Hotel press conference in Columbus, Ohio, the day before, postal workers "may strike" because of "inadequate" pay and postmaster general Winton Blount will resign because as Rademacher put it, "he can't have his own way." Evidence of the postmaster general's intransigence, Rademacher claimed, was Blount's "boycotting" congressional hearings on proposals for a government postal corporation along with a new postal labor-management law. Rademacher presciently predicted that this strike "would be wildcat and not condoned by the National Association of Letter Carriers." He then warned, "But we can't control unrest prevalent everywhere."[1] Both the strike and Blount's resignation, of course, would come to pass eventually—just not as soon as the NALC chief imagined. (Blount, on leave from his Alabama construction company to serve as postmaster general, would not resign that post until the end of 1971, after taking part in the reorganization of the USPOD into the USPS.[2]) And even though Rademacher implied rather than stated that this strike could be widespread, the "unrest" *would* prove hard to control throughout the United States—especially for him.

Crucial to creating the 1970 postal strike were the post office's high unionization rate and its existence as a national workplace. While federal employees overall were 43 percent unionized by 1968, postal workers, who represented the largest number of non-military federal employees, went from an astounding unionization rate of 84 percent in 1961 to an even higher

87.5 percent rate in 1968—including 97 percent of letter carriers. This was especially remarkable given their lack of full collective-bargaining rights or the right to strike. In 1968, the NALC was the largest postal union with 190,000 members, followed by the UFPC with 143,000, the NPU with 70,000, the NRLCA with 40,000, the Mail Handlers with 35,000, the NAPFE with 32,000, Maintenance with 21,500, Motor Vehicles with 8,000, and Special Delivery with 2,500.[3]

"Postal workers were the largest (25 percent) and the most militant group of federal employees," writes Charles Benda, noting that the "wage increases they won were generally extended to all federal workers."[4] Postal workers also had access to lobbying in Washington, D.C. But both their lobbying power and even their newly won partial collective-bargaining rights had limitations. In the first few months of 1970, expectations and impatience were rising among all postal workers. Most were dissatisfied about pay, management treatment, and their union leadership's ability to negotiate. And it was not just NALC Branch 36 members in Manhattan and the Bronx who were pushing for a strike vote: a district meeting of 1,100 Long Island letter carriers on February 28 also called for a March 16 strike, although district leaders did not implement their strike resolution.[5]

In early February 1970, postal workers became enraged when President Nixon deferred their scheduled July 1 pay increase until January 1971 and also threatened to veto any pay raise legislation that did not include reorganization of the post office as a corporation. There were cries that he was holding their pay raise hostage to his postal corporation plan, which now took the form of a compromise bill approved by the House Post Office and Civil Service Committee on March 12, 1970.[6] For postal workers, rising expectations after seeing positive results from other labor strikes and civil-rights protests clashed with the reality of stagnant postal wages, lack of full collective-bargaining rights, and authoritarian management styles. Many postal workers with families in major cities like New York and Washington, D.C., were drawing food stamps and welfare. The frustration finally boiled over with a militant mass march by over 2,000 postal workers on June 20, 1969, in front of the GPO in New York City, angry at President Nixon's 4.1 percent pay raise executive order—with inflation running at 5 percent and Congress voting themselves a raise. Many chanted "Strike!" and waved signs that read "Strike—July 1st." On the same day, 400 letter carriers protested in front of Grand Central while others rallied at the Brooklyn Post Office and in the Bronx. And there was the sick-out "wildcat" on July 1, 1969, in the Bronx.[7]

July 1, 1969, was the date that NPU members had tried to set as a national strike deadline at their 1968 convention.[8] In late June 1969, according to Tom Germano, "rumors spread like wildfire among the letter carriers in Manhattan and the Bronx that there would be a strike on July 1, 1969," after NALC President Rademacher attacked Nixon's pay raise and "publicly asserted the right of postal workers to strike." Questions over whether a strike would really happen on July 1, as their station delegate had suggested, prompted carriers at Kingsbridge Station to call the Branch 36 office in Manhattan and ask. "The union official who was the local vice president in charge of Bronx affairs told the Kingsbridge carriers, 'Today the Bronx, tomorrow Manhattan.'"[9] Germano and other sources note that a debate ensued over whether this meant the strike was on or not. There was a unanimous vote to call a sick-out as a compromise between those who wanted to strike and those who thought it was premature. The next day only five of the seventy-eight postal workers at Kingsbridge clocked in to work. The Post Office went into action: it sent postal inspectors to the homes of those calling in, and it sent certified letters to each absentee employee threatening "to suspend you from the Postal Service indefinitely pending investigation."[10]

Participating in the Kingsbridge sick-out were fifty-six carriers (all NALC members) and sixteen clerks and mail handlers (all MBPU members). The next day, those who had stayed out were not allowed to clock in to work. Carriers in Manhattan at the GPO heard about this and threatened to not return to work after lunch until convinced to by their station "delegate" (the term used for shop stewards before the advent of the USPS). Meanwhile at Throgs Neck, another Bronx station, sixteen carriers called in sick on Wednesday July 2, 1969. There were now seventy-two carriers and sixteen clerks "placed in a non-pay status and suspended indefinitely" from the two stations.[11] Both the NALC and MBPU protested, and all workers were allowed to return. Seventeen carriers in fact were subsequently exonerated, but the other postal workers were suspended for three weeks until July 22 without pay before being allowed to return to work. "The quality of mail service . . . was adversely affected during the suspensions," notes Germano. "Window service was reduced, deliveries were delayed and customer complaints increased."[12]

This was an important prelude to the 1970 postal wildcat strike. One of the 1970 strike organizers, Vincent Sombrotto, later called it "a dress re-

Manhattan-Bronx Postal Union (MBPU) members lead a march and rally on June 20, 1969, by over 2,000 clerks, carriers, and mail handlers at the General Post Office in New York City, protesting "Nixon's nothing" 4.1 percent raise executive order effective July 1. Front row left to right: Vicky Davis, John Townes, Tilford Townes, Silas McKendrick, and John Hawkins. There were also militant protests at the Grand Central Station Post Office and the Brooklyn Post Office. Courtesy of the NYMAPU Collection, Tamiment/Wagner Archives, NYU.

hearsal," also noting that this is when he first became involved in union affairs and began thinking about direct action.[13] For his part, Bronx postmaster Frank J. Viola had implemented the post office's "contingency plan," which provided for local postmasters to call substitutes, supervisors, and employees from other stations to help move the mail, and declare this sick-out an illegal strike. MBPU president Moe Biller and NALC Branch 36 president Gus Johnson had personally appealed to the postmaster general. The UFPC had condemned the sick-out. The MBPU blasted them. The MBPU, as Moe Biller recalled in a 1975 oral history, reimbursed two-thirds of the salary lost by members who had participated in the sick-out. Meanwhile, Branch 36 members demanded the same for their members who had been in the sick-out, as did MBPU for its members. But claiming lack of funds, Branch 36 leadership

Forty Brooklyn, New York, NALC Branch 41 letter carriers apply as
a group for welfare, October 1969, to dramatize low pay received
by postal workers. Many postal workers were actually eligible for
and received welfare and food stamps. Courtesy of NALC.

refused. In October hundreds of carriers applied for welfare in publicized
actions in Brooklyn, New York, and elsewhere. A caucus of rank-and-file
carriers began to meet as attendance grew in the November and December
Branch 36 meetings.[14]

On October 29, 1969, President Nixon issued Executive Order 11491,
"Labor-Management Relations in the Federal Service," which among other
things revoked "formal" and "informal" categories of representation for federal unions the following year, leaving only the "exclusive" category of representation for the top vote-getting union in each craft, thus marginalizing
the two most militant postal unions—the NPU and NAPFE. Both unions
expressed outrage. The NAPFE accused the AFL-CIO of supporting Nixon's
move to eliminate progressive independents like itself and the NPU.[15] In
December 1969 NAPFE, NPU, and other government employee organizations formed a new labor coalition to fight Nixon's executive order. NAPFE

Rising Expectations and Brewing Conflict

president Ashby Smith had been given strike authorization by his national executive board. He threatened "that he would use it if the White House doesn't change the order, or if Congress doesn't overrule it."[16]

Postal workers may have been denied the right to strike, but they could and did engage in legal "informational pickets." There had been pay raise rallies throughout the late 1960s in New York City and Washington, D.C.[17] According to Eleanor Bailey, an African American GPO distribution clerk and MBPU delegate, the MBPU turned annual pay demonstrations from routine affairs into festive protests. In 1967 they paraded around the Capitol building, blowing whistles on Congress, so to speak. In May of 1969, she said, "We went down there with 200 hundred pounds of peanuts . . . We walked around the post office [headquarters] and said 'no more peanuts, no more peanut salaries.'"[18] In a way, these were dress rehearsals for the actual picket lines that came with the 1970 wildcat strike. The unions rejected the proposed corporate model when they realized that it would deny them the right to strike.[19] NALC president Rademacher appeared before a meeting of Branch 36 in August following the Bronx wildcat strike and taunted members as to whether they would go through with a strike. He even pledged to lead a strike himself if a pay raise was not voted on by Congress. During the Christmas rush, Branch 36 members began talking about striking. They felt especially betrayed when word came that Rademacher had secretly met with Nixon and made a deal: a 5.4 percent wage increase in exchange for Nixon's postal corporatization plan.[20]

Rank-and-file members as well as leadership had been encouraged by the partial collective-bargaining rights that they had enjoyed since 1962 under EO 10988 but at the same time frustrated by their inability to collectively bargain over wages and benefits like unions in the private sector. Their desire to win those full collective-bargaining rights fits the description of what sociologists call "relative deprivation." For years postal unionists had lobbied, demonstrated in Washington, D.C., and engaged in postcard campaigns—all under the auspices of postal unions that represented the vast majority of those at work in post offices in all fifty states as well as U.S. territories. They watched as other unions, including public sector unions, struck and even won better wages and working conditions, while civil-rights groups demonstrated and won their demands. They heard their own union leaders make demands and occasionally even veiled strike threats. They were already organized as union members, but could only bargain with government over working conditions. They wanted more than that.

Branch 36 member Vincent Sombrotto, popularly referred to by most who knew him as "Vince" or "Vinnie," was a World War II Navy veteran and letter carrier at GCSPO. Prior to the strike, Sombrotto had never held any NALC office. After briefly serving as shop steward after the strike, he was elected Branch 36 president in December 1970, and eight years later was elected NALC national president.[21] Gus Johnson, then-president of Branch 36 was a striking contrast to Sombrotto. Johnson—who tried numerous methods to stop the strike juggernaut in 1970—had been vice president until 1968 when he was suddenly elevated to the presidency with the unexpected death of Philip Lepper, their longtime charismatic and progressive president. Lepper, who was Jewish, represented one of four ethnic groups who made up the majority of New York's postal workforce that included those of Italian, Irish, and African ancestry. Lepper himself was not only a strong trade unionist but a civil-rights advocate as well, playing a key role in the long fight against segregated NALC branches in the South. Each of those ethnic groups had its own advocacy group, respectively: the Jewish Postal Workers, the Columbian Society, the Emerald Society, with the NAPE (later NAPFE) both an ethnic advocacy group *and* a postal union for African Americans and others.[22]

Labor historian Aaron Brenner observes that Vincent Sombrotto was part of an already organized rank-and-file tendency within the NALC Manhattan-Bronx Branch 36 that began with "lunch-time meetings, work, and the Branch 36 bowling league," and later turned union meetings into mass meetings with attendance in the hundreds.[23] Tom Germano makes an important point in his study of postal workers and the strike having to do with the social relationships among postal workers in New York: he discovered conflict resolution among postal workers on an individual basis, while at the same time a widespread socializing within each craft, and even subcraft, as well as an "inter-craft association," both at the workplace and off the job. Branch 36 bowling leagues in the winter, along with softball and football leagues in the spring and summer, attracted postal workers across lines of craft, race, age, and ethnicity.[24] Most importantly, says Germano (himself a softball league captain), "They also served as training grounds for leadership."[25]

Paradoxically, even socializing *within* ethnic organizations served to strengthen the growing solidarity among postal workers. These political associations heightened social relations, and when union meetings became mass meetings, that became the most crucial element of all. Postal workers everywhere can attest to both workplace and off-the-job networks among coworkers, especially activities organized by the unions. Those relationships point to a social connection, deeper than that created through the unions, and powerful enough to create an organic undercurrent of solidarity preceding the strike.[26]

In late 1969 rank-and-file activists demanded that NALC national president James Rademacher and Branch 36 president Gus Johnson do for letter carriers as the MBPU had done for its member clerks and mail handlers who had participated in the July 1969 Bronx sick-out: "reimburse the disciplined letter carriers for lost pay."[27] Branch 36 union members approved the demands over the opposition of Rademacher and Johnson at their monthly branch meeting in January 1970. The rank and file, Brenner tells us, then won a vote rejecting the Nixon-Rademacher agreement while supporting their movement's motion that included "full government payment of pension, hospitalization, and life insurance premiums for both active and retired letter carriers, a twenty-year optional retirement, area wage differentials for cost-of-living differences, and the right to strike." If the NALC national office did not agree to this platform, the branch voted that they would strike.[28]

From there, events escalated as Congress considered postal corporatization, and Nixon let it be known that any raises would be linked to postal union support for his corporatization plan. Three major postal unions — the NALC, NPU, and the UFPC — voted to abolish the "no strike" clauses from their respective constitutions in their summer 1968 national conventions. The post office by then had crafted a strike contingency plan, as of July 1968, and sent it to all regional directors on March 4, 1970.[29] Postal inspectors were keeping close watch on Branch 36 strike meetings. But as a USPOD post-strike assessment later noted: "The Post Office Department was prepared for the walkout of Branch 36, but the rapid spread of the work stoppage and the dramatic support of other New York locals was unexpected."[30] This summary also points to an ironic problem in the Contingency Plan concerning instructions to regional directors "to update regional and local plans. . . . Unfortunately many of these instructions were caught in the pipeline and did not reach the local offices until after the strike."[31] The Contingency Plan also "called for drying up the mail flow in struck areas by use of embargoes and asking the public not to deposit mail to the affected areas."[32] Nowhere in the Contingency Plan was there any evidence of contingency planning to deal with a nationwide strike. USPOD general counsel David Nelson thought the first wildcat would begin on March 16 out on Long Island, with the Hicksville NALC branch (today part of Branch 6000). Nelson, while asking associate deputy attorney general George H. Revercomb for help with seeking injunctions against any striking unions and union leaders in New York, nevertheless had this comment: "If the Hicksville letter carriers do go out on strike next Monday [March 16] we anticipate that the national organization [NALC] will disavow the strikers and sever all ties with the Hicksville local. ... We do not believe that any postal employees other than letter carriers will participate in the strike."[33]

All of the events leading up to the strike make it even more remarkable that postal management and the Nixon administration were caught off guard by the nationwide strike. How did they imagine that the strike would never materialize beyond Branch 36? Or that it would not spread past New York City—which in itself would have devastated the financial center of the nation? And how did they so badly underestimate postal worker anger and the potential for united action? One has to wonder if officials ever considered that postal work is a complex operation and integrated system that takes time to coordinate, learn, and perform quickly and accurately across a variety of crafts. No amount of postal supervisors and military personnel could move that much mail on a daily basis once substantial numbers of postal workers struck.

Interestingly, despite opposing the strike as NALC president in 1970, as vice president Rademacher had previously warned in the May 1968 *Postal Record* that a strike might be a remedy for postal worker grievances, its illegality notwithstanding.[34] His contemporary accounts and a 2009 oral-history interview provide a perspective of a top-down leader negotiating with Nixon and trying to keep the rank and file under control. At the same time, he was doing his best to make good use of angry rank-and-file members as a bargaining chip, trying to head off the worst of the postal reorganization plans. One of those plans, for example, would have put grievance adjudication in the hands of a committee appointed by the Postmaster General and left many workplace issues entirely out of the hands of postal unions.[35] Most postal workers before the strike, including Rademacher, were understandably skeptical and even opposed to postal reorganization—then framed as "corporatization." They feared a loss of civil-service protections, lobbying power, and even the viability of the post office itself as a federal government institution providing universal service.[36]

Rising Expectations and Brewing Conflict

On the eve of the strike, starting annual pay at the post office was $6,176, and top pay was $8,422—after twenty-one years—which many never reached. Postal workers were becoming increasingly bitter at broken pay raise promises by presidents both Democrat and Republican.[37] Low pay was the main issue for those willing to risk their postal jobs by going on strike. Wages for postal workers had never been very high historically. This was a job that attracted those who wanted the security of a federal government job. Military service veterans could earn five extra points taking the civil service exam, and veterans with disabilities could earn ten points. By 1949, half of all postal workers were veterans—and by 1966 that figure had increased to three-quarters.[38] Immigrants and their descendants also found a niche at the post office, especially Irish, Italians, and European Jews. The post office was also historically a job magnet for African Americans shut out of private-sector jobs by racial discrimination, or in search of a flexible job where they could work another job or attend college.[39]

But in the 1960s postal workers, who had watched their wages recently start to keep up with those of police officers and fire fighters in New York, now saw their pay drop not only below those occupations but also below those of sanitation workers. What is more, they had seen New York City municipal workers join the nationwide strike wave and win wage and benefit increases. This was more than just a pay battle, however, as important as that grievance was. As labor historian Aaron Brenner has pointed out, the carriers of Branch 36 who struck in 1970 "organized around their rights, in large part because they were public employees whose wages and benefits were set through a political process carried out in the language and practice of rights."[40] One can also see in the narratives of strikers how low pay served as a marker for their feelings of general powerlessness and treatment as second-class citizens, barely able to provide for their families.[41]

Ironically, those who led the strike were those who arguably enjoyed their postal jobs the most—the letter carriers. These were postal workers who were out in public, wearing uniforms, some keeping the same routes for years, watching children grow up on those routes, and feeling a sense of pride contradicted by their treatment by Congress and postal management. Letter carriers enjoyed being usually "left alone" by management after they left the office to make their rounds—the part of the job that served to mitigate the often contentious relations on the shop floor with supervisors.[42]

Clerks and mail handlers meanwhile battled daily supervisor pressure in antiquated buildings that were freezing in the winter and unbearably hot in the summer.[43]

Writing two months after the strike ended, assistant secretary of labor for Labor-Management Relations William J. "Bill" Usery Jr. observed, "It was an historic event. It did not come about without warning. It was just that nobody seemed to believe it would ever really happen."[44] In fact, strike sentiment had been building for some time. Postal workers chafed at the new federal raise "guidelines" in 1966 pegged at only 2.9 percent, while at the same time the USPOD was now encouraging local postmasters to declare previous local contract provisions "non-negotiable." In September 1968 the *Wall Street Journal* reported on the post office's strike contingency plan along with news that the three largest postal unions (the NALC, UFPC, and NPU) had scrapped their respective constitutional "no strike" clauses at their conventions that summer. The NALC in August had passed a resolution (offered by Branch 36 president Gus Johnson) to "study the feasibility" of gaining the right to strike and "removing the no-strike oath." For its part, the NPU convention in June passed a resolution that authorized a July 1, 1969, strike deadline until president David Silvergleid overturned it as illegal. And UFPC legislative director Patrick Nilan warned Congress that postal union leaders were "sitting atop a live volcano."[45] As cautiously as these unanimous convention resolutions were phrased, they represented a growing rank-and-file resentment at their unions' inability to use workers' ultimate weapon—the collective withholding of labor. Strike momentum continued to build. Branch 36 rank and file tried to get their union to help cover strikers' back pay, as the MBPU had done for its members. Branch 36 meetings, not known for their high attendance, by the end of 1969 and into early 1970 had become mass meetings.[46]

Meanwhile, the NALC's "Save Our Service" protests to Nixon for higher pay, which included 3 million letters and postcards, prompted Nixon's request for NALC president James Rademacher to secretly meet with him on Friday evening, December 5, 1969, at the White House. When it was later discovered that Rademacher had agreed to postal corporatization "in exchange for a 5.4% wage increase," postal workers were outraged. There is no known official record of that December 5 meeting, but we are fortunate to have Rademacher's 2009 oral history to verify it, corroborated by a *Washington Post* article. Yet almost all scholarly and popular accounts wrongly date the meeting as occurring days later than the actual negotiating session.[47] White

President Richard M. Nixon and two aides meet with NALC president
James Rademacher, December 18, 1969. This short meeting followed prior
negotiations. Its purpose was to express Nixon's gratitude for Rademacher's
breaking ranks with other postal union presidents and agreeing to support
Nixon's postal corporation plan, craft a compromise that included a
pay raise, and take publicity photographs. Courtesy of NALC.

House special counsel Charles "Chuck" Colson in fact described the December 18, 1969, meeting as intended to be no more than a general discussion of "postal service problems and . . . Rademacher's background." Rademacher and Nixon's aides met just before Nixon arrived, as Colson notes in a December 18 memorandum following that morning's meeting: "[Henry] Cashen, [John] Ehrlichman, and I briefed the President on the agreement that had been reached with Rademacher for a compromise postal reform pay package." Ehrlichman's memo to the president the day before had stressed, "The meeting should be limited to the photograph and an expression of thanks. Substantive questions need not be discussed." And they were not, according to Colson's December 18 memo. The official presidential diary recorded the meeting with Rademacher as lasting only thirteen minutes—from 10:05 to 10:18 A.M.—which included having his photograph taken with Nixon as requested by Rademacher, to be hung in every post office and printed on the cover of the NALC *Postal Record*. (Rademacher was among the few union leaders who endorsed Nixon in the 1968 presidential election.) Nixon concluded the meeting, according to Colson, expressing hope that after this bill passed they would be given credit for hammering out the agreement.[48] A cordial correspondence continued between Rademacher and Nixon (and his aides) at least into 1973.[49]

Rademacher's claim that at the December 5 meeting he instantly convinced Chuck Colson to include binding arbitration and maintain Civil Service status for postal workers is curious considering that labor negotiations — especially something as huge as restructuring the post office — typically take time. Moreover, those elements were already in the original postal corporation plan (H.R. 11750) put together by Nixon and Postmaster General Blount, including collective bargaining rights over wages, benefits, and working conditions. Nixon had proclaimed all those features of his plan in a May 27, 1969, address to Congress promoting the passage of the Postal Service Act of 1969, which would remove the Postmaster General from the Cabinet, reorganize the USPOD as the United States Postal Service, and solve the post office's one-billion-dollar "financial crisis." The credibility of both Nixon and Rademacher were especially strained, Tom Germano notes, when the compromise plan showed up on Capitol Hill minus what the White House called "inadvertently omitted" pledges made to the postal unions.[50] It is hard to know what exactly Rademacher gained and Nixon gave up on this "compromise," which was essentially on Nixon's terms. One might say that the *real* compromise was Rademacher's meeting with Nixon to combine a 5.4 percent pay raise with corporatization. The other postal unions were predictably angry and denounced Rademacher for "breaking ranks" in addition to agreeing to such a small raise in exchange for backing Nixon's postal corporation plan. Many rank-and-file NALC members were especially furious at their president. "The split in labor's ranks," notes Vern Baxter, "was reminiscent of the split between 'public servants' and 'workers' in the post office at the turn of the century. James Rademacher was clearly a lobbyist and politician, and a model 'public servant,' while many of the young militants in New York identified themselves as class conscious workers."[51]

In Congress meanwhile there was a standoff. H.R. 4 had originally been introduced on January 3, 1969, with postal union support by the House Committee on the Post Office and Civil Service by its chair Thaddeus Dulski, and it called for postal reform and collective bargaining within the USPOD. Frederick Kappel refused to testify on H.R. 4, claiming it gave too much power to the unions. Instead he backed H.R. 11750 along with former postmasters general Lawrence O'Brien and John Gronouski, plus the Chamber of Commerce and other business interests. This Nixon-backed bill, notes Vern Baxter, solicited no feedback from unions or Congress and was "drafted by people with little or no postal experience."[52] But it was blocked 13–13 on October 8, 1969 by the House Post Office and Civil Service Committee.[53] "The meeting," Baxter concludes about the Nixon-Rademacher compromise, "was part of an administrative strategy to 'take on' the postal unions one at a time on the issue of postal reorganization."[54]

Rank-and-file Branch 36 activists had their own ideas. They were also responding to the militant MBPU leading the charge against postal corporatization, which included numerous informational leaflets. One of those claimed the Nixon-Rademacher plan flopped on guarantees of comparability (comparable pay to similar private sector work), compression (number of years until top pay), and civil service status. Typically, seventy carriers would attend Branch 36 monthly meetings — usually shop stewards. But the November and December 1969 meetings saw over 100 at each. At the January 1970 meeting, 200 carriers attended and proposed their own postal reform plan, which included the right to strike. They were also able finally to vote to compensate carriers who had been suspended for the 1969 Bronx sick-out.[55] Whatever traction Nixon hoped to gain from the deal made with Rademacher was lost by freezing postal wages until January 1971, citing inflation in his February 3 annual budget message. On February 12, Branch 36 held its regular meeting, where a turnout of 400 carriers debated and narrowly voted to strike March 15 — prompting branch president Gus Johnson to call instead for a "strike survey" whose results would be revealed at the next meeting on March 12. Tom Germano notes that the rank and file were coalescing from "a loose amalgam of dissatisfied letter carriers" toward a pro-strike uniting of factions: "young Turks" (including influential "informal leaders" like Germano), some senior letter carriers, and some union "delegates."[56]

Coincidentally March 12 was the same day that the Nixon-backed H.R. 11750 would be merged into the previously union-backed H.R. 4 and approved by a vote of 17–6 by the House Committee on the Post Office and Civil Service. This now-cannibalized bipartisan "substitute H.R. 4" was a blow to the postal unions, who still mostly opposed postal corporatization. Nixon approved it, and Rademacher helped write it with Representative Morris Udall (D-Ariz.). Dulski reluctantly gave his blessing to his gutted H.R. 4, seeing it as the only postal reform package possible. It was also the only pay-raise bill left standing, as H.R. 13000 on federal employee wage increases had stalled in the Senate. And Nixon had threatened to veto anything not attached to his postal corporation plan (including Dulski's original H.R. 4).[57]

Prior to the March 12 meeting, Branch 36 officials led by President Gus Johnson had done everything they could to sidetrack the brewing strike sentiment, including concealing the meeting time and place. Nonetheless, almost 800 carriers arrived on time and crammed into a West Side Manhattan hotel meeting room that only lawfully held 380, overflowing into the hallways. They demanded the results of Johnson's paper ballot "strike survey," which had only provided three choices. The results were: 2,083 would only strike if the national office called it, 486 would only strike locally, and 40 would not strike. Many shouted and booed as Johnson read Rademacher's letter aloud warning that any member or branch who struck faced NALC suspension. Johnson lost control of the meeting as members voted unanimously on a motion to convene a citywide strike meeting of clerks and carriers. He cited the lack of space anywhere to hold such a meeting. Carriers yelled back: "Use Central Park!" Reluctantly, Johnson agreed to meet with President Moe Biller of the MBPU the next day to set up that strike meeting. But according to Tom Germano, who was present and active at the branch meeting, this "mandate . . . was not implemented by the union leadership; instead of a strike meeting, the union leaders scheduled a strike vote only." They also did not meet with the MBPU leaders as promised, according to Germano.[58]

If Johnson and Biller did not meet, they at least corresponded across midtown Manhattan that month in an intriguing exchange. Biller wrote Johnson on February 5, calling Nixon's refusal of an adequate pay raise "a critical situation" for postal workers and noting the impossibility of the MBPU-NPU supporting Nixon's "Postal Authority or Corporation." He expressed his hope to meet soon to discuss restoring the New York postal unions' "solid front." Johnson wrote back on February 12, presumably after the Branch 36 monthly meeting, offering to meet "at the earliest possible time." He suggested an agenda including the Nixon-Rademacher legislation, some problems he had with certain MBPU "delegates," and "Strike Action at the LOCAL level ONLY." Biller wrote back, apologizing for the tardy response, pleading illness and then a sudden dash to Washington, D.C. He suggested they meet February 24. There is no evidence of Johnson's reply or that they actually met, but Johnson's offer to discuss a "local" strike with Biller is interesting, suggesting possible ambivalence.[59] Meanwhile, on Friday, March 13, *Miscellaneous Bulletin 80: Contingency Planning for Work Stoppages* was issued to postal inspectors, who in turn posted provisions of the no-strike law on employee bulletin boards throughout the New York area, while pursuing strike threats like the March 14 sick-out by eighteen carriers at the main post office in Far Rockaway. Gus Johnson, meanwhile, had scheduled a strike vote for Tuesday, March 17, St. Patrick's Day—a vote that he was certain would lose.[60]

BRANCH 36 VOTES TO STRIKE

Rank-and-file NALC members were meeting just prior to the March 17 strike vote. Vincent Sombrotto wanted to have a meeting before the vote, which actually would have been the proper procedure according to union bylaws. Germano was afraid of losing momentum if a strike vote was not called quickly. As it turned out later that evening at the Manhattan Center, Sombrotto's efforts to hold a meeting first were loudly rebuffed by the carriers who had assembled there to vote.[61] Branch 36 member William Roth still recalls pulling the lever in one of the six voting booths set up by the Honest Ballot Association (HBA) at the Manhattan Center on 311 West Thirty-Fourth Street. It was quarter to nine, and he had just gotten off work half an hour earlier at the Fort George post office. Roth was assigned to a collection route picking up outgoing mail from collection boxes and then driving it to a local mail distribution facility. But now he was taking part in an extraordinary event, along with almost 4,000 other letter carriers at the Manhattan Center. That night they were about to do something no postal worker had done in United States history. They would vote to go on strike. And they would soon be joined by thousands of other postal workers throughout the United States. Roth recalls that at the time of the strike he made less than $3 per hour and was working a second job driving a cab. This is a frequently told story by postal workers from that era. According to Tom Germano, 20 percent of New York's postal workers worked second or third jobs, including Germano, who was also married with four children. Another 20 percent had a spouse who worked. In addition, 10 percent were eligible for and received food stamps and welfare payments. Postal workers in other cities told similar stories. Striking was both risky and imperative, especially for workers with families.[62]

Roth had just turned twenty-seven the day before this strike vote. A carrier since 1967, his status was still Part Time Flexible (or PTF). He was hoping to soon "make regular"—which meant he could attain career employee status and be guaranteed forty hours of work per week. Postal workers who were not "regulars" could not begin work until given an assignment. But even "regulars" did not have financial security. About 1,800 miles west in Denver, Colorado, Vern Evenson, then a recently hired letter carrier described a similar situation: "Everybody had a second job." Evenson remembers carriers lined up at the time clock at the end of their shift, anxiously waiting to "clock out." There was no overtime then, he said, and many of them were getting ready to go straight to their next job. A twenty-four-year-old U.S. Army veteran, married with a one-month-old child, Evenson joined the NALC on Friday, March 20, and the night of Branch 47's debate and strike vote in Denver, as the strike made its way across the country. As in New York and elsewhere, most of those voting that night in Denver were also military veterans. And all postal workers were required to sign an oath that they would never strike. But now many felt that the government had violated its social contract by not paying them enough to support their families. Evenson and most of Branch 47 voted to join the strike: "And so the vote in Denver was: if these guys [in New York] are willing to do this for us, the least we can do is support them."[63]

Striking at the post office could have resulted in termination for Roth, Evenson, and thousands of others, not to mention $1,000 fines and jail terms of up to one year if convicted of what would have been a felony charge. It could have ended Roth's and Evenson's careers at the post office. Others had worked ten to twenty years, with some close to the standard thirty-year minimum time a postal worker needed to work in order to be eligible for retirement and a full monthly pension from the Civil Service Retirement System (CSRS). By Tom Germano's estimate, there were so many Branch 36 members waiting to vote that March night in Manhattan that as many as 1,000 became discouraged with the long lines and left without voting.[64] William Roth, however, was able to cast his ballot in what he described as a life-changing event: "And I'll never forget when I pushed that lever and I decided either we stand or we fall, and if we fall, I'm gonna fall fightin' for something that we need to do."[65] Frank Orapello, another Branch 36 member, had gotten to the Manhattan Center at six o'clock that evening. Most carriers had gotten off work at 2:30 that afternoon and had to wait around for the strike vote that had been scheduled for 6:35 to 9:00 P.M. Tom Germano reports that many went to nearby taverns for a beer to wait. Orapello feared the delay was intended by union leadership to suppress pro-strike votes: "You have got to understand the distrust we had for our local president Gus Johnson, who had too many ties to our national president James Rademacher," he recalled thirty-five years later.[66] Adding to that tension, the Manhattan Center doors didn't open until 6:45, after carriers banged on them.[67] Many of those who voted that night in midtown Manhattan stuck around the ballroom afterwards. The talk was loud and excited. The lines

Rising Expectations and Brewing Conflict

were slow, as mentioned earlier, and many went home without voting. But at 10:30 P.M., pandemonium greeted the results: 1555–1055 to strike. Branch 36 president Gus Johnson announced something that he had fought against, but now was obliged to declare: their branch was on strike as of 12:01 A.M. March 18, and as branch president he would lead it. He would not be seen again in public during the strike, but the courts nonetheless served him with injunctions later as if he were responsible for it.[68]

On the podium with Johnson that night was Brooklyn NALC Branch 41 president Jack Leventhal, who pledged his branch's important support, and MBPU president Moe Biller, who promised that his huge local would not cross picket lines and would vote later that week. Tom Germano agreed with a post office draft strike summary dated September 21, 1970: MBPU support *was* crucial to the success of the strike. The summary declared: "Carriers were well aware that mail could bypass the delivery stage with minimal inconvenience to the public but the system was completely inoperable should the clerks withhold their distribution skills."[69] In fact, carriers knew that striking *would* cause great public inconvenience. But they knew that striking by themselves would not shut down the post office. That would require cross-craft cooperation.[70]

Throughout the 1960s, joint demonstrations had been held in New York City by locals of the largest postal unions: the NALC, the MBPU-NPU, the UFPC, and the Alliance. Moe Biller and the MBPU had even held talks aimed at forming an expanded industrial postal union with local NALC branches — an effort that never came to pass. The "one big postal union" that many had called for but had never coalesced in formal terms now seemed to be happening on the ground among postal union members — not just in New York, but spreading rapidly across the country. Eleanor Bailey recalled that not long before Branch 36 voted to strike, one of the Tour I GPO letter carrier "routers" asked if she would support a strike if they walked out. She replied that she would. Bailey had come to the post office in 1964 during a spike of women's hiring, especially black women, whom she and others described as militant. This came a year after the Equal Pay Act (EPA) became law and two years after the Kennedy administration had banned gender-specific civil service job registries. The Kappel Commission reported that from 1959 to 1967, women's employment at the post office jumped from 11 to 17.4 percent. Young men were increasingly being drafted to fight in Vietnam, creating spaces for women's entry into government jobs. The women's movement was simultaneously beginning to grow as a political and social force. And the historical masculinism of the postal workplace was fading. Bailey quickly acquired a reputation for hardnose grievance negotiation with management as she "learned that contract back and forth," confessing with a laugh: "A couple of times I made up stuff!" Now she was helping lead co-workers off the job.[71] The USPOD September 1970 Strike Summary noted that, out of the entire shift of Tour I GPO carrier routers scheduled to begin work at 10:30 P.M. March 17, "all failed to report," and that among *all* GPO workers, while "5,809 employees were scheduled for Tour I, beginning at 11:00 P.M., 3,832 actually reported."[72]

How did postal management not see this strike coming? "The Post Office Department was prepared for the walkout of Branch 36," reads the USPOD summary, "but the rapid spread of the work stoppage and the dramatic support of other New York locals was unexpected." The next passage from the summary includes an assessment of known risks, attempted crisis management, and ultimately bureaucratic red tape hampering the USPOD's ability to respond to the strike. As the authors of the report belatedly recounted: "The Postal Inspection Service . . . had monitored the growing dissatisfaction of postal employees, particularly in the New York area, with the progress of pay legislation. Strike talk had been accelerating since Christmas. In response to this threat the Department had issued a supplement to the 'Contingency Plan for Work Stoppages,' published in July 1968, and had sent them to all Regional Directors on March 4, [1970], with instructions to update regional and local plans. (Unfortunately many of these instructions were caught in the pipeline and did not reach the local offices until after the strike.)" Realistically speaking, however, the "supplement" would have done little good because it detailed directions with only one scenario in mind: one craft striking. But this was the sound of many crafts striking.[73] The rank and file had spoken, despite the mutual agreement that Moe Biller reported later had existed between him, Johnson, and Leventhal not to lead their respective locals out on strike alone. Members of Branch 36 were exercising leadership from below.[74]

WHY NEW YORK?

"City of Strikes" is what the *Economist* magazine in 1968 called New York, and it could have been the title to the city's theme song for that decade. Strikes and labor organizing in the private sector had become common in this historically working-class city. Labor historian Joshua Freeman points to a postwar wave of both "called strikes" (those sanctioned by unions) and wildcat strikes in 1945 and 1946 that included longshoremen, tugboat

Rising Expectations and Brewing Conflict

operators, painters, teamsters, telegraphers, motion picture projectionists, elevator operators, garment workers, and hat workers. Part of a nationwide strike wave, it "revealed the power of New York labor as the postwar epoch began."[75] In the next big strike wave in New York, there were called strikes by unions of transit workers in 1966, sanitation workers in 1968, and teachers who walked out four times: 1960, 1962, 1967, and 1968.[76] "The offices, class-rooms, and hospital hallways of New York City," observes historian Nelson Lichtenstein, "proved the birthplace of modern public-employee unionism. Here was the Akron and Flint of a new labor movement."[77] Postal workers could not have helped but notice how millions of New Yorkers were affected by bus and subway closures in 1966 for almost two weeks, or the stinking mounds of garbage that piled up for nine days in 1968, or that fact that all the unions' job actions won significant gains in wages, benefits, and working conditions. Strikes were *not* illegal for public workers in either the state or the city of New York, but they were for federal workers employed in New York and elsewhere across the nation.[78] Freeman sees labor militancy in New York hitting its stride in the mid-1960s, and not just with private sector workers. "After World War II," he notes, "the number of public-sector workers in New York—employees of the city, state, and federal governments and public agencies like the Transit Authority—ballooned. In 1950 they totaled 347,400; in 1960, 408,200; and in 1970, 563,200." Most of these were city workers, which in 1970 outnumbered those in "the garment, banking, and longshore industries put together."[79]

New York postal workers felt like it was their turn. Vincent Sombrotto re-members that "protests were everywhere. . . . In our immediate area, workers, whether they were teachers, sanitation workers, transportation workers, all of them were taking some sort of job action. . . . And the carriers were look-ing at: 'When do we get our just rewards for our labor? And how are we ever gonna get a raise?'" Sombrotto's Branch 36 colleague Albert "Al" Marino declared, "The strike gave us identity and progress." Marino was thirty-nine years old at the time of the postal strike. "When we did go on strike in 1970 I had twenty-two years in the postal service, it was a risk. . . . We got tremen-dous public support. That helped us an awful lot."[80] Contemporary media re-ports and oral histories note the overwhelming popular sympathy that postal strikers received in March 1970, especially considering the inconvenience of the mail not moving. One of the key aspects of the strike was not only in how quickly it spread, but how many people were on the strikers' side. Striking letter carriers recall people honking their horns in support and their patrons telling them they backed their demands. What's more, they were surprised to see supervisors in some cases bringing out coffee and doughnuts, especially welcome where the weather was cold. Clerks and mail handlers either honored the picket lines or joined them, to the point where post offices in New York City were almost 100 percent on strike.[81] President Nixon quickly realized that attacking the strikers was not working. For someone who emphasized politics over everything else, with midterm elections looming and a presidential election two years away, fighting a popular wildcat strike by public servants that had taken the nation by surprise seemed doomed to failure.[82] Tom Germano in 1983 referred to the "vacuum" in Branch 36's leadership that provided room for the rank and file to take hold of a new narrative and strategy.[83] And Aaron Brenner has suggested these possibilities for why New York became the flashpoint of the nationwide postal wildcat strike: (1) "postal workers there faced the worst working conditions in the country and the highest cost of living"; (2) "the local leadership of the letter carriers union lacked experience and the respect of the membership, rank-and-file activists had the space to organize strike sentiment"; and (3) "the rank-and-file group in New York was particularly committed and well organized."[84]

Other factors to consider in New York's leading role would be the historical confluence of labor, left-wing, immigrant (Caribbean and European especially), civil rights, and African American activism in that city. New York was one of few cities in the 1960s where the NALC, NPU, and NAPFE held joint protest marches for better pay. Branch 36 itself had a history of activism, including fighting Jim Crow segregated branches in the NALC. Branch 36 strike activist Cleveland Morgan, who is African American, pointed out that he "experienced a lot [and] fought back" against racism from white coworkers when first arriving as a young man from rural Georgia in the 1960s, but he saw unity by the time the strike came. It could be argued that the century-long influx of African Americans to the New York post office (making up about one-third of its total employees) and the additional spike of black new hires in the 1960s helped mitigate "racial divisions" that might have otherwise derailed the strike and the rank-and-file movement that drove it.[85] As African American MBPU clerk Joann Flagler put it, "I think this is a labor city. [It was] because we have strong leadership. . . . We had strong union leaders."[86] For black New York postal strikers like Joann Flagler, Richard Thomas, and Eleanor Bailey to also assert that the strike "was not about color" or craft when those kinds of divisions frequently hampered labor movement success is more reflective of a long, hard-fought, black-led struggle for equality at the post office rather than some notion of labor solidarity based on "color-blind" class unity. Also underscoring the element of youth, Flagler, from a working-class South Carolina family, laughed at the idea of being fearful of going on strike: "I was young — I was nineteen years old! Who's afraid at that age? There was a *lot* of young people."[87]

A combination of organizing and spontaneity made this wildcat strike happen.[88] In some ways it resembled the black student sit-in wave of 1960 across the South against Jim Crow segregation. There was a "singleness of mind," Tom Germano observed. "Everybody felt the same way" was Vincent Sombrotto's recollection, seconded by numerous strike participants. Stories reported in the press and in oral histories talk of a "snowballing" effect coming across the country. Many spoke of walking out in solidarity with New York's postal unions, wanting to let them know they were behind them and would not let them down.[89]

3

The Strike Begins

Busy commuters rushing to work in New York City's five boroughs on Wednesday morning, March 18, 1970, heard the news on the radio or read it in one of New York's daily newspapers. "Strike Hits Manhattan, Bronx Mail," announced the *New York Daily News* headline at the bottom of its front page. A front-page headline in the *New York Times* read "Mail Carriers Go on Strike in Manhattan and Bronx," and the matter-of-fact tone of that article (similar to that of the *Daily News*) suggested a city used to strikes, including those by public sector workers: "What was apparently the letter carriers' first picket line formed shortly after midnight on the Forty-Fifth Street side of the Grand Central post office. The Fifty-First Street police station reported at 1 A.M. that there were 30 pickets there." The *Times* also cited Manhattan police reports that an hour later at the Murray Hill Station at 205 East Thirty-Sixth Street there were fifteen letter carriers picketing.[1] Picketing at the GCSPO (roughly 5,000 employees) was followed by walkouts and picketing from the GPO (over 10,000 employees) at Eighth Avenue and Thirty-Third Street. Strike veterans describe picket lines at the main post offices in the city as numbering in the hundreds. The snowball was rolling from Manhattan, the Bronx, Brooklyn, Queens, Staten Island, Long Island, across upstate New York, and into New Jersey. The postal strike was on.[2]

Pickets went up across the city in time for the morning shift (also known as "Tour II"), and by that afternoon virtually no postal workers had crossed them in New York City's five boroughs.[3] As mentioned before, picket lines were spreading from New York into New Jersey, Massachusetts, Connecticut, Pennsylvania, Ohio, Illinois, Michigan, Wisconsin, Minnesota, Colorado, and California, as over 200,000 postal workers (out of a workforce of 739,000) struck 671 post offices in dozens of cities and towns across the nation.[4] Entire branches or locals from the NALC, NPU, UFPC, NAPFE, as well as the smaller craft unions either struck or refused to cross picket lines. Members of eight postal unions (six of them AFL-CIO affiliates along with the independent NPU and NAPFE) were involved, while the NRLCA and its

NALC Branch 36 picket line at General Post Office, New York, March 18, 1970, after having voted as a branch to strike the night before, 1,555–1,055. Second from left is Tom Germano, picket captain, strike coorganizer, and author of a sociological study of the strike. Courtesy of Neal Boenzi/New York Times/Redux.

members were not. NALC Branch 36 members who worried about whether the rest of the country would join became encouraged by each news report of the rapid spread of the strike across the country, often conveyed by transistor radios, which became important portable, one-way communication devices for those picketing or holding meetings and strike votes.[5]

THE FIRST PICKET LINES

Just after midnight, Branch 36 and MBPU picketers at GCSPO moved the "sawhorse" wooden police barricades still in place from the St. Patrick's Day parade the day before onto the sidewalk in front of the building.[6] The police barricades thus became an innovative as well as a symbolic and defiant way of establishing a solid object complement to what would soon become moving picket lines across the city that included homemade signs in English or Spanish. These picket lines would grow across the city and much of the United States.[7] Vincent Sombrotto, who became a leading figure in the strike, had grown up in East Harlem (then called "Italian Harlem") and been neighbors with Frank Orapello. Sombrotto had served in the Navy during World War II, had started working at the post office in 1947 at Christmas, and "made regular" (become a full-time career employee) in 1949. A route that he carried out of GCSPO was renamed for him in 2014 (Branch 36's Manhattan office building and the NALC national headquarters in Washington, D.C., are both also named after him.) At the time of the strike, he was a forty-six-year-old father of six who drove a truck as his second job. In many ways, Sombrotto became the iconic public face of the strike. Sombrotto remembered getting oak tag out of the back of his pickup truck to make picket signs along with Eddie Morris and Charlie Springer, and watching "about a hundred" letter carrier routers, clerks, and mail handlers coming out of the building while those coming to work respected the picket line.[8] Cleveland Morgan, twenty-seven at the time and married with two children, proudly shared this recollection: "We went over to Grand Central, Sombrotto, some more guys that went over there, put up the [saw]horses . . . and that morning . . . we were picketing. . . . It was history!"[9]

At the GPO, Richard Luckstat, sent up from USPOD headquarters in Washington, D.C., told the *New York Times* that "21 routers were not on the job [for the night shift] but that 38 were working at 2 A.M. Of the latter number, he said, 33 had walked off and then returned. The first carriers begin work at 6 A.M." The *Times* reporter Damon Stetson, who wrote a number of articles covering the strike, prophetically added later on in this article: "If the strike is successful—and its effectiveness will not be known until this morning, when most carriers and other postal employees normally show up for work—it will seriously curtail mail service in one of the nation's busiest postal districts."[10]

Branch 36 strike veteran Barry Weiner also recalls that the first carriers to be affected by the strike were the "routers" in New York City. These were carriers who "cased" mail at night for letter carriers to deliver during the day, and were about two-thirds black and Latino. Pickets were rapidly going up at smaller stations as well. Barry Weiner worked at the Planetarium Station on the Upper West Side of Manhattan. A "good letter carrier friend" and router whose last name he remembers only as "Torres" showed up by himself at the station with a hand painted picket sign and "stayed there all night." When Weiner himself arrived for the morning picket line, he was surprised to see the NALC shop steward going in to work, so he went inside and talked him into coming out.[11]

As letter carriers posted picket lines throughout Manhattan and the Bronx by 6:00 A.M., the postal wildcat strike of 1970 had begun. Tom Germano, who had just turned thirty, noted the quick results at the GPO where he was picket captain: "By 8:00 A.M. only five of the approximately three hundred carriers assigned to Tour II at GPO had gone into work." On that first day, says Germano, about 20 percent of the clerks crossed the line, but "as the number of picketing postal workers grew, it became increasingly clear that the strike was successful."[12] The USPOD account noted that "attendance at GPO [and its twenty-one stations] progressively worsened with each tour."[13]

According to the 1970 USPOD post-strike draft summary, Assistant Postmaster General for Personnel Kenneth A. Housman met with postal union presidents at ten o'clock that morning and reminded them that by terms of the 1969 EO 11491, in event of a work stoppage, federal employee union heads were to take "affirmative action" to bring members back—and needed to file daily reports with him on what they were doing. The responses by postal union presidents varied. Probably the most sympathetic of the union chiefs to the strike was the NPU president David Silvergleid, who replied to Housman that he "only knew what he read in the papers," but that he was also heading to New York to get a firsthand assessment. The NALC's James Rademacher had perhaps the strongest antistrike response: he wanted to send a telegram suspending Branch 36 and recommend that his Executive Committee expel them, in addition to wanting to use USPOD headquarters to issue a news release and stage a press conference. Housman told him to talk to his lawyer and take any actions from Indiana Avenue, the NALC headquarters. The summary report speculates that Rademacher must not have subsequently sent the suspension telegram after all.[14] The USPOD Information Service for March 22, 1970, cited a story in the March 18 *Washington Star*: "NALC President, James Rademacher, calls emergency meeting of the union's executive council. Says he will ask it to suspend the defiant Manhattan-Bronx unit, any others that might vote to strike."[15] For his part, Francis Stuart ("Stu") Filbey of the UFPC declared that his union did not support the strike but would back any members refusing to work based on fear of physical harm from strikers.[16]

Picket lines in New York were also going up in Brooklyn and the Bronx. Branch 36 member John Phelan had voted to strike the night before at the Manhattan Center and has this recollection: "I showed up before 6 A.M. at . . . Morris Heights Station on Jerome Ave. in the Bronx" with "a couple dozen" other carriers and clerks "just milling around. We knew we had to set up a picket line but we had no 'on strike' signs." Phelan's solution to the problem was to bang on the "cargo area doors" until the station manager, Sandy Brewer, came out. "I asked for some assistance: poster paper, crayons or felt tip pens and broomsticks. . . . Surprisingly, within a short period, Mr. Brewer showed up with a load of material." Stories of supervisor cooperation during this strike are common, though not universal by any means. Phelan's conclusion is the same as other strikers I have spoken to: "Maybe Mr. Brewer figured that whatever we would get in pay or benefits he would get more, and he was right."[17]

Also striking that first day were carriers at the Central Islip Post Office in Long Island, New York, according to local branch member Jaime Rodriguez. Rodriguez, who is Puerto Rican, had been a member of Branch 36 before transferring to Long Island — as were most carriers in that small branch (now part of Long Island Branch 6000). He described the tension after hearing that Branch 36 had voted to strike. "While we cased mail the conversation on the floor was: do we go out with Branch 36 or do we wait it out?" Their supervisor, he said, actually gave them time to meet in the swing room to discuss it, "and after a go-around we decided to join Branch 36."[18]

Also striking on Long Island, in Massapequa, was Matthew Illicette, then the branch secretary of NALC Branch 4202 (now merged with Branch 6000). Forty-two years old, he had eighteen years of seniority and was married with five children. Initially opposed to the strike, he nevertheless joined it after the branch voted to strike at their meeting hall. "We actually walked out of the post office," he said, while the station supervisor was taking their pictures. All the carriers walked out, with the clerks joining some days later.[19] In Jamaica, Queens, the NALC Branch 562 had about 600 members. Anthony Parrotta said, "We knew it was coming," and tells of union delegates instructing carriers to walk out of the office that morning.[20] But in Flushing, Queens, Thomas Idoyaga, who had emigrated from Cuba in 1957 at the age of twenty-two, recalls that the strike came "as a total surprise" to his Branch 1094. As soon as they heard the news, they walked out, calling a meeting to vote to strike on Thursday.[21] Branch 3795 (now part of Branch 38 merged) in Springfield, New Jersey, went out that day also, remembers Dave McDonald, who said they took a vote in the post office swing room. Much to their surprise, their "conservative" Italian-American branch president called for a strike vote that he advocated, and they voted "unanimously." They got support from almost all residents, although the postmaster's wife drove by and yelled, "Get back to work you scumbags!"[22] In Paterson, New Jersey, Murray Ross was president of NALC Branch 120 at the time of the strike, and declared with pride that "in New Jersey we were the first to go out on strike and the last to go back."[23] He added an observation that many NALC strikers voiced: "In my opinion the strike was also against the NALC and the New

Jersey State Association," and for that reason Ross believes he "was not very popular with the national and state association officers."[24]

When we look at the USPOD list of stations going out the first day, including cities where the USPOD decided to "embargo" the mail, the strike moved from New York City and environs to New Jersey and then to Connecticut in the first sixty hours of the strike. From there, it extended to Philadelphia, Pittsburgh, Detroit, Minneapolis–St. Paul and Milwaukee, and then Chicago. Embargoes were rolled back in patchwork fashion more than reverse order, the last one lifted March 30 in New York, five days after the strike had ended.[25]

Across the country in San Jose, California, Mexican-American letter carrier Hector Gallardo was listening to music on the radio that morning while "casing" mail. Gallardo had been working at a sub-station in East San Jose at the time, having transferred from nearby San Francisco, where he was born in 1942. His father had been a union machinist who himself had been on strike more than once during his career. Still a "sub" and a "floater" (carrying regular carriers' routes on their days off) at the time, Gallardo was married "with two kids, one on the way," he said. He remembers that the music he was listening to on the radio that morning was interrupted with a "news flash of the New York City carrier strike. It was like a tidal wave!" He tried calling the branch president, but got no answer, so he walked out along with about twenty-five other carriers. Meetings were called later at the branch hall that he described as "hot" with "people letting off steam." Rank-and-file members were at odds with local officers, and "most military retirees were afraid of losing their pensions. . . . Everybody was caught off guard, but everybody was united" after the strike vote. Branch 193 was out, he recalls, until after Monday March 23, when they heard of another supposed Nixon-Rademacher agreement. Gallardo also noted they had local "support from the clerk unions."[26]

The USPOD first reported San Francisco stations walking out as of 10:00 A.M. EST (7:00 A.M. PST) Friday, March 20, but it seems within the range of possibility that some stations had walkouts during the early days of the strike without appearing on the quickly improvised USPOD daily lists that were marked with some variant of "The Following Post Offices Are on Strike." It was only halfway through the strike that there is evidence that the USPOD began issuing "status" and "summary" reports every few hours that were more in-depth—reflecting efforts by the USPOD to cope with the strike's staggering statistical tsunami.[27] Also on strike in San Francisco was

Alfred Chircop, a special delivery carrier, who reflected on some ironic advice his father gave him while he was deciding the previous year what kind of job to apply for: "I had a choice to make in 1969 at the age of 19. I could join the Teamsters Union—I was making $4.44 an hour as a lumper (casual)—or join the Post Office for $2.95 an hour. My father advised me to take the Post Office job because there were no strikes or layoffs. Less than a year later we were on strike!"[28]

Back in New York City, Mother Nature was not being kind to picketers. There had been a cold early-spring rain all day—something most letter carriers were used to—with temperatures topping out in the upper thirties. If all eyes (and ears) of the nation's postal workers were on New York, in the city itself picket lines were growing with carriers, clerks, and mail handlers, while the numbers crossing those lines were thinning to a trickle. "Only a handful of Tour I personnel showed up for work that evening," Tom Germano reported. "Two actually went into the post office, the rest joined the picket line. At about 1:00 A.M. the last pickets abandoned the lines. As far as the GPO strikers were concerned, the first day had gone well."[29]

Yet if history was being made that day at midtown Manhattan post office picket lines, there was also plenty of dramatic labor activity that night a few blocks away at the Statler Hilton on West Thirty-Third Street and Seventh Avenue. "It was fabulous! Everybody was on fire!" is how Eleanor Bailey, an African American GPO clerk, recalls the raucous meeting Wednesday night at the Statler Hilton. At least one-quarter of the MBPU's massive membership packed the Statler ballroom, even spilling out onto the street. Most members had refused to cross carrier picket lines since the first day of the strike. Bailey, known for stopping strikebreakers from sneaking into the GPO, even warned her father, who worked as a GPO mail handler and had gone to work after the strike began. "Dad," she told him, "I promise you—cross the picket line, I will break your legs!" MBPU president Moe Biller would also be on the picket line every day, but he was conducting this strike meeting based on strict adherence to union bylaws and would not allow a voice vote despite his sympathy for the strike.[30] A March 19 New York Times account of the MBPU strike meeting was actually understated: "About 3,000 members of the Manhattan and Bronx Postal Union, which has 25,000 members, demanded an immediate sympathy strike [with Branch 36 of the NALC already out] at a tumultuous meeting at the Statler Hilton Hotel last night. Shouting 'Strike! Strike! Strike!' the union members swarmed over the speakers' platform and forced the local president Moe Biller to flee through a kitchen.

MBPU strike meeting, Wednesday March 18, 1970, New York. Union militants seized the stage as part of a popular demand for a voice vote to join NALC Branch 36 on the strike as president Moe Biller called for a secret-ballot vote. The MBPU officially voted to strike that Saturday by a secret ballot count of 8,242 to 940, but members had already been observing NALC picket lines. Photograph by Donal Holway; courtesy of the NYMAPU Collection, Tamiment/Wagner Archives, NYU.

They refused to listen to his argument that union bylaws required a secret ballot in any strike vote."[31]

In fact, the crowd was probably at least double that size at about 6,500, according to the Associated Press and oral history interviews.[32] As John Walsh and Garth Mangum wrote in *Labor Struggle in the Post Office*, this was "one of the wildest meetings in postal labor union history."[33] Biller himself later recalled: "The situation on the platform was becoming more menacing by the minute." His call for a secret-ballot vote to be conducted later that week was shouted down. In photographs from the *Times*, strike proponents can be seen assembling on the stage, crowding around the podium where Biller was standing, with fists upraised in response to the cheering crowd. Things got ugly when someone pulled a knife on Biller before a union member got in the way and protected Biller. MBPU financial secretary Milt Rosner later recalled how people were throwing chairs from the balcony. Biller had to be escorted out by supporters and city police for his own safety. Biller's insistence on a secret ballot swam against the tide of the rank and file who objected to any delay in what looked to be an inevitable vote to strike.[34] But MBPU members were already out on the picket lines with the NALC. All that was missing was the MBPU's formal yet crucial vote in three days.

SNOWBALLING ACROSS THE COUNTRY

Strike votes were being held across the Northeast, with upstate New York, New Jersey, and Connecticut being some of the first to join New York City in striking and picketing post offices, and encouraging coworkers to not cross picket lines. Contemporary reports and later reflections by strikers frequently allude to the word "solidarity" with striking postal workers, but especially with those in New York who started the strike. Ron Nowark, who later became a tractor trailer operator and APWU member, at the time of the strike worked as a letter carrier in Hackensack, New Jersey. He reports that Hackensack, which struck soon after New York City's branches and locals walked out, only had one carrier cross the picket line.[35]

Soon after the strike began, attorneys for the United States acting under the direction of U.S. attorney general John Mitchell filed injunctions and temporary restraining orders against local NALC branches where members were on strike. USPOD regional directors filed affidavits against the strikers. In Connecticut, for example, sixteen NALC branches and their presidents were ordered by the district court to take no part in the strike, and "to in-

MBPU members and other strikers in New York City, possibly in front of the GPO, sometime during March 18–25, 1970, on the picket line behind police barricades. Courtesy of the NYMAPU Collection, Tamiment/Wagner Archives, NYU.

struct immediately all of its members to resume their normal employment in the Postal Department of the United States." Paul Daniels was a member of NALC Branch 227 in Meriden, Connecticut, a small town halfway between Hartford and New Haven. He describes a raucous branch meeting at the Knights of Columbus Hall on Willow Street that went on for roughly five hours on the night of Thursday, March 19 — following a contentious meeting the previous night. Daniels was one of those who had been pushing for a strike. The story he tells resembles that of many other striking postal union branches and locals:

We were split between the young kids that wanted to go on strike, and the older carriers that had legitimate concerns about their pensions. They didn't know if they were gonna go to jail. They didn't know if they were gonna lose their pensions. And losing their pensions was one of their biggest arguments they made for not going on strike. . . . And I'll tell ya, people at that time cared about each other. They weren't at each other's throat over old and young. They were making legitimate arguments about their legitimate positions, and at the end of the day they were letter carriers. And I'll tell you what happened. We voted on the second day of the special meetings. We had votes and votes, it kept getting voted down, no strike. . . . But I wasn't gonna give up. So the last day, the day of the strike when we're gonna go out . . . about eleven o'clock that night . . . everybody's tired . . . and they just want to go home. . . . It's about eleven-thirty at night. Last motion, one more motion: "I make a motion we go on strike only if Hartford [Branch 86] goes on strike." . . . How in the hell would you know what's going in Hartford? Guy's got a portable radio. Everybody's getting up and getting ready to go home . . . and he says, "Hartford just went on strike!" What? Boom! Everybody sit down! "In accordance with the motion that was just passed we're on strike as of midnight tonight!" Nobody was prepared for that. . . . There was four people that went out at midnight and started picketing. . . . And the next morning in Meriden, no one came to work. No one crossed the picket line.[36]

Paul Daniels later wrote in the branch's journal, the *Union Courier*: "There was no vote to return to work. When the sheriff finally caught up with President McAllister and served the Restraining Order, McAllister advised the membership that we had made our point and we should return to work on Monday March 23rd which we all did with our heads held high."[37] Meanwhile, Ernest Salamone was vice president at the time of Hartford NALC Branch 86. It had about 100 members—one of the largest in the state. About three-quarters of the branch supported the strike, and clerks honored their picket line. Twenty-nine years old at the time of the strike, Salamone said that "they arrested some of us picketing on High Street," but they went back on the picket line upon release, and became what he called "the only branch in the country that was fined" for conducting an illegal strike.[38]

William "Bill" Burrus Jr., who went on to be elected the first black president of the APWU in 2001, at the time of the strike was a clerk and Cleveland NPU local vice president. He recalls that they walked out on Thursday, March 19, a day after New York did. The much larger Cleveland UFPC Local 72 had about 2,000 members, and that night the UFPC invited NPU to meet jointly: "The message of the meeting was there would be no walkout in Cleveland, that what happened in New York was an aberration." But NPU local members had other ideas. "We were tired of what was happening in Washington," Burrus recalled. "We had no idea what collective bargaining meant at that time. We basically wanted more money. But it was a good punch line to say you wanted collective-bargaining rights, too." After the meeting, he said, "we convinced everybody to go, UFPC and NPU. The next morning [Friday], we had pickets in front of the post office. . . . Letter carriers relied upon our pickets of their facilities."[39] Another NPU striker in Ohio was James Mann in the western Cleveland suburb of North Olmsted. A Vietnam War veteran of the U.S. Navy who had just returned "young and hotheaded," Mann had started at the post office in 1968 as a combination "carrier/clerk" doing work that he observed would have been barred as "crossing crafts" (doing work across craft lines) since that time. Mann says that the carriers (who would have been NALC members) met at the local high school, and all of them voted to strike. "With that done we all returned to the Post Office, checked in, and went home to plan picket lines." Four carriers crossed the picket lines, which created bitterness for years afterward—a common story that one hears from strike participants. It also sparked a remarkably genial collective defiance despite the frustration, fear, and uncertainty. "The Postmaster was taking pictures of us with our signs," remembers Mann, "and we smiled and waved back although we could have all been sent to jail."[40]

For their part, Cleveland NALC Branch 40 members recall Friday, March 20, as the day when they went out. Branch 40 president Harold Loewe had called a meeting at the United Automobile Workers hall the night before to ask what they wanted to do. Former Branch 40 president Joe Vacca, who was now NALC assistant secretary-treasurer, came from the national office to try to talk them out of striking. "That place was packed," recalls Branch 40 rank-and-file member Bob Murphy. "We had nobody get up who did not want to go on strike."[41] And strike is what they voted to do, despite Loewe's objections, as reported by the UPI and AP wire services. When Loewe "tried to recommend to the Cleveland workers acceptance of the government's offer, he was booed and the workers voted to strike." This wire service story appeared in the *San Francisco Chronicle* of March 21, 1970, with the headline: "Workers Defy U.S. Back-to-Work Order—Leadership Helpless."[42]

Recollections by Bill Burrus, Hector Gallardo, and others paint the strike as a wave that moved swiftly. It is remarkable how many local strike votes were held that week around the country following that of NALC Branch 36 in New York City. Strikers relied on the mass media to get information about what other strikers were doing nationwide.[43] Despite the inconvenience to the public of a total mail stoppage, strikers enjoyed the support of the majority of Americans, as reported in both personal stories and news media polling. Strike veterans remember cars honking, and people waving or even bringing doughnuts and coffee to picket lines. "Right on, mailmen, you deserve your money," is what letter carrier Verle Craven recalls people shouting from their car windows as they drove by, encouraging NALC Branch 1111 strikers in Richmond, California, where the strike had spread by the weekend after St. Patrick's Day. The White House acknowledged that their *mail* response from Americans favored the strike by a ratio of ten to one—an ironic admission to have to make. And a nationwide post-strike survey found support for strikers at 61 percent to 25 percent opposed. President Nixon and his administration were quite concerned with poll numbers. Nixon's aide Charles Colson sent a telegram to the White House from New Jersey on March 27 informing them that the new Gallup poll was out, recording eight of ten Americans supporting a postal pay raise, 41 percent backing Nixon's independent postal agency plan, and 62 percent behind use of the troops to move the mail. Internal White House memos and meetings reveal apprehension with the views of labor, civil rights groups, and "minority communities" toward strikers and troops moving mail.[44] The strike had galvanized workers from coast to coast and across crafts and unions.

Within the same postal unions could be found activist members who opposed the strike, fearing the government would use it to break postal unions. Atlanta NAPFE official Samuel Lovett declared the strike "crazy," believing that strikers should have "stuck to the law" to resolve outstanding issues. Miami NAPFE official Sam Armstrong voiced similar objections. On the other hand, Countee Abbott, then a Chicago postal clerk who at the time of the strike was NAPFE District Seven (Midwest region) president, proudly proclaimed: "I participated in it!"[45] Ann Mariposa, a clerk who belonged to NAPFE and later joined the APWU after it was formed, recalls picketing the Berkeley, California, main post office.[46]

Meanwhile, over at the Chicago Plumbers' Union Hall, NALC Branch 11 was voting to strike on Friday March 20 over the objections of their president Henry Zych. "My first [union] meeting was the strike meeting," remembers Mildred Cross. "There were more letter carriers than you can imagine!"[47] In addition to NAPFE, NPU, UFPC, and other union members who struck in that city, this huge NALC branch of about 5,000 members was key to Chicago's short but crucial strike participation starting Saturday, March 21, and ending by the following Tuesday, March 24. It underscored the city's role as a key mail distribution center, which meant that postal workers did not have to shut down or disrupt the whole country, as Countee Abbott pointed out, but rather "major metropolitan areas" like Chicago, New York, Philadelphia, Detroit, and Los Angeles. Nevertheless, it helped the strikers' cause for Americans to see suburban and small-town postal workers shutting down their local stations, demanding a living wage and fair treatment. It demonstrated nationwide postal worker solidarity.[48]

That unity across craft lines was dramatically demonstrated in Detroit with a mass strike vote that Sunday morning at Cobo Hall. The vote took place after several days of picketing that had begun on the afternoon of Wednesday, March 18 — the same day that New York had gone out — and had already shut down Detroit and some suburban offices. There was a fifteen-minute meeting where about 3,000 postal workers voted unanimously to strike after the fact. Participants included nineteen-year-old NALC rank-and-file Branch 1 member Stephen Burt ("Most of my coworkers were World War II vets!") and NPU local president Doug Holbrook, who presided over the meeting ("I announced that we were officially on strike").[49] In nearby Pontiac, Michigan, Joe Chappellie, working as a clerk, recalled that they "were one of the first (if not the first)" post offices to strike in the Detroit area, adding: "We decided to all grow beards in support of it, and it must have gathered good P.R. because a photographer from *Life* magazine came by our office and took pictures."[50]

Back in the nation's capital, Postmaster General Blount had embargoed all mail going in and out of New York City, in addition to suspending private express statutes for that city and allowing for private delivery, "sealing" all mail collection boxes to protect "the sanctity of the mail," along with placing strikers in a "non-pay status." He also announced, however, that there was "no consideration for using troops to try to move the mail," an idea he dismissed as "impractical."[51] Another perspective was provided by labor attorney Jules Bernstein. Bernstein worked for both the National Postal Mail Handlers (NPMHU) and the union that it had affiliated with in 1968, the controversial Laborers International Union of North America (LIUNA), discussed more in chapter 6. He was part of the 1970 post-strike negotiations that would begin Thursday, March 26, 1970, the day after the strike ended. But Bernstein, who became a longtime friend of assistant secretary of labor William Usery Jr. (pronounced "US-er-ee"), remembers that the week before, probably on Thursday night March 19, he had asked Usery to get secretary of labor George Shultz directly involved in the negotiations. Bernstein said that joining him at that D.C. dinner meeting with Usery were James LaPenta, LIUNA Director of Federal Public Service (up until 1968 LaPenta had been USPOD Deputy Assistant Postmaster General, Bureau of Personnel), and Robert Connerton, LIUNA general counsel. "And we said to him, Bill, the secretary of labor needs to get in the middle of this . . . and end the strike." Usery and Shultz, according to Bernstein, were both reluctant based on what Usery cited as a non-interference protocol among Cabinet officers. Bernstein recalls that he convinced Usery to try and change Shultz's mind. Shultz personally knew LIUNA officials, most prominently its national president Peter Fosco, from when Shultz had been dean of the business school at the University of Chicago. Shultz subsequently did agree to get directly involved in negotiations. Bernstein maintains LIUNA was the main force that got George Meany to intervene in the post-strike negotiations, six of the seven "national exclusive" postal unions being AFL-CIO affiliates.[52]

As far as the Nixon White House was concerned, the strike was just now appearing on the radar in the notes of Nixon's chief of staff H. R. Haldeman, who wrote, "Start of a postal strike today that could spread beyond New York, [President] wants to be sure we do what we could."[53] What could have topped an illegal postal strike? According to Haldeman, a lot had been preoccupying the president since Tuesday, March 17: Kissinger's report on negotiating with North Vietnam at the Paris Peace talks; Nixon's preparation of a statement on school desegregation that would not imply support for school busing; worries about the chances of ex-actor George Murphy making a successful Senate bid as a Republican from California; and Kissinger's issues with secretary of state William Rogers over Israel and whether to bomb Laos. The papers of White House counsels Charles Colson and John Ehrlichman also fail to reveal awareness any earlier than Thursday: somehow they all missed the start of the postal strike. It was as if they could not believe that it had really happened.[54]

TRYING TO PUT THE GENIE BACK IN THE BOTTLE

Friday, March 20, found the worst fears confirmed at the Nixon White House: the strike had indeed spread beyond New York. "Postal strike still on," wrote Haldeman in his diary, "and P [President Nixon] got into some lengthy sessions with E [White House counsel and Assistant to the President for Domestic Affairs John Ehrlichman] on it. . . . P's first reaction was

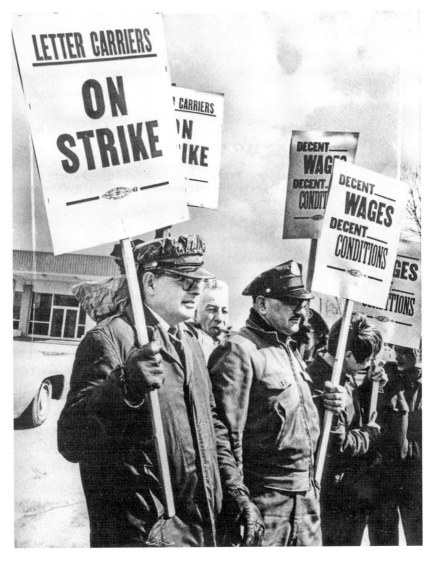

Dearborn, Michigan, NALC Branch 2184 picket line, sometime during March 18–25, 1970. Over 200,000 postal workers struck nationwide that week from coast to coast. Courtesy of the *Detroit Free Press*.

for really tough stand, examine the law, if people can be fired, fire them, if troops can be moved, move them. Wants to do something now, this morning, not going to tolerate Federal employees strike. Says suspend them if we can't fire them, all-out attack, not worried about the mail, it's the principle." Haldeman's next notes suggest a Nixon mood swing from anger to denial: "At midday, as P got better feel of seriousness and complexity of postal problem, he decided not to have the press conference today. Will probably do it in the morning. In discussing items with [White House Press Secretary Ron] Ziegler for briefing, P said, 'Hard-nose it at the moment, we'll have some good news before long.' Wants to be sure not to express concern, etc., about postal strike because that implies we're not in control, lack of leadership, etc."[55]

Presumably to get some of that good news, Nixon phoned secretary of labor George Shultz, according to Haldeman. Shultz "said he'd do anything [Nixon] wanted about meetings, statements, etc. He's anxious to get in command of situation."[56] An optimistic Haldeman next reported, "Postal problem settled in late afternoon when union leaders agreed to get workers back in, then negotiate. At least E[hrlichman] thinks this settles it." But Haldeman had his doubts: "I doubt that leaders can get workers back, since it's a wildcat strike to begin with."[57] By this time, the government had responded to the strike with court injunctions and threats of fines served on local union leaders, with public and private threats issues to break the unions of their power or even their existence. With that fear in mind, NALC President Rademacher, who had tried to stop the strike, on Friday, March 20, called 300 NALC state presidents and presidents of the largest branches to come to Washington, D.C. That represented about 80 percent of the NALC membership, out of a total of 6,000 branches. Wayne White was then president of the North Carolina NALC state association: "I was just a country boy, listenin' and watchin'. . . . It was quite an experience!" He vividly recalls those meetings where Rademacher and Usery tried to convince these state and local union leaders to give them more time to reach a settlement and end the strike.[58] Rademacher asked for their help in bringing the strike to a close, vowing to lead a strike in five days if they did not win what the strikers were demanding. He was not preaching to the choir. He was buying time. It is hard to imagine that he would have called a strike under any circumstances. But there was pressure on Rademacher to deliver. For the first time in NALC history, its 210,000 members—almost half of whom were already striking—were investing in their union president the power to call an official nationwide strike.[59]

Just before leaving for the meeting that morning, Rademacher had received a phone call from secretary of labor George Shultz, who told him, "We'd like to meet with you as soon as possible to try to settle whatever the problem is." Rademacher told him, "I'm sorry. I'm going to a meeting now to let you know what the problem is." Shultz replied that the administration was ready to talk. At the meeting of NALC branch presidents, Rademacher announced that he had "400 letters and telegrams [from branch presidents] telling me they'll support whatever action I take," while in his other hand he had "a message from the secretary of labor declaring he is ready to meet with us." Rademacher then recalled: "A delegate . . . arose and says, 'I move we give you five days to settle this. We'll go back to work.' It was almost unanimous. Because they didn't want to stay off [the job], but they trusted me, that I was going to do something. So I . . . told them, 'I'll be back at 1:00.' I went over to see Shultz. He set up the . . . meeting the very next day—Saturday."[60]

Postal union branches and locals continued to walk out that day as the strike spread across New England, New Jersey, and Pennsylvania. By ten o'clock Friday morning, March 20, a USPOD memo monitoring early strike activity affirmed that besides the New York City area, the entire states of Connecticut and New Jersey were on strike, as was the Philadelphia area. The memo, as with similar memos, was probably issued by the USPOD Head-quarters Control Center in their Washington, D.C., Bureau of Operations. But these USPOD reports were not yet standardized, possibly reflecting some institutional surprise. The rapid spread of the strike and the flying-by-the-seat-of-their-pants USPOD response was reflected in handwritten notations in this and other memos concerning cities like Detroit (following East Lansing and Dearborn) in Michigan, and San Francisco ("three stations out") in California added to the list along with Milwaukee, Wisconsin; St. Paul, Minnesota; and the Chicago suburb of Berwyn, Illinois.[61] By 11:30 A.M., Denver and Golden, Colorado, were handwritten into the updated typed list as cities experiencing "partial" strike involvement, along with three mail processing "sectional centers" in Pennsylvania, including Norristown, Doyleston, and Paoli—all in the Philadelphia area.[62]

In Philadelphia, clerks, carriers, mail handlers, and other crafts were hold-ing strike meetings and walking out. Members of the NPU's 5,500-member Philadelphia Postal Union (PPU) since Thursday March 19 had been "clam-oring all day for a strike," according to what their president Al Rosen told the press. One of those "clamoring" rank-and-filers was Greg Bell—a full-time college student working the evening shift as a PTF (Part Time Flexible) distribution clerk at the main post office at Thirtieth and Market. A young black "newly active member" of the PPU who had just started work at the post office in January, Bell recalls a bar across the street called Pete Richard's Tavern "where postal workers would go for lunch and socialize after work. During the strike, I remember that some of us would meet there and line up at the pay phone to call work to report that we would not be in." Bell, who later went on to serve as president of the Philadelphia APWU local, executive vice president of the national APWU, as well as other union offices, reports not only of the near-total effectiveness of the picket line at his post office, but also how on Sunday, March 22, both the PPU and NALC Branch 157 "defied the court order and pleas from their national leadership to end the strike, and voted to continue the strike."[63]

Thursday, March 19, was also the same day that members of the NALC Philadelphia "Keystone" Branch 157 voted to strike. The PPU rank and file refused to cross letter-carrier picket lines, and joined picket lines on Friday. On Saturday, March 21, only seventy-two clerks reported to work. Writing twenty-five years later in the PPU monthly newsletter, PPU treasurer Sally Davidow (later national APWU communications director) noted the crucial role of Philadelphia area strikers in shutting down mail in southeastern Pennsylvania and southern New Jersey. Even with injunctions slapped on them early in the strike, both PPU and NALC Branch 157 members voted on Sunday to extend the strike in defiance of those injunctions.[64] Nineteen-year-old letter carrier and Branch 157 member James Reilly was there that Friday morning in southwest Philadelphia. His story sums up the seeming randomness, combined with real-life dramatic discussions and actions — along with frequent lower-management ambivalence — that made labor solidarity work at street level:

> I come from a family of old union people. So I was brought up
> "union strong, union this, and union that." And being a PTF at
> that time, you didn't have a steady schedule. Right from the jump
> I got involved with the union. I talked to the guys. I seen guys
> older than me — one guy had seven kids. He actually had to collect
> welfare, food stamps, to make payments, to make it through. This
> is in Paschall Station in Philadelphia. . . . So my father drives me
> to work that day. And I was scheduled to come in at 8:30 [A.M.].
> . . . The guys were already out on picket. Everybody was out at my
> station, walking around Paschall Station. I looked at my dad. He
> says, "Well, what are you gonna do?" I said, "Well, I'm not gonna
> cross." He said, "Good, good." And then the shop steward came
> over said, "Jimmy, you better get in there, you're still on ninety-day
> probation." So I looked at my father. And he said, you know, "What
> are you gonna do?" I said, "I don't know." This steward said, "Jim,
> you better go in . . . You better go in or they're gonna fire you. *We*
> can be fired — [but] they'll definitely fire *you*." So reluctantly I went
> in. . . . My manager was an ex-carrier. He goes, "What do you want

to do?" I said, "I don't want to do nothing." He says, "Alright, just sit over there." So, I sat there for four hours, getting my four hours in and I left, and I went out and picked up my picket sign and joined my brothers.[65]

Joseph Hanlon was a letter carrier at the nearby Paoli, Pennsylvania, sectional center. (New Jersey and Pennsylvania were both part of the Philadelphia postal region.) He was also president of the tiny NALC Branch 4317, which as it turned out wielded a disproportionately large amount of power in shutting down mail for their entire region—a power that he and other strikers were quite aware of at the time: "There was only eight of us [carriers], but there were 300 clerks at this facility, and all those clerks joined the strike."[66] Samuel Miller, then twenty-seven and also from Branch 4317, thought it was funny that their small town of 5,000 actually had its mail embargoed, and recalls how they struck:

> March 20 was a Friday morning. We all went to work—there was only about eight to ten of us back in those days at our office. We sat in the swing room and it was getting close to clocking in. And we all knew what was going on in New York. And we just took an on-the-spot, off-the-cuff vote, and we said, "We're going out." We walked out, and the supervisor came over and he started reading a prepared statement. Basically it said we were all gonna get fired. So we went out and went to a little diner . . . and we decided to make up some placards. . . . We had $2.50 in our treasury so we blew all that on the posterboards and we went back and started to picket. . . . It's funny, we were the sectional center. So *all* the zip codes that started with 193 came through our place.[67]

In Pittsburgh, Joe Trenga of NALC Branch 84, who had come out of the military service in 1967 and started at the post office as a mail handler before transferring to carrier craft in 1968, remembers people telling strikers on the picket line: "They're going to fire you!"[68] Also striking in NALC Branch 84 was Howard W. Brandt Jr., working as a "sub" at the time of the strike, and just getting active in the union. Even though he had less job protection than "regulars," Howard said that his "real heroes" were those within a decade of retirement. He went on to observe, "The thing about the strike that was unusual was that nobody knew what was going on." The general chaos of the strike everywhere seemed to also inspire opportunity to create new possibilities. When Brandt went to his station he found everyone out, with the boss bringing out the coffee urn. They were all busy making sure there were pickets at the downtown post office and at the terminal annex where trains deposited and picked up mail. Many of their wives were doing picket duty. "It was person-to-person communication. All our union officers were gone. They were hiding [worried about being] served with papers."[69]

"The marshals were looking for us!" also recalls John P. Richards, then an NPU regional business agent from Pittsburgh. He has similar recollections of NPU officers successfully evading federal marshals while members walked the picket lines: "No one was served that I know," he said. Clerks and carriers walked out and observed picket lines with few exceptions. Richards himself had grown up in a family of union steelworkers where striking was not uncommon. As a boy he had even rolled cigarettes for his father to sell while on strike. Richards reports that the NPU president at the time, Oscar Leckman, had also been a steelworker, and that Pittsburgh as an industrial center was a crucial mail center to shut down, even if just for a few days. Another important observation Richards shared was echoed by other strike participants: the issue of personal sacrifice. Richards was bemused by those who said they struck but at the time had actually crossed the picket line and "clocked in, and then sat around because there was no mail to process," as the strike had shut down the nation's mail flow. It is not uncommon to hear stories of coworkers shunning strikebreakers for years afterward.[70]

According to USPOD strike reports, Pittsburgh was out as of Saturday, March 21, along with Chicago, Cleveland, and Detroit in the industrial Midwest.[71] The *Pittsburgh Post-Gazette*, like many newspapers, focused almost exclusively on the carriers while ignoring other crafts or unions. Their coverage shows NALC Branch 84 voting to strike Friday, then voting to return to work on Sunday. Interestingly, the *Post-Gazette* reported that the decision to strike was by a branch executive board vote of 8–4, while the choice to return was by referendum of over 1,200 branch members by roughly the same margin. Even more intriguing was the account of that Sunday, March 22, meeting at Soldiers and Sailors Hall, where the newspaper reported that "militants wanting to continue the strike booed at times and yelled, 'We're starving now,' and 'Sell-out!'" Branch president John O'Shea prevailed in convincing the great majority of those voting (which included only three women) to approve the "five-day cooling-off period" called for by NALC national president James Rademacher. But O'Shea managed to sound militant himself in announcing what became a familiar NALC branch president refrain, that "if negotiations bog down, I'll lead them out on a strike until hell freezes over."[72]

In the Midwest, Richard Schwarze of NALC Elmhurst, Illinois, Branch 825 (a different number then) also recalls walking out on Friday, March 20. Jim Sauer remembers that his suburban Des Plaines Branch 2076, just outside of Chicago, with about 120 carriers, went out Friday at six in the morning, and then took an official vote around three-thirty that afternoon at the American Legion Hall.[73]

Meanwhile, Barry Weiner of New York Branch 36, who said that prior to the strike he was a "sixties social radical" who had not considered the union "militant enough," provides a snapshot of what the mood must have been like on the first picket lines in New York City. They were waiting to see who, if anyone, was going to follow them out on strike around the country:

> It was easy to be "rah rah rah" leading up to the strike. But once you're there, now we're walking the picket line and we're thinking to ourselves, "Is anyone else in the country gonna go out on strike?" And we're listening to the news with these transistor radios. And at first we heard Brooklyn went out. Yay! Then we hear some branches in New Jersey it's reported are going out on strike. Yay! But that didn't really surprise us that much because we knew that on the East Coast there were a lot of people who were in the same financial situation. . . . Then we started hearing Boston, Philadelphia. On the West Coast, a couple of branches like L.A., San Francisco. We weren't really surprised about that. . . . I then heard on the radio that Minneapolis and St. Paul went out on strike. And I said to the people that I was picketing with . . . we're gonna win this thing. I've think we've got them. Because if they're going out on strike in the heartland of America, then this thing is gonna spread everywhere, and we're gonna wind up prevailing.[74]

Minneapolis and St. Paul already had a history of radical unionism that included postal workers. But being in the Upper Midwest kept them off many media radars of labor activism.[75] Meanwhile, the various stories from around the country reshape a common conception of the strike moving through space as well as time in a linear fashion. Modern technology that included telephones, television, and radio news, as well as print newspapers, made the strike news readily available. Workers arriving at their stations, some in earlier time zones who had heard the news before reporting to work, sometimes made spontaneous decisions to picket, regardless of whether or not they had time to hold formal meetings. Postal workers wanted to be involved, wherever they happened to be and regardless of their direct impact on the mail system. From big cities to small towns, the rapid and sponta-neous actions created a scenario of a nationwide postal worker solidarity that encouraged other postal workers and impressed the general public — as well as the USPOD.[76] Popular accounts of the strike note the unprecedented "em-bargo" or total halt the USPOD placed on all mail going in and out of New York City from the very first day of the strike, leaving out other cities in New York, New Jersey, Connecticut, Pennsylvania, as well as Michigan, Illinois, Wisconsin, and Minnesota that also saw embargoes.[77]

In Minnesota's Twin Cities, St. Paul went out Thursday, March 19, and Minneapolis followed the next day. Minneapolis letter carrier Mark Schindeldecker started at the post office in 1968. Married with children and in his mid-twenties, at the time he "had nothing to lose," with wages so low he thought he qualified for food stamps. He recalled that, inspired by Branch 36 and others already on strike, NALC Branch 9 in Minneapolis had their strike meeting that Friday night, and began picketing the next day. "I stayed in town and made all the strike signs for the Nokomis Station," he recalls. "It took me most of the night! I showed up in the morning with all the signs and I still had my postal uniform on. Found out from inspectors we couldn't wear our uniforms. I went down to my dad's house and borrowed his pants, size 42. I couldn't find a belt anywhere! The moral of the story is — try hold-ing onto a strike sign and your pants at the same time."[78]

The strike vote had not even been close for Branch 9: 1050–89 voted to strike.[79] The St. Paul NALC Branch 38 had already voted Thursday night to strike and began picketing early Friday morning. The UFPC, represent-ing clerks, and the competing NPU, which represented clerks, mail handlers, and other crafts, also participated in the postal strike in the Twin Cities. As in New York and other cities, the USPOD embargoed the mail in Minneapo-lis and St. Paul. The St. Paul Union Depot, as pointed out by the Minneapo-lis *Tribune*, was a major routing point in railroad mail distribution between the coasts.[80]

Back in New York, what had appeared to be the more likely New York postal union to have started the strike — the MBPU — was instead follow-ing on the heels of NALC Branches 36 (Manhattan-Bronx) and 41 (Brook-lyn). The MBPU was an industrial postal union that was mostly clerks but also included most of the mail handlers in the city as well as members of all crafts, even some letter carriers. After a tumultuous mass meeting Wednes-day night, the MBPU was set to take their secret-ballot strike vote on Satur-day, March 21, while area letter carriers were also rallying in support of the strike.[81]

St. Paul, Minnesota, NALC Branch 28 members after strike vote,
March 19, 1970, with branch member Robert Boltes holding picket sign.
Photograph by Pete Hohn; courtesy of the Minnesota Historical Society.

Ten o'clock Saturday morning, March 21, in Manhattan witnessed a mass display by letter carriers combining boisterous regional strike solidarity as well as disdain for all national officials working to derail the strike — whether it be the federal courts, President Nixon, or NALC president Rademacher. "Almost six thousand letter carriers filed into the Harlem armory between rows of armed U.S. servicemen," wrote Tom Germano. "Contingents of carriers from Queens, New Jersey, Long Island, and Brooklyn were on hand to voice support for the continuance of the strike. All agreed that the vote of Branch 36 would determine whether or not the strike would continue."[82] New York postal strikers in general and Branch 36 members in particular were emerging as the national leadership of the wildcat strike. There was drama as NALC Branch 36 president Gus Johnson first read out loud to the union members the court's back-to-work order, followed by President Rademacher's telegram that "outlined the agreement reached with the Secretary of Labor" and "implored the carriers to return to work in order to allow meaningful negotiations to begin."[83] Johnson, who had changed from strike opponent to strike advocate in the waning minutes of St. Patrick's Day with Branch 36's first strike vote, now reiterated his previous promise "to lead in their struggle," as Germano put it. To do so, however, Johnson had to wait until the subsiding of boos and catcalls that greeted each document he read out loud. "Before he could finish," said Germano of the back-to-work order, "the crowd began to scream 'Strike! Strike! Strike!' and then "Vote! Vote! Vote!': The vote was but a formality."[84] Many who subsequently filed out into the streets after the meeting to cheers from carriers from other cities then proceeded to march through Harlem "toward their respective post offices where they would resume picket duty." Some of those who had voted were wearing their postal uniforms, notes Germano. Letter carriers, in uniform or civilian clothes, were marching in the street to cheers along the way from many Harlem residents as well as a mutual exchange of the two-fingered V-for-victory sign.[85]

Meanwhile, in Chicago, letter carriers were walking out that same day after a boisterous meeting Friday night, March 20, at the Plumbers' Union Hall in that city's downtown "loop," where thousands of union members shouted "Strike!" when their president, Henry S. Zych, initially tried to dissuade them. But after the vote he proclaimed that the membership was so "angry" they would stay out "until hell freezes over." As Tom Germano, Countee Abbott, and others have pointed out, Chicago was *the* central mail distribution center in the nation. For New York to strike was immensely significant in itself. Now, with the strike spreading, if Chicago walked out it would be a game-changer. This has to be seen as a major momentum-builder for the strike. Postal workers also walked off the job in downstate Illinois and elsewhere in the Midwest in cities and towns in Minnesota and Wisconsin, besides going out in western cities like Denver, Los Angeles, San Francisco. There was no set pattern: some post offices across the country saw total carrier strike solidarity, while others saw ambivalence or even opposition. Some locations saw clerks and mail handlers honoring and even walking the picket lines, while in others they crossed lines or stayed home.[86]

Cornell Booker, a twenty-two-year-old Chicago native, was a Branch 11 striker who had just gotten home from military service in Vietnam in October 1969. He had worked as a mail handler in 1965 before being drafted. "I was skeptical about really going out on strike," he said, "but we had been hearing . . . about everything that was going on." A substitute or "sub" letter carrier assigned to parcel distribution on weekends, Cornell saw the picket lines Sunday night and joined them. On those Chicago picket lines was Booker Palmer, then twenty-four and originally from Huntsville, Alabama, who echoed a theme heard often from strikers: "It was really a good time for me, because . . . we were young, and it was like really a fun day . . . walking, talking, yelling, 'We on strike!' We didn't care about getting threatened."[87] Pearline Sanford, another Branch 11 striker, came to the Chicago Post Office in 1967, as she put it, through her husband, a Navy veteran who got a position as a letter carrier. Married with children, Sanford also had a sister who was a clerk. The post office in Chicago, as elsewhere, was an opportunity magnet for a lot of African Americans. Sanford remembers walking the picket line at her small station at Seventy-Ninth and Racine. "We were afraid about our jobs," she said, "but they kept saying this is the only way you're going to win."[88]

On the South Side, the Chicago Post Office had opened a new facility in 1965 called South Suburban P&DC (Processing and Distribution Center), then located at 7400 South Kostner Avenue, with over 4,000 employees. James Malone, UFPC Local 6591 president since 1968, called the local out on strike at midnight Friday. "The vast majority of employees walked off the job," he recalls. "Only probationary employees were allowed to cross the picket lines. . . . The Chicago Police, who were mostly sympathetic to us strikers, forced us off the streets, and the postal inspectors forced us off USPS [sic] property. We had approximately 90 percent cooperation from the work force that included all crafts."[89]

Back in New York on March 21, the MBPU vote was not even close at the

MBPU members standing in four lines arranged alphabetically
by last name on Saturday, March 21, 1970, as they voted to strike.
The vote was coordinated by the Honest Ballot Association, the same
organization that supervised the NALC Branch 36 strike vote on March 17.
Courtesy of the NYMAPU Collection, Tamiment/Wagner Archives, NYU.

Manhattan Center—the same place Branch 36 had voted to strike the previous Tuesday night. Once again, the Honest Ballot Association supervised
a postal strike vote, as MBPU members voted all day between 6:00 A.M. and
10:00 P.M. When votes by over one-third of their membership had been tal-
lied, the outcome in favor of striking was 8,242 to 940. The aftermath had
echoes of a religious rite: "Thousands of MBPU members joined in a candle-
light vigil around the [nearby] General Post Office, and hundreds of postal
workers became MBPU members during the ceremony," write Walsh and
Mangum in their APWU history. The MBPU would play a vital role in the
winning of the strike. And Moe Biller's ironic goal had been accomplished.
Like NALC Branch 36 four nights earlier, the MBPU, a legally constituted and
recognized federal government employees' union, had just conducted a legal
vote to conduct an illegal strike.[90]

If the media became an unwitting accomplice to the nationwide postal
strike, it also became the live broadcast drama: television anchors framed the
strike spreading to different cities, with exuberant striker interviewees ar-
ticulating their grievances to millions of viewers, providing vivid evidence of
government workers risking job loss, fines, and jail time for better living con-

The Strike Begins

ditions. In at least one broadcast, the TV camera cut away to USPOD head-quarters, with postal officials marking each reported strike outbreak on a map in their situation room.[91] At the White House, concern was also mount-ing, ranging from imagined fears of left radicals to a real mass labor action out of control. "The settlement didn't work," fretted H. R. Haldeman, "be-cause rank and file won't go back, have rejected leaders, and now SDS [Stu-dents for a Democratic Society] types involved, at least in New York. Walk-out has spread to many other cities, including Chicago, where they noted a strike. Real danger of national strike, with need then to call in troops to de-liver mail, and police to disperse pickets. Strategy is to do the least we have to do, but to insure [sic] the delivery of the mail."[92]

Nixon canceled his planned trip to the White House retreat in Camp David, Maryland, "to stay on top of the mail crisis."[93] Haldeman's diary had become consumed by the strike: "Threat now is of radicalization, a national strike, other walkouts, i.e. Teamsters, Air Traffic Controllers, etc., to cripple whole country at once. Would provide a real opportunity for leadership, but how to handle it? Overreaction could bring a real disaster."[94]

Out on the West Coast, the Saturday morning, March 21, *San Francisco Chronicle* would report that on Friday night "300 members of the local letter carriers—roughly one-fourth of the [NALC Branch 214] union's member-ship here—filed noisily into the ILWU [International Longshore and Ware-house Union] hall at 150 Golden Gate Avenue . . . to decide overwhelmingly on the strike vote." Members of that "Golden Gate" Branch 214, the *Chronicle* noted, had already begun walking off the job Friday morning. Branch 214 vice president Don Hackett and other local union officials faced "heckling" during the two-hour meeting for asking members who had already walked out "to return to work" and show "faith in their leadership." Hackett later called a press conference where he echoed the position emerging from the NALC national office, namely: go back to work, don't walk out, let us nego-tiate, we'll call a strike if that fails. Branch 214 president George Peralty was not in attendance at the branch strike meeting, because he was still in Wash-ington, D.C., where James Rademacher and NALC branch presidents had been meeting.[95]

STRIKE NOW COAST TO COAST

On Sunday morning, March 22, the *San Francisco Chronicle* proclaimed with a front-page headline: "Total Strike Monday by S.F. Carriers." The strike had now officially traveled coast to coast in about the same length of time that it took an average driver to cover that distance using the interstate highway system. Not only had NALC Branch 214 members voted 847–150 to strike Saturday night, but their president had sent a telegram from Washington, D.C., immediately afterwards that read: "Nobody works Monday. Nobody will do anything as far as negotiating till we get back in conference and come up with something." Another lopsided vote was reported in that same article: nearby Palo Alto carriers had voted to strike 125–10. Clerks were striking as well, as a "Post Office spokesman reported that about one-third of the 1,000 postal workers on the evening shift at Rincon Annex showed up last night. Rincon is the distribution point for all San Francisco incoming and outgoing mail." The *Chronicle* reporter figured that "Peralty's telegram ordering no work on Monday indicated a shift in the attitude of the union's national leadership." That speculation was premature, but it does suggest that not every NALC branch president came away from Friday's meeting with Rademacher ready to herd their members back to work.[96] With San Rafael in Marin County already seeing a work stoppage, this article also highlighted the general sense not just among postal workers but the general public of a strike still spreading, noting that San Jose, Berkeley, Daley City, San Mateo, and San Leandro were among the cities added to the list of those struck.[97] San Francisco was a city that was, after all, still amazed by what the *Chronicle* called the "unprecedented" four-day general strike of city employees that ended March 17 — the night Branch 36 in New York had voted to strike the post office and thus set off the nationwide wildcat strike.[98] A union seldom heard from during the strike — the National Postal Mail Handlers Union — weighed in with President Lonnie Johnson, announcing that "increasing numbers" of its members striking on their own would return to work on Monday, March 23, "on assurances" of amnesty and substantial pay raises.[99]

The Pacific Northwest has a long history of labor activism, but it also has been commonly assumed there was no postal strike activity in 1970. Yet there actually *was* some debate, voting, picketing, and pro-strike sympathy. NALC Portland Branch 82 and UFPC Local 128 both decided to hold strike votes with mail-in ballots. In neighboring Washington, NALC Seattle Branch 79 called two meetings — Tacoma Branch 130 held at least one — to debate and vote, while Everett and Bellingham indicated they would walk out if Seattle and Tacoma did. Portland UFPC Local 128 announced on Friday, March 20, that clerks would observe NALC picket lines if a strike were called. The Portland *Oregonian* had first reported on Friday that Branch 82 was set to meet that night on whether to strike, and later took a vote by mail Sunday to be tabulated the following Thursday. Local 128 did the same. On Sunday, March

The Strike Begins

22, the *Oregonian* carried a front-page story with the headline "Local Carriers Set Strike Vote," with the sub-headline "Ballots to Be Mailed Monday; 20 'Dissidents' Picket Office." The latter referred to letter carriers picketing Portland's main post office Saturday morning and calling for their own meeting in solidarity with strikers around the country. Branch 82 president Everett Mallon, who had just returned from meeting in Washington, D.C., with other branch presidents and NALC president James Rademacher, said members would cross any future "dissident" letter carriers picket lines. Ultimately, postal unions in the Northwest voted to not strike, but the media did report packed union meetings, frustration at frozen wages, anger at Nixon's use of troops the following week to break the strike, and a sense that if negotiations failed the following Sunday, they would strike if Rademacher told them to.[100]

Meanwhile, on Sunday, March 22, there also appeared to be two acts of desperation by two presidents — Nixon and Rademacher — to grab momentum from the strikers — both made at nationally televised press conferences. Sunday was a non-delivery day for mail, with window service typically closed as well across the country. So in strike-affected areas there were fewer pickets out than the previous days. President Nixon announced that if strikers were not back on the job Monday morning, he would be sending National Guard and federal troops to move the mail in New York. Also on Sunday, NALC president Rademacher made the bizarre public declaration that SDS (Students for a Democratic Society) members had taken the postal exam the year before and had infiltrated the New York City post office and Branch 36, as if to say that striking the government was disloyal and could only have been led by radicals or communists.[101] The ability of Branch 36 to quickly dismiss that accusation reflects the diminished power of anticommunist red-baiting once prevalent in organized labor — similar to the "outside agitator" trope used by white supremacists against civil-rights activists in the 1960s South. Branch 36 strikers rejected offers of help from groups like the far-left Progressive Labor Party (PLP). But the speed and intensity of that rejection also suggests the damage strikers knew could come with public assumptions based on any association with left-wing radicals. And even if red-baiting had lost much of its bite since the 1950s and '60s, it still personally stung the strikers at the time and for many years to come. Rademacher later wrote that he had received "bad information" and regretted the charge. In fact, SDS had collapsed as a mass New Left student organization well before March 1970, its remnants taken over by the PLP. Often forgotten in this controversy was Rademacher's threat at the same time to expel Branch 36 officers from the NALC if the branch stayed out on strike. The strikers' hostile reaction to offers of aid from groups that showed up on the picket lines also expressed strikers' alienation at being "used" by groups that had not previously expressed any interest in their struggles up until then. Strikers' rejection of support by groups like PLP was also based on their suspicion (as well as PLP's past practice) that these were not expressions of solidarity so much as attempts by a doctrinaire "cadre" organization to try and "organize" them.[102]

In Massachusetts, Sunday morning readers of the *Boston Globe* were greeted not just with the banner headline "Nixon Vows to Move Mail Monday," but the smaller headline story above that: "Wildcat Strike Cripples Boston Mail Service." There they learned that the day before in "Greater Boston . . . letter carriers and postal clerks joined a wildcat strike spreading across the nation." The 3,500 members of NALC Branch 34 and the 3,300 members of "Boston Post Office Clerks Union" (the UFPC, although NPU members in Boston also struck) walked out at the General Post Office and the South Postal Annex, and many surrounding small cities and towns like Cambridge, Brookline, and Waltham: fifty of seventy stations in the Boston postal district did not deliver mail that day. Boston voted Sunday to return to work on Monday, March 23, on a "wait and see" basis for five days while national negotiations for a 12 percent raise continued, as clerks and others followed. Many smaller cities and towns stayed out, and Worcester was still picketing.[103] The Monday daytime edition of the *Globe* reported that the Branch 34 strike vote on Sunday took place during "a stormy, one-hour meeting" of 3,000 members at the Bradford Hotel. So many carriers protested that they could not hear how the motion was worded that Branch 34 president Ralph Farrell promised a secret ballot Tuesday night. At that meeting Branch 34 voted 1284–448 to stay on the job during negotiations.[104]

In the Southwest, carriers and clerks almost struck in Arizona. On Saturday, March 21, Phoenix NALC Branch 576 and UFPC Local 93, both poised to strike Sunday, instead voted not to strike on advice from national leaders. On Sunday, presidents of Tucson NALC Branch 704 and the UFPC local declared they would "wait for a mandate from their national leaders," but would walk out by midnight Friday, March 27, "if a satisfactory settlement" was not reached.[105] In Denver, Colorado, NALC rank-and-filers voted to set up picket lines at post offices as discussed before. Paul Mendrick, a clerk sub and UFPC member who had been hired in June 1969 was working at the Terminal Annex at Sixteenth and Wynkoop. He recalls the strike "snowball" making its way west from New York but also hearing from postal dispatchers in Chicago ahead of time that this would be coming. Paul remembers walking out Thursday, March 19, and helping to set up picket lines. At twenty, he was like many young subs disgusted with the low pay and unpaid "swing time," where subs were kept from "clocking in" to work until there was enough mail to process. When Paul told his father—an upper-level postal manager in Pueblo—about his fear of being fired for striking, his father replied, "Son, you never cross a picket line." So with his coworkers he lined up at a bar's pay phone to make an ironic phone call to their supervisors. "Across the street was a bar called the Wazee Lounge," he laughed. "With one dime we called and said we didn't feel safe crossing the picket line." By shutting down the Annex they were able to stop mail from getting to the area stations. After management used mail trucks to bring strikebreakers to the Annex, one striker flattened the tires overnight with an icepick. Members of the UFPC, NPU, and the maintenance, motor vehicle, and special delivery unions (future APWU merged unions) later met downtown at the Carpenter's Union Hall at 2011 Glenarm Place on Saturday, March 21, and "there was nearly a riot" as union members debated and voted to strike over warnings from UFPC leaders.[106]

There were also strike threats in the Southeast. A hastily typed USPOD memo on Saturday, March 21, at 4:00 P.M. declared that the situation in the Atlanta postal region was "normal," as were the Dallas and Memphis regions, along with the non-southern regions of St. Louis, Washington, Wichita, and Seattle.[107] But the more organized "Status Report" updates that began appearing at 2:00 P.M. Sunday, March 22, suggested that things were not altogether normal. That status report noted, among other things, that in the Atlanta region, "Miami carriers voted no strike; the results of clerk vote this P.M. not available at this time; report later. No significant change in other major offices."[108] The city of Atlanta itself and other cities in that region—specifically those in Florida—were not quiet when it came to the postal strike, although it is not known why that USPOD document reported a Miami NALC no-strike vote on Sunday, when the vote was held Monday night. In any case, interviews with NALC Branch 1071 activist Matty Rose along with contemporary newspaper accounts reveal a workforce divided but with many ready to strike. There were strike votes in Jacksonville in north Florida; in St. Petersburg and Tampa in central Florida; and Key West, Ft. Myers, and Miami in south Florida. Carriers and clerks voted as members of their local unions against striking, but carriers voted to strike if NALC president Rademacher called one later. The St. Petersburg post office's officer-in-charge advised postal customers to hold their mail, pointing out:

"It would just pile up if you mailed it." The NALC president of Miami Branch 1071, Anthony Montanez, even predicted on Sunday that his branch would vote to strike the following day when a massive strike meeting and vote was scheduled for Bayfront Park. Ft. Myers postal clerks (who would have been either UFPC or NPU members) voted to strike that coming Friday, March 27, "if the situation is unchanged," a spokesman said, and carriers said they would not cross their picket lines if they did.[109]

Providing us with an inside view of strike efforts in Miami is Matty Rose, who later became president of his local NALC branch before becoming a national officer. Rose was a Vietnam War veteran who had started at the post office in 1966, carrying mail in Hollywood, Florida, located between Miami and Ft. Lauderdale. He worked for a year and a half as what was then called "Temporary Indefinite" before becoming a career carrier, and was active in the union: "The best part about working for the post office for me was being in the union. I felt a sense of security." Rose recalls his small Hollywood NALC branch voting to strike if the larger Miami Branch 1071 (which Hollywood later merged with) struck. Thousands of letter carriers in the Miami area had a meeting and took a strike vote, where the mood actually leaned in the direction of striking. From its national office, the NALC sent field representative Tony Huerta, who was from Florida, along with their legal counsel Moe Rattner. Rose expected them to call a nationwide strike, but "they talked us out of going on strike. They said, 'Everyone here will be getting fired. The leaders will go to jail.'" Rose himself was targeted by the local postmaster for being part of a pro-strike faction. An unreal scene unfolded where the postmaster called him a "traitor and communist," and seized his SF-46 (federal government driver's license) the following week before summarily firing him a month later. Rose sought help from the NALC to file an "adverse action" (this was before grievances came into effect in 1971) and regained his job six months later, but with no back pay. "I made a vow to myself: either I'm 100 percent union, or I'm quitting the post office," said Rose, wryly concluding, "My claim to fame is that I'm the only letter carrier in America fired for *not* going out on strike!"[110] There were NALC branches in the South and elsewhere that had voted to walk out but were willing to wait and follow Rademacher, who pledged to lead a nationwide strike if an agreement was not reached in five days.[111] Southern votes to strike, such as the one by Atlanta NALC Branch 73, were conditional on Rademacher's word, if and when he said so, according to Charles Windham, Jr. Windham, a Vietnam War veteran and branch "representative" who later became a NALC regional administrator, backed Rademacher's position at the time. "There must have been 250 of us," Windham said of a shop floor meeting at the Federal Annex during the first few days of the nationwide strike. "And of course the agitation was: 'Strike, Strike, Strike!' Because the rest of the country was going out on strike. We didn't want to be left out." Unreported in the local media, Atlanta's vote to strike by 78 percent (Windham's estimate) was impressive even though it was contingent. Furthermore, Windham declared, "[If a] national strike had been called, then we certainly, I think, would have walked."[112]

Other postal union branches and locals in the South took strike votes. Some of them even wanted to participate immediately. Strike votes were taken in southern and "border" cities like Atlanta, Houston, New Orleans, Baltimore, Miami, Nashville, Chattanooga, Knoxville, Birmingham, Memphis, Washington, D.C., Charleston (West Virginia), Winston-Salem, Charlotte, Chesapeake, Norfolk, and Richmond. In Richmond, NALC Branch 492 president Lawrence G. Hutchins told the *Richmond Times-Dispatch* on March 24, after his union voted unanimously to strike in that city March 28, "We will have pickets at the main post office at 12:01 A.M., Saturday, if an agreement is not reached."[113] Joyce Robinson, an African American postal clerk who later became APWU Education Director, was a Richmond UFPC member in 1970. Along with many other UFPC members, she was ready to walk out and recalls, "We took two strike votes."[114] Special delivery messenger Vern Baxter (later an author and sociologist) provides a written recollection that suggests other spontaneous walkouts in the South may have happened that have yet to be chronicled. "Many Richmond postal workers walked off the job in solidarity with the wildcat post office strike in March 1970," he writes. "I joined the strike in the middle of its second day."[115] And the *Charlotte Observer*'s coverage of the rapidly evolving national strike on March 20 noted that almost half of that city's 400 letter carriers "indicated that they would go along with a national strike. A telegram from the [NALC] asked the local mailmen not to take a strike vote pending a strategy-meeting today. But cheering assent was given to the direct question, 'Are you willing to strike?' There was not a dissenting voice."[116]

The southern cities that displayed strike interest were all in states that had lived under "right to work" laws since the 1940s and '50s (with the exception of Maryland), which prohibited "union shops," banned collective bargaining and strikes by public sector employees, and in general depressed union membership and activity. These were also cities that had seen black-led campaigns against NALC Jim Crow branches. All of these things make those southern strike votes and activity all the more remarkable.[117] In Louisville,

Kentucky, on Monday morning, March 23, the *Courier-Journal* published two remarkable front-page, above-the-fold articles. The first, from news wire services, outlined the gravity of the situation, with President Nixon on the verge of calling up troops for use in several cities to move the mail while postal officials expressed skepticism that they could actually perform that function. The other article, by a *Courier-Journal* staff writer, bore this headline: "In Louisville: Strike May Begin Saturday."[118] The latter, which included a large photo of Saturday's NALC Louisville Branch 14 strike meeting, was actually becoming a typical occurrence in many postal union branches and locals this late in the strike, with reports of heated debates by postal unions and votes to strike that Saturday if a national agreement was not reached. "A thundering chorus of angry 'ayes' cut through the smoke of a crowded meeting room yesterday and promised a postal strike in Louisville beginning at 12:01 A.M. Saturday [March 28] unless national negotiations are completed by midnight Friday," began this report that colorfully characterized a spirited meeting of almost 500 letter carriers at the Iroquois American Legion Post. But before the vote, there had been voices calling for the branch to "go out now" and "support our brothers in New York." The article further noted that "Local 4 of the United Federation of Postal Clerks has agreed to honor picket lines in the event Louisville letter carriers do strike." NALC Branch 14 president Carl Meiman also pledged to lead the strike if necessary, as members also shouted solidarity with New York and other cities on strike.[119] Elsewhere in the state, Newport and Covington NALC branches also voted to strike that Saturday "if union leaders in Washington do not agree on terms."[120]

In Gary, Indiana, letter carriers and clerks voted to strike "if postal workers in neighboring Chicago are still on strike." And in the state capital of Indianapolis, the NALC branch approved a strike vote for that coming Thursday, March 26.[121] Interestingly enough, appearing next to the strike-vote article as it continued on the back page was an article headlined "Montreal Mail Strike Creates Cabinet Crisis" concerning the two-week-old strike by Canadian postal workers in that city in solidarity with contract mail-truck drivers.[122]

At the White House, things were going downhill, as H. R. Haldeman reflected, "A busy day as the postal issue got worse. Most of us were in several sessions with P[resident] and with Shultz, etc. No action today, will see what the workers do in the morning. If they don't come back, P[resident] will move with troops, consequences may be bad." Nixon's time was split between two domestic crises: "P[resident] spent whole day at EOB [Executive

Office Building] on this and with [aide Bryce] Harlow on the school [desegregation and busing] statement. Wants tomorrow cleared to finish statement and be prepared to act on strike."[123] Nixon had already threatened that weekend to call out the troops. Some cities were just walking out, like Chicago, Denver, San Francisco, and Los Angeles. Now Nixon felt he had to follow through.

By Monday, March 23, the USPOD status report for ten in the morning said of the Minneapolis region: "Nine offices are out including Minneapolis, Milwaukee and St. Paul. Little activity other than a Milwaukee vote to be taken at 10 A.M. today. Minneapolis clerks voted [at a ratio of] 5 to 1 on March 22, 1970 to go out on strike." On Monday, the USPOD reported that clerks and carriers were both slated to vote on whether to return in Minneapolis, whereas in St. Paul, carriers had voted to return, but it was the NPU that had voted to strike and were asking carriers to not cross their picket lines. Clerks and carriers in the Twin Cities did not return until the last day of the strike, Wednesday, March 25.[124] Mike Mazurkiewicz, a retired St. Paul clerk and APWU member, has collected numerous stories and photographs from NPU strike veterans. Mazurkiewicz's father was a St. Paul letter carrier and NALC member who was involved in the strike.[125] Some of those NPU strike stories echo those told in other cities. For example, Larry Gervais, then editor-at-large of the NPU local newsletter, recalls that "we had a meeting on Sunday with all the other unions and voted overwhelmingly to support the strike, about 800 yes to 80 no. The unofficial strike headquarters became Sugar's Bar [now Station 4]."[126] Don Freestone added a similar observation: "We used to meet at Venagilas bar [now Kelly's Pub] and call in. One of us would call, then pass the phone down the line to the next person and so on."[127]

Other NPU strikers, including both men and women, recalled postal inspectors photographing picketers, support from students, and only a handful of strikebreakers—one of whom stayed inside the post office for the entire strike. Freestone commented on NPU and UFPC member fraternization on the line: "Through picketing and mutual support during the strike we realized that the other guys weren't so bad after all! That was important because after the strike we merged into the new APWU and had to work together."[128] These stories resemble those told across the country, conveying a combination of excitement and anxiety at what they were doing that crossed lines of age and seniority. Lola Reed, who later became a local APWU president, picketed while her husband took care of their six children. She says that she "was a sub at the time. We referred to ourselves as 'sub-humans' because that's how we were treated! We could be told to go home before we punched in if the mail volume was light. . . . Working conditions and pay were awful and many postal workers were on welfare."[129] Another striker who later became an APWU local president was Rex Johnson. "Of course we were concerned about losing our jobs," he said. "In the end though we all took pride in what we were doing and felt we were doing what we had to do."[130] For his part, Mazurkiewicz, then age fifteen, remembers "several carriers coming over to our house one evening during the strike. They had been picketing downtown and formed human blockades in front of the dock entrance. I remember the sense of pride they had in what they were doing."[131] It should not be surprising to see an industrial-labor stronghold emerging in the post office in the Twin Cities, where solidarity was almost unanimous and militancy grew over the short life of the strike. However, just as it happened back east and elsewhere, postal union local officers in the Twin Cities were either threatened or actually served with restraining orders and injunctions to cease striking—a major factor causing strikers to return to work, in addition to promises of a settlement that involved substantial raises. And there was also the issue of the troops called up by President Nixon on Monday, March 23, to move the mail in New York City.

4

The Strike Ends

On Monday, March 23, in an effort to break a nationwide strike that seemed to be gaining momentum with each passing day, President Nixon issued a proclamation and an executive order that mobilized 26,007 U.S. military troops for what was called "Task Force New York." They were to move the mail in New York and thus demoralize strikers into returning to work. But New York was the last city to see strikers return — doing so after Nixon withdrew the military strikebreakers — while other cities were threatening renewed walkouts. The rank and file were still the wild card.

Service personnel in this mobilization were drawn from the Navy, Marine Corps, Naval Reserve, Marine Corps Reserve, Air Force, Air Force Reserve, Air National Guard, Army, Army Reserve, and Army National Guard, of which 16,836 were actually ordered to be "engaged in augmentation of the Post Office Department," as the Department of Defense (DoD) called it. The DoD preferred that neutral language over "deployment," which suggested coercive military action.[1] "We were told no helmets and no guns," said Army specialist Tom Stokinger, sent with his unit from Fort Dix, New Jersey, to New York to help try and get the mail moving again. The contrast was stark between uniformed troops rolling in on buses or military vehicles past striking postal workers who were not allowed to wear their uniforms on the picket line — the letter carriers anyway. The public was used to seeing both as representatives of the federal government but in quite different capacities, military and civilian. And there was no mistaking what the troops were there for.[2]

At the White House that morning, there was a sense that Nixon's order and the very visible troop occupation of New York post offices was turning the tide in favor of the government. "Maybe an historic day," is how Nixon aide H. R. Haldeman put it. "P[resident] ordered troops into New York to take over essential services."[3] The mood was upbeat, as if this was going to do it and really end the strike. There had been a long debate that included Postmaster General Blount, labor secretary George Shultz, Nixon aides John

Ehrlichman and Herbert Klein, and press secretary Ron Ziegler. Shultz, according to Haldeman, "was the last holdout but finally agreed we had to do it." Troops would be sent in to major cities to move the mail, starting with New York, with Boston and Philadelphia listed on the original DoD plan, and preparations made for a total of deployment to thirty-six cities if needed. These were designated as "first priority cities" and "second priority cities" across the country, with proposed "troop strength" exceeding "manpower requirements" in key postal centers from Atlanta to Chicago to Houston to Seattle and points in between.[4]

That morning, President Nixon issued Proclamation 3972 declaring "a national emergency" that began: "Whereas certain employees of the Postal Service are engaged in an unlawful work stoppage which has prevented the delivery of the mails and the discharge of other postal functions in various parts of the United States . . ." It noted that the results of that "work stoppage" had interfered with "the performance of critical governmental and private functions, such as the processing of men into the Armed Forces of the United States." Besides interfering with the orderly "processing" of men into the military, Nixon stated the work stoppage was also blocking the processing of tax and tax collections, "transmission" of Social Security and welfare checks, along with "important commercial transactions." The proclamation directed "the Secretary of Defense to take such action as he deems necessary."[5]

At the same time, Nixon issued Executive Order 11519, Calling into Service Members and Units of the National Guard, "to respond to requests of the Postmaster General for assistance in restoring and maintaining Postal service and to execute the Postal laws of the United States."[6] But Nixon did not read from either document in his national address at 2:15 P.M., which took just a few minutes. Instead, he read from prepared remarks that featured an interesting mix of metaphorical carrots and sticks. On the one hand, he displayed sympathy and praise for what he called the hardworking and underpaid postal workers. But for strikers—about 25 percent of the postal workforce—he combined criticism with public shaming for their shutting down essential services. Nixon also implicitly blamed Congress for having allowed this crisis to happen by not passing his postal reform legislation. He seemed to almost praise strikers with their "legitimate grievances" for having provoked this impasse. "But that crisis is here and it has brought additional grievances to the fore," he declared. "The country has recognized these inequities in postal pay and benefits." And he maintained that since his first day in office, he and the postmaster general had worked "to eliminate the source

The Strike Ends

of those grievances, that is, the obsolete postal system itself, a system that no longer serves its employees, its customers, or the country as it should." The new post office would mean "increased pay for postal workers . . . increased benefits . . . [and] compression by 60 percent of the time it takes a worker to move from the bottom to the top of the pay scale." There was no explicit mention of unions, but there did not have to be—it was implied in his call for negotiations. He also made it clear that he had no sympathy for public-sector strikers who interfered with "essential services," concluding, "What is at issue then is the survival of a government based upon law."[7]

Millions of Americans watched, including many strikers who later recalled that Nixon was ranting and angry. Viewed today, Nixon seemed to have adopted a calm but resolute demeanor, which was evidently his intent. But to the strikers, his words seemed menacing. They felt like rocks had been thrown at them, unfairly casting them in a negative light when it seemed to them that it was *his* actions in freezing their wages for the past year that had provoked them to go out in the first place and risk their jobs and livelihoods. Yet regardless of how he felt about the strikers, this performance suggests a Nixon who knew that there was widespread public support for postal workers. It was a Nixon who wanted workers' trust, and also saw an opportunity to get his government postal corporation bill passed by Congress. Nixon did not publicly share his initial private rage. And it was a far cry from the visible anger displayed eleven years later by President Ronald Reagan towards PATCO strikers, although on the last day of the 1970 postal strike Nixon would be dealing with a crisis brought on by about 2,000 PATCO members who had begun a two-week sick-out in protest of poor pay and working conditions.[8]

Sometime after Nixon's statement, a press briefing on the troop deployment to New York was held in the White House Roosevelt Room with Press Secretary Ronald Ziegler, Secretary Shultz, and Postmaster General Blount—who did most of the talking. Blount's remarks, like Nixon's, concealed any private anger, instead modeling what he called the administration's "restraint." He echoed and extended Nixon's remarks: the troops were to serve as a "supplemental" workforce to "restore essential services," although mail delivery was not one of those services. He would not "talk about blame," instead faulting "the system" that needed "drastic restructuring." Blount was encouraged by major offices like Boston and Philadelphia returning, but acknowledged that "over 100,000" workers were still out, including all of New York City. Before leaving for a meeting, the historically more conciliatory Shultz reminded reporters that this was still an illegal strike, declaring that negotiations could not happen "with people who are in the process of violating the law. . . . *There's an old adage in the field of labor relations: that 'there's only one thing worse than a wildcat strike, and that's a successful wildcat strike.'*" Blount then concluded by calling for strikers to return to work and Congress to act on the "unique" pairing of postal pay and reform—whose "collective bargaining procedures would have obviated this kind of strike."[9] Nixon administration officials were all publicly on the same page, and they were also visibly concerned by the power of the strikers.

Most postal workers were military veterans, many having served in World War II, the Korean War, or the Vietnam War. Twenty-three-year-old Richard Thomas, an African American and an MBPU member at the time in New York, recalls starting at the GPO in 1968 as a mail handler after military service in Europe. The post office "was like a dropoff point out of the military. . . . You went in and you just continued on with the federal government. We even wore our khaki outfits, our fatigues on the work floor. . . . Most of us were veterans, and most of us were angry." The response by many veterans on the picket lines to Nixon's order was more disdain than fear: "We were already former troops," observed Thomas. "Some of them were former postal workers—the ones that were in the National Guard. We were standing our ground!"[10]

Many postal strikers publicly expressed scorn toward Nixon's action. Those watching him on television in groups, and filmed by NBC-TV, booed his remarks and shouted at the television sets. But others felt dread. Many picketers who witnessed the troops enter New York City in trucks bound for the GPO, Grand Central, Chelsea, Murray Hill, Morgan, Brooklyn, and other postal facilities expressed uneasy feeling at what seemed like military occupation in New York with the possibility of other cities seeing troops as strikebreakers. Branch 36 striker Barry Weiner recalls the scene at the Manhattan GPO: "I was there when the military vehicles first showed up. And it was very eerie. Because in those days you would see those things happening in South American countries where there were soldiers in military vehicles lining the streets of the main post office. And soldiers in uniform walking up the steps of the main post office to go in per Nixon's order. But we all knew they wouldn't have that much success."[11]

Some of the first troops to arrive in New York City on Monday night found themselves driving right past Madison Square Garden on Eighth Avenue, across the street from the GPO, just as a basketball game crowd was letting out at 11:30, according to the army's report. Who was playing remains a mystery, as college tournament games had ended, the Harlem Globetrotters had not played there in over a year, and the New York Knicks had ended the regular season the night before in Boston with their first playoff game set for Thursday at the Garden. Meanwhile, the Ringling Brothers and Barnum and Bailey Circus was pulling into the Garden on Monday morning for forty-nine days beginning Tuesday, and the *New York Times* reported a striker shouting as the parade of elephants and other animals passed by the GPO picket line: "We've been working for peanuts for years, too." And as it happened, Cazzie Russell and Michael Riordan, star reserve players for the Knicks, were both part of the National Guard call-up to work mail at the post office in New York, which made Knicks management frantic about being able to have them available for team practice sessions. A photo, retrieved from the *Chicago Tribune*, of Russell in uniform with his rifle at the Bronx Armory is one of the few published photos from the strike that included armed troops.[12]

The Department of the Army's report *The Postal Work Stoppage, March 17–26, 1970 (Operation Graphic Hand)* reported that this massive troop utilization had begun at 6:26 P.M. with "thirteen buses carrying 525 Air Force military personnel" to the Brooklyn Army Terminal "for assignment and deployment to a postal facility." Other units were headed to other post offices by nine o'clock that night. Six hundred troops arrived at the GPO in Manhattan by buses at 10:45–11:00 and 11:25 P.M. "No fanfare or problems" were reported at the Brooklyn GPO or Church Street Station in Manhattan, "but unexpected circumstances occurred" when troops arrived at the Manhattan GPO. The report noted that "the vehicles would turn onto 33rd Street to enter the enclosed transportation deck area of the post office, thousands of people exited from Madison Square Garden from a basketball game.... Crowd control became a delicate problem. Police were on hand ... directing traffic. The crowd was noisy but good humored. Members of the military and the crowd entered into an exchange of waving and amiable banter."[13]

It was a short work night for the troops ordered into strikebreaking activity. The Army's *After Action Report* (with the same *Operation Graphic Hand* subheading as the document entitled *The Postal Work-Stoppage*) notes that all military personnel left the postal facilities at 1:35 A.M. —at the same time that "student type agitators were on hand" at the Manhattan GPO. The Army reported with some satisfaction: "The picketing postal employees told the recalcitrants that they did not need or desire their participation."[14] The *Postal Work-Stoppage* report makes other references as well to "agitators," "radicals," and "revolutionary or subversive groups" who were attempting to participate in the strike.[15]

National Guardsmen brought in as strikebreakers to move mail in major New York City post offices, sometime between the evening of March 23 and noon of March 25, 1970. Courtesy of the National Postal Museum.

Some of the soldiers mobilized by Nixon to move the mail had been postal strikers just before being called up as reservists or guardsmen. Striker John Alversa of NALC Branch 294 in Flushing, New York, exclaimed: "We lost two-thirds of our pickets because they were in the National Guard. That was their second job!"[16] Jeffrey Chester was among the hundreds of military service members inside the GPO during the strike, having been called up from McGuire Air Force Base in Wrightstown, New Jersey, where he had been serving as an MP (Military Police). Chester had just turned thirty when the strike happened: "The plastic containers of letter mail would come down in front of you, and you would pull out a handful, and one by one you'd put 'em in the pigeonhole [case] by zip code. And it was like, 'You gotta be kiddin' me!'" Fifteen years later, after retiring from the Air Force, Chester was hired by the post office in California as a letter carrier. Chester also joined the union that had started the strike — the NALC — in their North Highlands Branch 133 in Sacramento County.[17]

Chester corroborated frequently repeated stories of troops being unable to quickly master mail-sorting. "It was a joke," said Tom Stokinger from

The Strike Ends

Quincy, Massachusetts, an Army veteran of the Vietnam War also deployed to New York. "They had baskets of mail, chock full, and a wall of slots where we placed the mail. It was an unbelievably slow process of finding an address in New York City. Everyone immediately understood that it was an impossible task."[18] That job normally required clerks to "case" (insert) mail into pigeonhole case slots organized by streets and carrier route numbers at the rate of "40 to 60 letters per minute." The back page of the March 25, 1970, *New York Daily News* included a photograph of Stokinger and other uniformed members of his unit with piles of mail in front of them trying to quickly absorb the "schemes" (memorized sets of address and routing information) that normally took many hours of training and practice, including passing a scheme training test. But it was just a few hours of training that military service personnel like Chester and Stokinger received.[19] Chester, Stokinger, and others have also pointed to troops feeling uncomfortable in their role as strikebreakers, being unwilling to effectively move the mail, and even demonstrating sympathy and solidarity with the strikers. "Don't worry, we're not really helping anything" is what Stokinger called out the bus window to pickets outside the post office where he was deployed.[20]

On the subject of National Guardsmen and other troops handling the mail during the strike, NPU official Philip Seligman would reveal to an oral-history interviewer six years later: "My son-in-law happened to be in the National Guard. . . . He was telling people to mis-box a lot of mail." Also speaking on the troops and their mail-sorting attempts, Elsie Resnick, a striking MBPU member, later remembered in a 1976 interview that "they threw mail into any bag just to get rid of the mail."[21] Barry Blank was a U.S. Marine Corps reservist sent to the Brooklyn General Post Office. Blank pointed out that, despite his regret at being sent to break the strike, he and his fellow reservists "benefited because of an obscure DoD order which granted reservists activated in national emergencies the opportunity to go inactive for the 6th and final year of obligation."[22] Blank's unit was the Eleventh Communications Battalion "based during the mail strike at Chapel Street, Brooklyn, right at the Brooklyn Landing of the Manhattan Bridge."[23]

Meanwhile, twenty-six-year-old MBPU member and distribution clerk Raymond Smith, an African American, had begun his career in 1962 at age eighteen at the Morgan Annex mail processing facility. His father was a federal employee who worked in customs, and had told him he should apply and take the civil service exam for a post office job, which he did, but a 1967 fire at Morgan moved mail processing to the Brooklyn Army Terminal (BAT) on Fifty-Eighth Street for the next few years. It was there that Smith and other

clerks refused to cross the picket lines—only to see military personnel arrive Monday to their facility: "Many of us reported for duty, but refused to
cross the line. Then President Nixon called out the National Guard to fill in
and move the mail. . . . Needless to say we were all quite apprehensive, not
knowing if we would get suspended or get our jobs back. I remember the
army trucks loaded with National Guardsmen yelling encouragement and
support for us as they made their way inside BAT. They were wishing that we
could get back to our jobs as they were not pleased that they had to do this,
just following orders. . . . As you can imagine, our work areas were in a total
mess, no blame to the National Guard who could not have processed the
mail correctly, especially on short notice."[24]

There were also conflicts within the Nixon administration between
civilian and military authorities over strike response. At the White House,
Haldeman would write later that night: "[Postmaster General Winton] Red
Blount got into a flap with the Army over who's giving orders. E[hrlichman]
had revised Red's timing and quantity of original troop movement. I had
to call Army and tell them to take orders from PMG [Postmaster General]
only. E[hrlichman] of course concurs." There seemed to be a renewed confidence in Nixon, according to Haldeman: "P[resident] again completely
cool, tough, firm, and totally in command; fully aware of it, and loving it."
Haldeman was upbeat as he noted, "First results appear to show some success as some of the big locals vote to go back to work. But New York still
out, and troops moving in tonight. Strike could easily spread back out across
country and into other unions."[25]

Monday, March 23, became the day when most striking postal union
branches and locals across the country were starting to go back to work, although some were actually just starting to go out. Chicago was still out, even
after Nixon's speech, which was followed by NBC-TV news anchors David
Brinkley and Chet Huntley reporting that NALC president Rademacher
was calling for members to cross picket lines and return to work. (No other
postal union president received as much media attention during the strike
as Rademacher.) Some of those just going out on strike were those in the
Southwest and the West Coast.[26]

In San Francisco, Martin Curtan had arrived in 1968 from Colorado
aboard a freight train, exclaiming in retrospect: "I was a hippie!" He began
his career as a mail handler at the Rincon Annex in 1968 before switching to
letter carrier in the Sunset District, a job he liked better: "It was much freer,
getting to know the people on your route." When he arrived at the post office
on one of those days soon after the strike had started in New York, he re-

called, "I started for the door and they said, 'We're not going on in. We might be going on strike.' . . . We made up picket signs and stopped other carriers from going in." A branch delegate from a nearby station had brought them news of New York City, "and we were gonna support them."[27]

Lowell Turner was also in San Francisco during those days, working as a PTF letter carrier driving mail collection routes from 4 to 8 P.M. on weekdays around the city, and depositing outgoing mail at Rincon Annex. Having come from Los Angeles to the Bay Area in 1969 with a BA in international relations from Pomona College to work with the American Friends Service Committee, Turner decided he needed a job that paid better than social activist gigs, but one that also allowed him to continue doing that kind of work. The post office hired him just a few weeks before the strike started. Today a political science professor at Cornell University who researches comparative labor issues, Turner looks back fondly at the "ragtag bunch" he said he worked with, who themselves were often activists looking for a part-time job that they could "get by on" with some job independence as well. "I watched the strike come across the country," he recalls, in a kind of mirror image to the "snowball" that Manhattan-Bronx NALC Branch 36 strike veteran Frank Orapello described. It was a few days after the strike in New York started—certainly no later than, and most likely on, Friday, March 20—that Turner reported to work to get his keys and his postal vehicle, only to hear his fellow carriers debating whether to go on strike. Someone said there was a picket line at Rincon Annex, and somebody else asked what the issues were. Lousy pay, it was agreed. But are we ready to lose our jobs over this, someone replied? Finally, said Turner, a collection driver whose dialect identified him as a native New Yorker exclaimed, "There's only one issue: are we gonna support our brothers in New York or what?" Turner said at that point they all turned in their vehicle and collection box keys to go join the picket line. What seems remarkable in retrospect was not the solidarity that the drivers exhibited in striking when they could be fired and lose everything, but the fact that they did so despite what Turner called the lack of interest NALC Branch 214 displayed in organizing them as part-timers. That changed quickly after the strike. He and the others joined the union as new leadership swept in, and Turner himself went on to become elected shop steward, then chief steward, and also "scribe" (editor) of the branch monthly newsletter, the *Voice of Golden Gate Branch 214*.[28] Helping lead clerks on strike in San Francisco was Alice Lindstrom, a window clerk who had become a UFPC shop steward soon after she started at the post office in 1966 as a distribution clerk. "We just did it out of desperation," she recalls. "If we lose the job or worse . . . it's what happens. . . . Something had to be done." She heard about New York going out from the chair of the UFPC shop stewards council, and "it was just like wildfire. . . . We had three strike meetings and I chaired two of them [at Howard Presbyterian Church]." They set up picket lines. And she took posters around to all thirty-eight stations in the city along with Sidney Rollen, an African American postal-truck driver from Augusta, Georgia, with the National Federation of Post Office Motor Vehicle Employees (NFPOMVE). "The truck drivers didn't vote to strike," he said. "We voted to honor picket lines." And they did, especially after Rollen and Lindstrom parked a fifty-five-gallon oil drum and picket sign in front of the truck yard, which he said kept drivers from moving mail in or out of the city during the last days of the strike. (Rollen moved on to other jobs sometime after the strike, while Lindstrom stayed on, retiring after twenty-seven years in 1992, still a shop steward. Today she is an APWU delegate to the San Francisco Labor Council.)[29]

In suburban Los Angeles, Kathy Rubly was walking the picket line in Montebello. Just out of high school in 1969, she began carrying mail for the post office. "They teased you a lot," she recalled of male carriers she worked with. But her feeling was that "you had to take it with a grain of salt . . . because they were there to help you." Echoing what other strikers have reported, she said that since her parents had been union, "I figured, that's what you did! Somebody went on strike, you stuck together." Rubly said there was no meeting or vote by her local Branch 1100 — she and nine other carriers just went out, although she noticed while picketing that the senior carriers were still in the office. Meanwhile, not too far away in Orange County, Huntington Beach, and Anaheim, stations were also going out that Monday morning. Orange County may have been long considered a conservative political bastion, but newspaper articles and photos show letter carrier pickets protesting low pay and walking off the job against the pleas of their national and local NALC presidents. Even Yorba Linda, Nixon's hometown, saw letter carriers walk off the job for one day. Sidney Harriman Jr. was one of those striking in Huntington Beach. A Detroit native whose father had worked at a Chevrolet plant, Harriman was a Vanderbilt University graduate who had come to the post office in 1963. "We went out for one day," he remembers, "after the branch president Brian Farriss wanted [to get a strike vote in solidarity with New York City]."[30]

Meanwhile, Orange County newspapers as well as the *Los Angeles Times* reported that in metropolitan Los Angeles, members of the NPU were stopping the mail flow.[31] The *San Francisco Chronicle* noted on Sunday March 22 that "the clerks' union [NPU] called a membership meeting for today to decide what to do about the spreading national postal strike. The Los Angeles Postal Union represents 3,500 of the city's 8,000 mail clerks."[32] The follow-up story came the next day, when the paper announced that Los Angeles's NPU had voted to strike, effective Monday.[33] Already active in the Los Angeles Postal Union was Carl Jensen: "I was recruited by [NPU local official] Ben Evans," said Jensen, "and worked on the graveyard shift grievances if I remember right from 1967 to 1973."[34] Jensen was one of those NPU members picketing the Terminal Annex, called "the most modern and efficient" postal facility in the nation by the *Los Angeles Times* when it opened in 1940. Terminal Annexes were central mail processing facilities built near downtown railroad stations.[35]

In other parts of the country, smaller branches and locals wanted to go out in solidarity a day before going back in what looked like the end of the strike approaching. Significantly, this was the first use of military troops in fifty years to try to break a civilian strike by doing the work of strikers, according to the USPOD Draft Summary. Although the paper does not name the incident, it must be referring to the "West Virginia Mine Wars" of 1920–21. Most studies of the postal strike instead point for precedent to President Grover Cleveland's administration for calling U.S. Army troops to suppress the 1894 Pullman railroad strike, in part to keep mail trains from being delayed during that national strike of over 150,000 workers. Both cases involved troops firing on and killing strikers. But the 1970 postal strike, unlike either of the others mentioned, involved unarmed troops, with government officials referring to them euphemistically as a "supplemental work force" for "essential services." The USPOD Draft Summary commented on this use of strikebreakers against striking federal employees: "The most amazing aspect of the precedent-setting incident was the very routine manner in which the operation was accomplished. There were only token statements by George Meany and other labor leaders protesting the action. Editorial comment was also muted."[36]

Strike veterans recall a mixture of fear and defiance among strikers in reaction Nixon's use of uniformed military personnel. Those troops failed to move the mail, but as Tom Germano notes, "although the deployment of the military in the New York City post office had little direct effect on the strikers and virtually no effect on the movement of mail, it did serve to isolate the New York City strikers and frightened postal workers in other parts of the country."[37] The exhilaration of striking in defiance of federal law was tempered by federal marshals serving injunctions on union officials and uniformed troops occupying their workplace.

What impact did the postal strike have on the United States? It is worth quoting at length from an article published in the weekly newsmagazine *Time* on March 30, 1970 — five days after the strike ended — but actually written halfway through the strike. Entitled "The Strike that Stunned the Country," it included words like "devastating" to describe the effects of the strike: "Many of the country's largest corporations are headquartered in the city; most depend upon the mails for conducting their business. Paychecks destined for branch offices were frozen. The strike . . . prevented banks, insurance companies and Government offices from sending out bills or receiving payments." On Wall Street, "checks, stock certificates [and] bonds . . . failed to arrive, hampering business and forcing officials of the New York Stock Exchange to consider a market shutdown." There was disruption to mail-order houses, periodicals, the garment industry, and department stores. If the strike continues, pensioners expecting Social Security payments early in April will have to do without. . . . The Defense Department estimated that more than 500 tons of mail destined for U.S. military personnel and their families round the world were already tied up."[38] This article also related the many personal inconveniences to individuals, businesses, and agencies, similar to how other news stories from that time period captured anecdotally this "disruption" to the nation's communications system that everyone had seemingly "once taken for granted." They did not even mention that income tax returns would be due to be mailed to the Internal Revenue Service in just a few weeks — this of course being years before anyone could file an online return. The *Time* article expressed sympathy for the wage demands of postal workers and predicted the failure of any use of troops to move the mail. But it also decried the use of the strike weapon by public employees, concluding with a ghoulish image that also further reinforced the popular image of this being a "mailmen's strike" that the media helped create: "Until they go back to work, however, the corpse that they carry in their mailbags can only be that of the public interest."[39]

Meanwhile, the title of *Newsweek*'s cover story, "The Day the Mail Stopped," echoed the 1951 American science fiction thriller, *The Day the Earth Stood Still*. Interestingly, this article noted how efforts by the Nixon administration to pull postal workers off the picket lines by the end of the week — Friday March 20 and Saturday March 21 — were loudly rejected across the country, from New York, where the strike started, to the Midwest and West

Coast, where it was now spreading. By the time many had read either of the articles in the two major American weekly newsmagazines, the strike would have ended, but it was still "to be continued" when they were published.[40]

Events had already far outpaced the writing and publication of the *Newsweek* and *Time* articles, but like many media stories they did manage to highlight the strike's effect on American society. In a way they also fore-told the combination of promises and threats that would be employed by both the Nixon administration and postal union leaders who would have to somehow coax back to work thousands of public servants whose strike some news magazines were already referring to as the "Revolt of the Good Guys." Sympathetic descriptions of postal strikers like these provided an interest-ing counterpoint to frequent mainstream newspaper and magazine editorial denunciations, sometimes within the same publication.[41]

TROOPS MOVING MAIL?

More troops were brought in on Tuesday, March 24, to work in Manhattan at the GPO along with "Morgan, Church Street, Grand Central, Madison Square, FDR, Murray Hill, Cooper, Old Chelsea and Canal Street Stations, from approximately 10:00 A.M. to 7:00 P.M.," with further plans "to man all three tours beginning at 7:00 A.M. on March 25."[42] Altogether, seven-teen stations in New York City saw military personnel at work from March 23 to 26.[43] As military personnel in New York offices struggled to process mail, there was verbal combat in the White House—this time between staffers and top postal officials, according to H. R. Haldeman: "Blount and his Deputy [Postmaster General] Ted Klassen, trapped me in late morning about White House staff interference in Post Office negotiations, especially [Special Counsel Charles] Colson," he complained. "They were really mad. Three-hour meeting this afternoon at Post Office. Finally got Blount to agree to [William] Usery (Labor) as the chief mediator in charge. Hard to beat the Post Office down, they are determined to have full control in their hands."[44]

Elsewhere at the White House, Charles Colson worried in a memoran-dum to John Ehrlichman of the "political damage" that might befall them, especially since his estimate of the strike was that "there is little chance of it being settled quickly." The Democrats stood to score political points, he said, and the public would blame the strike on Nixon. Colson's idea for regain-ing the initiative was to have Nixon ask "Congress to enact H.R. 4 at once," since it "represents the same position the Administration has held since last December." He ticked off all its advantages: an 11.1 percent pay raise, "compression from 21 to 8 years," and "meaningful collective bargaining (with compulsory arbitration) [so] that they would have no reason to strike."[45] Colson no doubt meant what Ehrlichman called the "substitute" H.R. 4 that was now Nixon's "Postal Authority" plan.[46]

Colson need not have panicked, as it turned out. In between Rademacher's Friday, March 20, meeting with NALC branch presidents and Nixon's sending troops to move mail in New York the following Monday—not to mention the steady drumbeat of government injunctions, restraining orders, and fines on postal union officers—most of the nation's postal strikers, including those in Chicago, were starting to return to work by Tuesday. According to USPOD status reports and the more detailed Summary Reports updated every few hours, most of the Chicago region—which included Detroit—was still on strike as of nine o'clock Monday night, with less than 10 percent of both clerks and carriers reporting for duty. That report also had forty-five out of seventy-nine offices in the wider Chicago region returning. The 5:00 A.M. status report on Tuesday, March 24, affirmed that "50 percent of the clerks were working in the main post office in Chicago." But by noon Tuesday, the status report noted that "in Illinois all employees are reported back to work except at Aurora." The same entry then added: "It was reported that Lansing, Michigan employees struck this morning and picket lines are up."[47]

And they were on the fence in Pittsburgh until Sunday night. Howard Brandt Jr. recalls NALC Branch 84's meeting, where many were in favor of staying out as long as New York did. Federal marshals were at that meeting looking for the officers, so rank-and-file members were convening meetings. "We picked out the biggest guys" in the branch, he said. These men confronted the marshals and told them they had no business coming in. There were no violent confrontations, but this kind of "muscular unionism" must have felt satisfying to postal workers who for so long had felt disrespected and disempowered. That night, Branch 84 voted to go back Monday, Brandt recalls, because "Rademacher came out on TV and he said they had a tentative agreement," although "there was a lot of skepticism."[48] Vern Evenson saw similar results in Denver: "Rademacher got the word out to the local presidents ... [to] give them five more days to finish negotiations."[49] Strikers began returning, but NALC branches and other postal union locals not on strike were poised to walk out if negotiations failed, increasing pressure on Rademacher and Nixon administration negotiators.[50]

Tuesday night, March 24, Postmaster General Blount called his second press conference of the strike. It was ten thirty, and he apologized to reporters for the late hour, "but there has been a significant continuing development in the situation as far as the postal work stoppage is concerned." There was a "trend," he said, of strikers returning to work, prompting him to announce that he had "sent a telegram to the presidents of the seven national postal unions"—meaning those who had exclusive bargaining rights, but leaving out NAPFE and the NPU, the latter providing one-fourth of all strikers. The telegram "suggested" that "assuming this trend continues we meet tomorrow, Wednesday, at 2:00 P.M., at the Laborers' International Union of North America, AFL-CIO, 905 Sixteenth Street NW, Washington, D.C., the place agreed upon last Friday for such a meeting."[51] One of the first questions reporters posed to Blount was an awkward one: "You indicated this afternoon that the key to the situation was New York City. Now you have not reported men going back to work in New York and yet you are willing to start negotiations. What has changed this pattern?" Blount reiterated that he thought this "trend" would continue, adding, "I happen to be an optimist by nature." The grilling from reporters continued, but Blount was adamant. He maintained there had not been any preconditions to negotiating, although Nixon had said there would be no talks until strikers returned to work. Blount vaguely predicted that soon "we will not be in a walk-out situation and we should get on with these discussions."[52] There seemed to be an atmosphere of flexibility, not something that Blount was known for.

Meanwhile, back at the White House, H. R. Haldeman reflected on that afternoon's meeting between administration and postal officials, his remarks exuding both confidence and apprehension of the wild card that had become federal employee rank-and-file unionists. "At meeting looked as if we were in pretty good shape externally," he exulted, "problems all internal, mainly ego. All unions basically back, except New York, and their leaders are here and anxious to meet. We seem to have the upper hand. Problem is to keep it, and move on from here. Also air traffic controllers threaten walkout tomorrow, a disaster if they do." It was a day of political battles both domestic and foreign. That same day, Nixon "reaffirmed his support of desegregation and his opposition to busing," a contradiction he would never resolve.[53] And Haldeman's final diary entry that day reported: "Poor K[issinger], no one will pay attention to his wars, and it looks like Laos is falling." The next day's entries would be of a piece: postal negotiations would begin at two o'clock that afternoon while worries continued about a PATCO "sick-out." Finally, in another historical irony, Nixon "made clear in meeting this morning that under no circumstances would he declare a national holiday for Martin Luther King."[54]

On Wednesday, March 25, New York was the last stronghold of the postal strike. But even in New York some postal workers were starting to return. There was confusion and skepticism among strikers. Among those returning were those who were persuaded that a deal was imminent, and that if it was not, President Rademacher would lead a national NALC strike. Strike participants from around the country talked about the confusion during the strike, which worked both for and against them. But in New York, there was also anger. Vincent Sombrotto recalled that Brooklyn NALC Branch 41 president Jack Leventhal came back with a list of proposals supposedly agreed upon by the Nixon administration that were intended to get them back to work. But they had no basis in fact, Sombrotto continued: "[Leventhal] wanted it to be true. . . . I don't think that he was part of a conspiracy. . . . He truly believed . . . what Rademacher told him was correct. Rademacher later denies that he ever told him that. I think I can make a case for both of them." Sombrotto said Leventhal had brought back what many began to call a "phantom package." And Sombrotto recalled that Branch 36 "didn't even have a membership meeting to say we accept it; they just did it." Meanwhile, he added, major media outlets promoted the story that strikers were all going back and that a deal had been reached. That was the same media that strikers had relied upon for news about other branches and locals walking out in other parts of the country, as well as to deliver the news of their plight to millions of Americans wondering why the mail had stopped.[55]

The strike ended on Wednesday, March 25, when union leaders convinced the remaining strikers—mostly in New York—that a deal had been struck and asked them to return to work during negotiations with Nixon administration officials. Accounts differ as to the veracity of the agreement that had been reached with administration officials in order to coax them back to work. There were debates over duplicity versus wishful thinking and misunderstandings. In the city where the strike began and ended, Moe Biller, Gus Johnson, and other postal union officials—whether for or against the strike—were telling postal workers that they had won their demands, and strikers, however skeptical, began returning to work. Branch 36 president Gus Johnson told MBPU president Moe Biller that carriers were returning based on Secretary Shultz's "agreement" that called for a 12 percent pay raise retroactive to October 1969, paid health benefits, "compression" of top pay from twenty-one to eight years, the "area wage" calculation, full collective bargaining, and amnesty for strikers. Meanwhile, fines were being threatened both to Johnson and Biller along with their respective local unions beginning at five o'clock on March 25 if they did not agree to end the strike. Those fines would have been substantial amounts that would have hurt both union locals: $10,000 a day, with an additional $10,000 on top of that for each day that members stayed out. Johnson himself stood to have an added personal daily fine beginning at $500 a day.[56]

According to Tom Germano, all but three members of Branch 36's seventy-five-member executive board had already voted on Tuesday to end the strike. Jamaica and Brooklyn NALC branches had already voted that day to go back on Thursday, mostly on the word of the two New York congressmen who had been at the previous Friday meeting with Rademacher and presidents of 300 major NALC branches. One dissenting Branch 36 member protested that union bylaws required a membership vote, but Johnson maintained there was no time for that.[57]

Meanwhile, Biller liked the agreement offer that Johnson relayed to him, according to Walsh and Mangum's APWU history. But Biller wanted to first verify it personally with Postmaster General Blount. Biller felt that he had already been "sandbagged," as he later put it, by Johnson and Branch 36 leadership just before the strike began. He could therefore be forgiven for his skepticism. He said he wanted workers to stay out one more day while he kept trying to reach the Postmaster General. But Branch 36 was heading back to work Thursday, March 26. Biller felt compelled to announce to the membership his recommendation that they vote to return, but would not vouch for the agreement until he and union attorneys first went to Washington, D.C., to find the postmaster general to substantiate the agreement, as Blount was apparently not answering his phone. This was the era of exclusively landline telephones, of course. We should not make too much of technological contingency here, but it is tempting to picture Blount's phone ringing unanswered, with Biller having to fly there in person to speak to him about the agreement to end the strike.[58]

At a Wednesday afternoon meeting at the New Yorker Hotel on Eighth Avenue, Gus Johnson held a press conference. Speaking both to the press and about 1,000 postal workers—most of whom were letter carriers—Johnson announced an end to the strike and asked his membership to return to work the following day. Germano tells us that cheers greeted Johnson's announcement, although there were some voices of protest that members should get to vote an end to the strike. Johnson's reply was that he was "acting without a vote because the package was so good."[59] Biller spoke an hour later to about three thousand MBPU strikers on the Thirty-First Street side of the GPO and

MBPU president Moe Biller on the picket line, New York City, sometime during March 18–25, 1970. Courtesy of the NYMAPU Collection, Tamiment/Wagner Archives, NYU.

called for a vote. This was not the secret ballot Biller had insisted the MBPU use to decide on striking eight days before. He read the agreement out loud, recommended acceptance, and promised to lead members out again in five days if that agreement was not kept. The vote was by acclamation.[60] Tour III workers headed inside for the evening shift, followed by Tour I before midnight, and Tour II on Thursday morning. Moe Biller had been the highest-profile postal union leader involved with the strike, not to mention leading the largest postal-union local in the strike. But even before going to that meeting, he expressed his feelings about the strike's continuation to Detroit NPU president Doug Holbrook, who remembers: "Moe Biller called me . . . and he told me that this strike has got to end because we can't afford to lose our dues checkoff."[61]

The wildcat strike ended as it had begun eight days before: for the most part decided by rank-and-file postal unionists democratically, collectively, and locally, but influenced by national events, including the actions of other strikers. But the final day of the strike saw the last of the strikers voting to return to work based on promises that were more like works-in-progress. And it also saw power moving from the streets back to the bargaining table. Yet

The Strike Ends

this in itself was a first in postal labor-management relations: both sides sitting down to hash out *all* issues even before the Postal Reorganization Act was voted on later that year to take effect in 1971. As clerks and mail handlers on Tour III that started at 3:00 P.M. began their shifts, the last of the troops mobilized to move the mail in New York City were getting ready to leave. Service personnel in the city were given a "warning order for withdrawal" at 1:35 A.M. on Wednesday. At 4:05 P.M., the *US Army After Action Report* chronology noted: "Regular Navy/Marine Corps augmenting personnel depart General Post Office [in Manhattan]."[62]

EXACTLY HOW MANY DID STRIKE?

To this day there is an absence of certainty as to exactly how many struck. That total tally matters as a reflection of the enormity of the strike contributing to its success, including its demonstration of which regions saw strike activity. Figures vary considerably on the numbers of workers and offices involved in the strike. The USPS gives the number of about 152,000 strikers (which seems low) in 671 offices.[63] On the other hand, Tom Germano has claimed about 230,000 nationwide strike participants, which seems a bit high.[64] USPS sources peg the final strike tally at "an estimated 152,233 employees [who] were absent without leave [AWOL]."[65] But that would leave out the strikers who were non-scheduled (NS), on paid annual leave (AL), on paid sick leave (SL), or on leave without pay (LWOP), and those who were allowed to clock in and out and picket by sympathetic station managers. Moreover, management typically determines employees as AWOL if they neither report for work nor phone in. But we know that some strikers called in sick and therefore would not have been included in their figures. In addition, how many striking substitutes were NS during that week and not counted among the strikers? As to figuring the total number of employees, according to the *1970 Annual Report*, which includes postal labor figures for 1966–70, there were a total of 739,002 employees as of June 30, 1969. That includes 192,821 "substitute employees" alongside 546,181 full-time career, or "regular," employees. A year later that total number barely moved, but the percentage of "subs" for 1969 was at 26 percent, and remained roughly the same for all five years cited (except 30 percent for 1966), which was typical for that era but nonetheless staggering. What further complicates any attempt to get an exact strike figure is the 1970 USPOD "Draft Report" calling the 152,233 number "30 percent of the total post office complement," which suggests they were just counting career or "regular" employees. But even that would be 38,738 fewer than the 546,181 actual "regulars," unless they were not counting those considered NS, AL, SL, or LWOP.[66]

How will we know how many postal workers struck in 1970? I think it is possible to at least make an estimate based on the USPOD's own figures compiled during the strike. The Files of the USPS Historian, at their L'Enfant Plaza headquarters in Washington, D.C., include status and summary reports for most of the strike days — most critically the final ones. What is especially interesting are grids marked "Prepared by POD Control Room." They were updated every few hours, and reveal the increasing numbers as well as the leveling off of strikers involved. The high-water mark of the strike seems to have come between midnight March 23 and 1:00 P.M. March 24. In the latter, the "Strike Summary" records 640 offices having been struck by 208,694 workers. That includes 132,642 clerks (and presumably other non-carrier crafts), or 64 percent; along with 76,052 carriers, or 36 percent. The postal regions most affected (with numbers of local post offices struck in parentheses) included New York (220), Philadelphia (215), Chicago (84), San Francisco (51), Boston (31), followed by Minneapolis and Cincinnati (14 each) and Denver (11). Regions unaffected were Atlanta, Dallas, Memphis, St. Louis, Seattle, Washington, D.C., and Wichita. A total of 35,206 clerks and 22,534 carriers in 270 offices had returned to work by midnight March 23, ramping up to 60,039 and 52,878, respectively by 1:00 P.M. March 24. With the USPOD revising the Cincinnati region's figures upward by the 5:00 P.M., March 24, Summary Report, the total number of strikers nationwide could be put as high as 209,185. Minneapolis, Denver, San Francisco, and Cincinnati regions had also revised their total strike participant figures upward between midnight March 23 and 1:00 P.M. Tuesday, suggesting not just mathematical error correction but also more workers walking out. For example, the 7:00 A.M., March 24, Status Report notes that Toledo, Ohio, clerks "walked off the floor at 2:30 A.M.," and in St. Paul, Minnesota, "the NPU voted to strike."[67]

It is also useful to compare strike activity by craft, city, and region. The Post Office Status Report Number 7 from March 23 at midnight lists the percentages of striking offices by region and city. In Chicago region, for example, 12 percent of clerks had returned along with 11 percent of carriers; 66 percent of Boston's clerks and 54 percent of its carriers; for New York it was 1 percent versus 4 percent, respectively; Philadelphia 73 percent versus 79 percent; Cincinnati, 0 versus 5 percent; Chicago, 12 percent versus 11 percent; Minneapolis, 16 percent versus 11 percent; Denver, 38 percent versus 96 percent; and San Francisco, 35 percent versus 44 percent. As for *cities*, Detroit reported 19 percent of its clerks but none of its carriers back at work by that date. Cleveland had 2 percent of its clerks and none of its carriers back at work. Brooklyn had the same figures. Los Angeles had 68 percent of its clerks and 95 percent of its carriers. Denver had 50 percent of its clerks and no carriers, while Minneapolis had no clerks or carriers back by then.[68]

Why such uneven figures across crafts and regions? That remains a mystery absent more research. There are probably a variety of elements at work, such as influence of local formal union leadership or a history of local rank-and-file activity. At the very least, the patchwork effect of those striking and returning by craft refutes any larger narrative that carriers or clerks overall were the most steadfast strikers. We can also get an idea of how frantic the Nixon administration must have been at the social and economic disruption that lay ahead if the strike was not quickly resolved. What was also in the strikers' favor was the fact that the strike hit its largest offices, although the sight of small offices on strike throughout the country cheered the strikers in large urban areas, impressed the public, and concerned the Nixon administration. By July 1967, 88 percent of all postal workers worked at only 15 percent of its offices. The ten largest offices employed more than 22 percent of all workers, in order from the largest: New York (Manhattan), 41,406; Chicago, 28,229; Boston, 14,195; Los Angeles, 13,588; Philadelphia, 12, 014; Washington, D.C., 11,349; San Francisco, 10,228; Detroit, 9,865; Cleveland, 9,242; Brooklyn, 8,638.[69] All of these offices struck except Washington, D.C., which probably would have seen letter carriers go out if NALC Branch 142's voting results had not been falsified, according to its former president Joseph Henry.[70]

Another remarkable feature of this wildcat strike was that the return to work was so uneven. In the Post Office's Status Report Number 12 for March 24 at 1:00 P.M., on the seventh (and next to last) day of the strike, 384 offices had returned to work out of 640. That means 40 percent of the original striking offices were still on strike: 200 in the New York region alone (which includes New Jersey), 29 in the Philadelphia region, and the rest scattered around the country. It is interesting to note that while there was steady movement back to work twenty-four hours after President Nixon called up troops to move the mail in New York City, close to half of the nation's striking offices were still out. Some offices were just going out while others struck in defiance of Nixon's call-up.[71] This was a huge national wildcat strike that in general terms spread quickly and enthusiastically and went back slowly and reluctantly. Those who returned did so after assessing the risks to staying out, often first engaging in local union debates and votes, asserting their power and defying notions that they were just giving up.

A good argument can be made, then, that over 200,000 postal workers struck at some time during March 18–25 across eight postal regions and including every geographical region except the South—where there were nonetheless rumblings of strike activity. The number of strikers was between one-quarter and one-third of all postal employees. It included "regulars" close to retirement as well as "subs" with just a few months of service and seniority. New York City was crucial, as was the New York *region*. As of 2:00 P.M. on March 22, 85 percent of the region was on strike, and as of the 11:00 A.M. USPOD *Summary Report* on March 24—the first day military strikebreakers began work—there had been 72,000 New York regional postal workers on strike that week: *over one-third of all strikers*.[72]

RESUMING "NORMAL OPERATIONS"?

The first chronological entry for the U.S. Army *After Action Report* for Thursday, March 26, notes: "All post offices resumed normal operations except for operations in Chicago which were hampered by a 10 inch snowfall." By 2:25 A.M., "New York City postal authorities determined that there was no requirement to employ service personnel."[73] Air Force MP Jeffrey Chester would be headed back to Ft. McGuire, while Army specialist Tom Stokinger and USMC reservist Barry Blank would be returning with other soldiers to Ft. Dix. That same day, employees at every U.S. post office were back to work, backed-up mail was starting to move again, and the entire nation saw how much its business and civic life could freeze when the mail did—and how vital postal workers were to the movement of mail. What are we to make of this strike? Was it successful? What were its limitations? In many ways it was really not over yet. Negotiations, conflicts, and threats of strikes characterized the post-strike period from March 1970 through the end of 1971 in what was about to become the new era of the U.S. Postal Service. Those issues will be discussed in the next chapter.

Aftershocks and
Postal Reorganization

How did the postal strike lead to postal reorganization and with it the most liberal collective bargaining regime won by any public-sector workers to that point? Was this the promise of a new era, change for the worse, or a mixed bag for postal labor? It is interesting to consider different sides of the conflict during the strike aftermath. We can see Nixon administration (including USPOD) officials and top union leaders negotiating an end to a government labor crisis while engaging as if they were private-sector adversaries. Both sides seemed to also be forgetting that the tens of thousands of postal unionists who had just struck the government and were about to be granted amnesty had compelled the Nixon administration to negotiate with their union leaders. Many of those workers were also threatening another strike, thus renewing the crisis that both administration and union officials hoped they had solved.

After the strike ended on March 25, there were only three more entries in the diary of White House aide H. R. Haldeman relating to it, but they are instructive. The weekend after the strike was Easter, and Nixon and his aides were in Key Biscayne, Florida, where Haldeman noted Nixon's "continuing concern re [Judge Harold] Carswell [Supreme Court] nomination, postal negotiations, and the possibility of a 'sick-out' being called by the air traffic controllers." Arriving back at the White House on Monday, March 30, Nixon and Ehrlichman met with Postmaster General Blount, and Nixon appeared "fairly encouraged about postal negotiations."[1] After a week in crisis mode, Haldeman exuded confidence on Thursday, April 2, 1970: "Settlement day. Postal agreement. Knew we had it at noon when Usery made deal with [George] Meany, but had to go through motions of negotiating session. Now have to sell it to Congress. Came out pretty well, P[resident] especially anxious to get positive interpretation on it."[2] That Nixon was moving on to other things can be seen one paragraph later, where Haldeman dis-

President Nixon, cabinet officials, and union presidents wrapping up post-strike negotiations at the White House, April 2, 1970. Original NALC *Postal Record* caption reads: "President Richard M. Nixon discusses wage settlement with key participants of negotiations in the Cabinet Room. Shown in the photo, among others, are from center to right: [NALC] President Rademacher, AFL-CIO spokesman James Gildea, Assistant Secretary of Labor W. J. Usery, Secretary of Labor George Shultz, [AFL-CIO] President [George] Meany, President Nixon, Postmaster General [Winton] Blount." Other meeting attendees listed in the presidential daily diary include other postal and labor department officials plus representatives from all other postal unions except the NPU and the NAPFE. Courtesy of NALC.

played a calculated political pragmatism based on postal workers' (especially letter carriers') place in society. There was irony in Haldeman's words: "The air controllers problem goes on and the plan now is to fire a bunch of them, especially after postal settlement, to prove government employees can't win by striking. *Theory is that the mailman is a family friend, so you can't hurt him,* but no one knows the air traffic man. Also they make a lot more money, hence invoke a lot less popular sympathy."[3]

Nixon had been put in a bind with the postal workers' strike, but he was not going to allow any other government employees to "win" like that. The postal strike that he was now getting credit for ending constructively is one that in fact Nixon had done much to provoke in the first place by holding postal wages hostage to his reform plan. He was not going to fire the mailman, so to speak, but memorandums and meetings in the aftermath of the strike show fear and caution in the executive branch. How to negotiate and take advantage of this window of opportunity to combine a pay raise and postal reform, discipline the strikers, but not provoke another strike? The postmaster general's general counsel David Nelson made a list of possible sanctions the day after the strike against strikers and unions alike, but recommended instead: "Let everything remain in status quo . . . no pay for the time

Aftershocks and Postal Reorganization

they were out, but . . . no other penalties."[4] At the March 28 White House meeting, John Ehrlichman recorded a discussion that among other things observed that they faced "[in]experienced neg[otiators] for unions," the poss[ibility] of union double cross after table agreem[en]t," and a "*very* delicate" meeting the following week with the "NPU [and] Alliance [NAPFE]" with their "large #'s [numbers], the "Alliance" being a "big civ[il] rts [rights]" group.[5] These notes were probably typed into the memo soon after, titled "Base Position for Negotiations," which included "providing Health benefits only as a final yield to get reform," arguing that "Amnesty" for strikers should be "a big yield that "should be hooked to reform. We will give this anyhow but could make it a big concession," and concluded tellingly: "In general, I think the only way the Administration can save face is to tie any pay and benefit concessions to reform. As you know all Federal employee organizations are watching the negotiations to determine if wildcat strikes are the way to get pay."[6] At 9:00 A.M. there was a meeting at the White House with Blount and Klassen from the USPOD and Secretary Shultz, with Ehrlichman taking notes, discussing the importance of "good PR [public relations] posture." They were joined on the phone at 9:35 A.M. by Nixon from Key Biscayne, who noted that "whatever [is] done will have Gov[ernment]-wide effect," sharing his concern that, as with the "Air Controllers, this [is] a precedent."[7]

THE SCENARIO SHIFTS

All of the remaining strikers as it turned out—not just Moe Biller—had been sandbagged by the purported administration deal that was relayed to Biller by NALC Branch 36 president Gus Johnson. Mikusko and Miller in their NALC history point out that "the 'phantom package' was simply NALC's proposal—a retroactive 12 percent pay increase, fully paid health benefits, an eight-year pay scale, collective bargaining with binding arbitration, and full amnesty for strikers."[8] But the part of the agreement that *was* factual was significant: top pay would indeed be "compressed" from twenty-one to eight years; collective bargaining and binding arbitration would take effect whenever negotiations broke down; and amnesty would be granted for all postal workers who had been out on strike. On the other hand, full payment of health benefits by the government proved to be in the "phantom package" category, along with "area wages" (higher pay depending on the higher cost of living in geographical areas like New York City). Also, the "12 percent pay raise retroactive to October 1969" turned out to actually be 6 percent retroactive to December 27, 1969, and another 8 percent effective whenever the postal reform bill was enacted, according to the April 2, 1970, "Memorandum of Agreement" between the USPOD and the seven "exclusive" postal unions.[9]

Collective bargaining with arbitration was a key union demand, according to a USPOD document titled "Work Stoppage Settlement: Negotiation and Agreement." It was put on the table along with the pay raise, compression, amnesty, and other demands. At two o'clock on Wednesday afternoon, March 25, as the strike was ending, Assistant Secretary of Labor William J. Usery Jr. called a negotiating meeting to order as chief mediator. As corroborated by H. R. Haldeman's notes of White House meetings with Postmaster General Blount, postal officials were not going to take a back seat to the Nixon administration in strike negotiations: "Confronted with the dilemma of an unjustifiable strike resulting from legitimate grievances, the Postal Service management sought a means of quickly ending the strike action without appearing to reward the strikers."[10] Toward that end, Usery was joined by principal negotiator for the USPOD, Deputy Postmaster E. T. Klassen, along with Kenneth Housman, Assistant Postmaster General for Personnel, and James P. Blaisdell, a "postal labor-relations consultant." Undersecretary of Labor James D. Hodgson represented the U.S. Department of Labor.[11] Representing postal labor were the seven craft unions that had "national exclusive" representation. NAPFE and NPU representatives were barred as industrial unions that did not enjoy any "national exclusive" bargaining rights under Nixon's EO 11491. But they were not barred by Nixon's negotiators. "The administration would like to include the (industrial unions)," this USPOD document quotes Usery telling the excluded unions, "but the other unions would not permit it."[12]

After the strike, Brian J. Gillespie in the Post Office Labor Relations Division of the Bureau of Personnel sent a memo to the division's director, John N. Remissong. In it, Gillespie urged caution but at the same time prevention of future work stoppages: "Eliminate NPU and Alliance [NAPFE] in struck locals."[13] Ironically, the NAPFE leadership had prided itself on publicly opposing the strike, even as many of their members had participated. About one-quarter of all strikers had been NPU members, along with key local officials like Moe Biller in New York and Doug Holbrook in Detroit—the only fulltime NPU local leaders. But neither Gillespie, nor Remissong, nor anyone else in the USPOD needed to worry about taking drastic action in the "struck locals." AFL-CIO president George Meany was adamant that the post-strike scenario meant the Nixon administration should only negotiate with and grant "exclusive" bargaining rights to the postal unions who held that status nationwide under Nixon's EO 11491. That meant everyone but the NPU and NAFPE, although those unions argued that the USPS was a brand-new entity and therefore they should be allowed to compete for representation. The other postal unions concurred to the contrary along with Meany, including the independent NRLCA.[14]

It is worth highlighting the congressional hearings held in April 1970 (after post-strike negotiations had ended), where members of the Post Office and Civil Service committee were astonished at this exclusionary policy. They pushed Meany to explain why he opposed the NPU and the NAFPE having a place at the bargaining table based on new elections. Representative Frank Brasco (D-N.Y.) at one point commented to Meany: "As I interpret it, this would take away dues checkoff from any union that does not have national recognition." Without hesitation Meany replied, "That is exactly what I mean."[15] The scenario indeed had shifted. Whose strike was this, anyway?

Tom Germano points to the remarkable "fact that the strike lasted eight days without formal leadership and no support from organized labor" as an indication of their collective "resolve" and internal solidarity.[16] "One must consider," he acknowledges, "that it was difficult for any national, particularly AFL-CIO affiliated union, to publicly support the strike not only because it was illegal but also because it was a wildcat strike not sanctioned nor supported by its own national leadership."[17] In fact, there were many instances of rank-and-file workers in AFL-CIO and non-AFL-CIO unions supporting the strikers or refusing to cross picket lines — such as the truck drivers loading and unloading mail. Germano also recalls that the American Federation of State, County, and Municipal Employees (AFSCME) New York District Council 37 supported strikers with $5,000, along with passing out coffee and doughnuts to picketers. Victor Gotbaum, president of District 37 — the largest of all municipal unions in the city — called a press conference to back the postal strike as being a blow for all government workers' rights. Also in New York City, the International Longshoremen's Association (ILA) stymied Nixon's plan to use New York City's piers to park vehicles carrying strikebreaking troops. The ILA's threatened work stoppage forced Nixon to route the vehicles instead to the Brooklyn Army Terminal.[18] In Detroit, there was support from the United Automobile Workers (UAW), which had left the AFL-CIO in 1968 to form the activist ALA (Alliance for Labor Action) along with the Teamsters and some smaller unions (the ALA dissolved in 1971 and the UAW rejoined the AFL-CIO in 1981). Doug Holbrook, Detroit NPU president and local postal strike leader, recalled the

UAW's support, which was both remarkable and ironic, given the issues the UAW leadership had with wildcat strikes among their own membership in the late sixties through the early seventies. Holbrook noted the many postal strikers who had once been UAW members like himself and Detroit NPU vice president Henry Tapsico—a veteran of the bitter but successful 1941 Ford strike for UAW recognition. And during the 1970 strike Holbrook met with UAW officials Douglas Fraser and Emil Mazey.[19] Yet here was George Meany exercising control over the future of the postal labor movement. It is worth comparing Meany's approach to those who had just brought the post office to a standstill.

HOW DID THEY DO IT?

How did some 200,000 postal workers suddenly strike the post office for eight days in defiance of their own national union leaders, shut down the nation's mail, and emerge without individual terminations or union dissolutions by government, and win pay raises and collective bargaining that included arbitration should contract negotiations break down? And how did they win the support of many if not most Americans despite the disruption that it caused in their lives? It was something that grew through a barely synchronized network of union members, including many local union officials. And it was more effective in some regions and cities than others. The Northeast, Midwest, and West Coast saw varying levels of strike activity, and strike votes were also held in the South where there was very little strike activity, although nationwide television viewers of NBC news March 20 would have seen postal officials at USPOD headquarters in Washington, D.C., on the phones and monitoring a "Work Stoppage Status Board" with lights on for various cities, suggesting a strike blanketing the entire country.[20]

Countee Abbott, Chicago NAPFE branch president at the time of the strike and also a strike activist, observed that what was most important was the shutting down of major mail distribution centers, which the strikers did. Chicago, the nation's main mail distribution center, only shut down for three days—from Saturday, March 21, through Monday, March 23. But from both a logistical and morale standpoint it was highly effective as the strike spread westward.[21] Also critical to the strike's success was widespread public sympathy for postal workers as government service workers making so little money that many were working second and even third jobs. President Nixon wanted to defeat this strike and was afraid of the precedent it had set for other federal employees. His administration even exerted efforts to ask major media outlets to frame the strike as his "domestic equivalent to the Cuban missile crisis," but failed.[22] But it was much more successful in immediately applying legal pressure on the postal unions — in particular the branches and locals that either voted to strike in defiance of the federal-employee strike ban, or just members participating in the strike. Postal employees' high rate of unionization is all the more remarkable when we remember that the post office was a nationwide "open shop" (a workplace where employees were not required to join unions with collective bargaining rights) — an issue that would come into play in the post-strike negotiations.[23]

Sympathy for strikers despite the inconvenience of up to a week's worth of curtailed mail was a two-way street, reflecting a longstanding relationship. Both the media and the public largely viewed the postal strike as a "mailman's strike" not just because the first postal workers to strike were letter carriers, but because that craft was the most visible expression of not only the post office but the federal government itself. Clerks and mail handlers participated and were crucial to the strike's effectiveness — and made up the majority of strikers. Like carriers, they and their families were part of community networks. But daily interaction between postal patrons and carriers laid the groundwork not just for overall sympathy for all postal strikers, but it also dramatized the public service component of that job — the men and women who daily visited homes and businesses in a job where, even in a carrier's grumpiest moments arguing with a supervisor or backing away from a menacing dog, there was always an awareness of performing a socially necessary task. The 1970 mass rebellion against a lack of adequate compensation for doing that job also reflected postal worker impatience with government's overall delivery of that service. "Social movement unionism" is how sociologist Paul Johnston terms this kind of public service labor activity that resembles private sector strikes for improving material benefits while going a step beyond.[24]

"I loved my job!" declared letter carrier Vern Evenson in 2014, who also had been an NALC shop steward in southwest Denver. Being a shop steward meant learning how to argue with management on behalf of carriers. But he was also mindful of what his career was about: "I worked for the post office for thirty-five years," he said, proudly. "I missed two days sick. I enjoyed my job. I enjoyed the people. I had a route — I had a little first grader on it. When I left that original route, *she* had a first grader."[25] This is a common sentiment heard from strike veterans. Benjamin Lopez, also from Denver NALC Branch 47 declared, "I'm a 'people person.' I just loved it. . . . That was the big deal: serve the public." Latino letter carrier Juan Medina from

Galesburg, Illinois, NALC Branch 88, agreed: "I did love my job. I was a sub for five years and then got assigned to a route. Carried for thirty-two years. . . . Grandsons [on my route later] had kids . . . They're family is what they are."[26] John Alversa from NALC Branch 294, Flushing, New York, echoed a similar sentiment: "It was our route, our people. . . . We treated our people like they were family."[27] Leroy Thompson from Cleveland, NALC Branch 40, concurs: "I loved carrying mail, being outside and meeting people all along your route."[28] And Richard Schwarze, a member of NALC Branch 825, Elmhurst, Illinois, sums up the appeal of independence combined with personal contacts with patrons: "When we got out of the office and got on your own route you were your own boss and they didn't harass you that much then. You could . . . deliver your mail and get it done and I really enjoyed it. I was on the same route for thirty-five years. Seen them . . . grow up and get married, and their children."[29]

People who received mail not only looked forward to seeing their letter carrier every day, but often chatted with them or even confided in them. This connection between carriers and patrons was wrapped up in the collective historical memories of *carriers* as daily bearers of their personal news and information. "I loved the carrier job," recalled Tom Germano, one of the NALC Branch 36 strike organizers. Germano had worked as a clerk, special-delivery messenger, and then as a carrier in Manhattan. He carried two different routes, one being a business route, and the other a primarily residential mixed route: "I had a lot of 'people contact,' especially on the residential part. I delivered to the neighborhood I had grown up in." The social contact among carriers, between carriers and members of other crafts, and between carriers and the public was something Germano also studied.[30] And buried in the Army's *Postal Work-Stoppage* report was this remarkable summary observation: "The most noteworthy aspect of the postal strike, considering the scope of the work stoppage and number of employees involved, is the complete absence of any significant disruptive incident involving postal employees. Acts of violence did not occur and field reports relate that in most locations, a good humored air of camaraderie existed among the picketing employees and patrons."[31]

"REVOLT OF THE GOOD GUYS"

In retrospect, the strike could be said to have lasted just long enough to forcefully make their point and set the gears in motion for the administration to negotiate and Congress to legislate, while at the same time ending just in time before potentially losing its momentum nationwide and thereby appearing weak with little leverage. Despite reports by some NALC officials and congresspersons, "the actual settlement took five months to negotiate." Postal workers in the end won a 14 percent wage increase: 6 percent retroactive to December 1969, and 8 percent in August 1970 when the PRA was signed. Twenty-one years became "compressed" to eight years as the minimum possible amount of time for attaining top pay.[32] And it was Rademacher, himself a strong opponent of the strike, who looked back in 2009 in an oral history interview and proudly proclaimed that "the strike put us on the map . . . that we're a union now."[33]

The 1970 postal strike was part of a labor upsurge of the late 1960s and early 1970s—a period frequently associated with President Nixon and construction worker "hard hats" clashing with antiwar protesters in New York City, and the AFL-CIO in 1972 snubbing South Dakota Senator George McGovern, the Democratic Party's presidential nominee, by refusing to endorse his candidacy. But during this period, multiracial private-sector wildcats and union-approved strikes, plus public-sector strikes, were becoming more common. This particular wildcat strike was inspired by other labor struggles and in turn inspired yet others to come, as part of a larger public service worker assertion of rank-and-file power and demands. It was not, however, "just as much a strike against national postal union leadership as it was against the government," as is often argued. Postal union leadership varied in their reasons for opposing the strike or their actual sympathy, but all were afraid of postal unions being broken as a result. It was the federal government that was the target against whom union members were striking for better pay and conditions. But by failing to lead that popular mass action, the national unions made themselves a target of protest and reform efforts.

One of the most interesting if overlooked features of the wildcat strike was that it was often initiated by planned strike votes at special union meetings called by local leadership at the union hall or borrowed halls. There were often multiple meetings—including votes on going back to work. Reports of these meetings are widespread: from participants themselves to union records to media accounts to the periodic status reports issued by USPOD headquarters in Washington, D.C. These were meetings demanded by the rank and file that were organized by both new ad hoc leaders and elected local leaders, which could include anyone from shop stewards to local presidents. Out on the picket line, the signs (homemade at first and often in both English and Spanish in New York and elsewhere) had the union branch or local number proudly displayed. There was a high level of participation.[34] Labor secretary George Shultz, at one point during the strike declared to NALC president Rademacher: "The only thing worse than a wildcat strike is a wildcat strike that is successful."[35] Both in specific and general terms, Shultz's remark (with the implied assumption that Rademacher would agree) suggests official dismay at labor union leaders' inability to exercise discipline on their members—to serve as mediators, in effect, between labor and management. The strike by all accounts was more successful than Shultz feared. It was both spontaneous and organized. Union officials were threatened by this mass cross-craft rank-and-file eruption, but at the same time they were able to use it as leverage.[36]

After the strike was over, the unions became stronger with the growth of rank-and-file caucuses producing local and national leadership within a decade, supplanting those who had opposed the strike. There was widespread sympathy among the general public for the strikers. Even Nixon found himself compelled to publicly express sympathy for postal workers' demands, even as he attacked them for striking. Nixon was finally forced to turn this crisis from a botched paramilitary solution into something that would look phenomenal today: consensus among labor, management, and both political parties supporting reform of postal operations and labor rights.[37]

Was the strike a success or a failure? Labor union and labor histories generally refer to it as a victory. The popular media account at the time was summed up in the first sentence of a front-page *New York Times* article on Wednesday, March 25, 1970, the last day of the strike: "The postal strike began to crumble yesterday." Ironically, this article was placed next to two iconic photographs of "a soldier from Ft. Dix, N.J., sorting mail at Brooklyn General Post Office yesterday," his jaw dropped wide open and appearing clearly overwhelmed at trying to find where a piece of mail belonged in the metal case in front of him.[38] On the other hand, when Tom Germano wrote of the 1970 strike being "broken" after eight days, he was reminding readers to be realistic. "Labor-management relations" do not form a level playing field. Striking workers typically fear being fired or replaced, and in this case we should add fined or jailed for striking the federal government. Even strike "victories" can face unintended consequences. Those can include higher productivity agreements demanded by management in return for wage and benefit increases, or the closing or moving of the business.

In this context, Germano was talking about a wildcat strike in which postal workers won most of their demands, while it was at the same time "ultimately broken . . . by the lack of formal leadership . . . dealt the coup de grace by trusted representatives of the strikers."[39] The strike was along union lines but without its elected leaders in charge. It was national in scope but uncoordinated. And it was solidly united in certain regions but divided nationally by region as to whether or when to strike. New York strikers, in many ways isolated at the end, began returning to work with promises of settlement coupled with threats of union dissolution and punishment of union officers.[40]

It was only a matter of time before an illegal wildcat strike that was feeling pressure from both executive and judicial branches of government was "broken." But there was no sense among strikers that they had lost or been crushed. And the experience of a democratic rank-and-file action propelled those caucuses to national union leadership within the decade in the NALC and the APWU, with both unions widely considered to be as strong if not stronger than most private-sector unions. As a harbinger of future conflicts, during the early summer months after the strike the NALC Branch 36's rank-and-file activists obtained a copy of the USPOD's "Five Year Plan" (which the caucus then made public) that declared how the plan for this new formation, called the U.S. Postal Service, would make it self-supporting, increase productivity, and cut jobs.[41] In the strike's aftermath there was debate in the NALC's *Postal Record* between branch "scribes" over regional strike involvement, loyalty to the national office, and "area wages."[42] Striker John Susleck from San Francisco wrote in the May 1970 *Postal Record*: "I would ask of my fellow branch scribes in the southland, 'will the south rise again' or were you too busy drinking those mint juleps."[43] In the September issue a Winston-Salem scribe noted his branch had split on striking, asserting, "Some of you think that just because we did not walk out and you did, you deserve more; well, you don't. And put this in your pipe and smoke it — if our National Officers (all of them, not just Gus Johnson), call a walkout, we will be right there, pounding the pavement just as all the good brothers here in the South will be doing."[44] Similar contingent future strike support also came from NALC scribes in Birmingham and Houston.[45]

THOSE WHO STRUCK

Who were the people who forced the federal government to the bargaining table and compelled Congress to act on postal reform legislation? The value of first-person accounts is considerable. They not only inform, but also reveal what the participants thought and felt about what they were doing.[46] The stories point to a real diversity of postal strike experiences, as well as a lot of similarities. Once the strike started, for example, many local union officers received help from members in "disappearing" to avoid being served with court injunctions. Some letter carriers took the "case strips" from their large metal address cases before walking out to prevent strikebreakers from being able to "case" or carry their routes.[47] And older postal workers nearing retirement were often as likely to strike as young people.[48]

Rank-and-file leadership was often exercised by those with little or no practice in daily union affairs. Strikers' only communication was by telephone, word of mouth, or through news reports. It is common to hear them express pride in that fact, in contrast to the dizzying ubiquity of instant communications today: "We didn't have cell phones or the Internet back then," they will often say, as if to highlight this strike as an "old-fashioned" grassroots action. Yet the postal strike in today's language could be called a late twentieth-century "flash mob" of social protest that "went viral." Postal workers who went on strike across the country voted in union halls, bars, veterans' halls, in post office break areas (known as "swing rooms"), or even on the workroom floor. In some cases they simply walked out without even taking a vote. These local strike actions often took place after heated discussion and debates that lasted anywhere from a few hours to several days. Sometimes it was spontaneous. It was coordination by inspiration. Few had experience in striking. There was nothing routine about spending union or personal funds to buy placards and write "Strike!" And there was no automatic assumption that this dispute would be resolved by negotiation with no management retaliation. Strike veterans remember feeling concern for their future. Many thought they had nothing to lose, while at the same time all knew they had a lot to risk, especially those close to retirement with pensions saved. Half a century later, postal strike participants still carry vivid memories of 1970, and never tire of discussing and debating what happened.

This was a strike by postal union members and their locals, not by the national postal unions. That made it a strike in defiance of national postal-union leadership. It was a collective democratic action driven by the rank and file. While it gave rise to local leaders, it remained leaderless at the national level, which became both its strong and weakest point. The fact that so many local votes were taken in the postal unions (especially the NALC, the NPU, and the UFPC), and that so many local officers and especially shop stewards were involved also made this a unique kind of wildcat strike that complicates any notion that it was led *entirely* by rank-and-file workers, even though, for the most part, it was.[49] This was an *organized* wildcat strike, even though that sounds like an oxymoron, as wildcats are typically spontaneous in addition to being unapproved and unsupported by the national unions.

Aftershocks and Postal Reorganization

The strike's dual nature (local unions striking, their national unions officially opposed) hampered the government's ability to identify it as union-led. That distinction did not stop federal judges from issuing injunctions against postal unions and their officers and threatening to impose fines. But in the courtroom of public opinion, this was an understandably desperate mass action by underpaid civil servants, despite the fact that it inconvenienced the public. Most wildcats are over working conditions, not major contract issues like pay as was this one, with postal workers effectively demanding *all* issues be collectively bargained. Strikers were beyond the control of their union leaders as well as postal management, yet were still able to mobilize the most important union resource of all—the rank and file.[50]

The strike was also nothing if not dramatic, which adds to the curiousness of this major labor event being largely ignored today. Imagine the spectacle of President Nixon, at the height of the Vietnam War (and antiwar protests), dispatching thousands of troops in transport trucks—seen by millions in media photographs and videos—that rolled through the streets of New York en route to its largest post offices to try to move the mail and break the postal strike. The Post Office's post-strike draft summary cheerfully concluded that while "there was not much preferential mail to be worked, the military cleaned it up by the middle of the second day. The military sorted, bundled, and packaged over 20 million pieces of mail and delivered more than two million pieces during their short stay."[51] The Army's Operation Graphic Hand was equally sanguine. But neither assessment could quite square with what postal workers found after the strike, or what witnesses reported during the strike in New York offices where military personnel worked the mail. Operation Graphic Hand also reveals an even greater initial contingency plan should the strike have become prolonged, or involved violence, with twenty-five "First Priority" and ten "Second Priority" cities requiring approximately 115,000 troops to potentially cover if the strike continued and spread. Many of those cities were in fact struck, including New York, San Francisco, Los Angeles, Minneapolis–St. Paul, Detroit, Cleveland, Boston, and Philadelphia.[52]

"PRESIDENT OF THE WORKING MAN"?

What are we to make of the role of President Nixon in the postal strike? Jefferson Cowie points to the significance of Nixon's deliberately avoiding even officially terming this labor action a "strike," which would have required legal action against the strikers. Instead he referred to it as a "work stop-

Black female letter carrier casing mail in 1970s wearing uniform with the new USPS bald eagle logo on the sleeve, replacing the previous post rider emblem, which had been used since 1837. The sonic eagle replaced the bald eagle logo in 1993. For decades, carriers have arranged letters and flats in these cases but have done less manual casing after the 1990s, when Delivery Point Sequence (DPS) mail began to arrive at their cases presorted. Courtesy of NALC.

page." It is possible this was also because he realized he was not likely to win, given the widespread sympathy for the cause of underpaid postal workers, and he saw an opportunity to concede higher wages and collective bargaining to employees in a key government agency subject to government corporatization, which was already on his agenda. Could it also be seen as part of his attempt to paint himself as "president of the working man"?[53] That is certainly how he sounded at the PRA signing ceremony on August 12, 1970, as he amplified his support for what he referred to as hardworking government employees and good-paying union jobs, both of which he said would be enabled by the PRA.[54] And when NALC president James Rademacher, in Hawaii at the NALC national convention and unable to attend the signing ceremony, suggested NALC member Joseph Kleapach as a substitute, Nixon agreed—his aide Charles Colson suggesting it would be "a very nice touch to have just an ordinary carrier in off the streets so to speak."[55]

Nixon's right-wing populism was typically aimed at white workers with conservative views on race and the Vietnam War. Nixon surely must have

Aftershocks and Postal Reorganization

known that the postal unions whose members were involved in the strike leaned liberal and Democratic, especially those in New York City, and that large numbers of African Americans were employed in urban post offices — in many cases majorities or near-majorities. But if his general political strategy was to separate white workers from the Democratic coalition, his restraint after the postal strike was contingent. It reflected not just his focus on defusing a crisis and winning his postal corporation after all, but also being influenced by administration officials who argued for negotiation, not termination — most notably labor secretary Shultz and assistant secretary Usery. What if they had *not* prevailed over Nixon's initial command to his aides that they should "attack" the strikers, and that "if people can be fired, fire them"?[56] We might instead be talking today about Nixon the postal union-buster who created chaos by firing those who could actually move the mail.[57]

Contradictions ruled Nixon's response to the strike. His unprecedented offer of negotiation subject to postal workers returning to work failed, which led him to send troops to try and break the strike, or at least to nudge them back. Nixon on the one hand publicly termed the strike a threat to "the survival of a government based on law."[58] And his administration even tried to get media stories planted that the strike was Nixon's "domestic equivalent to the Cuban missile crisis," in a clumsy attempt to seize the public sympathy factor back from the strikers and highlight this as a national security issue rather than a labor conflict.[59] In a 1990 oral history interview, William Usery Jr. confirmed Nixon's commitment to collective bargaining for federal employees as well as a lack of desire to fight the postal strikers or unions in general. Usery reflected on his sudden and unusual elevation to chief negotiator between government and postal unions and the responsibility that entailed: "I'm now appointed by the President, and who have I got to straighten out — the Postmaster General, the Secretary of Labor, the Deputy Postmaster General." The fact that Nixon gave Usery — an assistant secretary of labor sympathetic to unions — mediation powers to end the strike that were greater than those of other administration officials suggests Nixon's intent to put postal unions back in charge of their membership to ensure labor peace at the post office. It was also part of an expansion of union rights in the federal government. Despite seeing unions in general as his "political enemy," Nixon acknowledged to Usery that they were "a powerful force" that were "part of America" with whom government should "get along."[60] And it was obviously union members who were on strike, so only the unions could bring them back to work. But Nixon pointedly did not back legislation that would have provided collective bargaining in a reformed USPOD, rather than his "postal authority." If he did, then how could he deny similar demands for collective bargaining by other federal government employees?

As Aaron Brenner describes it, even the Shultz-Rademacher collaboration (approved by Nixon) failed to drive the strikers back into the control of union leaders. Nixon's subsequent use of the military then proved incapable of acquiring the requisite labor-intensive skills fast enough to move the huge volumes of mail in New York City—the flashpoint of the strike.[61] The military entered the picture when most of the striking postal workers were starting to return to work except for New York and a few other key cities—but it was a situation in flux, as some cities were just starting to go out. The military presence sent some strikers outside New York back to work while giving pause to others who had just gone out or had considered striking. There were also those who struck just for a day to make a statement. Cooler heads in the White House realized that strikers were "going for broke" by striking when they knew they could be fired, fined, and jailed. The so-called post office "contingency plan" developed in July 1968 to handle potential work stoppages had proven to be hardly a plan at all.[62] One could argue that the strikers made negotiation inevitable and mass termination untenable. They had suddenly shut down the nation's premier communications network with no alternative labor to keep it going.

While American presidents, including Nixon, have often made rash and even irrational choices with devastating consequences, in this case Nixon and his administration were pragmatic in working to bring three-quarters of a million federal government workers into the collective bargaining system, while seeing to it that no other federal workers were allowed those rights.[63] Furthermore, in exchange for negotiating with the postal unions, Nixon achieved his goal of postal reorganization. Jefferson Cowie sees this effort as no fluke, but rather part of what Nixon's aides called their "blue-collar strategy" for Nixon to become the "workingman's president."[64] Nixon could thus align himself with popular sentiment in favor of striking postal workers. Strike veterans like Cleveland Morgan and Richard Thomas—both of whom had little use for Nixon's policies in general—expressed amazement that Nixon accepted such a radical conversion of the post office that actually gave postal unions more power.[65] The unions had to learn how to negotiate in a new format but on the same unbalanced playing field that favored management. AFL-CIO negotiator James Gildea had this to say at a collective bargaining conference two months after the 1970 strike. "The postal negotiations were a monumental first step in bringing first class citizenship to postal workers in the workplace," he proclaimed triumphantly. "The President and

Aftershocks and Postal Reorganization

the Postmaster General have served notice on them [postal supervisors] and the Congress will do so shortly — that they want first class treatment of their workers and first rate labor relations in providing that treatment."[66] Was his optimism well-placed?

The PRA indeed called its "basic function" the "obligation to provide postal services to bind the Nation together."[67] But the law was a government-labor compromise after a mass postal worker uprising. Aaron Brenner puts it in context: "The Post Office strike and the larger militancy of which it was a part represented a break in the pattern of postwar labor relations. Both employers and workers found themselves in an unfamiliar situation, one of declining economic prospects. Employers responded with a productivity drive and efforts to hold down wages and benefits; rank-and-file workers countered with organized activity to maintain and improve their work and living standards, often without the approval of their union leaders."[68]

The post office, one of the nation's "largest businesses" and "principal employers" (in the words of the 1968 Kappel Commission report), was about to begin directly dealing with the postal unions.[69] But the end of the strike revealed both the strengths as well as the limits of rank-and-file struggle. While the Nixon administration was deploying military troops that were more effective as theater than as a replacement workforce, news reports indicated that strikers were going back across the country, and union leaders were assuring them that talks had produced an agreement with the administration. Tom Germano said of those still on strike: "The prospect of isolation and the fear of vulnerability began to overwhelm them. The strike, even in Manhattan and the Bronx, could not continue without a new surge of support and strong formal leadership."[70] Postal strikers were no different from any other labor or social movement: they wanted leadership that was effective. Leadership was needed to negotiate the end of the struggle on the best possible terms for postal workers. That could not be done alone by some 200,000 postal strikers. It was the formal leadership of postal unions that negotiated the end of the strike and laid the groundwork for the U.S. Postal Service — minus two large, militant, and influential postal unions, the NPU and NAPFE. But rank-and-file activism had already begun the process of working to assume formal leadership of the postal unions. They would be successful in the NALC and the yet-to-be formed APWU. One might surmise that Nixon's show of force caused the strikers to capitulate — until we consider that some strikers around the country were already returning while others were just going out. In New York, where troops proved ineffective at moving the mail, postal workers were not budging. The strike ended when union leaders convinced strikers that a deal had been struck and asked them to return to work during negotiations with Nixon administration officials. But the drama was just beginning.

STRIKE THREATS, UNION LOCKOUTS,
AND REORGANIZATION

After the strike, how did former strike adversaries resume working relations on what would become a new basis? And what direction forward would the postal unions take? Rank-and-file militancy was forcing change in the post office and the unions. But that meant both good and bad news for postal workers. Overall a change in the workplace atmosphere could be detected. MBPU strike organizer Eleanor Bailey remembered that lower and middle supervisors "stayed off their case for a while" after the strike, keeping the harassment to a minimum. During the strike, said Bailey, "my supervisors, every night they would send me out a list of people that came in . . . because the only way they got a raise is when we got a raise. . . . So we could 'dog' those people [the strikebreakers] the next day. I was out there [at the GPO in Manhattan] from six to eight in the morning to make sure my folks would not go in to work."[71] Bailey's rank-and-file strike leadership actually had lower management helping her enforce strike discipline on union members based on those managers' self-interest.

Yet even though the picket lines had come down on March 25 and the mail was moving again, the conflict was by no means over. "The mood of the letter carriers was particularly positive," recalls Germano. "As they resumed their duties they spoke of their importance as workers and the 'dignity' they had recaptured through their strike action."[72] But after the high of the strike, labor-management relations seemed stuck. "In fact," writes Germano, "all that had occurred at the negotiations was an agreement in principle between the Post Office and the unions." Rademacher's strike threat had come and gone "with no action from him in spite of stalemated negotiations [and] the government hardened its position" on issues including retirement and medical benefits; pay increases; and the "compression" of years necessary to reach top pay.[73]

The Nixon administration did not want to move on the amnesty issue in the postal strike until it had resolved the PATCO wildcat strike of over 1,500 air traffic controllers on sick-out.[74] The April 2, 1970, memorandum of agreement that had been hammered out between the post office and the seven unions still required Nixon's signature. There was delay and drama over the

136   *Aftershocks and Postal Reorganization*

next two weeks when Nixon finally signed the pay bill on April 15.[75] There would be more action and acrimony involving the unions, the rank-and-file, and Congress all through the summer months up until the signing of the PRA on August 12, when there would be nothing but smiles and accolades for the news cameras at the signing ceremony.

The only movement in Congress that April while postal unions and the USPOD were negotiating concerned the 6 percent retroactive pay bill (the one that had already been in the pipeline and would apply to all federal employees). By April 9, the day the House approved it on the day after the Senate had, over 2,000 NALC Branch 36 members were back for a union meeting at the Manhattan Center in New York. This represented an astounding turnout for a monthly membership meeting, but these were still extraordinary times, as many carriers began demanding another strike. Debates at that meeting yielded a "compromise" between officials and members that directed Branch 36 president Gus Johnson, accompanied by a rank-and-file representative, to meet with other big NALC branches to coordinate a strike if demands were not met by April 30. There was no mention of NALC president James Rademacher, no coordination with the national office, and the Branch 36 executive board even met later that day with delegates from the MBPU.[76]

The two industrial independent unions—the MBPU (and its parent union NPU) along with NAPFE—protested being squeezed out by what the MBPU called a "sweetheart deal" whereby bargaining units would be determined on a *craft*, rather than *industrial*, basis. There was a feeling of betrayal. The MBPU called for an industrial postal union in New York City of all crafts, including members of other postal unions.[77] The House Post Office and Civil Service Committee listened sympathetically as NPU and NAPFE leaders related how they had been excluded from negotiations with the government. By this time, H.R. 17070 was the new compromise postal reform measure, representing details hashed out post-strike. NPU president David Silvergleid testified on April 27, 1970, and protested H.R. 17070 because, he said, "if unchanged, [it] would almost certainly destroy our union and the possibility of ever achieving one industrial union of all postal employees. Although ours is the third largest union in the postal service, we were excluded from the so-called negotiations that took place between the AFL-CIO and seven craft unions on the one hand, and the Post Office Department on the other. *And just as we were excluded, so was the National Alliance of Postal and Federal Employees with substantial postal membership.*"[78]

Using the third-person singular to refer to himself, the committee's chair,

Thaddeus Dulski interrupted: "So was Dulski. Go ahead." Silvergleid quickly acknowledged that Dulski, too, had been marginalized, and then pointed out how 55,000 NPU members out of a total of 80,000 had participated in the strike — about one-quarter of all strikers in fact. For its part, NAPFE represented the fourth-largest postal union in 1970 at about 45,000 members, and yet much smaller unions were seated at the table just by virtue of being AFL-CIO craft unions like the Special Delivery Messengers, at about 2,500 members. Silvergleid also questioned the Mail Handlers representation as a subsidiary of LIUNA, "although the status of that organization under the existing Executive order has been called into question."[79]

The discussions and negotiations from which NPU, NAPFE, and even Representative Dulski, had been excluded, had begun the month before on March 26, 1970, at LIUNA headquarters in Washington, D.C. Jules Bernstein was an attorney working for LIUNA from 1967 to 1987, and at the time also represented its affiliate the Mail Handlers, which had only marginally participated in the strike. He remembers being called out of one of those meetings by a LIUNA security guard to take care of a disturbance on the ground floor of the LIUNA building. The next thing he knew, MBPU president Moe Biller had come up to the eighth floor by elevator, and was angrily demanding entry to the meeting. Bernstein went back inside to get William Usery to "calm him down," which Bernstein said he did, but Biller was still denied entrance.[80] It would seem like the deck was stacked against the two militant independent postal unions.

But in fact there was a diversity of viewpoints among politicians on that and other issues having to do with postal labor. It is remarkable to read the transcripts of the House Post Office and Civil Service hearings held in April 1970. At the time, both Democrats and Republicans on the committee for the most part operated under the same set of assumptions, all of which related to postal union empowerment. Besides outspoken labor advocates already mentioned — Dulski and Brasco, both representing New York State — other Democratic congressmen like North Carolina moderate David Henderson and California liberal Jerome Waldie, and even among Republicans like Idaho's James McClure, appeared to sympathize with the NPU and NAPFE's right to representation. Representative Waldie, in questioning NAPFE's president Ashby Smith, even wondered if Smith's vocal opposition to the strike had caused the "exclusive" unions to shut them out: "I am inclined to think your opportunities would have been greater had you been more militant," he suggested. Smith provoked laughter from the room when he observed that the "most militant group" in the post office, the NPU, was

Aftershocks and Postal Reorganization

also excluded. Waldie was not deterred, adding: "I would . . . suggest a review of your position in terms of the ability to negotiate a right to work provision," the union shop being something Waldie argued should at least be on
the table. This was a touchy subject. Smith had already denied that NAPFE
supported "right to work" (no mandatory dues checkoff) at the new USPS,
and Henderson, representing a western district in North Carolina, a "right
to work" state, sought to support Smith's disavowal of that term by seeking
to substitute "the right to join or not to join." Later, NAPFE vice president
Wyatt Williams, still not happy with his union being tagged with the antiunion "right to work" label, sought to amplify what Smith and Henderson
had already asserted, citing what had always concerned NAPFE with "white
trade unionism" generally, not just that in government service. "I think what
we are talking about is not so much the right to work but it is compulsory
unionism more than the closed shop," he said, and then offered this caution-
ary note: "We are also talking about the closed shop and the compulsory
unionism that has denied employment for millions of black workers. So we
have a dangerous precedent." The NAPFE's objection was that the "union
shop" proposal for the USPS, rather than protecting union rights, would only
enable representation for "franchise" AFL-CIO postal unions that had won
pre-strike representation elections under the soon to be defunct EO 11491 —
the successor to the 1962 EO 10988. They argued that this would fence out a
historically black union formed in the Jim Crow era that included segregated
unionism. The NPU, NAPFE, and pro-labor House committee members were
not opposed to the principle of the "union shop." But the post office was a
unique workplace that in eight decades of postal unionism recognized AFL
postal unions (and AFL-CIO postal unions after their 1955 merger) as well as
independent postal unions.[81]

By 1970 the NPU was indisputably the most militant postal union, while
NAPFE was the most militant on civil-rights issues. Yet both were being
squeezed out by a process that had allowed them to promote progressive
agendas operating outside the AFL-CIO. The exception to the rule whereby
AFL-CIO postal unions enjoyed a virtual national (but not regional or local)
representation monopoly was the independent NRLCA, numbering about
30,000 members. The NRLCA maintained their national exclusive bargaining
rights for rural letter carriers, never having had any competition for representation in that craft. The NRLCA in fact had always resisted calls to merge
with the NALC or any other union, the NRLCA typically being described as
a conservative union. That had mostly to do with the rural letter carrier, as
described by Tom Germano as being a "private entrepreneur" who histori-

cally had "relied on his political connections when seeking to achieve goals or adjust grievances. Having obtained his position through politics, most often sponsorship by a local Congressman, the rural carrier has tradition- ally been loyal to the parochial principles of the politician or political party which dominates in his hometown."[82] President Nixon and Postmaster Gen- eral Blount stopped all future USPOD appointments on February 5, 1969, in- cluding postmasters and rural letter carriers, with the final abolition of pa- tronage on August 12, 1970.[83]

Meanwhile, on the other side of the political debate over "right to work," the National Right to Work Committee through its newsletter on April 15, 1970, was assailing proposed postal reform as betraying free choice for postal workers as promised in the platform of the Republican Party. Germano ar- gues that the price the Nixon administration had to pay to get the AFL-CIO on board with postal reorganization was the "union shop." As it was, that provision was eliminated in the final version of the House bipartisan bill sponsored by Morris Udall (D-Ariz.) and Edward Derwinsky (R-Ill.). The final bill (H.R. 17070) also did not allow for the right to strike, area wage differentials (supported by many urban postal unionists, especially in the Northeast), or recognition for the NPU and NAPFE. The absorption of the NPU into the newly formed APWU in 1971 downgraded the importance of independent industrial unions to postal workers. Even the issue of the union shop, while significant, was not a deal-breaker, since the post office con- tinued to have the highest unionization percentage in the federal govern- ment. Dues checkoff, while voluntary, had been and would still be automatic for almost nine of every ten postal workers. The experience of both losses and gains during negotiations led to a formalization of the rank-and-file postal union movement.[84]

The April 2 "compromise" that Vern Baxter outlines that finally took place between unions and government was one that "combined a postal pay raise with postal reform" as the answer to the dispute between government tying raises to reorganization and unions demanding raises *before* reorgani- zation.[85] But unions, he argues, also engaged in "intense lobbying" that "pre- served the bargainability of issues related to technological change."[86] Profes- sor of management Joseph Loewenberg notes that the offer of an 8 percent raise on top of a 6 percent raise was a game changer for the unions.[87] Political scientist John Tierney agrees with that assessment, but adds that the govern- ment's proposal to the unions "included an offer to have the unions partici- pate in formulating the details of the reform plan," as well as a provision for "third-party binding arbitration—a provision the unions had sought as compensation for the reduction in Congress's role in making postal policy."[88] Readers by now would be justifiably confused as to why it took over a year and a strike to hammer out an agreement if Nixon already supported collective bargaining and third-party arbitration in principle from the beginning. But those were concessions Nixon was willing to make *only* if unions first agreed to his postal corporation plan: even raises were off the table without it, and he was apparently hoping raises would remain low. The devil is always in the details in the world of labor-management negotiations, but two things stand out here. One is that collective bargaining and third-party binding arbitration would be considered normative for corporations (not government) by a conservative Republican president, which reflects unions' political power then as well as Nixon's pragmatism. The second is Tierney's reminder that on March 24, the day before the end of the strike, "Postmaster General Blount announced that the administration was willing to discuss all issues involved in the strike, and that postal reorganization would not necessarily be a prerequisite to pay legislation."[89] In other words, the strike moved the needle.

By contrast, James Rademacher's recollection of a post-strike meeting among union presidents reveals a top-down attitude by those at the top who forgot how it was a wildcat strike from below that made negotiations over the PRA and postal raises possible. At an April 6 meeting of Rademacher and six other postal union presidents, plus AFL-CIO president George Meany, Rademacher rejected the offer by Meany (effectively serving as Nixon's intermediary) of a 6 percent raise on top of the 6 percent raise all federal government employees were receiving. Rademacher said they needed at least 8 percent. Meany agreed, and Rademacher recalls, "So we bought reorganization which was what I was fighting for years, but I opposed it constantly because I said, 'We're not going to give them this for nothing.' So we got 8% in addition to 6%, which is 14%. . . . We [also] agreed on 8 years to the top [pay] with the help of President Nixon."[90] John Tierney confirms that "further negotiations continued for two weeks in an attempt to develop a reorganization package that would have the support of the Post Office and the unions alike. On April 16 the parties finally reached an agreement on the terms of a postal reorganization proposal."[91] Nixon sent the measure to Congress where it passed right away, facing some delays in the Senate over "postal rate-making machinery." By August 6, as the House completed work on the bill, Postmaster General Blount marveled at how, eighteen months before, "nobody held out much hope . . . for reorganizing," but now all the "conflicting opinions" had been accommodated.[92]

There were still conflicting views in the labor movement, however. According to labor historian Martin Halpern, the AFL-CIO historically had not demonstrated much interest in winning collective bargaining rights for federal workers before the 1970 postal wildcat strike. So it was understandable that many postal workers would be angry at the post-strike behavior of Meany, who convinced not only the six AFL-CIO postal unions but also the independent NRLCA to *only* negotiate on pay raises, not other issues. He even went so far as to urge the House of Representatives to drop the retroactive part of the 8 percent postal pay raise, along with automatic wage adjustments, when considering the PRA in exchange for allowing the "union shop" to be considered in negotiations. (Meany's action led to the overwhelming defeat of a resolution at the NALC national convention that August in Hawaii commending him and the AFL-CIO for their strike support — with Branch 36 president Gus Johnson leading the floor speakers denouncing Meany. The convention just minutes before had overwhelmingly voted for a resolution to support the campaign for a federal holiday honoring the famed civil rights leader Dr. Martin Luther King Jr., who had been assassinated in 1968.) The final House version disallowed the union shop provision while keeping the pay increases intact. The bill signed by Nixon was essentially the same as the memorandum of agreement signed by the USPOD and the seven "exclusive" postal unions on April 16.[93] But according to Vern Baxter, postal unions significantly maintained the right to keep collective bargaining rights over technological changes (i.e. mechanization) that would affect jobs and working conditions.[94] Unfortunately for the two independent industrial unions, the Nixon administration also implemented the PRA with only the previous winners of national exclusive bargaining status — which meant everyone but the NPU and NAPFE. The two unions picketed, protested, and even disrupted the preliminary talks in the year following the strike. They demanded inclusion, and filed suit against the USPS and the seven "exclusive" postal unions.[95] NPU and NAPFE national officials testified before a congressional committee in 1970 as to the unfairness of this exclusion.[96] But bipartisan sympathy on the committee for their plea was to no avail.[97]

New York City postal workers, the first to go out on March 18 and the last to go back to work in the late afternoon of March 25, 1970, never quit conducting labor actions or talking about striking again during the rest of 1970 and into 1971.[98] GPO letter carriers refused overtime to clear the backlog of mail from the March 1970 strike, for example. On October 6, 1970, 300 NALC members from across the country came to New York to hammer out a rank-and-file platform. The issues put forward had to do with both postal work and union democracy. They included more union branch autonomy and local officer accountability, and better safety, health, retirement benefits, and full medical and dental insurance paid by the USPOD.[99] The summer of 1970 had already seen rank-and-file New York postal workers threatening strike activity as debate on the final version of the bill began on June 15 in the House. Postmaster General Blount, meanwhile, acting in some ways like a loose cannon, declared that same day his opposition to amnesty for strikers and a retroactive pay increase. The pay bill bogged down in the Senate, as Majority Leader Mike Mansfield (D-Mont.) blocked the movement of all legislation until the Nixon administration had answered questions about why U.S. troops were in Cambodia. By this time, NALC president James Rademacher was threatening to lead a strike if improvements were not made by June 30. Branch 36 got ready for a strike vote on July 1, 1970. Past strike threats by Rademacher had come up empty, but on June 29, with the end of the fiscal year only a day away and appropriations bills also hung up, the Senate began debating. "As the clock struck twelve on the night of June 30, enough 'positive action' had transpired for the letter carriers' union leaders to rescind their strike threats," which included Branch 36.[100] Suddenly congressional movement quickened. An amended version of H.R. 17070 cleared the House committee on July 30, the Senate bill S. 3842 on August 3, the full House on August 6, and was signed by Nixon on August 12.[101] Compared to Nixon's original 1969 plan and the subsequent 1970 Nixon-backed H.R. 4, Joseph Loewenberg says of the final bill, "the labor-management sections were more elaborate than they had originally been, but fundamentally no different."[102]

THE STRANGE BIRTH OF THE USPS

A jovial President Nixon welcomed his official guests into the Great Hall at the Post Office Department building at 9:45 A.M. on a humid Washington, D.C., summer morning of August 12, 1970: "Mr. Vice President, Members of the Cabinet, Members of the Congress, former Postmasters General, Mr. Postmaster General, all of our distinguished guests on this occasion. As the Postmaster General has very eloquently pointed out, this is an historic occasion, because this particular Department goes back earlier than the Constitution itself."[103]

For the PRA signing ceremony, Nixon chose the headquarters of the USPOD, then located on Pennsylvania Avenue between Twelfth and Thirteenth Streets NW, just a few blocks from the White House. It was a stately structure that symbolized the central role the post office played in American communications culture. The new USPS headquarters that would take its place in 1973 would be a modern office building, two miles away at 475 L'Enfant Plaza.[104] Nixon's lofty rhetoric matched the older building's architecture, although there is no shortage of ironies contained in the words he spoke. Within just a few years, both he and vice president Spiro T. Agnew, along with attorney general John Mitchell, would be forced to resign their respective offices in disgrace after committing acts that flouted the Constitution. The senators and representatives who had backed this measure, many of whom were in attendance, included staunch pro-labor liberals and lifelong conservative segregationists.[105] Almost five months before, in a televised March 23 address calling up troops to use as strikebreakers to move the mail, Nixon had criticized striking postal workers for threatening "the survival of a government based on law." His speech then, however, was as conciliatory as it was impatient, conceding that "the . . . fine Americans in the . . . Post Office Department . . . are underpaid and they have other legitimate grievances." Had union leaders led the strike, or the public not sympathized with striking postal workers, Nixon's position might have differed. This was quite a turnaround from a president who in March had privately told his aides that he should just "fire them all."[106] Despite having illegally struck the federal government, these postal workers were, in Nixon's narrative, deserving of labor union rights.[107]

Nixon had credited postal workers with making this law come to life, although he failed to acknowledge the role of the wildcat strike that almost a third of them had participated in. For his part, James Rademacher years later would look back and claim that "the reorganization did not result as a part of the strike. It resulted as part of our negotiations."[108] Nixon's omission of the strike's impact on reorganization is unsurprising, but Rademacher's dismissal is astonishing, yet revealing of a top-down approach to union leadership. Nixon's words also sharply clash with the dominant view in the Republican Party of the early twenty-first century that openly disdains government enterprises that employ well-paid career union employees. It is strange, then, to hear Nixon in 1970 express concern for government employees and improving their labor conditions.[109] And even though he could not resist joking about how a letter he sent three days prior across town to the Postmaster General had probably not yet arrived, nevertheless, with a final flourish, Nixon beamed: "As we look to that past, a very proud past, I think what we all feel today is that hundreds of thousands of people in the Post Office Department can look to a better future, a better future for them, and as the future is better for them it means better service for all of the American people."[110]

INSTITUTIONALIZING CONFLICT, REGIMENTING LABOR

As a result of the strike, that venerable center of American communications since 1775 found itself transformed by the PRA into the U.S. Postal Service on July 1, 1971, with its workers the only federal employees to enjoy full collective-bargaining rights—except the right to strike.[111] Writing twelve years after the birth of the USPS, Tom Germano captured this paradox in observing that the PRA "institutionalized major conflict within the postal service. Since 1971, the salaries of postal workers have risen dramatically while postal management has increased its control of the workforce through the application of scientific management."[112]

A decade later, Vern Baxter revealed how business principles were embedded in the PRA and the USPS that it created: "After 20 years it seems clear that the top-down reform process and many changes in management structure failed to fundamentally transform the postal management culture."[113] The list of examples is daunting. Top postal managers were replaced with private-sector executives with no postal experience. The Board of Governors drew two-thirds of its members from the business community from 1971 to 1992. Westinghouse was called upon to draw up job-evaluation studies that included measuring workloads, which led to a new job classification system that replaced the Civil Service system in 1973. "Postal management," Baxter concludes, "tried to use its expanded authority to compress internal job ladders and create a system of bureaucratic roles."[114] We can understand why Nixon was so jovial at the August 12 PRA signing: he got the essence of his original postal corporation after facing the first nationwide federal employee strike in U.S. history on his watch.

The 1970 postal strike inspired other government employees, in addition to benefiting them directly, which made the Nixon administration fear its setting a precedent. All government employees were now entitled to the same 6 percent raise the postal workers won in the bill that was quickly passed and signed on April 15, 1970.[115] In addition, three major government unions saw their members clamoring to strike: the American Federation of Government Employees, the National Federation of Federal Employees, and the National Association of Government Employees.[116] PATCO, founded just two years before, saw about 2,000 of its members go on a nineteen-day, nationally planned sick-out.[117] Postal strikers had been influenced by labor and civil-rights struggles of the 1960s and now in turn inspired rank-and-file democratic action occurring in other unions. Within a decade, the NALC and APWU would become two of the largest, strongest, and most influential unions in the AFL-CIO.[118] The 1970 postal strike created possibilities. It challenged certain assumptions about the power and voice of members within unions. Far from being an isolated event, the 1970 strike represented the extension of a "democratic movement culture" (to borrow a term from Lawrence Goodwyn, the preeminent historian of American populism) that had been brewing over the previous decade in conflict with what was frequently described as an authoritarian bureaucracy. This rank-and-file postal unionist culture used the historical experience and collective memory of the strike to maintain pressure on the USPS and its unions to change. Surely, as a "modern" entity the USPS would be open to the necessity of change, especially when confronted by strong, united postal unions. Tom Germano has argued that Moe Biller and Vincent Sombrotto carried the rank-and-file spirit of the strike and democratic reforms into their respective union infrastructures (APWU and NALC), while at the same time making compromises with democracy, in addition to returning to the lobbying of Congress because of the limitations of the PRA. What Biller, Sombrotto, and others had once decried as "collective begging" reemerged as an important pragmatic weapon in the arsenal of self-preservation for the postal unions.[119] The hybrid government agency/corporation that was supposed to centralize labor relations in the same autonomous body found itself with new conflicts and new versions of old ones.

Aftershocks and Postal Reorganization

6

The U.S. Postal Service
and the Postal Unions
in the 1970s

The strike aftermath was complicated. The first contract negotiations for what would become the new USPS were acrimonious against a backdrop of fraught internal union politics, with NALC Branch 36 and the MBPU both ready to strike. In the NALC, strife mixed with insurgency. The NAPFE was locked out from collective bargaining by the exclusive unions, while the NPU was absorbed into the new APWU, where triumphalist merger combined with heated debate over its future direction. The NRLCA remained conservative and above the fray. And the NPMHU was still mired in issues of corruption and undemocratic representation. In 1971 the NALC slapped a trusteeship (took over operations) on Branch 36 that had begun the strike, and a decade later the NALC and APWU almost struck during contentious contract negotiations with the USPS — just weeks before the ill-fated PATCO strike that saw President Reagan fire over 11,000 striking air-traffic controllers. The 1970s at the post office saw a 1974 wildcat strike (and management lockout) at the huge New York Bulk and Foreign Mail Center in Jersey City, New Jersey. Bulk mail centers (BMCs) saw a wave of slowdowns protesting safety issues, schedule changes, discipline for accidents, and mandatory overtime, leading to a 1975 rally at the San Francisco BMC, and a July 24, 1976, walkout at the Philadelphia BMC. A rash of BMC wildcats broke out in 1978 in Jersey City, San Francisco, Los Angeles, and Washington, D.C., demanding those issues be included in contract negotiations — which themselves had the possibility of becoming a nationally called strike.[1] Postal labor relations and postal unions were evolving in turmoil. The rank and file were not done fighting for reforms, starting with their own unions.

Threats to strike by rank-and-file postal unionists throughout 1970 and into 1971 were not the only forms of militant activity. Late in 1970, rank-and-file caucuses at major NALC branches were not only meeting and communicating together, but were running slates of candidates that swept local union offices in Minneapolis, New York, Boston, and Philadelphia, among others. The spontaneous communication links that had constrained 1970 strike coordination were now given time to grow and mature. Local union election confrontations in New York also included letter carriers "crashing" other post offices to campaign for office in the "swing rooms" where employees took their breaks. With support from dozens of carriers gathered to hear them, the candidates refused orders to leave from management, who brought administrative charges against some of them.[2] In direct confrontation with postal management, more than a thousand Branch 36 and MBPU members on March 1 and 2, 1971, demonstrated outside the office of the USPS Regional Postmaster General, located in Manhattan's GPO, after local negotiations became stalled. About 150 protesters occupied the Regional Postmaster General's office for seven hours in what was then a popular form of social-movement protest—especially in the civil rights, Black Power, women's, and antiwar movements—although rarely seen any more in the labor movement that had helped pioneer that form in the 1930s. The postal union demonstrators did not leave, notes Germano, until management agreed to restart local negotiations—even after postal inspectors had threatened occupiers with arrest.[3]

All this activity happened just before the seven exclusive postal unions began negotiating on a national contract with USPOD management on January 20, 1971. For bargaining purposes, the unions formed the Council of American Postal Employees (CAPE), and for the next six months they negotiated with a management that refused to make a single concrete wage offer. CAPE's attorney was Bernard Cushman, a labor lawyer with three decades' experience in collective bargaining, who later reflected that he had never seen "a situation where management refused to make even a token offer on wages and fringe benefits." APWU historians John Walsh and Garth Mangum noted that the unions initially offered sixty-three items. They quote APWU's first president, Francis Filbey, as calling management's counterproposals those "designed to take away protections already enjoyed by employees and to set up a system by which all phases of a new contract would be subject to arbitrary decisions of management."[4]

Getting negotiations off to a rocky start the week before January 20, Postmaster General Blount had issued a "gag rule" prohibiting postal employees from contacting congressional members on any postal affairs— which Congress rejected and Blount did not enforce. That same month, a three-judge federal panel shot down the NPU and NAPFE's request for a temporary injunction to block collective bargaining as long as they were excluded—which led to the NPU merging into the APWU two months later. Meanwhile the stalemate at the bargaining table continued. The unions refused management's request for an extension past the April 19, 1971, deadline. But the Postal Reorganization Act, besides providing a framework for negotiations also mandated a fact-finding phase. This meant the Federal Mediation and Conciliation Service appointed a panel that met but was unable to arrive at recommendations.[5]

NALC Branch 36 and the MBPU in New York both voted to strike, this time on July 1, 1971, by huge margins at the Manhattan Center. The twin strike votes followed a pre-strike rally of about 12,000 postal workers on June 30 at the center, which included as honored guest speakers longtime local labor leaders Harry Van Arsdale and Victor Gotbaum.[6] The MBPU press release proclaimed that joining them were presidents of NPU locals in Chicago, Los Angeles, Boston, and Philadelphia, as well as officials from their national office in Washington, D.C. Also included was Vincent Sombrotto of NALC Branch 36. Sombrotto, widely hailed as a principal leader of the 1970 wildcat strike, was now president of Branch 36 after defeating Gus Johnson on December 2, 1970, in what was described as "the largest election turnout in the history of the N.A.L.C." There had still been a lot of resentment by rank-and-filers toward Johnson for having tried to block the 1970 wildcat strike vote.[7] Branch 36 was now challenging the NALC national office by rallying in solidarity with the MBPU in calling for a strike because, as the MBPU press release put it, "The Postal Service was callously trying to strike a bargain: They would put a money offer on the table IF the unions would give up JOB SECURITY—IF THE UNIONS WOULD AGREE TO WIPE OUT FOREVER THE POSTAL WORKER'S RIGHT TO CIVIL SERVICE PROTECTION."[8] The contrast could not have been starker between that demonstration and a rally of about 150 people in Washington, D.C., in support of negotiations by national NALC president James Rademacher. Tom Germano outlines what must have been a humiliating experience for USPS officials and encouraging for the rank-and-file postal workers on July 1, 1971: "As the Post Office band played on the steps of Manhattan's General Post Office for a bevy of political and postal officials gathered to celebrate the birth of the United States Postal Service, thousands of postal workers were only a few hundred yards away at Manhattan Center voting to authorize a strike against the new agency."[9]

Like the thunderstorms that rolled through the city that day, postal rank-and-filers were raining on the USPS parade. But there was even more to this spectacle than rallies, rainfall, heat, and high humidity in the New York City summertime.[10] The vote to strike by NALC Branch 36 was leading by a ratio of about 20–1 when all the ballots were suddenly seized by federal marshals and impounded by an injunction of the U.S. Circuit Court of Appeals on behalf of Rademacher and the NALC national office. MBPU members were not under that injunction, and voted 10,645–608 to strike. On July 1, 1971, the APWU formally came into existence based on the merger of the UFPC, the NPU, and three smaller craft unions: National Association of Post Office and General Services Maintenance Employees (NAPOGSME), the National Federation of Post Office Motor Vehicle Employees (NFPOMVE), and the National Association of Special Delivery Messengers (NASDM).[11]

On July 1, with the federal panel unable to help, "crisis bargaining ensued."[12] USPS and postal union negotiators had hoped to announce a contract agreement that same day—the first day of the USPS. But with the "organized militancy" of New York postal workers, suddenly, management's "final offer" started including bonuses, wage increases, and a cost-of-living increase, "enough to diminish the discontent of most postal workers," although many were still opposed to the eventual July 20, 1971, agreement for its allowance of "crossing crafts" and President Rademacher's refusal to submit the agreement to the membership.[13] "The contract also contained a job security clause," notes Tom Germano, which significantly "guaranteed that there would be no layoffs of employees for any reason during the life of the contract." Furthermore, "unresolved issues would be negotiated at the local level" rather than wading through the more cumbersome process of binding arbitration. Top pay at the end of the two-year contract would jump from $8,442 annually to $11,073.[14] This was the first time wages and benefits, formerly subject to congressional discretion, had been negotiated by federal employees and a government agency. It represented a milestone, especially with two important provisions that would become permanent fixtures in postal labor relations: a no-layoff clause and a formal grievance system. Shop stewards—a concept borrowed from private-sector unionism—would replace the old system of union "delegates" and "representatives" who

The first U.S. Postal Service collective bargaining agreement was signed July 20, 1971, and included the American Postal Workers Union (APWU), National Association of Letter Carriers (NALC), National Postal Mail Handlers Union (NPMHU), and the National Rural Letter Carriers Association (NRLCA). NALC president Rademacher is seated, with (*left to right*) Postmaster General Winton Blount and Assistant Labor Secretary William Usery looking on. Courtesy of NALC.

enjoyed far less power on the shop floor.[15] Former Pittsburgh APWU local president (and NPU local officer before then) John P. Richards highlighted the contrasts between grievance procedures before and after the 1971 contract. Under the old system, the local grievance committee consisted of three members, two of whom were chosen by management, the third by the union. For over a decade before the new system, said Richards, "I could not win a single case!" Once that changed, his average of victories ran over 95 percent.[16] Within the APWU, a growing overall militancy was heightened by the presence of the previously independent industrial NPU whose members had helped start the 1970 postal strike. It would take less than a decade for former NPU members to ascend to national leadership and the organization begin to operate similarly to the former NPU.[17] There were some tensions at the first APWU convention in 1972 between the former industrial NPU (bringing about 80,000 members in) and the other craft unions that had merged together to number about 300,000 members. But agreements also included two key democratic measures promoted by former NPU members: final contract ratification would be made by membership, and national officer elections would be by referendum rather than at the convention.[18]

Overlapping the drama of national contract negotiations was the battle between the NALC national office and Branch 36. President Rademacher began what turned into a six-month campaign to place dissident Branch 36 in trusteeship on June 25, 1971, out of fear that it was getting beyond the national control with its strike rallies and votes. "Local officers," writes Tom Germano, "refused to surrender their positions."[19] The national office sought an injunction from a federal judge but failed. They appealed. This was the backdrop for a rally of 12,000 postal workers at the Manhattan Center on June 30, 1971.[20] On December 3, 1971, a year after Vincent Sombrotto defeated Gus Johnson to become NALC Branch 36 president, national officers appeared at Branch 36 headquarters in midtown Manhattan with their attorney, police officers, and a writ to impose trusteeship. Sombrotto, along with newly elected executive vice president Tom Germano and recording secretary John Cullen, were stripped of their full-time branch positions and returned to their stations carrying mail. They were replaced by the trustees, which included Gus Johnson, NALC national officer Bernard Murphy, and NALC New York state association president Frank Merigliano. The branch did not recognize them, however, as officers.[21] It was a dual-power situation. Germano argues that a major motivating factor for putting Branch 36 under trusteeship was a desire to halt the campaign by the National Rank and File Movement (NRFM)—whose stronghold was in New York—to put "one man one vote" decision-making on the ballot at the 1972 NALC convention.[22] What followed was two weeks of embarrassment for Rademacher and the national office. One day during that period, over 2,000 Branch 36 members picketed their union office—then located in the Times Square Hotel at 261 West Forty-Third Street. An agreement was reached after a series of negotiations. Rademacher made and then retracted an offer. Branch 36 asked the U.S. Supreme Court to hear their appeal. Rademacher finally gave in to

The U.S. Postal Service and the Postal Unions in the 1970s

Branch 36's demands and agreed to rescind the trusteeship—five minutes after Branch 36's attorney filed an appeal.[23] But the damage had been done to the burgeoning rank-and-file movement. By placing Branch 36 under trusteeship, along with merging seventy-five Long Island branches, Rademacher was able to stop the NRFM "from attaining the required number of endorsements necessary to present the question of referendum voting for national officers to the total membership prior to the national convention."[24] In 1974, the year before the NRFM's decline, supporters of Rademacher "stole the thunder" from the NRFM by proposing resolutions that both passed, allowing voting on national officers by mail rather than being restricted to convention attendance, as well as membership voting for contract ratification.[25]

MAKING THE APWU, JOINT BARGAINING, AND PRO-EQUALITY ACTIVISM

The making of the APWU began with maneuvering behind the scenes between the UFPC and NPU. Merger talks were going on at the same time as the NPU and NAPFE lawsuit was being filed against the USPS and the seven exclusive postal unions in October 1970. That lawsuit lost, announced the January 27, 1971, *Federal Times*.[26] On March 3, 1971, the NPU was brought on board with the UFPC and three other craft unions representing maintenance, motor vehicle, and special delivery employees (NAPOGSME, NFPOMVE, and NASDM, respectively) to announce the formation of the APWU pending rank-and-file approval in all five unions. The UFPC's monthly *Union Postal Clerk* announced the forthcoming merger in its April 1971 issue in an article titled "World's Largest Postal Union Hinges on Rank-and-File Vote." The editors exulted: "These final steps toward the creation of the long-anticipated One Big Union were launched in Washington on March 3 when the leaders of the five unions, including the UFPOC [UFPC], signed an historic merger agreement."[27] The NAPFE meanwhile shrank in membership but expanded its scope as a federal employee union, even as it had lost collective bargaining rights at the post office.[28]

The American Postal Workers Union (APWU) formally came into existence on July 1, 1971, with the merger of two former rivals and three small craft unions. That happened to also be the day the USPS came into being, superseding the USPOD. The meeting of the five union heads had come four months earlier on March 3, with a triumphant announcement made in the NPU's monthly union journal, the *Progressive*. The NPU, which not long before had joined with the NAPFE to blast the AFL-CIO and the Nixon administration for not allowing recognition of the third- and sixth-largest postal unions, respectively, had decided that merger was the better part of valor, and buried the hatchet with the second-largest postal union, the UFPC. The NPU may have been the fastest-growing postal union, but it was also doomed to be quickly headed nowhere without being part of a government-recognized union. Now it was a key player in the new APWU, which was also the world's largest postal union with over 300,000 members.[29]

Meanwhile, NAPFE rejected offers to merge with the APWU in what would have been by all accounts a kind of "civil rights division" of the APWU. NAPFE president Robert White that same month declared that "the National Alliance has no intentions of even discussing merger with any other union." NAPFE national officer Countee Abbott remembers White warning that if they merged they would be "submerged." Former NAPFE president Ashby Smith continued to blame Nixon's EO 11491 for damaging the NAPFE in abolishing the "formal" and "informal" recognition categories — as well as the exclusive category at the local and regional levels — previously available under President Kennedy's EO 10988. More black postal workers, including those who had held dual memberships for years, now left the NAPFE. There was no financial incentive to pay dues to an organization that could not formally represent them.[30]

The legacy of the 1970 strike included an impulse for the next decade for postal unions to threaten called (and still illegal) strikes during periodic contract negotiations. The four postal unions negotiated jointly in 1971, 1973, and 1975. In 1978 the NALC, APWU, and NPMHU bargained together as the Postal Labor Negotiating Committee. By 1981 the NALC and APWU had decided to bargain without the Mail Handlers after what they considered a disastrous outcome in 1978 bargaining alongside that union. They formed the Joint Bargaining Committee (JBC) for the 1981, 1984, 1987, and 1990 contracts.[31] And in general, postal labor gave as good as they got at the bargaining table. At a press conference during the 1975 negotiations, NALC president James Rademacher even boasted (along with Mail Handlers Union chief negotiator James LaPenta) of intimidating USPS negotiators: "We put up this finger and told them, we can put this finger on the phone and tell them [postal employees] to be calm. Or we can put this finger on the phone and — dial-a-strike." The result was a favorable contract for labor, with union leaders only complaining that Congress needed to give them the right to strike.[32]

Meanwhile, despite being left out of postal collective bargaining, the NAPFE was an important part of the movement in 1972 to amend Title VII of the 1964 Civil Rights Act to allow federal employees to file civil suits for discrimination.[33] With the NAPFE leading the way into the 1960s, pro-equality activism at the post office had picked up, as the competing NPU made it one of their hallmarks. Raydell Moore, an African American clerk in the Los Angeles area, became adept at handling EEO cases for the NPU on the west coast, and was active in the Los Angeles area during the 1970 strike.[34] Following the strike and the 1971 APWU formation, black APWU activists like Eleanor Bailey and Josie McMillian in New York City formalized their advocacy for women postal workers—first by helping form the Coalition of Labor Union Women (CLUW) in 1974, and in 1979 establishing the Post Office Women for Equal Rights (POWER) group.[35] In Durham, North Carolina, Jimmy Mainor, a Vietnam veteran of African American and Lumbee Indian descent from eastern North Carolina, was hired in 1971 as a letter carrier and joined the NAPFE. But he wanted to join the craft union that could negotiate contracts and file grievances. He kept demanding entry into the all-white NALC Branch 382 until they relented in 1975. Ten years later Mainor was elected branch vice president, and in 2001 he was elected president, serving until 2004. His legacy includes his campaign for more blacks and women to be hired by the Durham post office, which became majority-black by the time he was first elected vice president. In 2004 Mainor pointed with pride to Durham's having been a test site in 1998 for what became the USPS's nationwide Dispute Resolution Process, in conjunction with the postal unions to reduce the number of grievances from around 100,000 to 4,000.[36] Yet discrimination continued: in 1982 testimony before a House committee, Postmaster General William F. Bolger conceded to Representative William Clay (D-Mo.) that blacks in the USPS were fired or suspended almost four times as often as whites. By the 1990s, instances of black workers being "removed from service" were still double those of whites.[37]

MAIL HANDLERS AND LIUNA

In 1968 the NPMHU, a predominantly black and increasingly militant postal union with a black president, Lonnie Johnson, had voted to affiliate with the Laborers International Union of North America (LIUNA) that according to government reports was influenced by organized crime. In 1988 the NPMHU temporarily lost its autonomy to a trusteeship imposed by LIUNA.[38] For its part, LIUNA was forced to operate under a consent decree with the U.S. Department of Justice (USDOJ) from 1994 to 2001, based on the USDOJ's complaint "alleging that La Cosa Nostra crime families dominated the 800,000-member union, and alleging 100 predicate racketeering acts."[39]

Work for mail handlers was changing as well. Richard Thomas, who became an officer in NPMHU Local 300 in New York City after participating as an MBPU activist during the 1970 strike, and who with Jeff Perry challenged the national leadership many times, noted the change to greater mechanization and automation in the years after the strike: "When I started off in the sixties everything was done manually.... Eventually the mail went on wheels [large metal carts that ran on tracks].... Now it comes containerized, and all we have to do is take it off the truck, put it on the elevator.... It's a vast improvement."[40] Thomas also talked of how his facility, the GPO, "was definitely a factory-type operation."[41] The same was going to be true of BMCs and other mail-processing facilities planned in the 1970s, where increased automation would ultimately speed the mail as well as trim jobs from the workforce, and create major safety issues.

BATTLE OF THE BULK, PART I: THE 1974
NEW YORK BULK LOCKOUT/WILDCAT

Almost a year after the strike ended, the USPOD decided to make major changes in mail processing. On March 11, 1971, Postmaster General Blount announced a one-billion-dollar plan to construct a network of BMCs to handle parcel post and third-class bulk-rate mail. They would be built at a cost of around $1 billion in taxpayer money in suburban areas near air, rail, and truck lines that Blount claimed could save the USPS up to $500 million a year and improve efficiency, making it more competitive with the United Parcel Service. Federal Express (called FedEx since 1994) had just been launched as a private carrier that year by Fred Smith, who was to become a major proponent of postal privatization. The new construction would also include thirty Preferential Mail Facilities (PMFs) along with the BMCs (today called Network Distribution Centers). BMCs were like highly mechanized mail factories. Mail handlers would unload tractor-trailers full of bulk mail and transfer it to clerks to process. Clerks would type (or "key") onto "keying machines" the first three digits of the zip code of each parcel corresponding to a particular Sectional Center Facility, as it moved on a conveyor belt. From there it would be sent to the appropriate chute for other clerks to separate by zip code, and load into big gray sacks with draw strings — the same kind that had been used for a century at the post office. Bundles of bulk-mail letters and flats, meanwhile, would be sent to other conveyor belts where clerks sorted bundles also into large gray sacks for distribution by zip code.[42]

The USPS decision in the early seventies to build BMCs was similar to strategic moves made by auto manufacturers who had begun moving urban factories to suburban and rural areas, often in different states, following black-led wildcat strikes in Detroit, Newark, and elsewhere in the late 1960s and early 1970s.[43] In fact, there was widespread suspicion about the timing of this post-strike movement of postal jobs from mostly black cities to mostly white suburbs. Congressional hearings were held on this issue, and five months after Blount's announcement, NAPFE president Robert White attacked "the moving of postal services . . . where blacks and other minorities are situated to suburban areas."[44]

New York Bulk, located in Jersey City, New Jersey, was the first of the twenty-one BMCs to open, and remains the largest in the world, at 1.6 million square feet with 292 cargo bays. It cost $193 million to build—more than $100 million over its original projected cost. About 900 clerks and mail handlers were hired when it opened August 3, 1973, to work in the foreign mail and military mail sections. They would be followed by the opening on January 21, 1974, of the bulk mail section, where about 1,200 postal workers were hired to handle parcel post along with second- and third-class mail—everything from advertising circulars to magazines.[45]

On January 21, 1974, New York Bulk workers, most of them members of the New York Metro Area Postal Union (formerly MBPU, now NYMAPU or New York Metro, the largest local in the APWU) found themselves locked out of their facility while at the same time engaged in an illegal wildcat strike after refusing to report at their new times. Instead they were reporting to work in protest at their originally scheduled start times that had been arbitrarily changed by postal management less than two months before, to be effective that day.[46]

This conflict was both a management lockout and a workers' wildcat, as described by John Walsh and Garth Mangum in their APWU history, as well as by Moe Biller in a 1976 oral history interview. At the time of the wildcat/lockout, Biller was New York Metro president—the new name for the MBPU after Jersey City postal clerks had voted to join in 1973. Many of New York Bulk's workers had been encouraged by management in 1973 to leave their Brooklyn Army Terminal and other New York City jobs for day-shift (Tour I) postal positions and bid that shift at New York Bulk if they had enough seniority. But once the facility had opened, the new manager discovered that most mail came after four in the afternoon, so he changed the schedules to force most workers to start after 4:00 P.M., and all workers to start their shifts later. This was a work site "out in the middle of nowhere," as workers described it. Public transportation was not very accessible after midnight, and most of the workers were women. Automobile transportation became a necessity — and this was during the gasoline shortage and price spike because of the Arab Oil Embargo.[47] Biller told his interviewer how management had only told him in late November or early December 1973 of their plans to change the shifts for all workers at New York Bulk to three hours later in the morning shift and four hours later for the afternoon shift. Those shift changes were to be from 7:00 A.M.–3:30 P.M. to 10:15 A.M.–6:45 P.M. for Tour I; and from 3:15–11:45 P.M. to 7:00 P.M.–3:30 A.M. for Tour II. What took place over the next four days was a bizarre drama that included all New York Bulk workers in a lockout/walkout stalemate ultimately resolved by negotiation and a pre-arbitration agreement. A total of 511 clerks and 306 mail handlers were now assigned to late shifts starting at 7:00 and 11:00 P.M., but no one hired before January 1, 1974, for the original 7:00 A.M. day shift could be forced to start later.[48]

There was also at that time a radical-left organization of postal workers that called themselves "Outlaw" and led opposition to what they called a "sellout" by Biller and union officials. Outlaw was not unique. Emerging from the Revolutionary Union (which became the Revolutionary Communist Party in 1975), it represented one of many such workplace concentrations of left-wing organizing. Many members of competing left organizations — often described as part of the 1970s "new communist movement" comprised mostly of young former college students — obtained factory and warehouse jobs across the United States to try and build their respective organizations and working-class struggle in general. Ideological dogmatism and sectarianism kept those efforts isolated and mostly unsuccessful. The Outlaw group at New York Bulk and other BMCs from 1974 to 1978 may have been one of the more successful, relatively speaking. Their footprint included a periodic newsletter, confrontations with New York Metro officers at union meetings, and the election of Kenny Leiner, a leading Outlaw activist, to not only chief steward at New York Bulk, but also to a national APWU office in 1978, vice president representing mail handlers.[49]

Ironically, James Gildea, who had been an AFL-CIO negotiator following the 1970 postal wildcat strike, now represented the USPS and helped negotiate an end to the four-day 1974 lockout/walkout in a compromise settlement, with Francis Filbey and Moe Biller representing the APWU. Biller in his 1976 oral history acknowledged that "40 to 50 percent" of New York Bulk workers ultimately still had to change their shift times after the walkout, but he nevertheless claimed victory. The largest APWU local, despite being handcuffed by the continued ban on federal employee strikes, nonetheless in this case managed to make good on the strike threat. They could do so without repercussions because they were now covered by federal labor law provisions that included mediation and arbitration of labor disputes, which they had not enjoyed before the 1970 strike and postal reorganization. Similarly, management's lockout worked as an intimidation tactic but was also constrained within the limitations of mediation and arbitration. Management's duplicity had not impressed Federal District Court Judge Lawrence Whipple in Newark, who heard the case. Whipple rejected management's argument that the unions should be punished for conducting an illegal job action. This "wildcat strike" was not quite that, at least in in the eyes of the courts. And yet it *did* represent defiant direct action by postal workers angry at having their schedules changed arbitrarily. It was a large-scale work stoppage — the first since the 1970 strike.[50]

This was still primarily a *local* action, but it was resolved nationally. Tom Germano points out the context of the New York Bulk dispute: local unions that were "particularly concerned about impending technological changes and the effect such changes might have on employee classifications and work assignments."[51] Along those lines, in 1973 the MBPU (later NYMAPU) and the NALC Branch 36 each separately petitioned — and lost — before the NLRB to have their own seats in future collective bargaining. Branch 36 President Vincent Sombrotto, seeing this as an issue affecting all postal workers, was issued a restraining order when he appeared at the 1974 New York Bulk wildcat strike to offer support on behalf of his 9,000-member union. Ultimately, however, the agreement was arrived at between the national APWU and USPS management. The latter chose to term this job action a work stoppage, the former calling it a lockout, with Moe Biller and others in New York Metro calling it both.[52]

In 1974, the specter of the 1970 wildcat still lingered. Without that legacy and the new format, there could have been hundreds fired and possibly New York Metro and APWU broken. Instead, the APWU and NALC would be able to successfully invoke the still-illegal strike threat as a bargaining tool through July 1981 — just before President Reagan broke the PATCO strike only two days after it had been called on August 3. That would be one of the last times that postal union leaders would threaten a strike, although the postal unions would continue to bargain in many ways as if they had the right to strike. Increasingly and ironically, they would also be returning to the past practice of lobbying Congress. They would also be using rank-and-file union members to lobby the public.[53] Both sides — but especially postal unions—during subsequent contract negotiations came to rely upon a crucial right actually won by postal workers in the 1970 Postal Reorganization Act: mediation and binding arbitration, should collective bargaining break down.

BATTLE OF THE BULK, PART II:
1978 WILDCATS ON BOTH COASTS

Four years after the 1974 lockout/walkout, a wildcat strike broke out at New York Bulk on July 21, 1978. This time the grievances were national, not just local. Both the APWU and NALC membership rejected the 1978 contracts, a right that both unions in that decade had voted for themselves at convention. Postal workers at large mail distribution facilities had their own workplace issues and most were frustrated with the USPS offer, but that week a concerted wildcat broke out at four BMCs and an L&DC (Logistics and Distribution Center). The 1978 wildcat at New York Bulk in Jersey City was soon followed by a walkout at the Meadows L&DC, a mail distribution facility in Kearny, a suburb of Newark, New Jersey; along with the Philadelphia BMC; the Washington, D.C., BMC in Largo, Maryland; and the San Francisco Bulk and Foreign Mail Center in Richmond. A total of about 5,000 workers struck over four days, and 200 were fired by Postmaster General William F. Bolger under the administration of President Carter. Many of those fired never got their jobs back. The issue over whether the APWU should have called a strike, and whether they did enough to help the fired strikers get their jobs back, tarnished Moe Biller's image but did not stop his winning the APWU presidency two years later. Biller expressed regret for what he called his mistake in not calling a strike as president of New York Metro APWU as he redoubled his call for more union militancy.[54]

Jeff Perry was one of those fired by the USPS during the 1978 wildcat, although he got his job back in 1980, after extensive legal action and proving that his picketing did not occur on his work shift. Perry had been a member of Local 300 of the NPMHU from his start date at New York Bulk in April 1974. (He was also a member of APWU New York Metro until 1978.) The APWU at the time represented all the clerks at New York Bulk, who made up most of the workforce, but also represented "the vast majority of mail handlers" in New York, according to Walsh and Mangum. This was by agreement with the NPMHU parent union, LIUNA, to allow NPMHU Local 1 to *jointly* represent mail handlers in New York with the local agreement "which stipulated 'no raiding'" by the APWU.[55]

160   *The U.S. Postal Service and the Postal Unions in the 1970s*

Perry himself was locked in a bitter dispute with the NPMHU national office that disapproved of Local 300's militancy, which extended beyond craft issues into explicitly confronting white supremacy—for example, the considerable power at New York Bulk invested in the ethnic Italian-American social club called the Columbia Association. Perry recalled the explosive combination of hot weather and heated labor relations and working conditions. "We were working six, seven days a week—ten, twelve hours [a day]," he said, in reference to "mandatory overtime" commonly invoked by management in those days. "Conditions were very rough. The place was a powder keg. The day after the [USPS-postal unions] contract expiration, it actually didn't take much to pull people out, it was so hot and oppressive." Perry himself was not in favor of striking, and had been part of a New York Bulk workers activist meeting the night before that voted not to strike. Monroe Head, himself a former 1968 wildcat strike leader with the United Black Brothers organization at the Mahwah, New Jersey, Ford auto plant, and now a mail handler at the New York Bulk, cautioned Perry and others not to wildcat, as this appeared to be a "setup" by management to break the union.[56]

But hundreds walked out in those facilities, resulting in 200 removals, 116 suspensions without pay, and 2,500 "letters of warning."[57] Walsh and Mangum argue that the Outlaws provoked the wildcat. Noting that BMCs failed in their goal to compete with the United Parcel Service "because their costs were so high that it was impossible to set competitive rates," the BMCs, Walsh and Mangum observe, had "caused a massive migration from other post office stations," and "the so-called 'Outlaws'" figured prominently among those migrants." Walsh and Mangum cite Biller's regret "that he should have called a strike as soon as the workers were fired, but that he was busy in Washington." But besides being dissatisfied with the USPS offer, BMC workers were also angry at mandatory overtime, speedup, and hazardous working conditions.[58] Tom Germano points to one of the 1978 wildcat strikers' leaflets claiming the 1970 wildcat strike spirit as a motivating factor: "We know from experience that unless we, as rank and file members, walked out, management and the National Unions would work together to make ratification of the sellout contract a sure thing. . . . We had hoped for support from other locals, especially New York City, *that would lead to a nationwide strike for a new contract.*"[59]

During the July 1978 contract negotiations and subsequent brief BMC wildcat strike, Biller had seen his priority as intervening in Washington, D.C., with the three union heads negotiating with the USPS: James La Penta of the NPMHU, Joe Vacca of the NALC, and Emmett Andrews of the APWU.[60]

What followed the BMC wildcat and mass firing debacle was a high-profile campaign by Biller and APWU members to get the fired strikers their jobs back by not only picketing USPS headquarters in the nation's capital, but also Bolger's home in suburban Springfield, Virginia. Most of the 200 fired workers did not get their jobs back, but that campaign probably helped Biller win the APWU presidential election two years later.[61] Harvard University professor James J. Healy was appointed mediator and then arbitrator in a "hybrid dispute resolution process called 'mediation-arbitration.'"[62]

In 1978 Healy wound up awarding slightly higher annual raises, a significantly "uncapped COLA [Cost of Living Allowance]," and amending the original 1971 "no-layoff clause" to now apply to those hired on or before the award date (September 15, 1978) or hired after that with six years of service. This was not a bad outcome for postal labor considering that the USPS had come into negotiations with a $3.5 billion deficit at the end of fiscal year 1977 and a 10 percent workforce decrease since 1970 — with "step four" grievances (those having been appealed) almost doubling between 1971 and 1977 from 5,000 to almost 10,000 — and the NALC losing 87 percent of 3,022 discipline cases arbitrated from 1975 to 1977. The collective-bargaining process had turned out to be successful for the postal unions, ironically, with all the elements involved, including a problematic original contract, rejection by the rank and file, threats of isolated wildcats, and finally, mediation and arbitration. The days of "collective begging" Congress for raises and benefit increases were seemingly long gone. In January 1979, Vincent Sombrotto, taking office as national NALC president and alarmed at legislation introduced trying to merge Social Security with the Civil Service retirement fund, revived the NALC's lobbying campaigns in Congress.[63] On December 15, 1979, BMC conditions that had been an accident waiting to happen took the life of twenty-five-year-old mail handler Michael McDermott at New York Bulk; he was crushed to death by a conveyor belt whose safety device had been disabled to speed up production. There were leaflets of protest over his death circulated at the Denver BMC where the author started as a distribution clerk in February 1980, as well as resistance to mandatory overtime and speedup.[64]

NALC TURNS TO SOMBROTTO, APWU TO BILLER

The rise of Vincent Sombrotto in 1978 and Moe Biller in 1980 to the presidencies of the NALC and APWU, respectively, is part of the mythology and heroes' tale of the 1970 postal wildcat strike. In the broadest terms it represents a validation of the rank-and-file activity that began to follow their leadership in 1970 during the strike, and later into union democracy efforts that dovetailed with their determined leadership defending postal workers' rights against the USPS management. Both exuded charismatic qualities, leadership skills, and a fair number of mistakes and controversies concerning their commitments to union militancy. Matty Rose of Florida recounts with pride his participation with Sombrotto (who left the Rank and File Movement) on the NALC Committee of Presidents (COP) as a "grassroots effort," whereas Tom Germano, Sombrotto's colleague in Branch 36, saw the COP as a deviation from rank-and-file unionism.[65]

Biller and Sombrotto were both engaged in union service within a service occupation—which meant managing rank-and-file demands, political compromises, and fulfilling their own careers. Despite the messiness of union politics, both acquired a kind of sainthood in their respective unions over time. This is often the case with charismatic leaders who participate and articulate the aspirations of the people in whatever movement they serve. Veterans of the strike themselves are iconic figures routinely honored at national conventions and in publications of the APWU and NALC.[66]

Some NALC 1970 postal-strike participants also remember Sombrotto's participation at 1972, 1974, and 1976 NALC national conventions. They tell stories of Sombrotto's being combative as a speaker from the floor, to the point where President James Rademacher would cut off his microphone. Sombrotto could draw boos as well as applause, admiration and disdain, but he also evolved into a more effective public speaker and the voice of the rank and file who began the strike and wanted to move the union in that direction. In 1972 the Rank and File Movement managed to win an end to proxy voting effective in 1974, which is when they won resolutions that would allow voting on national officers by mail rather than restricted to convention attendance.[67] It was Joseph Vacca's bad luck to occupy the NALC presidency during the 1978 contract year, when the USPS had dug in its heels. The August national convention followed the July contract that the membership rejected, sending the contract to binding arbitration.[68]

Significantly, after the strike there was an upsurge of rank-and-file activity nationwide in the postal unions. In the years following the 1970 strike, members could vote for national officers and on contracts directly. The use of the strike threat, whether it was by union leaders or suggested by membership rejection of a contract, was more than idle posturing. It energized the membership and represented defiance of the strike ban after they had won full collective-bargaining rights. It also represented a continuation of the 1970 strike as a collective assertion that striking is what *real unions* had the right to do, and they were going to do it. What if another national postal strike broke out—either called or wildcat? That was never tested. If it had, it might have resulted in another administration being forced to the negotiating table—or the strike being broken with the unions defeated and possibly even decertified by the government. It would have been a high-stakes gamble. But the strike threat alone was sufficient for now. In interviews conducted with 1970 postal strike veterans, some remember what it was like to "almost" strike in 1978: for example, moving branch funds to personal checking accounts, making picket signs, and being ready but also worried about the outcome. There was no element of surprise this time, and there was the exact opposite of any government promises of amnesty for striking. This would not have been an illegal wildcat, but rather an illegal *called strike* that likely would have resulted in mass terminations and loss of collective bargaining rights for the AFL-CIO postal unions.[69] The inexperienced collective bargaining team of Emmett Andrews (APWU), Joe Vacca (NALC), along with James La Penta (NPMHU), produced a disastrous contract that wound up undoing the presidencies of Andrews and Vacca.[70]

Surprisingly, in 1978 former president Rademacher, who had defeated Sombrotto in 1974, switched his endorsement to Sombrotto from Joseph Vacca—his preferred successor—who had defeated Sombrotto in the 1976 election. After Sombrotto won, he began instituting union reforms in 1979 as soon as he took office. NALC historians Brady Mikusko and John Miller observe that Sombrotto and most of his slate won by mobilizing the same rank-and-file forces that had fought for and won reforms like the one-person-one-vote national election ballots, members having the final say on contract agreements, and attention to working conditions. Sombrotto and his administration began instituting more union reforms the following year.[71]

Vacca's candidacy in 1978 had also already been weakened by member frustration at the huge backlog of grievances, a remarkably high grievance arbitration loss rate of 87 percent from 1975 to 1977, and his failure to secure a good contract in 1978 bargaining with the USPS. The NALC had just won a significant 1976 arbitration ruling overturning the USPS "Kokomo Plan" of computerized time-and-motion study. It is quite possible that the win raised letter carriers' expectations for workplace gains even higher. Meanwhile, Sombrotto, who had joined others to speak out on the convention floor on Kokomo and other issues, would serve as president for twenty-three years.[72]

Something similar happened in the APWU after the 1970 strike. Moe Biller, like Vincent Sombrotto, was both a deliberate and an accidental leader

Vincent Sombrotto, 1970 NALC Branch 36 postal strike coorganizer, speaking out in 1976 from the floor at the 50th biennial NALC national convention in Houston, Texas. Courtesy of NALC.

of the 1970 wildcat. But unlike Sombrotto, who was new to union politics, Biller had been at it already for over two decades prior to the strike. His ascendancy post-strike, similar to Sombrotto's, was not merely personal but symbolic: representing a progressive thread with the old NPU militancy. That was now validated in the 1980 ticket he led.[73] Biller used rank-and-file upsurge to win the APWU national presidency in 1980, after battling internally over issues of militancy for almost a decade. Unlike Sombrotto, he did not mount a challenge to the incumbent president in 1978: Emmett Andrews in fact won a three-way race but remained very unpopular over the 1978 contract fiasco, even facing off against an angry two-hour demonstration on the convention floor.[74] The two best-known leaders of the 1970 strike in New York were now national presidents of their respective postal unions, which had become among the strongest in the AFL-CIO. They made joint appearances not just on current postal labor issues but also in strike retrospectives. Joining Biller on that 1980 ticket as executive vice president was Bill Burrus, along with John P. Richards as Director of Industrial Relations. According to Burrus: "We ran against the status quo, and we revolutionized the political process and the collective bargaining mindset. . . . We thought that everything was possible."[75] Burrus and Richards would later have differences over staff and contract negotiations with Biller.[76]

LABOR-MANAGEMENT RELATIONS POST-STRIKE

By the 1980s, the post office had become a relatively secure job magnet—especially for African Americans. But many 1970 strike veterans have expressed concern about their coworkers becoming too complacent in defending what past struggles and negotiations by unionists at the post office have won for them, including health benefits, retirement, a no-layoff clause for those with at least six years of service, and a median annual salary in 2018 of $58,760 ($28.25 per hour).[77] Labor-management relations—frosty enough in the USPOD era when management seemingly held all the cards—now often became quite contentious, as postal labor unions attempted to exercise their full bargaining rights. Contracts that often had to be won through mediation and arbitration contained increasingly liberal provisions such as the "no-layoff" clause for employees with at least six years of seniority. The first USPS contract in 1971 calling for no layoffs of "regular" employees gave way in 1978 to a provision that established a cutoff of 1978, after which employees would have to be full-time for six years to be immune from layoffs: an important job security provision.[78]

Late twentieth-century postal technological development was contradictory. The standard mail-sorting "pigeonhole case" was finally being replaced by mechanization leading to computer automation. The early 1960s saw LSMs (letter sorting machines), and facer-cancelers (aligning mail before "canceling" stamps). Computerized OCRs (optical character readers) and BCSS (barcode sorters) were installed in 1983, a year before Zip+4 expanded on the original 1963 five-digit zip codes. In 1991 the USPS adopted wide-area barcode readers along with DPS or "delivery point sequence" mail processing, whereby most mail would arrive presorted by street address. Less "raw mail" was now arriving at the route case for carriers to "put up," and which they now had to collate into the presorted DPS mail, increasing the amount of delivery time. In 2006 Intelligent Mail barcodes with sixty-five bars were instituted for sorting and tracking mail. Automation increased productivity, sped up service, and decreased the number of postal clerk positions. But the total number of postal positions, including clerks and mail handlers through the 1990s, actually *increased* as mail volume and the growth of postal delivery "territory" continued to rise. The postal workforce, while

The U.S. Postal Service and the Postal Unions in the 1970s

Female clerk in 1965 operates the "Keytronic Mail Sorter," a Single Position Letter Sorting Machine (SPLSM), which evolved to the Multi-Position Letter Sorting Machine (MPLSM) as the post office became increasingly mechanized to handle huge volumes of mail. Automation replaced letter sorting machines with Optical Character Readers in the late twentieth century, which were replaced in the early twenty-first century by Carrier Sequence Barcode Sorters. Courtesy of the National Postal Museum, Smithsonian Institution.

dropping slightly in the 1970s, grew steadily from the 1980s until peaking at 905,766 total employees in 1999, after which it began to decline to 621,837 in 2015, rebounding by 2017 to 644,124.[79] From 1976 to 2006, the USPS invested billions of dollars in automation that could process almost all of the mail, according to Christopher Shaw. But in 2005, APWU executive vice president Cliff Guffey observed that the USPS in the 1990s, as it was spending $18 billion on automation, had also "decided it could generate more business and save money by providing temporary discounts for companies that applied bar codes themselves and pre-sorted their mail." (This work was done by low-waged non-postal workers.) Guffey estimated that with "private companies . . . still applying bar codes and presorting approximately 80 percent of the mail," the USPS "bought 80 percent too much capacity and overspent by $14.4 billion."[80]

Yet even as clerk and mail handler work was being automated, home and business mail delivery had changed little since its 1863 inauguration, except for the reduction of home mail from frequent daily trips to just once daily in 1950. Then, in 1974, the USPS began a campaign to control letter carrier jobs—something that it had also done during the early twentieth-century Progressive era that included the "scientific management" theories of Frederick Winslow Taylor, in which "efficiency experts" would conduct "time and motion studies" to measure work output. Supervisors gauged how fast letter carriers could "case" and carry mail on the street. "Route inspections" were still based on the stopwatch and clipboard measurement that the NALC unsuccessfully fought long ago.[81] Shortly after the formation of the USPS in 1971, postal station managers and carrier supervisors "put carriers under unprecedented pressure to deliver their routes at break-neck speed. Unresolved grievances piled up in response to this new speed up." This speedup was followed in 1974 by a "pilot work measurement system called LCRES—Letter Carrier Route Evaluation System"—also known as the "Kokomo Plan" for the Indiana city where it was to be tested. But unlike the previous confrontation decades before, the NALC was able to take this new issue to arbitration and win in 1976, based on arguments that the Kokomo Plan was a violation of the National Agreement and reasonable work standards.[82] Collective bargaining, while a marked improvement over "collective begging" to Congress in the past, frequently came down to the wire or had to be settled by arbitration. Brief isolated wildcats broke out in 1978, significantly in a few of the new BMCs that were deliberately built outside of urban areas after the strike, and also were workplaces where disputes between management had broken out over arbitrary shift changes, mandatory overtime, and unsafe machinery.[83] In 1975, the APWU and the NALC had embraced the slogan "No Contract No Work."[84] And indeed, they would be able to successfully invoke the strike threat as a bargaining tool through July 1981—just before President Reagan broke the PATCO strike, which followed postal union contract negotiations. That would be the last time postal unions would threaten to strike.

Almost Striking Again, Arbitration, and Automation, 1980s–1990s

In 1981 the NALC and APWU again came close to calling a nationwide strike when contract talks broke down with USPS negotiators.[1] But this was not 1970 or the 1970s, even though the postal unions had become stronger and more democratic since then. Republican Ronald Reagan, elected president in 1980 in a massive conservative political upsurge, did not repeat Richard Nixon's attempt to woo or at least get along with labor unions. Hostility to labor unions was in fact part of this wave of antiliberalism.[2] That hostility extended to the USPS's seeking to automate more work functions and trim union power. The 1970 wildcat strike by rank-and-file postal workers was a "surprise attack" labor action. But postal unions now faced the limitations of trying to behave like "normal" unions with full collective bargaining rights except the crucial right to strike. Could they manage a "called" strike this time as a deliberate action? What would be the consequences if they did? Would binding arbitration, written into the Postal Reorganization Act (PRA), become a hindrance or a firewall?

THE ALMOST STRIKE OF 1981

In 1980 Moe Biller had defeated the increasingly unpopular incumbent APWU president Emmett Andrews by an almost two-to-one margin at their Detroit convention, while hundreds of members in Chicago that summer conducted a half-hour walkout over safety conditions in the old, swelteringly hot main post office with few fans. Vincent Sombrotto had won his NALC presidential reelection handily that year, and now expectations were high for the two 1970 New York wildcat strike "war heroes" to go toe-to-toe with the irascible postmaster general William F. Bolger and his USPS negotiating team in what Tom Germano said promised to be "the 'armageddon' of all the postal conflicts yet." Both union presidents promised to call strikes if basic demands were not met, such as an uncapped Cost of Living Allowance (COLA). Meanwhile, the NALC had tried to "raid" (recruit) rural letter carriers who belonged to the NRLCA, while the APWU tried to decertify LIUNA, which had taken over the NPMHU. Both efforts failed, but the NALC and APWU still represented 80 percent of postal workers. Postmaster General Bolger then sent letters to all postal employees in April 1981, informing them that the USPS had filed a petition with the NLRB asking it to determine bargaining units because union "raiding" had created too much uncertainty. Bolger proposed that contract negotiations be postponed. Despite those talks being slated to end by July 20 with contract expiration, he wanted them extended past that date. Bolger failed to get his NLRB petition approved on April 30, so he appealed, only to lose again June 11. But Sombrotto and Biller meanwhile had issued a furious letter in response to Bolger's letter, accusing him of duplicity. Labor-management relations had hit a new low. The USPS and the two unions took turns filing appeals with the NLRB; the USPS publicized the fact that they had taken a quarter of a million job applications; both sides attacked each other in the media; and the NALC and APWU dubbed June 25 Postal Action Day (later Postal Solidarity Day). They called on members to demonstrate in front of their local post offices to support union negotiators.[3]

Collective bargaining began June 16, 1981, with so little headway that, by July 15, Biller and Sombrotto accused Bolger of stonewalling and trying to provoke a strike. The initial USPS offer contained no wage increases. On July 17, Bolger used the mail to notify all postal workers that termination awaited them if they struck.[4] The USPS then led with an unsatisfactory proposal: limited COLA increase and $100-per-year raises over a three-year contract. The NALC and APWU rejected it, as over 100 union representatives had gathered in the L'Enfant Plaza Hotel, conveniently located across the street from USPS headquarters in southwest Washington, D.C. Predictably, negotiations ran down to the wire, with both sides agreeing the night of July 20 to "stop the clock." This was a common practice in the private sector and already used in 1978 during postal negotiations. It pretended that time froze and the contract was still in force until an agreement could be reached — or not. Included in the process (outside the bargaining room) was the APWU's Rank and File Bargaining Advisory Committee, who held veto power over approval. They were not happy with the lack of health and safety, discipline, and grievance provisions — and not even a written proposal. Even if the contract was approved, it had to be ratified by the membership of both unions.[5]

The July 21 *New York Times* was already announcing the possibility of a strike after talks broke down at midnight. "We are on a collision course with a strike" is what Sombrotto told their reporter, who noted that "Mr. Biller echoed that opinion." Readers were reminded that "such a strike is illegal." Furthermore, "at the Pentagon, officials were studying the possible use of 100,000 military personnel" to move the mail along with "private carriers."[6] Fourteen years later, Moe Biller would reflect at the Smithsonian Postal Museum's twenty-fifth anniversary retrospective of the 1970 wildcat strike what his thoughts were during these 1981 negotiations. Biller feared that both Bolger and the Reagan administration were trying to make examples of the postal unions and break them by provoking them to strike.[7] Firing striking government workers was something that Reagan would do to PATCO — a union that had backed him in the 1980 election but which on August 3, 1981, would go on strike over wages, safety, and scheduling.

Whether it was desperation, fatigue, or wishful thinking, Biller and Sombrotto fell into that time-honored trap of accepting a *verbal* agreement by management and recommending it to union officers outside the negotiating room. After securing an enthusiastic agreement from NALC officials but warier support from their APWU counterparts, NALC negotiators began notifying the media as well as many of the branches around the country who had been engaged in "strike vigils" that an agreement was imminent.[8] Thousands of postal workers across the country were on a "strike watch" listening for the news on the night of July 20, and early the next morning of July 21, 1981, to see whether they should report for work the next day. There was a sense that this is what "normal" unions can do — take direction from national union leaders negotiating a contract, and withhold their labor if that was their recommendation. But this was not 1970. What if Reagan and Bolger responded with fear tactics and strikebreakers — and won? Sombrotto and Biller had helped to lead a wildcat "from below" in 1970, and had threatened postal management with called strikes after the formation of the USPS. Now they were warning union members of the dire consequences that could come from exercising the right that postal workers knew they did *not* have but most probably felt they deserved — namely the right to strike. Few knew the drama going on at the L'Enfant Plaza Hotel, as the two sides continued to bargain throughout the day. The news on radio and TV the morning of July 21 had declared that an agreement had been reached, leading postal workers and the general public to assume that was the case. It was not, and with strikers heading to work instead of the picket line, as Tom Germano points out, the USPS negotiating team was now able to back the two union teams into a corner with a much smaller offer that the NALC and APWU wound up agreeing to. Union leadership that had only days before been calling on members to be ready to strike subsequently felt compelled to vigorously sell this offer to their membership, as mail-in ballots went out for them to decide on the proposed contract. Only about 10 percent of NALC members voting opposed the settlement, while roughly 25 percent of APWU respondents rejected it. Substantial majorities were not ready to strike.[9]

On Tuesday morning, July 21, on the East Coast, postal workers on Tour II were getting ready to go to work, so there were no labor "troops" for the unions to use as a bargaining chips. John P. Richards said his Pittsburgh APWU local, like others were ready to walk if a strike was called, and had already made picket signs: "We were going to be the tough guys!" Moe Biller, he said, was "rattling sabers." But when Sombrotto and Biller came back into the Washington, D.C., hotel room with officers of both unions and announced a deal, Richards and others had to call home to "release" members there from a strike.[10]

There was no deal. Instead, Biller, Sombrotto, and their teams had to return at about 5:00 A.M., Tuesday morning, in Tom Germano's words, to a "fresh and feisty" Postmaster General Bolger. The union leaders, like most others on the union negotiating team, were quite sleep-deprived. They would wind up spending most of July 21 not finalizing contract terms, but instead arguing with Bolger and the USPS team. The two sides finally agreed on $300-per-year wage increases with three annual bonus payments of $350 each, "uncapped COLA" pegged to the Consumer Price Index, and maintenance of the no-layoff clause. It was less than the original, now-phantom verbal offer that the USPS claimed it had never made ($750 raises the first year, $600 for the next two years, plus the uncapped COLA formula from the previous contract). Now Biller and Sombrotto found themselves in the awkward spot of urging their respective memberships to vote to ratify management's offer, because rejecting it would lead to the declaration of an illegal strike.[11]

There was some serious opposition among APWU members, and many urged rejection of the contract. Ultimately, despite more reservations on the APWU side, the vast majority of both unions, casting their votes by mail at about the same time that President Reagan was firing 11,000 striking PATCO members on August 5, 1981, overwhelming approved the contract: 147,692–

36,595 for the APWU, and 124,316–20,856 for the NALC. For those who voted not to strike, the stakes seemed way too high, despite the unsatisfactory agreement. The breaking of PATCO overall would have an enormous damp- ening effect on organized labor strikes nationwide. Strikes that had averaged 300 per year over previous decades would shrink to 30 per year by 2006.[12] Meanwhile, the conservative NRLCA and the LIUNA-affiliated NPMHU would continue to win gains in the shadow of the APWU and NALC, with few internal reforms to speak of. The APWU and NALC, on the other hand, bene- fited from the widespread involvement of members, both in mass lobbying of Congress and advocating change in their respective unions. Ironically, the NPMHU did better by asking for fact-finding and binding arbitration after the other two unions had already begun bargaining. Their complaints had to do with wage increases, inadequate COLA formulation (not "rolling in" pre- vious increases to overall salaries), and health and safety issues.[13]

Like the 1978 negotiations, the 1981 strike threat was hesitant compared to the 1970 wildcat. There was no shock element by postal unions, either in 1978 or in 1981. There were now rank-and-file advisory councils assisting negotiations for both teams, a legacy of the strike and post-strike reform movements in the APWU and NALC. But these were not rank-and-file ac- tions like the 1970 strike. The 1981 "almost strike" has also strangely been examined by few labor historians — mostly notably John Walsh, Garth Man- gum, and Tom Germano. Walsh and Mangum believe that "the major ques- tion raised by the 1981 negotiations was the use of the strike threat to pres- sure the USPS. . . . How often could the unions 'cry wolf' and get away with it?"[14] They argue that any strike would have failed because of Reagan admin- istration hostility to strikes by government workers. And they quote APWU counsel John O'Donnell as doubting the efficacy of a strike then "because postal workers don't have the same sense of injustice" as those who struck in 1970. Finally, they conclude that, with no actual implementation, postal union strike threats began to disappear after 1981. And because postal jobs were now well-paid, we could also add to that list the absence of widespread public sympathy for striking as there was in 1970.[15] For his part Tom Ger- mano concludes his study by noting the significant gains made by postal workers in the decade following the 1970 strike, and conflict management better controlled through the Postal Reorganization Act, evidenced by five negotiated agreements between 1971 and 1981 (with two of those mediated: 1975 and 1978). But he also points to the decline in postal unions making gains in wages and working conditions, along with the return of congres- sional lobbying. Germano thought postal unionists needed to revive that spirit of 1970 to push for more union reforms and thus be able to take on the USPS in the Reagan era.[16]

Democratic president Bill Clinton was much more sympathetic to labor in general and in particular postal labor during his two terms, for example signing the Hatch Act reform bill which, as Mikusko and Miller point out, gave government employees the "right to work in partisan campaigns, hold party office, serve as delegates to political conventions and speak out for the candidate of their choosing."[17] But two things must be remembered here. First, Clinton, like Jimmy Carter and many other Democrats, also shared with Republicans certain neoliberal policy tenets such as free trade, deregulation, privatization, balanced budgets, social spending cuts, and workforce "casualization" that negatively impacted labor.[18] Secondly, the USPS Board of Governors, not the president, has appointed USPS postmasters general, beginning with Winton Blount in 1971 (Blount had been appointed USPOD Postmaster General by Nixon in 1969). Postmasters general, therefore, set their own agendas.[19]

It is possible that the USPS's aggressive collective bargaining in 1981 reflected a desire to provoke a strike and break the unions. Or it could have just been aggressive collective bargaining, combined with a wish to avoid the arbitration built into the PRA that had helped postal unions achieve decent outcomes in the past decade. The firing of PATCO members had a negative effect on any thoughts by postal workers of striking. The 1970 strike had propelled rank-and-file reform movements within the NALC and APWU and achieved a certain measure of success with Sombrotto and Biller's reform slate election victories in 1978 and 1980, respectively. However, there was controversy even within the larger reform movement, with NALC NRFM members seeing the formation of the Committee of Presidents (COP) as an ill-advised compromise coalition within that union that watered down their reform agenda. For their part, the APWU had at their 1980 convention amended their constitution to provide for a Rank and File Bargaining Advisory Committee with "full veto power over the proposed National Agreement"—an important role in negotiations.[20]

LEARNING TO LOVE ARBITRATION

What was the USPS's reward for "playing hardball" in 1981, if indeed there was one? The breakdown of contract talks three years later resulted in the 1984 comprehensive arbitration award that was actually favorable to the postal unions. This possibly led to a relatively amicable settlement with the unions in 1987 as the Reagan era was about to close.[21] The 1981 postal union strike threat had by 1984 become almost perfunctory. In August of 1984, both the NALC and APWU held conventions in Las Vegas, Nevada. While waiting for arbitration to settle the contract impasse with the USPS, the APWU membership gave their executive board permission to take "whatever steps" it deemed necessary, although delegates interviewed by the *New York Times* admitted that there was no strike appetite. NALC delegates also gave Sombrotto what he called "the power to call a strike."[22]

This was the second straight set of contract talks that Postmaster General Bolger had begun by calling for a wage freeze. The month before, after talks stalled, "the Postal Service announced it would begin hiring new clerks and letter carriers at about 20 percent less pay. The move was blocked by a Congressional amendment to an appropriations bill."[23] Not only had Bolger in 1981 similarly asked for a wage freeze, but he had also "asserted that the employees are paid wages [$19,900] commensurate with similar workers in private industry, such as bank tellers."[24] That was a strange comparison: bank tellers are rarely unionized, and their labor does not exactly resemble that of postal employees. There had barely been a decade of full collective bargaining between the USPS and the postal unions. And yet by now the postmaster general seemed to be daring the unions to strike. The USPS was setting a combative tone for future negotiations with unions that had become stronger since the 1970 strike. At the heart of that conflict was what had set off the 1970 strike, and around which other demands revolved: wages.

Postal workers may have been denied the right to strike, but the PRA provided for a mediation and arbitration safety net should contract negotiations break down. Almost as many NALC contracts since the birth of the USPS have gone to arbitration (1984, 1990, 1995, 1999, and 2013) than have been negotiated by the two sides (1971, 1973, 1987, 2001, 2006, and 2017), with 1975 and 1978 being mediated.[25] The APWU has a somewhat similar contract settlement history: arbitration in 1984, 1990, 2000, and 2016; negotiated settlements in 1971, 1973, 1998, 2005, 2007, and 2011; with mediated settlements in 1975 and 1978.[26] What happened to union coalition efforts? All four unions: the NALC, APWU, NPMHU, and NRCLA, bargained together in 1971, 1973, and 1975. All but the NRLCA bargained jointly in 1978, while the JBC of the NALC and APWU held through 1981, 1984, 1987, and 1990.[27] When unions bargain separately, of course, it affects strategy by both labor and management. Roughly the same number of contracts went to arbitration with joint bargaining as did with single-union bargaining. More research is needed to determine if joint bargaining played any kind of role in causing management to stiffen its resistance to forging negotiated agreements. The spirit of 1970, while muted in many ways since that year, also provided a loyal following in the NALC and APWU, where members expected results—not just at the bargaining table but on the shop floor whenever grievances needed to be filed and won as often as possible. "Charismatic" leadership alone, the kind that sociologist Max Weber theorized, was not enough and in fact is not even particularly applicable here.[28] No one in the two unions saw Sombrotto and Biller as possessing supernatural powers compelling them to follow in pursuit of common goals. Leadership by those two men and others had to be effective and invested to be trusted by membership.[29] Origin myths of the largest two U.S. postal unions—or perhaps "rebirth myth" is a better term—may have conferred heroic status on those leaders. But it was based on the historical idea of a post-strike transition from relatively weak government-employee associations (or unions) forced to lobby more than conduct face-to-face bargaining with management—to strong unions with full collective-bargaining rights. Finding a way to put that rank-and-file upsurge legacy into daily practice has been the enduring challenge.

LABOR-MANAGEMENT AND LABOR-LABOR RELATIONS

Before the 1970 strike, only a handful of elected federal officials openly supported postal privatization—at a time when even a conservative Republican like Nixon was proudly promoting postal expansion, modernization, and innovation. But in the first three months of 1978 alone, Congress saw more than fifteen bills proposed with the goal being "repeal of the postal monopoly on first class letters," though none of them passed. The USPS and postal unions were at least united in fighting off such attempts to diminish public postal service.[30] Three years later during the 1981 contract negotiations, there was a similar "flurry of activity on Capitol Hill regarding postal employees," including budget measures to reduce cost-of-living adjustments for postal and federal employees and a USPS 1982 budget reduction.[31] In 1982 the USPS received its last government subsidy.[32] Political activity on Capitol Hill in 1987 reveals instructive parallels to the 2009 postal financial crisis. "Part of the plan to create a semiautonomous postal corporation," Vern Baxter observed in 1994, "was the removal of the USPS from the federal budget in 1974." But in 1985 the administration of President Reagan put the USPS "back on budget," ostensibly to meet "productivity and accountability goals." Critics saw this as an act intended to "create a potential scapegoat for higher federal deficits or a future source of budget surpluses" that could help mitigate future deficits. Baxter goes on to point out, "As part of the Budget Reconciliation Act of 1987, the OMB [Office of Management and Budget] ordered the Postal Service to pay $350 million in increased payments to the Treasury for retired workers' health benefits." There were consequences, then as now, including substantial curtailment of capital investment and new facilities construction, delaying the USPS automation program and fostering "a crisis atmosphere."[33]

For their part, the postal unions did not always operate as a united front, both before and after reorganization in 1971, when nine unions became the "Big Four" recognized by the USPS as exclusive collective-bargaining agents for postal workers. There were periodic campaigns among postal unionists for "one big postal union," but they never gained traction.[34] The APWU and NALC, under Biller and Sombrotto, formed a JBC in 1981 to negotiate a new contract with the USPS.[35] During the 1990 contract negotiations, according to Mikusko and Miller's NALC history, the USPS tried to use increased automation as a rationale for proposing lower wage and benefit increases, a lower-waged tier of new hires, and more temporary workers. The NALC and APWU rejected the offer, and though the arbitration panel did not give management its most severe wage cut proposals, it demonstrated enough sympathy for their automation-flexibility argument to lead the NALC to vote to the dissolve the JBC during the 1994 negotiations because, according to Mikusko and Miller, "postal automation was creating an insurmountable wedge between the union and the APWU, leading to sharply diverging positions on key workplace issues."[36] Former APWU president Bill Burrus's 2013 autobiography contains this recollection of the NALC's termination of the JBC: "The announcement did not come as a major surprise, but it was disappointing to the APWU. Moe [Biller] and his disciples truly believed in the concept of one union, and if joint bargaining was the closest we could get, it was better than nothing. The Letter Carriers could not achieve their highest priority, a universal upgrade, with three hundred thousand clerks, vehicle, maintenance, and special delivery employees who had to be included in any pay package."[37]

Burrus made an interesting observation about the JBC's being for Biller the closest thing to the old NPU goal of a single industrial postal union. In fact, the "one big union" campaign after 1971 had become a movement on the margins, sealed by objections from NALC president Rademacher (apparently with the support of most of his union) that the NALC would lose

APWU/NALC Joint Bargaining Committee protest at USPS headquarters, L'Enfant Plaza, Washington, D.C., July 10, 1987. APWU president Moe Biller (wearing ball cap) and NALC president Vincent Sombrotto are in the middle— both iconic 1970 strike leaders. Today in Washington, D.C., the APWU national headquarters is called the Moe Biller Building and the NALC national headquarters is the Vincent R. Sombrotto Building—also the name of the NALC Branch 36 building in New York City. In 2014 Congress voted to rename the Grand Central Station Post Office the Vincent R. Sombrotto Post Office. Courtesy of NALC.

control over not only craft interests like seniority, but also its insurance and real estate assets. Biller's predecessor, Francis Filbey, had even proposed that year to merge postal unions with the 650,000 member Communications Workers of America.[38] Clearly there were differences over merger versus maintenance of existing postal union autonomy.

By 1990, the USPS, after a decade of "breaking even," was asking for major concessions from the postal unions, citing greater costs associated with automation, and the need for more contingent labor. Mikusko and Miller note that arbitrators, while not agreeing to the USPS's two-tier wage proposal, did sympathize with its call for greater "flexibility" with greater automation, and not only allowed more PTFS (Part Time Flexible employees) and "casuals," but added a new category called TEs or "transitional employees." Compared to casuals who could work ninety-day terms, TEs could work for a year, with the chance to renew for another year. Both would be paid considerably less than career employees for doing the same work.[39]

Almost Striking Again, Arbitration, and Automation

In 1994, the NALC, besides separating from the APWU in the JBC over automation, was also demanding a wage upgrade for letter carriers from Grade 5 to Grade 6 (the highest for hourly employees), based on what it called the additional workload and skill required to manage the new DPS (Delivery Point Sequencing) automated mail. This was letter mail that arrived presorted at carriers' cases, ostensibly ready to be taken directly to the street. But there was still residual mail that had not arrived presorted, and flats (large envelopes and magazines) also still had to be "cased." The result was carriers having to juggle several bundles during delivery. The NALC's demand for wage upgrade failed in the 1994 arbitration award after negotiations broke down, but succeeded in 1999 after the 1998 contract failed to see a negotiated settlement between the NALC and the USPS. This was the first time since 1863 that carrier and clerk pay scales had diverged.[40] But Burrus noted in his memoir that in 2006 he was able to win an upgrade for APWU members similar to what the NALC had won seven years earlier for their members.[41]

Rural carrier non-career "associates" (RCAS) had existed since 1987, and the clerk-craft contingent labor known as PSEs or Postal Support Employees became effective in 2011, taking the place of NCAS or Non-Carrier Assistants. Mail handler assistants (MHAs) and City Carrier Assistants (CCAs) were inaugurated in 2013, and Assistant Rural Carriers (ARCs) in 2015. CCAs as of 2017 made $16.41 per hour to start.[42] The APWU and NALC found themselves forced to accept lower starting salaries in arbitration awards for new hires: both the NALC and APWU in 1990, the APWU alone in 2012, and the NALC alone in 2013. In a kind of de facto two-tier wage scale, new hires were merged into the pay schedule that arrives at top pay in 12.4 years for carriers. In 2016, however, the APWU announced that the clerk craft had actually grown for the first time in ten years. The NALC grew as they added members among the CCAs (who are paid less than regular or PTF carriers), successfully winning through arbitration a pathway to full-time regular status for them.[43] For its part, the USPS official history does not discuss labor relations during the post-strike period, but it does provide a straightforward narrative of the development of mechanization and automation as institutional responses to increased demand.[44] Automation has affected mostly clerk and mail handler positions, although a "no layoff" 1971 contract clause (amended in 1978 to protect those with at least six years of service) has mitigated job loss to some extent. Postal union histories on the other hand have focused on both automation and outsourcing of postal jobs to the private sector over the years as threats to jobs and union membership.[45] They also reveal a four way tug-of-war involving the unions, the USPS, Congress, and the executive branch.

Exceptions to combative labor-management relations included experimental conflict resolution processes between the USPS and the NALC ("Employee Involvement" and "Quality of Work Life" or EI/QWL) that were intended to ameliorate the ongoing contentious grievance process based on the post office's historically rigid work rule and disciplinary procedures. These proposals were initiated by Postmaster General Bolger, whose tenure was marked by union accusations of bad-faith bargaining, unjust firing of wildcat strikers, and resistance to safety reforms at bulk mail centers. EI/QWL programs were controversial within the NALC, and were opposed by the APWU as conceding too much to management outside the contract.[46] Vern Baxter argues that with EI/QWL, the USPS attempted to move from an "authoritarian" to "a more participative management culture" in 1981, with the NALC and NPMHU on board, but rejected by the APWU as a "cooptative mechanism designed to undermine the collective bargaining process."[47] Ironically, the USPS quit EI/QWL in 1996 following NALC resistance and protests against USPS rigid policy measures on TEs, route adjustments, and how carriers should handle automated (DPS) mail.[48]

Some other examples of union-USPS cooperation and clashing can be seen in 1979. That was the year the NALC filed suit against the USPS for massive overtime violations based on Congress's extending that year to federal employees protection under the 1938 Fair Labor Standards Act. The NALC won a $400 million settlement in 1982. The year after the NALC filed their suit, they combined with the USPS to reduce the number of grievances in a program called "Operation Shakeout," taken from the term for workers emptying mail from sacks and pouches.[49] The NALC and USPS also worked together in 1987–88 to successfully defeat the Reagan administration's efforts in Congress, which would prevent postal rate hikes as well as cuts in service and capital improvement.[50] There was even a joint declaration by Postmaster General Bolger, NALC president Vincent Sombrotto, and then–vice president of the APWU William Burrus calling for an end to what postal scholar Dale L. Ferguson has termed an "adversarial relationship." But the 1980s also saw the USPS rolling out a transformation plan, which included a 1986 structural "realignment" that abolished forty-two districts, established seventy-four divisions, and increased automation in the workplace.[51] As a reminder

Almost Striking Again, Arbitration, and Automation

that congressional oversight still exerted considerable power over *both* postal labor and management, a bipartisan bill in 1982 sailed through Congress over NALC lobbying to place new postal and federal employees hired on or after January 1, 1984, under Social Security rather than the CSRS.[52]

By the 1990s, presorted DPS mail and handheld scanners combined to save costs and regiment letter-carrier work in a craft that had previously been insulated from automation-driven downsizing. Scanners have gone through several iterations since then: in 2014 the Mobile Delivery Devices began replacing the paired scanner/cellphone Intelligent Mail Devices. Scanners were designed to improve service by tracking "accountable mail" (mail checked out to the carrier for which they are accountable) like express, certified, and registered mail; CODs ("collect on delivery" or "cash on delivery" items paid for by addressee), and postage-due mail. They would later be used by the early 2000s for arranging parcels in delivery order, and by supervisors for tracking carrier location.[53] For its part, the USPS was rebuffed by Congress in the 1990s in its attempts to expand service that would have included electronic services, although postal scholar Christopher Shaw points to the USPS as not being proactive in promoting new services as well. Shaw notes significant blockage of new services like low-cost packing services by trade associations who lobbied the Postal Rate Commission, along with numerous complaints by FedEx and UPS — the latter objecting to the USPS's 1998 new secure email server as unfair competition with its own. But if the USPS was constantly being told to "stay in their lane," Shaw also points to many blown service opportunities. Union officials tried to intervene, but NALC president Joe Vacca provided this telling observation in 1977 as he lamented the USPS failure to introduce electronic transmissions during that decade: "I am confirmed in my conviction that this newly assembled group of expert businessmen not only lack a commitment to service, but they also lack the prime requisite of business, a will to compete . . . [suggesting] an unexpressed desire to preside over the demise of the U.S. Postal Service."[54]

Congress also found the USPS "an easy target" in the 1990s when attempting to "siphon off USPS funds to mask the ballooning federal deficit."[55] In 1987, President Reagan convened a twelve-member President's Commission on Privatization to study converting government agencies to businesses, including the USPS, but the initiative found no popularity in Congress. The APWU filed lawsuits to stop corporations trying to exploit this growing postal privatization atmosphere. The USPS itself backed corporations like React Postal Service in Salt Lake City, Utah, in 1982 that violated the postal monopoly protecting stamped letters on postal routes. The USPS also set up pilot programs in 1988 at select Sears Roebuck stores, where their employees sold postal products using postal equipment—an outsourcing project disrupted and ultimately abandoned by 1989 after the APWU launched a mass media campaign that included members sending thousands of letters to the chairman of the board of Sears threatening a boycott.[56]

Labor scholar (and former APWU shop steward) Sarah Ryan wrote in 1999 of growing postal privatization advocacy in the 1980s and 1990s as fundamentally one that "reflect[ed] the interests of large businesses to enter a huge, previously government monopoly."[57] Those interests, however, were not strong enough to pass the 1997 Postal Reform Act (HR 22)— a "moderate" privatization initiative introduced by Representative John McHugh (R-N.Y.). This bill, if enacted into law, would have capped postal rate increases to the Consumer Price Index (and thus capped wage increases), separated "competitive" from "monopoly" products, substantially lowered the competitive price restriction, and created "a postal employee-management commission that would alter the current collective bargaining procedures."[58] Postal union lobbying helped shut the Postal Reform Act down, but Ryan argues that the NALC and APWU missed opportunities to lobby the public against postal privatization as postal unionists did on wages and working conditions in the decade leading up to the 1970 strike.[59] Ryan also notes how the USPS kept the unions in the dark on "strategic decisions" like the 1993 Priority Mail "redesign," about which the USPS had met with private business leaders but failed to tell the unions until 1996 that it might be outsourcing that work. Moreover, in 1997 the USPS awarded a $1.7 billion contract to Emery Worldwide Airlines to operate ten Priority Mail Processing Centers.[60]

When Vincent Sombrotto stepped down as NALC president in late 2002, reform of the Postal Reorganization Act that he had argued for to make the USPS better able to compete with private carriers was still not on the horizon.[61] Moe Biller, meanwhile, had stepped down in November 2001 after serving as APWU president since 1980. He died in 2003, followed a decade later by Sombrotto. Biller was succeeded by Bill Burrus, the first African American elected APWU president, in a year that saw the terrorist attacks of September 11, 2001. That fall saw an unrelated case of individual terrorism: anthrax attacks on the mails—made worse, Burrus pointed out, by the USPS practice of using compressed air to clean postal equipment, a practice carried out in defiance of union protests.[62] Biller and Sombrotto served longer than almost any national presidents of any postal union. Both brought their rank-and-file 1970 wildcat strike experiences to national office. The

Almost Striking Again, Arbitration, and Automation

rank and file played a crucial role in crafting *them* as the trade union political leaders they became. In the process, both unions moved beyond solely economic demands to national and international labor solidarity, committing those unions to the fight for equality, and mobilizing members to oppose service cutbacks. Meanwhile, the contract arbitration process built into the 1970 PRA as a fallback to negotiation impasses has become a safety valve for union negotiators facing USPS intransigence and its attempted rollbacks of benefits. If changing work rules and advancing automation has been crucial for the USPS, safeguarding jobs and workplace autonomy has been equally important for unions to protect. For the USPS it meant balancing its narrow revenue-surplus margin with its statutory service mandate. But what made the first four decades of postal labor–USPS management clashes even more contentious was the postal financial crisis on the heels of the Great Recession of 2008. This was part of a global financial crisis that saw millions unemployed, homes foreclosed, business and bank failures, social service cuts, and national economies in "free fall," as economist Joseph Stiglitz called it, driven for the most part by reckless and unregulated investment banking in the United States. Business losses and cutbacks in the communications industry hurt the USPS short-term, but that was not what caused its 2009 financial crisis.[63]

Downsizing, Financial Crisis, and the Challenge for Postal Labor, 2000–2019

It was March 18, 2010, forty years to the day after the 1970 postal strike began. Phillip Herr, Director of Physical Infrastructure Issues for the Government Accountability Office (GAO), was testifying before a congressional subcommittee on the USPS financial crisis with these sobering statistics and assessments: "As mail volume declined by 35 billion pieces (about 17 percent) in fiscal years 2007 through 2009, USPS's financial condition deteriorated, with close to $12 billion in losses, and it does not expect total mail volume to return to its former level when the economy recovers. This volume decline was largely due to the economic downturn and changing use of the mail, with mail continuing to shift to electronic communications and payments. In July 2009, we added USPS's financial condition and outlook to our High-Risk List and reported that USPS urgently needed to restructure to address its financial viability."[1]

There is no doubt that this was a serious situation. But the losses cited by Director Herr as being "close to $12 billion" do not include the lion's share of the USPS deficit: the annual payments to the U.S. Treasury beginning just three years before, as mandated by the 2006 Postal Accountability and Enhancement Act (PAEA). Despite the real challenges of online services and the Great Recession, the USPS financial crisis that began in 2009 is still ongoing as of this writing because of that mandate, which required the USPS to set aside about $5.6 billion a year for the next decade toward future retirees' health benefits. It was a requirement not seen in any other government agency or private corporation—and not even amortized over forty or fifty years, as one might expect. This mandate has created a $15 billion debt for the USPS.[2] Why would Congress saddle the USPS with such a fantastic debt burden?

Before discussing the particulars that preceded the PAEA, we must consider the history of postal privatization campaigns that focused their criticisms on public-sector employee collective-bargaining rights. These campaigns included politically conservative and libertarian institutions like the *National Review*, the Cato Institute, the American Enterprise Institute, the Heritage Foundation, the Public Service Research Council, the *Government Union Review*, the *Government Union Critique* newsletter, along with the private delivery carriers United Parcel Service (UPS) and FedEx, whose founder and president is also on Cato's board of directors. The Cato Institute began promoting the story of a collapsing USPS in need of privatization as early as February 12, 1985, in a paper by James Brebard titled "The Last Dinosaur: The U.S. Postal Service." Cato Institute books that followed were based on conferences in the 1980s and 1990s that included the Heritage Foundation, corporate heads, government officials (including a postmaster general), and sympathetic scholars. These discussions argued three major themes: (1) the USPS is costly and inefficient and needs to be privatized before it unfairly squeezes private competition any longer; (2) 80 percent of postal costs are labor, and therefore excessive; and (3) there is a crucial need to advance pending legislation too often blocked by "powerful trade unions" in the post office.[3] Beside the issue of wages, "hostility to unions," explains Sarah Ryan, is rooted in the idea that unions stall privatization because "they have tended, historically, to initiate and defend public ownership in a variety of areas."[4]

What effects did this privatization movement have on the USPS? For years, conservatives and private delivery competitors had openly complained of having no influence in Congress with legislation along those lines — until the 2000 presidential election of George W. Bush. Bush, a Republican, took office in 2001 and appointed a presidential commission to study postal reform. In 2002, as if responding to greater talk of privatization, Postmaster General John Potter issued the *United States Postal Service Transformation Plan*, which called for changes in the USPS to meet the challenges of the digital age. In the Executive Summary, Potter argued that three choices faced the USPS: revert to a "Government Agency," become a "Privatized Corporation," or transition to a "Commercial Government Enterprise wholly owned by the federal government." Potter favored the third option because he thought it would carry the "businesslike tradition" of the PRA "to the next level." And, he declared, this way "the universal service obligation might be met under contract between the government and the Postal Service. A new labor model would be probable."[5]

The ambiguous phrase "new labor model" must have given pause to the postal unions. Indeed, the NALC and the USPS have published different reactions to President Bush's 2003 postal commission report. The USPS history saw that commission's report, called *Embracing the Future*, as palatable to a broad coalition of postal management, labor, mailer, and consumer interests. By contrast, the NALC history reported NALC president William Young's criticism of the report as an attack on wages, benefits, and collective bargaining. A close reading of *Embracing the Future* finds the presidential commission essentially agreeing with the USPS *Transformation Plan*, although the commission called for a reduction in postal monopoly and was more explicit about workforce management. The commission even went so far as to recommend "that the private sector become more involved in the delivery of the nation's mail."[6] *Embracing the Future* did acknowledge the role of the 1970 postal strike and its effects on reorganization—even referring to the PRA and collective bargaining as "positive." The old post office was outmoded, the report said, but the Internet age had made the PRA outdated as well. Any sympathy from the commission for past low-waged government employees quickly faded to a critique of the present in which strong postal unions were able to bargain collectively or win demands through arbitration, a situation that had become too expensive in the commission's view. The report noted that no other government agency had those rights.[7] The commission also soberly observed that in 2001 the post office had 400,000 applicants and no turnover. *Embracing the Future* used terms like "pay for performance" and "right-sizing" in calling for facility consolidation, more outsourcing, consideration of benefits as wages in determining "comparability," and cutting back on so many arbitrated settlements. It expressed satisfaction with the reduction of 40,000 postal jobs in the previous year through attrition and the imminent retirement of thousands more postal workers. Support for downsizing emerged as part of the goal of the subtitle to chapter 5 of the report: "Designing a Smaller, Stronger, New Postal Network."[8]

The attitude of the Bush administration and the USPS toward downsizing postal services largely paved the way for the 2009 postal financial crisis. Historian Kevin C. Brown points to a 2002 Office of Personnel Management report that found the USPS had actually *overfunded* its annual pension payments, possibly by as much as $100 billion. Postal scholar Steve Hutkins points out that the 2003 Postal Civil Service Retirement System (CSRS) Funding Reform Act would have saved the USPS money and increased the federal deficit "by as much as $41 billion. . . . In other words, if the Postal Service were to reduce its payments into the CSRS (to avoid overpaying and creating a surplus), the federal budget would take a big hit and 'cost' the federal government over $4 billion a year [over ten years]. Congress was having none of that." Instead, Hutkins notes, Congress did three things to alleviate this "problem": (1) made the USPS (instead of the Treasury Department) responsible for postal military veterans benefits; (2) forced the USPS to use its pension savings to pay off a Treasury loan; and (3) required the USPS to tell Congress how it would use its future savings. In other words, Congress was using the USPS to subsidize its balanced budget. The Bush administration was meanwhile running up huge deficits caused by tax cuts that especially benefited wealthy income earners, and by wars in Iraq and Afghanistan. President Bush insisted that legislation such as postal reform be "budget neutral" and not contribute to the deficit. Postmaster General Potter told Congress that if the $27-billion-dollar postal military pension payment were transferred to the USPS from the Treasury, it would actually *increase* the federal deficit. Why not instead keep those payments in the Treasury in an account called the Postal Service Retiree Health Benefits Fund (RHBF)? This set the stage for the PAEA, the first major postal-reform law since 1970. It also changed the postal rate system, gave the renamed Postal Regulatory Commission (PRC) more power, and for the first time in a postal-reform law, employed the term "business model" as a desirable if ambiguous goal.[9] On December 20, 2006, President Bush signed the PAEA into law. The crisis would not take long to develop.[10]

THE CRISIS BEGINS

NALC president William Young issued a statement on January 30, 2009, on the effects of the 2008 Great Recession on the post office that disputed Postmaster General Potter's call for five-day delivery as a solution.[11] The USPS Office of the Inspector General on February 2, 2009, reported bleak economic figures for FY 2008 in a blog post entitled "The Postal Service Financial Crisis."[12] And on the morning of March 25, 2009, an Associated Press wire story carried this alarming headline: "Call for Help: Postal Chief Says Agency Crashing." It cited the USPS's loss of $2.8 billion in 2008, and quoted Potter warning a House subcommittee that morning, "We are facing losses of historic proportion. Our situation is critical." Potter repeated the possibility of delivery cutbacks, which he had posed in January, adding that layoffs were possible. The USPS would be offering 150,000 employees early retirement. Closing "small and rural post offices" was suggested by PRC chair Dan Blair.[13] By the summer, wire reports like the one published on August 9 in the Raleigh, North Carolina, *News and Observer*, with the headline "Postal Service Will Cut Costs and Offices," were becoming commonplace.[14] What caused the crisis? Did President George W. Bush's administration seek to deliberately sabotage the USPS and force it to privatize, as one popular suspicion maintained?[15] Did it represent bipartisan good intentions gone wrong? Addressing the former, postal researcher and retired postmaster Mark Jamison doubted that an actual conspiracy existed "to bankrupt the Postal Service, but the consequences of what they were doing were pretty clear." Where did the PAEA's authors think the USPS would get the funds to make such huge annual payments, especially when that same legislation imposed a "new pricing regimen with the CPI [Consumer Price Index] cap on market-dominant products?" (Market-dominant products are those like first-class mail, standard mail, periodicals, etc., where the USPS faces little competition.) Jamison concludes, "The RHBF . . . really ended up having nothing to do with its stated purpose. It was basically designed as a mechanism to keep the bill budget neutral . . . (hence the ten year window—the same reason the Bush tax cuts expired after ten years)."[16] Jamison notes how the postal retiree health insurance liability would have been a nonissue if federal employees under 1984 legislation had been *automatically* added to the Medicare rolls upon reaching retirement. If that enrollment had been required, "just like almost every employer plan in the country . . . then the retiree health benefit unfunded liability melts away to about $3 billion. That's the testimony of Jeffrey Williamson, the Chief Human Resources Officer of the Postal Service. . . . [Representative] Darrell Issa has even acknowledged that it solves the problem."[17]

The PAEA passed both the House and Senate in 2006 with Democratic support when Republicans enjoyed majorities in both chambers. How did the postal unions and others not see this disastrous law coming? The question "where were the voices of opposition in 2006?" is one that Kevin C. Brown tried to answer—despite few forthcoming congressional sources—in a 2012 "Remapping Debate" website analysis: "For one thing, the significance of the change in the [PAEA] legislation between the House and Senate versions and the final version was not immediately apparent to members of Congress or to observers. And most people don't want to talk about it. . . . 'I'm not aware,' said Representative [Peter] DeFazio [D-Ore.], 'of any discussion by anybody (at the time that) we were looking at a massive ten year funding obligation. . . . I think a bunch of Democrats got suckered on that one,'" a decision that was made by voice vote during the 2006 lame-duck session of Congress. "They didn't realize how radical the changes were."[18]

Brown also quotes Senator Tom Carper (D-Del.), author of the leading piece of postal reform legislation in 2016, as well as one of those backing the PAEA a decade earlier: "While the payments were larger than my colleagues and I would have liked, we had no reason to believe that the Postal Service would not be able to afford them. At that time, mail volume was at its historic peak and the Postal Service indicated the payments were affordable."[19] The authors of the NALC's official history, Brady Mikusko and John Miller, concur. Their 2006 edition of *Carriers in a Common Cause* discussed support by the NALC, the USPS, mailers, and both Democrats and Republicans in Congress for postal reform, starting as early as 1994. The debate became considerably altered when the incoming Bush administration in 2001 supported USPS "freedom to place its products and organize its core business" but also "attacked the pay and benefits and collective bargaining rights of carriers and other craft employees."[20] Mikusko and Miller concluded that earlier edition by observing that "the full Senate had yet to consider postal reform as 2005 came to a close."[21] By the 2014 edition of *Carriers in a Common Cause*, the NALC had more to say about what actually had transpired by 2006. The NALC felt that the "Senate bill unfairly singled out postal employees receiving workers' compensation."[22] The 2014 edition explained NALC president Young's "reluctant" decision to neither support nor reject the "compromise" bill: "Despite its limitations, the bill protected bargaining rights for letter carriers and other postal employees, preserved the USPS in the public sector and retained universal service for the American people, funded by a regulated postal monopoly. The NALC president also assumed, as did Congress and virtually the entire postal community, that the legislation's limited pricing and product flexibility provisions would stabilize the Service's finances. Unanticipated circumstances and a largely overlooked provision dashed these modest expectations."[23] This is an understatement. The authors' conclusion is a familiar one to those who were blindsided by that "largely overlooked provision" also known as the "prefund requirement." That huge annual payment "did not appear to be an immediate problem when the law was enacted," they wrote, summing up the exigencies of a government corporation still accountable to Congress: "Postal revenues were increasing, and management was able to build the cost of pre-funding payments permanently into postage rates during the special rate proceeding authorized by the law to occur within one year of enactment. But as the nation's economy fell apart in 2007 and 2008, the Service chose not to raise rates. As a result, the Service paid more than $12 billion between the beginning of 2007 and the end of 2009 to pre-fund future retiree health benefits, turning its healthy balance sheet deep red."[24]

Neither the "deliberate sabotage" theory nor the "good intentions" theory is satisfactory. The PAEA's basic intent more strongly suggests a Bush administration desire to (1) relieve its financial responsibility for owing money to the USPS for pension overcharges; and (2) effectively force the downsizing of the USPS, which the presidential commission and the postmaster general were already in agreement about.[25]

THE GREAT RECESSION AND THE POSTAL CRISIS

In 2008 the APWU and NALC had high expectations for a pro-labor presidency and endorsed former community organizer and senator Barack Obama (D-Ill.) for president, as did the AFL-CIO.[26] Whereas President Nixon governed with Democratic majorities in Congress as well as on the basis of shared political assumptions of labor rights and government services, President Obama was hampered by Republican majorities (the House, beginning in 2011, and the Senate, in 2015) and obstructionism, as well as a marked decline in previously shared positive postal-service assumptions. Obama's certain veto constituted a firewall against Republican postal downsizing and privatization legislation, if any had ever gotten that far. But a 2011 NALC web article criticizing Obama's support for cutting Saturday delivery also reflected postal labor's disappointment in his concession to austerity advocates.[27] With Obama entering office in 2009 determined to end the Great Recession, the postal unions, followed by the USPS, were calling attention to the postal fiscal crisis. The postal unions — chiefly the NALC and the APWU — pointed to the PAEA prefunding mandate as the chief culprit behind growing amounts of USPS red ink. For its part, the USPS, following FY 2009 losses, placed principal emphasis on the recession and the competition posed by electronic communications. Postmaster General Potter concluded the USPS's November 2009 report with a plea to Congress to pass legislation that would alleviate "the impossible demands of prefunding future retiree health benefits at current levels of more than $5 billion annually; the barriers to matching delivery frequency with declining mail volumes; and the ability to leverage the Postal Service's logistics, distribution and retail networks to create new revenue streams."[28] Potter was asking for more than debt relief and product expansion: he also wanted a break from

Eleanor Bailey, interviewed on May 14, 2015, by a reporter and surrounded by other APWU activists outside the GPO (today the James A. Farley Building), New York City, as part of the National Day of Action one week before the APWU collective-bargaining agreement was set to expire. These rallies were called to demand a fair contract and the preservation of postal jobs and service. Bailey was a 1970 postal strike activist with the MBPU, an APWU predecessor. This was the same post office she struck in 1970. She was shop steward for thirty-one of her thirty-two years at the post office and later held positions as Legislative Director, Human Relations Director, and Chair of the Trustee Board of NYMAPU Local 10-APWU. Courtesy of APWU.

certain service and workforce obligations that cut into USPS profits. A year later he announced his retirement.[29]

By 2011 more serious media coverage, combined with a national organized protest in September by the postal unions, had begun to alter the larger narrative of a feckless USPS to one that was capable of otherwise earning profits yet unfairly burdened by this huge annual financial obligation.[30] The USPS position, however, began to appear more and more erratic, to the point of desperation, with proposals ranging from cutting back to five- or even three-day weekly service — all in a futile effort to meet what had now become an ongoing fiscal crisis in the billions of dollars, with attempted solutions that would only save millions while compromising its mandate, namely, dependable universal service at inexpensive uniform rates. A new postmaster general, Patrick Donahoe, took office on December 6, 2010. By 2012 the USPS had staked out a firm position that treated postal unions as an obstacle to USPS financial recovery.

To date there has been minimal scholarship on the postal crisis, but two postal-history books published in 2016 reveal opposite sides of the debate. Devin Leonard's *Neither Snow nor Rain*, the first comprehensive history of both the USPOD and USPS, paints the RHBF and PAEA as common-sense measures, and expresses doubts about the USPS's future.[31] By contrast, Winifred Gallagher's *How the Post Office Created America* — even more comprehensive in its sweep — argues that the PAEA has needlessly damaged the USPS, and advocates for a public postal service future rooted in its long past.[32]

While the USPS was supposed to complete its annual $5.6 billion payment to the RHBF by FY 2016, it has been unable to make those payments to the Treasury, starting with FY 2011. Meanwhile, it appears to have been trying to mollify a critical and predominantly conservative Republican Congress by aggressively pursuing a policy of downsizing its network, including infrastructure, delivery, service, and personnel.[33] As former Postmaster General Donahoe told journalist Devin Leonard in 2011, "Some people say if you crash the system, then people will pay attention to you." Leonard's interview with Donahoe for *Bloomberg BusinessWeek* seems to confirm popular suspicions of Donahoe's proposing and conducting labor and service cuts in exchange for the hope that Congress would agree to forgo the prefunding mandate. Donahoe thought he could turn a profit by cutting Saturday delivery, using attrition rather than layoffs to slash the workforce by 20 percent, and moving postal retail services into convenience stores and supermarkets.[34]

In 2013 the USPS unilaterally declared that Saturday delivery would be abolished, before protests by the public and Congress made it back down. Meanwhile, mail processing centers were reduced by 50 percent through consolidation. Hundreds of urban and rural post offices — some with great historic value — have been closed, sold off, leased, or had their window hours cut, and neighborhood cluster boxes and curbside boxes are increasingly replacing home delivery. These cuts have already compromised service and eliminated jobs.[35] Innovative ideas like the Office of Inspector General's proposal to restore a postal banking system, which ran from 1911 to 1967 and if restarted would likely be on both digital and brick-and-mortar platforms, have yet to be publicly embraced by the USPS. Yet despite missed (and denied) opportunities to seize new technology-based services in addition to cutbacks in existing services, the USPS ironically continues to expand services in response to demand. Those include Intelligent Mail tracking and Informed Delivery service, $301 million in online sales, 35.5 million "Click-and-Ship" labels sold online, along with 36.8 million computerized address changes processed in 2018 (16 million of those online), 83.4 million money orders sold, and 6.8 million passport applications handled.[36]

THE ONGOING CRISIS AND EFFECTS ON COMMUNITIES

The USPS has used up its maximum borrowing power from the U.S. Treasury Department at $15 billion, which it needed to make earlier payments.[37] To indicate just how much the USPS actually rebounded since the Great Recession, however, between 2012 and 2015 mail volume seemingly stabilized at 154.2 billion annual pieces. The same was true of total first-class volume at 62.4 billion pieces, and standard (advertising) mail at 80 billion pieces. Packages actually *rose* to 4.5 billion pieces (with an increase of 11 percent in the first half of FY 2016), while delivery points rose to 155 million in 2015. Not counting the prefunding mandate expenses, total 2015 revenue was $68.9 billion, a $1.2 billion revenue increase, with a $1.4 billion revenue increase over the previous year. By FY 2017 total volume had slipped to 149.6 billion pieces, with $69.6 billion in revenue, followed in 2018 by a drop in volume to 146.4 billion pieces, but with a billion-dollar revenue increase to $70.6 billion.[38]

In response to the USPS financial crisis and the failure of Congress to lift or ease the PAEA mandate, the USPS has closed 150 mail-processing facilities since 2012, with 70 more slated for "consolidation." It scrapped a 2011 plan to close 3,700 post offices, but its subsequent "POStPlan" slashed hours at 13,000 rural post offices across the country.[39] The stated purpose was to cut costs and avoid default, which many have pointed out was self-defeating, as postal service and business both suffer with job and service cuts. Meanwhile, if not for the RHBF debt, the USPS would have demonstrated revenue surpluses every year since 2013.[40] But in addition to the 2014 defeat of the abolition of Saturday delivery, Steve Hutkins noted in February 2016, "Thanks to public protest and pressure from Congress, there appears to be an unofficial moratorium on post office closures." Yet there continue to be what the USPS calls "emergency suspensions" of post offices that it has deemed inoperable—that number now runs to almost 600.[41]

What are the effects on communities, workers, and their families with postal-job and -service cutbacks? How are some communities more affected than others? We know that the post–Civil War post office was a target career for increasing numbers of Americans, including military veterans and immigrants. This job niche was especially valuable for African Americans after the Civil War, when they were first allowed to work at the post office, and where the hiring possibilities overall were greater than in the private sector. By World War I, African Americans made up about 10 percent of the postal workforce, in spite of President Wilson's efforts to purge and segregate them. By the 1960s they were at their present percentage of the workforce: approximately 21 percent. Many urban post offices had large African American components by 1960 (at least 30 percent), which have grown since then. This includes New York, Cleveland, Detroit, Philadelphia, Houston, Cincinnati, Memphis, and Atlanta. Meanwhile, other urban offices have been majority-black since 1960, including Chicago, Los Angeles, Washington, D.C., and New Orleans.[42] Black postal workers over the years were typically homeowners, married with children, often with college degrees and/or veteran status, and usually male, until the 1960s saw a spike in black women's employment at the post office.[43]

Economists Leah Platt Boustan and Robert Margo in 2009 discussed the steady rise of African American postal employment from 1941, with the black-to-white-employee ratio growing to two to one nationwide by 1970 — and much higher in some urban areas. Boustan and Margo also reported that "by 2000, the [statistical] mean black postal worker remained in the top 25 percent of black earners and above the median for the nation."[44] And Timothy Williams of the *New York Times* wrote in 2011 at the height of the postal financial crisis that "about one in five black workers have public sector jobs, and African-American workers are one-third more likely than white ones to be employed in the public sector." He further noted that losses of public-sector jobs including the USPS have proportionately greater effects on the black community. There are a number of negative effects that follow collective job loss, as we are witnessing today. It affects families, certainly, but in this case also communities where postal workers are homeowners, parents of college-age children, consumers, and activists. Historically, this has especially been true in the black community, where postal workers have both been seen and operated as part of the black middle class.[45]

The fight for equality at the post office, led by African Americans, helped open up the post office to women, who now make up 37 percent of the workforce, as well as Latinos and Asians, who each make up about 8 percent of all American postal workers today. Even though the percentage of African Americans at the post office is probably the same since large-scale job elimi-

Downsizing, Financial Crisis, and the Challenge for Postal Labor

Female letter carrier making a residential delivery, Minneapolis, Minnesota, 2012. Women today make up 37 percent of the postal workforce and over 30 percent of letter carriers—up from only 92 carriers in 1956. In the NALC they make up about one-quarter of national convention delegates and over 9 percent of union retirees, and hundreds serve as local, regional, and national officers. Courtesy of NALC.

nation began in 2009, it is the *number* we should be especially concerned with. Thanks to union contract provisions dating back to the 1970s, career postal workers with six or more years of seniority cannot be "laid off," but their *positions* can be abolished. When jobs are eliminated and postal workers are given the choice to transfer (sometimes at prohibitive distances), retire, or resign, and when future postal-career opportunities dry up, there are negative ripple or "multiplier" effects on communities.[46]

Women of all communities will also be negatively affected by postal job loss — whether as individuals or breadwinners (or co-breadwinners) in families. The percentage of women at the post office was only 17.4 percent in 1967, 73 percent of whom were clerks.[47] In 1956 there were only 92 total female letter carriers, compared to over 58,000 today when women make up over 30 percent of all carriers and 37 percent of all postal workers. Today, women in both the APWU and NALC have also won union positions numbering in the hundreds in each union, a legacy of what labor historian Dorothy Sue Cobble refers to as the "labor feminists" of the 1960s. One of those activists was Josie McMillian. McMillian, a 1970 strike veteran who led shop floor actions at the GPO after the strike and was the first woman elected New York Metro APWU president in 1981, put it this way: "We wanted women to go to union meetings and not be afraid to speak, to let their feelings be known."[48]

Technological change — including the automation that began rendering so many postal jobs redundant in the early 2000s — forces us to confront a larger question: does our society see it as a positive good to ensure the availability of well-paying public sector unionized jobs for all who are willing and qualified to do them? This would include training workers who have invested years in that career for other positions in the postal service. But according to a 2015 Pew Research Center report, the general trend since 2009 has been public-sector job elimination, including the USPS: "Government payrolls at nearly all levels also have been cut. Local governments have shed 446,000 jobs, about 3% of their total workforce; state governments have cut a net 121,000 jobs, with small growth in education more than offset by cuts elsewhere. *And while the federal government has added 62,700 non-postal jobs, the Postal Service has reduced its workforce nearly 18%, or 129,400 jobs.* The Postal Service now employs fewer than 600,000 [career] people, its smallest payroll since 1964."[49] In FY 2017 those USPS employment figures showed a rise for the third straight year after a decade of decline, with 503,103 career employees and 141,021 non-career employees, for a total of 644,124 employees.[50] The USPS in 2018, with 146.4 billion pieces of mail worked, was still below 1969 employment levels, when 739,002 total employees worked 85 billion pieces of mail. Non-career employees at the time of the 1970 strike (192,821) were about 12 percent of the workforce. In FY 2018, the figures dipped for career (497,157), non-career (137,290), and total employees (634,447). This means that about 22 percent of employees are non-career, paid considerably less with fewer benefits for doing the same work as full-time career colleagues.[51] And in 2018, journalist Jake Bittle found rural postal service collapsing under the weight of cutbacks and labor shortages, rural carriers (almost half now part-time) working extra hours without extra pay, and the NRLCA enduring pay cuts in collective bargaining.[52] With still no PAEA reform in sight as of 2019, the debt-induced crisis has become chronic. What does the future hold for the USPS, the postal unions, and postal workers?

LOOKING BACK

The post office's functions have expanded and changed greatly over time. But it is worth comparing the tenuous situation of postal workers, their unions, and the USPS today with the pre-strike era. In some ways, it has come full

Downsizing, Financial Crisis, and the Challenge for Postal Labor

circle, while in others it is even more challenging. The APWU and NALC remain among the strongest unions in the public sector, which enjoys a much higher union density than the private sector, according to labor historian Joseph Slater. As of 2019, the NALC had 288,000 members, the APWU approximately 232,000. Both figures include retirees, but the APWU's drop in membership behind the NALC reflects the constant elimination of clerk jobs.[53] The 1970 wildcat strike in defiance of union leadership strengthened the postal unions and contributed to the USPS being a well-paying job open to more people of color, women, and young people. By 2002 this job had an astonishingly low "quit rate" of less than 1.5 percent.[54] The USPS continues to enjoy the highest citizen satisfaction rating of any government agency, as it has for years. A 2014 Gallup poll noted an unexpectedly higher favorability among young versus older users — this despite USPS service cutbacks. The 2019 Gallup poll pointed to the USPS's being on top in those succeeding years, with 74 percent of Americans rating it as "excellent/good."[55] This presents the question: what will be the long-term effects of the ongoing crisis on service and employee morale?

Discussions of the future of postal labor are dependent on whether society deems the post office itself valuable. That debate is contingent on popular demand and habits, as well as innovations that encourage new uses of trusted institutions. The future of postal labor is bound up in the fate of the USPS. When Americans contrast their vastly increased personal and business use of the Internet to their declining use of stamped letters, it is worth considering that this change began long before the Internet. By 1963, the same year zip codes were introduced, 80 percent of postal volume was business mail. Two decades later, household-to-household mail made up only 4.8 percent of total domestic mail volume, dropping down to 3 percent by 2006, to 2.8 percent in 2012, and 2.5 percent in 2014. By contrast, nonhousehold-to-household rose from 55.5 percent in 1987 to 75.4 percent in 2014, and household-to-nonhousehold mail dropped slightly during that period from 6.4 to 4.5 percent. First-class business, second-class newspaper and magazine, and third-class standard mail have been the overwhelming engines of postal revenue since before the postal strike.[56] In 2015 the USPS Office of Inspector General said this about mail and the 2008 Great Recession: "While single-piece First-Class Mail has been in decline since about 1990, commercial First-Class Mail—what business mailers send—remained a growth product until 2008 when it fell by 1.6 percent. It has declined every year since then *until this year.* . . . It's no coincidence that 2008 was the turning point for commercial mail volumes. That year marked the first full year of the Great

Recession, which roughed up the housing and financial sectors in particular. With limited cash flow, those sectors—heavy users of First-Class Mail for advertising—cut back on marketing, including direct mail."[57]

There is also a larger question about the future of work itself with the steady de-employment trend in modern capitalist society. The downsizing of the USPS and its services has profound, negative implications for American society. Those include: frustrating postal consumers with the relaxation of service standards (slowing down even local first-class mail); longer lines at the post office; forcing longer travel time to post offices after nearby ones close; and communities losing post offices and jobs. Tom Germano traces these kinds of negative actions back to the "corporate culture" that accompanied the creation of the new USPS in 1971.[58] Where should the money come from to operate a universal service? Tension exists in a society that combines capitalist economic relations with government-sponsored public service. Is the postal service still necessary and viable? Should it be expanded to provide other communications-related services that compete with the private sector? Is there a future for well-paid government employees doing those kinds of jobs in service to the public?

Postal labor in 1970 used a nationwide strike to force the issue of poorly compensated, skilled labor and inefficient, authoritarian management. Even a 2016 blog on the website of the USPS Office of Inspector General includes a positive and admiring narrative of the strike.[59] But though the USPS has continued to meet new delivery demands, it has become a target for elimination or privatization. Opposition forces that could not gain traction against the former U.S. Post Office, or its self-supporting successor, the U.S. Postal Service, have seemingly found the perfect means for dismantling public postal service through the inability of Congress (still as of 2019) to repeal the PAEA.[60]

Congressional inaction concerning the postal financial crisis reflects a new set of general assumptions in government and management. Joseph McCartin has argued that these were first brought into being with President Ronald Reagan's firing of about 11,000 striking PATCO members in 1981, which in effect proclaimed that management has no obligation to ensure strikers' jobs, and that labor unions are no longer necessary for managing workplace control. Since that time, we could add another common assumption which declares labor should be contingent, low-waged, and in the private sector.[61] Writing in 1994, Vern Baxter came to this conclusion: "The real substance of the postal privatization campaign is an attack on postal workers—their wages, working conditions, and labor agreement."[62] Mark

Jamison similarly refers to postal policies during the 2009 postal financial crisis as part of "a war on workers" that somehow "either forgot or never understood what service really meant."[63]

AMAZONIA

First hired at $15 an hour (about $8 an hour less than fulltime carriers) in March 2013, City Carrier Assistants (CCAs) would become the part-time workforce the USPS would rely upon later in the year when it signed a Negotiated Service Agreement (NSA) with Amazon to provide a discount to a company whose name was becoming synonymous with online shopping *and* shipping. Amazon utilized its twenty-five sort centers and more than seventy fulfillment centers to bring presorted parcels directly to the post office when it was not otherwise shipping via United Parcel Service and FedEx, both of which would in turn rely on the USPS to deliver them on the "last mile" of their journey. (Amazon also rolled out its own contract delivery service in 2018).[64] Embedded in the controversial NSA between the USPS and Amazon.com, the CCAs were a product of the January 2013 arbitration award which came halfway through the 2011–2016 NALC-USPS contract period. CCAs would take the place of the Transitional Employees (TEs), and there would also be a phasing out of PTFs (Part Time Flexibles) in favor of full-time career employees. As Brady Mikusko and John Miller point out in *Carriers in a Common Cause*, this arbitration award was in part a response to the NALC's "proposals to create an all full-time career workforce," in addition to "giving the CCAs the opportunity to fill available full-time career positions, an option transitional employees never had." It also followed the previous "APWU pattern" by not only creating a new lower-paid "assistant" category, but also pushing back starting salaries with lower "steps" for letter carriers.[65]

How big a boost was this to the USPS? "USPS revenue was just about the same in 2017 as it was in 2005," but parcels now accounted for 28 percent of total revenue—a jump of 25 percent. That increase, noted Jake Bittle in a 2018 *Nation* article, was "attributable almost entirely to e-commerce," with Amazon the most prominent shipper.[66] Whole parcel routes for CCAs were created for carrying the huge influx of Amazon packages. Vehicle accidents and injuries increased, along with CCA turnover and a quick morale dip as carrier assistants could not keep up with the strain of a seven-day week. (And this is occurring at a time when most of the USPS fleet of right-hand-drive Long Life Vehicles or LLVs are past their twenty-four-year life expectancy, with LLV fires now "an Internet meme.")[67] The NALC notes in its history how its membership was finally "leveling off" rather than dipping, as it recruited new CCAS as members and fought for quicker conversion of the part-time carrier assistants to full-time career employees.[68] By 2014 the USPS had agreed to begin making Amazon package deliveries on Sundays.[69] Sunday mail delivery had been banned in 1912 during the Progressive Era of workplace and urban reforms by the Mann Sunday Closing Act, to give carriers an assured weekly day off.[70] For years, special-delivery messengers were the only postal employees Americans could expect to see on Sunday, with the exception of the occasional Express Mail delivery. But by 2017 it was commonplace to see postal delivery vehicles delivering Amazon parcels on Sundays.[71] Ironically, the year before Sunday parcel deliveries began, "bipartisan congressional opposition" forced Postmaster General Donahoe to back down from his plan for five-day delivery—which had also been in President Obama's 2013 budget.[72]

A further irony followed a successful December 2017 holiday delivery period for the USPS, with President Donald Trump's ill-informed Twitter posts decrying the USPS's billion-dollar losses and low parcel rates for Amazon.[73] Trump tried and failed to pressure Postmaster General Brennan to increase rates to Amazon and other shippers.[74] On April 12, 2018, Trump issued an executive order for the government to conduct a review of the USPS, asserting without evidence, "The USPS is on an unsustainable financial path and must be restructured to prevent a taxpayer-funded bailout."[75] Trump's actions have served as a reminder that the USPS remains vulnerable to executive as well as congressional whim. Trump's privatization proclivities have not boded well for either the USPS or its unions since he took office in 2017.[76] His first budget proposal in May 2017, for example, called for the elimination of Saturday delivery.[77] On the other hand, Trump's proposal to sell off the USPS and privatize it—with fewer weekday deliveries to cluster boxes and lower-waged workers drawing fewer benefits—has so far won few backers.[78] Trump's "Task Force on the United States Postal System," established in April 2018 to review the USPS, finally released a seventy-page report in December that is revealing in its reform proposals, which suggest more privatization measures and even an embrace of wholesale privatization. The report barely mentioned the PAEA's huge annual employee health benefits mandate and did not even cite it as a cause (let alone the main cause) of the resulting massive USPS deficit. But after first asserting the mandate's normalcy, it curiously recommended that "the $43 billion in pre-funding payments that the USPS failed to pay . . . must be restructured . . . based on the population of employees at or near retirement age." The task force used the phrase "business model" no less than seventy-three times to argue for a profit-oriented fix to what it called the "unsustainable" USPS, primarily through reducing labor costs. This included a radical call to "remove USPS compensation from collective bargaining"—a right postal workers won in the 1970 Postal Reorganization Act after the strike.[79]

OUTSOURCING AND RESISTANCE

President Nixon and others who cheered the "bright future" of the USPS on the day he signed the PRA in 1970 might not have seen the Internet Age coming, or the rise of private carriers like FedEx and UPS. But it is worth mentioning that those two corporations combined only cover a fraction of USPS delivery territory: approximately 20 million, versus the 157 million homes and businesses for which the USPS is responsible. Privatization forces also did not predict the Internet actually *generating* revenue for the USPS, with more people shopping online and UPS transferring parcels to the USPS for "last-mile delivery." The arguments of inevitable public postal service failure in the age of the Internet and low-waged workers have not accounted for three successive years — 2013 to 2016 — of USPS revenue surpluses, including a $610 million "operating profit" in FY 2016.[80] Christopher Shaw notes that FedEx and UPS are powerful political donors with enormous political clout, having "worked to keep the Postal Service's offerings in the parcel and express delivery markets as noncompetitive as possible," such as blocking the USPS's proposed 1997 Global Postal Link program that would have moved parcels more quickly through customs.[81]

The USPS since 2001 has made regular use of FedEx jets in addition to the regularly scheduled airlines, even as it has failed to develop electronic mail initiatives and has allowed its private sector competitors to outdistance it in a USPS invention—overnight express mail.[82] But closing post offices, which have long fostered rural and urban communities, has become a way of erasing the memory and legacy of postal service. Self-inflicted mediocrity of a long-trusted government service makes its infrastructure look weak and irrelevant. Disregarding widespread protests against slowing down mail or centralizing postal delivery in "cluster boxes" further diminishes patrons' feelings of security and convenience, and could take down the favorable ratings previously enjoyed by the USPS above all other government agencies.[83] In 2013 the USPS outsourced retail work from trained government employees to low-waged workers in over 500 Staples office-supply retail stores. That outsourcing gave rise to an active boycott led by the postal unions and citizen groups, crucially joined by the millions of members of the nation's two largest teacher's unions—the American Federation of Teachers (AFT) and the National Education Association (NEA). An NLRB ruling against the USPS-Staples partnership on January 4, 2017, was not appealed by the USPS, nixing the deal.[84]

Popular protest possibly influenced the NLRB ruling against that partnership, yet three years before and with less publicity, the USPS signed a deal with the *Goin' Postal* "franchise chain of retail shipping and receiving stores based in Zephyrhills, Florida" to be placed in 2,000 Wal-Mart stores across the country.[85] The corporate name harkens back to a number of incidents at post offices across the country beginning in 1986 and running into the 1990s involving postal workers shooting managers and coworkers. The popular expression "going postal"—meaning to fly into a sudden rage—began circulating after those shootings. It was based on a stereotype of violent postal workers (especially Vietnam veterans) driven to murdering supervisors and coworkers as a result of a combination of personal mental-health issues and job stress. While studies showed the post office to be no more violent a workplace than others, the number of incidents called into question postal work culture as well as the screening process for postal job applicants. The adoption of this expression as a corporate name is a cynical, gratuitous poke at postal workers that nevertheless trades on the dependability of the postal "brand," with the USPS itself still apparently looking for cheap retail outlets to sell its products and services.[86]

The USPS, delivering 146 billion pieces of mail in 2018 out of 34,772 offices, is unique in its positioning at the center of a huge mailing industry of over 7.5 million workers. It is the nation's second-largest civilian employer (behind Wal-Mart) with $70.6 billion of operating revenue, $1.0 billion more than the previous year.[87] It enjoys monopoly status (first-class mail and mailbox exclusivity) and constraints (most innovations must go through Congress and may be lobbied by competitors like FedEx and UPS, who also depend on USPS services). By 2016, in response to the postal financial crisis, a concerted nationwide postal worker–consumer coalition emerged, including public forum "field hearings" in five major cities.[88] The four postal unions (NALC, APWU, NPMHU, and NRLCA) formed an alliance not commonly seen in the first four decades of the USPS. The unions did so first in September 2011 with a nationwide "Save America's Postal Service" campaign, followed in early 2014 with a "grand alliance" that included dozens of national labor and community-advocacy groups, highlighted with a proclamation to "end the attack" on postal jobs and services, and thereby preserve and protect an innovative "*public* Postal Service."[89]

This movement expanded in 2018 with an additional coalition calling itself Communities and Postal Workers United that included rallies, local organizing, and reporting on USPS-APWU contract negotiations—where APWU negotiators and demonstrators were joined by the presidents of NALC, NPMHU, AFL-CIO, and the NAACP's Washington, D.C., Bureau Director. Invoking the 1970 strike, APWU president Mark Dimondstein argued against the "three-tier wage and benefit structure" and service cutbacks. And in October 2018, in response to the Trump administration's postal privatization proposals, the postal unions called a nationwide demonstration under the slogan "The U.S. Mail is Not for Sale" that later became an ongoing "worker-led campaign sponsored by the American Postal Workers Union and the National Association of Letter Carriers . . . to fight plans to sell the public Postal Service to the highest bidder." Meanwhile, lively local union newsletters like the *Union Courier* (NALC) in Meriden, Connecticut, or the *Postmark* (APWU) in St. Paul, Minnesota, typify commitment to rank-and-file issues and 1970 strike historical memory in the two national unions, as seen on their websites. In the city where the strike began, NALC Branch 36's newsletter and New York Metro APWU's *Union Mail* (in its sixty-second year in 2019) reflect the use of online media to inform and mobilize members, often invoking the legacy of strike veterans, many of whom remained active throughout their lifetimes.[90] Individual union activists hired in the 1970s and 1980s have testified how the 1970 strike veterans inspired and influenced them to continue the campaign for workplace rights and union democracy. Patricia Williams, an African American distribution machine clerk hired in 1979 at the Los Angeles Terminal Annex, recalled, "I was mentored by Raydell Moore, Liz Powell, Judy Beard, Shirley Taylor, Debbie Zeredy" en route to her serving first as shop steward and local recording secretary, then National Business Agent, and finally the first woman elected Assistant Director of the Clerk Division at APWU headquarters in Washington, D.C. The stories of the post-strike generations of postal union activists are still waiting to be told.[91]

When postal workers struck in 1970, it was at the height of labor rank-and-file activism across the country, along with other social movements demanding change. As an illegal wildcat strike, it had the elements of surprise and autonomy, combined with national union leadership negotiating with the Nixon administration almost as a third party. Public-sector

NALC Branch 36 members lead a protest against USPS plans to cut Saturday delivery, New York City, forty-three years after the 1970 postal strike, March 24, 2013. Courtesy of NALC.

unions today have surpassed private-sector unions in size and representation. Union membership dropped from 20.1 million in 1983 to 10.7 million in 2017; but public-sector unionization in 2017 reached 34.4 percent (7.2 million workers) compared to a 6.5 percent private-sector union rate (7.6 million workers), with nonunion worker weekly earnings at 80 percent of those unionized.[92] At the same time, many government employees are denied the right to strike and public-sector unions are steadily losing members as the public sector strips itself of employees. In the twenty-four states controlled by Republican legislatures since 2014, antiunion laws, spearheaded by the conservative networks American Legislative Exchange Council (ALEC) and the State Policy Network (SPN), have eliminated collective bargaining rights and automatic dues checkoff for public employee unions. In 2018 the U.S. Supreme Court in *Janus v. AFSCME* ruled that public employees not belonging to unions do not have to pay fees for collective bargaining under so-called fair-share provisions. Yet 2018 also saw public school teachers in West Virginia, Kentucky, Oklahoma, Colorado, Arizona, and North Carolina conducting wildcat strikes and walkouts that to varying degrees successfully pressured their respective legislatures to increase teacher salaries and school funding. By early 2019, teachers in Los Angeles, Oakland, and Denver had already struck. For anyone pronouncing the strike tactic dead in the United

States, there were more strikes in 2018 than in the previous three decades, including unexpected strikes by fast-food workers.[93]

In 2019 the unorganized resistance and highly publicized misery of 800,000 federal workers furloughed or forced to work without pay helped force President Trump to back down after he had partially shut down the government from December 22, 2018, to January 25, 2019, over his demands for Congress to fund his border wall with Mexico. Transportation Security Administration agents had been calling in sick by the hundreds, with the rate rising to 10 percent of the workforce by January 20 (three times the percentage at the same time the previous year). Sick calls from air traffic controllers, especially in the Northeast, were decisive in forcing Trump to reopen the government. Unlike the 1970 postal strike, these sick-outs were apparently unplanned and uncoordinated. Meanwhile, hundreds of unionized federal workers along with pilots, flight attendants, and other unionized airline employees, demonstrated during the shutdown in Washington, D.C., Chicago, Boston, Dallas, Raleigh, and other cities.[94]

The crisis of the USPS is politically constructed, with a huge negative impact on its financial health. The roots of the crisis lie in the way the post office was reorganized after the 1970 strike. Since its 1971 origins, the USPS has wrestled with the contradiction of how to balance revenue and universal service in a competitive field. A financial crisis before the creation of the USPS would never have been existential because Congress was obligated to support the post office — and this crisis was imposed by Congress. Congressional oversight of the USPS shows no signs of going away — nor should it, as long as that oversight is fair. But congressional or executive-branch consideration for postal patrons/customers and workers has always been politically contingent. In addition, this stunning downsizing of a government service and its workforce was enabled by the USPS's semi-autonomy, its powerlessness in the face of congressional politics, and a prevailing ideology that regards universal service and well-paying, unionized postal jobs as problematic. "Congress should have fixed the prefunding problem back in 2009 or 2010," Steve Hutkins points out, "as soon as it became clear that the size of the payments was unmanageable in a recession. Unfortunately, privatization advocates in Congress (like Darrell Issa) wanted to use the crisis as justification for legislation designed to dismantle the Postal Service." We have a stalemate, Hutkins concludes, because "fortunately, there were others, Democrats and Republicans, who saw the value of having a vital public postal system."[95]

On November 11, 2014, the USPS announced that Postmaster General

Donahoe would be stepping down in February 2015, to be replaced by chief operating officer Megan Brennan, a former letter carrier from Lancaster, Pennsylvania, and the first woman to be appointed Postmaster General. A *Washington Post* article summed up part of Donahoe's legacy: "Donahoe oversaw aggressive cuts to the heavily unionized postal workforce . . . losing about 220,000 through attrition and buyouts. . . . He grew the agency's reliance on part-time and contract workers, who get lower pay and benefits than the career employees they replaced. He closed mail-plants and some post offices and reduced hours at thousands of others."[96] That same day it was reported that while the post office earned revenue of $569 million for FY 2014, it remained $5.5 billion in debt for that same period.[97]

Moreover, as a reminder that political stakes are high in filling vacancies on the eleven-member USPS Board of Governors (BOG), it has only *two* presidential appointees as of 2019 — in addition to the postmaster general and the deputy postmaster general, whom the BOG selects. The BOG has been shy of a quorum since 2014 and has been operating since then under a "Temporary Emergency Committee." Any senator can block a nominee with a "secret hold," and, ironically, Senator Bernie Sanders (I-Vt.), who has caucused with the Democratic Party, blocked several of President Obama's BOG candidates because of their support for job cuts and privatization.[98] The USPS cannot be abolished outright without a major overhaul in federal statutes, and there are still plenty of USPS mail products and services used on a daily basis, both domestically and internationally, that are crucial to the economy and social fabric of the country. The reality that the USPS handles 47 percent of the world's mail in a globalized age should give pause to any thought of trusting this public enterprise to private concerns.[99] The dominant American historical impulse instead has been to preserve the post office as a government agency that staffs trained, accountable employees (including the only civilian government employees most Americans see on a daily basis) whose labor is trusted to help make those global communications connections possible. Mark Jamison observes that Postmaster General Brennan's strategy lacked Postmaster General Donahoe's "fast and obvious service cutbacks" and instead "let things degrade at their own pace, allowing expectations to diminish."[100] But Brennan reappeared on the public radar in June 2019 when she issued preliminary proposals for a ten-year business plan. That plan would include devastating cuts in service, pensions, and paid leave while expanding the temporary workforce and resuming closure of mail-processing plants, contingent upon congressional approval.[101]

What does the future of the USPS look like? Will it continue to be a universal service that delivers the nation's mail, is accountable to both the general public and the federal government, and is provided proper stewardship by the government that safeguards contractual and traditional obligations to its workforce? This book began by asking how the 1970 strike happened, how it succeeded in reforming the post office, and how the reformed postal service became threatened in its fourth decade of reorganization. After the establishment of the USPS and the conclusion of the first contract negotiations, it settled into a new protocol with four postal unions. Collective bargaining had been a union demand long before the strike, along with higher wages, better benefits, and more control over working conditions. Collective bargaining, including a grievance system, had also been understood by both major political parties and the USPOD as a necessary replacement for postal-union lobbying of Congress. Over five mostly contentious decades, the USPS has treated postal unions as formidable adversaries and partners, which is to say, no worse than private-sector manufacturing has treated its unions. "The fact that labor costs actually increased after postal reorganization," concludes Vern Baxter, "demonstrates the contingent nature of change in social institutions. Organized labor has provided a consistent . . . alternative institutional vision that has profoundly influenced the process of change. Postal workers fought to establish and enforce bureaucratic mechanisms to classify jobs, cover training, reassignment, bidding on new positions, as well as wages and discipline." Baxter adds that postal unions have won their "share of battles in the political process of postal reorganization."[102] Today, 92 percent of the USPS workforce is covered by collective bargaining agreements in the nation's largest unionized workforce.[103]

In 2009, after briefly appearing to side with its unions following the onset of the postal financial crisis, the USPS joined with forces attempting to undercut union power, increase privatization, and slash unprofitable services. That was the kind of predicament feared by the workers who struck in 1970 for labor reform while resisting corporatization. The 2009 crisis of the USPS had its roots in the 1970 strike, subsequent postal reorganization, and postal labor–management clashes; as a manufactured crisis, it represented a political opportunity to downsize unionized government labor and the USPS itself. The 2009 postal financial crisis has threatened a permanent austerity regime in the USPS that is part of a general attack on public institutions. It is no accident that, with a notable increase in temporary employees to 130,000 in 2016 (about one-fifth of the workforce), the USPS Office of Inspector General found that year a "combined annual turnover rate for all four non-career crafts [at] 42.7 percent," with the cost of hiring replacements at $95.1 million. Exit interviews highlighted the main reasons for leaving: management abuse, scheduling inflexibility, inadequate training, low pay, and lack of benefits.[104] These are eerie echoes of the pre-strike era of postal worker grievances. What is *new* is the strong traction gained by a conservative narrative that declares postal service and postal workers obsolete and expendable — a narrative that ignores constitutional and congressional mandates as well as postal history. For all its contradictions, the post office is a dynamic institution that has grown with the nation and which in the future should be expected and allowed to meet changing habits and needs by combining and expanding hard-copy and digital communication services.[105] "The Internet was going to challenge the viability and composition of physical mail," Mark Jamison notes. "But somehow the USPS and Congress forgot what the USPS really was — infrastructure. . . . The idea of having an email address tied to a physical address, of voting by mail, of a shift towards electronic bill presentment and remittance while preserving the robust physical network would have sustained the Postal Service while addressing security, privacy, and monopoly issues on several fronts."[106] In 2016, the USPS Office of Inspector General cautioned that despite reducing labor costs "by over $10 billion during the last 9 years," the USPS "also reduced both its service quality and capital expenditures . . . that could undercut its long-term performance."[107]

The downsizing and threatened privatization of the USPS and its services has profound negative implications for American society that has long depended on it. There have also always been contradictions between the declared democratic purpose of the post office and the lack of democracy for its employees — between the visionary universal service and the bureaucratic government agency. The "business practice" of keeping labor costs low was a hallmark of the USPOD. Historical struggles over labor and service issues carried over from the USPOD to the USPS, where the government and corporate halves of a contentious hybrid have managed to coexist for fifty years. Today, the USPS as a threatened institution is the canary in the coal mine for American labor and government services.[108]

Half a century after the 1970 wildcat strike, we live in a time when ideological assumptions (neoliberal *and* conservative) have combined with historical amnesia to threaten to push public institutions like the post office and postal unions to the margins of our modern communications network.[109] But that strike in fact produced new paradigms in workplace organizing, especially in the public sector, with its continued service commitment.[110] For the first time in the history of federal government employee unions, a strike won full collective bargaining rights and a pay raise. Rank-and-file agitation in the NALC and the then-new APWU made them both stronger, more democratic unions, and better able to represent members in conflicts with postal management. The strike was something that suddenly empowered tens of thousands of postal workers who saw possibilities based on what other unionized workers were enjoying in the public and private sectors. In the end, the strikers did their best to force government and union leaders to negotiate in response to their demands. Rank-and-file postal workers have not enjoyed such power since.

It was, after all, rank-and-file strikers who seized the stage, so to speak, after their union leaders and congressional allies had struggled to stop the momentum of the Nixon-Rademacher compromise. That compromise had already eliminated the original 1969 "Dulski bill" that would have provided full collective-bargaining rights within a reformed USPOD rather than a corporatized government agency. Passage of Representative Thad Dulski's bill (H.R. 4) along with living wage increases might have even averted the 1970 strike. But collective bargaining for other federal employee unions besides the postal unions was not what Nixon had in mind. The PRA that created the new USPS was a compromise between Nixon and the postal unions, although it was still more of what Nixon wanted than the unions' preference for the USPOD to remain a protected government agency whose solvency and integrity would never be in doubt. Instead, the USPS would be self-supporting and semi-autonomous but continue to face congressional oversight. By 2009 the postal financial crisis would compel postal unions to begin to lobby and then mobilize to protect themselves and the USPS against political attacks. If Congress ever repeals prefunding and enacts postal reforms that reject privatization, it will largely be due to the combination of lobbying and public activism efforts by the NALC and APWU.

For eight days in March 1970, starting in New York, over 200,000 postal workers staged an illegal wildcat strike for better wages and working conditions. They defied court injunctions, threats of termination, and their own union leaders. In the negotiated aftermath, the U.S. Post Office became the U.S. Postal Service, and postal workers received full collective bargaining rights and wage increases while continuing to fight for greater democracy within their unions. Born of frustration and rising expectations, and part of a 1960s-1970s global rank-and-file labor upsurge, the strike transformed the post office and postal unions. It also led to fifty years of clashes between postal unions and management over wages, speedup, privatization, automation, and service. The current manufactured postal financial crisis threatens the future of a vital public communications institution as old as the republic itself. If this crisis ends with the replacement or radical revamping of the USPS, it could quite possibly end collective bargaining for the postal unions and deliver a historic blow to organized labor in the United States. Saving the USPS and its unions from an undelivered future will probably require a combination of union bargaining, political negotiation, public outcry, and especially rank-and-file militancy in the spirit of the 1970 postal wildcat strike.

The 1970 Postal Strike:
An Artist's Interpretation

Thomas Germano III

My interest in depicting labor subjects developed from my childhood environment. The Postal Service was the employer of my father, grandfather, uncle, and godfather, and even at the age of six, I listened attentively to the conversations in my home concerning the postal strike, in which my father was deeply involved. Twenty-five years later, I felt the desire to communicate visually the experience of the strike—the Great American Postal Strike of 1970.

My intention in making the *Great Postal Strike · 1970* painting was to present a montage of events that occurred through the course of the strike and its aftermath, using characters and places that, though based on real individuals and physical structures, took on universal meaning. In the painting are represented some of the major figures and key strike players in the New York area, but I consider these to be more than just portraits. They are symbols of those who supported the strike nationwide.

The central figure in the painting is Vincent Sombrotto, represented here as a rank-and-file letter carrier in uniform as he rejects the phantom return-to-work package from Postmaster General Winton Blount. Similarly, the physical setting of New York City depicts more than just that city, as important as it was in the strike. The building is the General Post Office, located

Note: Thomas Germano is a full professor of art and art history at Farmingdale State College–SUNY and also teaches a graduate seminar at the New York Academy of Art in New York City. Article and reproduction reprinted with permission from author and the University of Maryland. Originally published in *Labor's Heritage* 7, no. 4 (Spring 1996): 18–19.

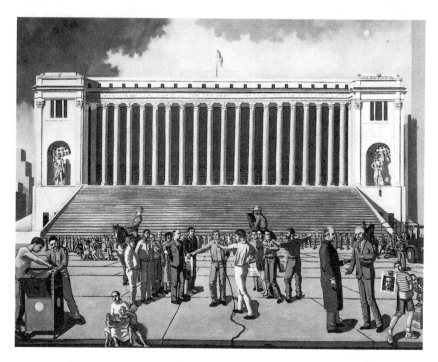

Thomas Germano III, *The Great Postal Strike • 1970*, oil on canvas,
66 x 52 in., 1995. Reproduction courtesy of the artist.

on Eighth Avenue at 33rd Street in New York, but I see this building, with
its imposing Greek revivalist neo-classical style, as an icon of the postal service in general.

One of the two large figures in the front foreground represents a worried
Gus Johnson holding the vote tally that indicates the decision of Branch 36
of the National Association of Letter Carriers (NALC) to go out on strike.
Johnson, president Branch 36, converses with Moe Biller, who is president
of the New York City clerks' union. Biller stands firm and offers the support
of his union to honor the letter carriers' picket lines. A third union official,
Jack Leventhal, president of NALC Brooklyn Branch 41, is shown leaning
into the composition to pick up a copy of the *New York Daily News* with
President Richard Nixon's portrait on the cover; Nixon is announcing the
use of United States troops to move the mail. Leventhal's key support helped
cripple the city's mail service, which made the strike effective.

Members of the National Guard are shown arriving at the General Post
Office in the rear right. In the left background, a picketing letter carrier ex-
pels a group of radical students, members of Students for a Democratic So-

ciety (SDS). The letter carriers refused the support of special interest groups so as not to distort the motives behind the strike.

In the left foreground, my father, Thomas J. Germano, is writing on top of a locked letter box. Germano, who was a letter carrier and chief organizer of the strike's activities at the General Post Office, also documented much of the strike activity, history, and its later repercussions in *Delivering the Dream*. I have represented my father as the poet and an architect of the strike.

The family group, consisting of a distraught mother and crying children, symbolizes the impoverished salaries that made many of the New York City postal employees eligible for welfare. The family represents despair and just cause for asking for a decent living wage for postal employees. That is why members of the Letter Carriers are picketing at the base of the stairs of the post office. The post office contains a quote on its façade reading "Neither snow, nor rain, nor heat, nor gloom of night stays these couriers from the swift completion of their appointed rounds." Throughout the painting I have represented the many means by which those rounds were accomplished, by horse, truck, and plane. The quote, however, appears as an irony because here the mail was stopped, not by weather or darkness, but by postal workers' quest for dignity and fairness.

Two invented allegorical figures appear in the niches of the General Post Office. They represent *Virtue* and *Victory*—two important concepts which I have always associated with the justice of the Postal Strike. The mounted police officers represent the impending threat to imprison striking government employees and the organizers of the walkout. Elected union officials were banned from picketing, which resulted in the rise of a rank-and-file labor movement that produced new leaders who were elected to office, first at the local, then the national level.

ACKNOWLEDGMENTS

I could not have written this book without people who shared their stories, sources, information, support, and guidance. They helped bring this story to life, and I was lucky enough to be able to interview dozens of those involved in the strike, the vast majority of whom remained active in their respective unions. Every one of them told me their story for a reason, and I tried to make sure that I mentioned every one by name at least once. Ultimately it was because of them that I decided I had to write this book. A big shout-out is also due (again!) to all my former coworkers at the post offices where I worked in Denver and Lakewood, Colorado, and Raleigh and Durham, North Carolina, from 1980 to 2000 (nine months as a clerk and almost twenty years as a letter carrier). I also owe great debts of gratitude to scholars of the post office and postal labor who never failed to answer my questions quickly and on point. Tom Germano, Jeff Perry, Lowell Turner, Richard Kielbowicz, Steve Hutkins, Mark Jamison, and Patricia Williams all provided me with background history, analysis, suggestions, and resources. Tom Germano, Steve Hutkins, Mark Jamison, Gordon Mantler, Victor Devinatz, Craig Phelan, and Jeff Perry also offered invaluable critiques of manuscript drafts. Tom spent the equivalent of an eight-hour shift plus overtime going over it on the phone, and his son Thomas J. Germano III provided the iconic cover art. Jennifer Lynch, USPS historian, has been an indispensable source of advice, answers, and resources, as was Meg Ausman before her. Vital assistance was rendered by the National Association of Letter Carriers (NALC) national office, especially staff historian Nancy Dysart, chief of staff Jim Sauber, *Postal Record* editors Philip Dine and Michael Shea, and editorial assistant Jenessa Kildall. Valuable help also came from the American Postal Workers Union (APWU), its late president William Burrus, retired communications director Sally Davidow, current communications director Emily Harris, and digital communications specialist Ashley See. Important resources also came from NALC local activists Mike Mazurkiewicz (Minnesota), Kathy Rubly (California), Paul Daniels (Connecticut) and Matty

Rose (Florida). NALC president Fred Rolando generously allowed me to interview strike veterans at their 2014 biennial convention in Philadelphia, and put me in touch with many more, as did the APWU national office. Archivists and librarians at Duke University, New York University's Tamiment Library and Robert F. Wagner Labor Archives (particular thanks to Michael Koncewicz!), North Carolina A&T State University, the USPS Library and Archives, the Smithsonian Institution National Postal Museum and Library (particular thanks to Nancy Pope and Bill Lommel), the U.S. Department of Labor's Wirtz Labor Library, Georgia State University, Emory University, the University of Maryland, the Hennepin County Library in Minneapolis, and New York Metro Area Postal Union, helped me find what I needed to tell the fullest and most accurate story possible, including amazing photographs. Independent researcher Scott Russell found and copied for me some amazing documents from the Nixon Presidential Library and Museum, where archivists Jason Schultz and Dorissa Martinez were always quick to respond with suggestions. Filmmakers Greg Poferl and Ann Sutherland were helpful sharing their resources and documentary works, and Denver Branch 47 NALC (one of my former branches) provided me with a DVD of interviews they did with strikers.

So many people like those I've listed not only steered me to what I needed to read, but also helped me make sense of postal matters. The late Jimmy Mainor—the first African American elected president of Durham, North Carolina, NALC Branch 382 (also my former branch) generously appeared with me on radio talk shows during the postal financial crisis, and helped bring me up to speed on what was driving that crisis. My editor, Chuck Grench, with the patience of Job, gave me the guidelines I needed to get the job done, assisted by Jay Mazzocchi, Dylan White, Jessica Newman, Cate Hodorowicz, and everyone else at UNC Press, including the two outside readers and their enormously useful comments and suggestions and copyeditor Matthew Somoroff. I am also indebted to the History and Political Science department as well as the College of Arts, Humanities, and Social Sciences at North Carolina A&T State University for providing some financial support for the research and writing of this book, my colleagues for their encouragement, and my students, who keep asking questions and reminding me why I do this. My family and friends never failed to offer encouragement. Finally, my wife, Paula, gave me crucial feedback, help with editing, and moral support. For that, I can never thank her enough.

NOTES

ABBREVIATIONS

APWU   American Postal Workers Union
LIUNA   Laborers' International Union of North America
NALC   National Association of Letter Carriers (NALC)
NAPFE (NAPE)   National Alliance of Postal and Federal Employees/
  National Alliance of Postal Employees
NAPOGSME   National Association of Post Office and
  General Services Maintenance Employees
NAPOMVE   National Association of Post Office
  Motor Vehicle Employees
NASDM   National Association of Special Delivery Messengers
NFPOC   National Federation of Post Office Clerks
NPLM   Nixon Presidential Library and Museum
NPMHU   National Postal Mail Handlers Union
NPU   National Postal Union
NRLCA   National Rural Letter Carriers' Association
NYMAPU   New York Metro Area Postal Union
NYT   *New York Times*
PR   *Postal Record*
PRA   Postal Reorganization Act
SFC   *San Francisco Chronicle*
SLA   Southern Labor Archives
TWA   Tamiment/Wagner Archives
UFPC   United Federation of Postal Clerks
USPOD   United States Post Office Department
USPS   United States Postal Service
WP   *Washington Post*
WWL   Willard Wirtz Library
WPRL   Walter P. Reuther Library

1. Mikusko and Miller, *Carriers in a Common Cause*, 72; and author's interview with Sombrotto, Orapello, and Marino.

2. Germano, "Labor Relations," 184. See also extensive author telephone conversations with Germano, June 20–22, 2018, for which I am extremely grateful. Since 1976 Tom Germano has been extensively involved in the field of industrial and labor relations. He has been a mediator, arbitrator, labor studies professor, and program director and has conducted over 2,000 public hearings in both the public and private sectors.

3. Germano, "Labor Relations," 145.

4. See USPOD, Status Report, March 24, 1970, 12:00 P.M., and Summary Report, March 24, 1970, 5:00 P.M.

5. Nixon, "Remarks on Signing the Postal Reorganization Act, August 12, 1970," from *The American Presidency Project*, http://www.presidency.ucsb.edu/ws/?pid=2623. This useful website has other Nixon proclamations on the post office, including a 1969 official visit to postal headquarters to "lobby" for postal reform. From 1969 until the 1970 signing ceremony, Nixon made at least eight public proclamations on postal reform. See also Mikusko and Miller, *Carriers in a Common Cause*, 73.

6. Postal Reorganization Act, *Statutes at Large* 84; and U.S. Postal Service, *United States Postal Service*, 40 (quote), 39–40, 52, https://about.usps.com/publications/pub100.pdf.

7. Mikusko and Miller, *Carriers in a Common Cause*, 131.

8. Mikusko and Miller, *Carriers in a Common Cause*.

9. USPS, *FY 2017 Annual Report to Congress*, 2. See also Rubio, "Organizing a Wildcat"; Office of the Inspector General, "Be Careful What You Assume"; and Mikusko and Miller, *Carriers in a Common Cause*, 126–29.

10. Winslow, "Overview: The Rebellion from Below," 1.

11. Winslow, "Overview: The Rebellion from Below," 1, 2–3, 10–11, quotes on 2 and 3, respectively. See also Lichtenstein, *State of the Union*, 186; and Zieger and Gall, *American Workers, American Unions*, 230–39.

12. McCartin, "'Wagner Act for Public Employees,'" 123–48, quote on 123.

13. See for example Lewis, *Hard Hats, Hippies, and Hawks*; and Joshua Freeman, *Working-Class New York*, chap. 14.

14. See Shaw, *Preserving the People's' Post Office*; Mikusko and Miller, *Carriers in a Common Cause*; Walsh and Mangum, *Labor Struggle in the Post Office*; Germano, "Labor Relations"; Conkey, *Postal Precipice*; Leonard, *Neither Snow nor Rain*; Baxter, *Labor and Politics*; McGee, *Negro in the Chicago Post Office*; Tennassee, *History of the National Alliance*; and Tierney, *Postal Reorganization*.

15. Baxter, *Labor and Politics*, chap. 6, quote on 101.

16. See President's Commission on Postal Organization, *Towards Postal Excellence*; and the Postal Reorganization Act. See also Baxter, *Labor and Politics*, chaps. 5–6 (quote on 95), 226–27; *Postal Accountability and Enhancement Act* (2006), https://www.govtrack.us/congress/bills/109/hr6407/text; Mark Jamison, "By Default or Design"; and USPS website, http://about.usps.com/news/national-releases/2014/pr14_031.htm, where they note a 2014 fiscal-year second-quarter loss of $1.9 billion, a $379 million revenue gain, and an inability to pay the September 2014 retiree health benefit prefunding annual installment, along with a regular feature on their website called "USPS Sets the Record

Straight," rebutting claims of privatization, among other things: http://about.usps.com/news/electronic-press-kits/usps-sets-the-record-straight/.

17. Besides the works mentioned, see Brodie, "Revolution by Mail"; and Germano, "Labor Relations." The official history of the National Rural Letter Carriers Association is by former NRLCA president Lester F. Miller, *National Rural Letter Carriers Association*. Labor historian Greg Geibel is reported to be working on a history of the NPMHU. See the *Mail Handler* Special Convention Issue, 2012, http://www.npmhu.org/media/magazine/body/13342_MHSmr12_low-res.pdf. The NPMHU did not respond to my telephone and email requests to interview staff and research documents at their Washington, D.C. national headquarters (April 9, 2016). See also the NPMHU website at https://www.npmhu.org/.

18. U.S. Postal Service, *United States Postal Service*.

19. Windham, *Knocking on Labor's Door*, 3.

20. Windham, "Author's Response," 102, part of a larger debate in the journal issue's "Bookmark" section, 77–106. See also Cowie, *Stayin' Alive*.

21. Fletcher and Gapasin, *Solidarity Divided*, quotes on 59 and 94, respectively. The authors are describing features embedded in neoliberal ideology.

22. See Germano, "Labor Relations"; Freeman, *Working-Class New York*, 249; Winslow, "Overview: The Rebellion from Below," 10–11; and Brenner, "Rank-and-File Rebellion," chap. 3, 112–46.

23. Germano, "Labor Relations," 7, 452, with quote on v; and email to author, May 20, 2015. See also monthly journal editions of the *American Postal Worker* (APWU) and the *Postal Record* (NALC) from 1971 to present, increasingly devoted to issues of domestic and global labor rights campaigns in addition to union and postal business in the last decade. Thanks to Emily Harris and Ashley See for sharing recent copies of the APWU journal. The NALC's *Postal Record* is available online going back eight years.

24. Brenner, "Rank-and-File Rebellion," 112–46.

25. Rubio, *There's Always Work*, chap. 10.

26. Some references to the strike are contained within larger studies: see Loewenberg, "Post Office Strike of 1970"; and Halpern, *Unions, Radicals, and Democratic Presidents*, chap. 5. See also Rubio, "Organizing a Wildcat"; Stephen Shannon, "Work Stoppage in Government," 14–22; Zieger and Gall, *American Workers, American Unions*, 211–12; Brecher, *Strike!*, 258–60; and Aronowitz and Brecher, "Notes on the Postal Strike," 1–5.

27. Fine, *Sit Down*.

28. See for example Hill, *Black Labor*; Fletcher and Gapasin, *Solidarity Divided*; Brenner et al., *Rebel Rank and File*; Halpern, *Unions, Radicals, and Democratic Presidents*, chap. 8; Rubio, *There's Always Work*; and Rubio, *History of Affirmative Action*, chaps. 4–6. On Taft-Hartley, see Labor Management Relations Act; and Zieger and Gall, *American Workers, American Unions*, 52–59. "Closed shops" required workers to join the union before hiring, while "union shops" required workers to join the union after being hired.

29. In 2019 a Google search of the term "Great Postal Strike" on the first page finds use of it by those organizations going back at least to 1994. See also Germano, "Labor Relations," for use of that term in 1983.

1. Author's interview with Sombrotto, Orapello, and Marino. Quote is verbatim.

2. Baxter, *Labor and Politics*, 68; Brenner, "Striking Against the State," 6–8 (quote on 6–7); Germano, "Labor Relations," 43–44, 133–34; and Mikusko and Miller, *Carriers in a Common Cause*, 61–62.

3. Baxter, *Labor and Politics*, 68; Brenner, "Striking Against the State," 6–8.

4. See EO 10988 (1962).

5. See for example Rubio, *There's Always Work*, 154, for 1961 congressional criticisms of postal working conditions.

6. Rubio, *There's Always Work*, chap. 6. See also Mikusko and Miller, *Carriers in a Common Cause*; and Walsh and Mangum, *Labor Struggle*.

7. McCartin, *Collision Course*, 33.

8. Rich, *The History of the United States Post Office*, 42; USPS, *The United States Postal Service*, 7–11.

9. John, *Spreading the News*, chaps. 1–2; and USPS, *The United States Postal Service*, 7.

10. Brodie, "A Revolution by Mail," 3, 41 (quote on 3).

11. See John, *Spreading the News*, 3–6. Quote is from *Statutes at Large* 1: 354, sec. 28.

12. John, *Spreading the News*, 3–6, quote on 6. Unofficially housed in the executive branch, the post office in 1872 became officially part of that branch. See also Mikusko and Miller, *Carriers in a Common Cause*, 2–3.

13. U.S. Postal Service, *United States Postal Service*, 15–16.

14. Mikusko and Miller, *Carriers in a Common Cause*, 4. See also U.S. Postal Service, *United States Postal Service*, 11; and Olds, "Public Service and Privatization," 13, on postmasters and clerks.

15. Mikusko and Miller, *Carriers in a Common Cause*, 4. See also USPS Historian, "Delivery: Monday through Saturday Since 1863," June 2009, http://about.usps.com/who -we-are/postal-history/delivery-monday-through-saturday.pdf; and U.S. Postal Service, *United States Postal Service*, 20, which included the 1862 *Annual Report* reference. See also *Statutes at Large* 12, chap. 71, 701–9. Postal salary reference is from sec. 11, 703; and the quote and other reform examples are from sec. 13, 703–4 of that statute. See also Briggs, Joseph W., entry, *Encyclopedia of Cleveland History*, http://ech.case.edu/cgi/article.pl?id =BJW.

16. Baxter, *Labor and Politics*, 225.

17. See Mikusko and Miller, *Carriers in a Common Cause*, 4, 9–10. See also Gannon, *Won Cause*.

18. See Mikusko, *Carriers in a Common Cause*, 31, 64–65; and Spero, *Government as Employer*, chap. 7. On African Americans and the GAR, see Gannon, *Won Cause*. See also McConnell, *Glorious Contention*; Dearing, *Veterans in Politics*; and a synopsis of the GAR on the website of the Sons of Union Veterans of the Civil War, http://www.suvcw.org/gar .htm.

19. See Mikusko and Miller, *Carriers in a Common Cause*, 13; and Rubio, *There's Always Work*, chap. 1.

20. U.S. Postal Service, *United States Postal Service*, 15; and Nancy Pope, "150th Anniversary of Railway Mail Service," August 28, 2014, http://postalmuseumblog.si.edu /railway-post-office/.

21. Baxter, *Labor and Politics*, chap. 3.

22. Rubio, *There's Always Work*, 27–33.

23. *See Statutes at Large* 1, chap. 48, sec. 4, 1802; and Litwack, *North of Slavery*, 57.

24. See Rubio, *There's Always Work*, chap. 1.

25. See also Van Riper, *History of the United States Civil Service*, 162, who notes: "There are no figures showing the precise extent to which veterans came into the public service before 1900." See also Lynch, "African-American Postal Workers"; and Boyd and Chen, "History and Experience."

26. See, for example, Glenn, *History of the National Alliance*, 348; Litwack, Trouble in Mind, 161–62; and Rubio, *There's Always Work*, chap. 1.

27. See Bennett, *Shaping of Black America*, 259–64; and Harris, *Harder We Run*, 25–26.

28. Baarslag, *History of the NFPOC*, 18; and "APWU History."

29. Baxter, *Labor and Politics*, 58–61; "APWU History"; and Walsh and Mangum, *Labor Struggle*.

30. Franklin and Moss, *From Slavery to Freedom*, 432. See also van Riper, *History of the United States Civil Service*, 104.

31. See also Logan, *Betrayal of the Negro*; and *The Negro in American Life and Thought*. On the origins of the Civil Service (with its roots in 1871 in the administration of President Ulysses S. Grant, 1869–1877), its built-in inequality, its adoption by states and municipalities after the 1883 Civil Service Act, and the importance of the term "merit" to the act's passage, see Gottfried, *Merit System*, chap. 5, esp. p. 7.

32. See USPS Historian, "African-American Postal Workers in the 20th Century," https://about.usps.com/who-we-are/postal-history/african-american-workers-20thc .htm. See also Tennassee, *History of the National Alliance*; APWU website, https://www .apwu.org; and Harris, *Harder We Run*, chap. 2.

33. Glenn, *History of the National Alliance*, chap. 1; and Paul Tennassee, "NAPFE: A Legacy of Resistance and Contributions 1913–1999," *National Alliance*, October 1999," 12.

34. See Glenn, *History of the National Alliance*, 17, 20. Glenn's history includes not just his narrative but also verbatim reprints of selected articles from the *Postal Alliance*, official documents, and union correspondence.

35. Paul Nehru Tennassee, "Research and Education Corner: Individuals to Remember: James Foster Spencer, Henry T. Ellington, Ernest M. Thomas, Henry Lincoln Johnson," *National Alliance*, June 1999, 12.

36. See for example Ortiz, *Emancipation Betrayed*, 174.

37. Rubio, *There's Always Work*.

38. Glenn, *History of the National Alliance*, chap. 5. See also Bates, *Pullman Porters*, 36–41, 126; and Paul Tennassee, "Governance, The House of Labor and Black Nationalism: A Review," *National Alliance*, March 2001, 24. Many NAPE (NAPFE) officers like President James B. Cobb held degrees from Howard University.

39. Author's telephone interview with Castilla.

40. Dittmer, *Local People*, 20, 30, 42, and 229. See also Glenn, *History of the National Alliance*, 295; George Bell, "Mississippi," *PR*, September 1941, 412; and Convention proceedings, *PR*, October 1941, 567.

41. National Urban League, *Negro Membership*. See also Ortiz, *Emancipation Betrayed*, esp. 173.

42. See Rubio, *There's Always Work*, chap. 1.

43. Mikusko and Miller, *Carriers in a Common Cause*, 28–30.

44. See Rubio, *There's Always Work*. See also author's telephone conversations with Germano for his recollections of meeting black southern NALC members who regretted losing their black branches despite Jim Crow.

45. Cushing, *Story of Our Post Office*. I am indebted to Jennifer Lynch for referring me to this source. Paraphrase and quote are from pages 15 and 18, respectively; and reference to employee table is from page 11. (Cushing's source is *"The Blue Book* by Dr. John G. Ames.") Photo of Cincinnati Post Office found on p. 176. The information on mail handlers is also from Jennifer Lynch, taken from the *Annual Report* in 1944. Email to author, August 6, 2015.

46. U.S. Postal Service, *United States Postal Service*, 22–25; and Miller, *National Rural Letter Carriers' Association*, chap. 1.

47. U.S. Postal Service, *United States Postal Service*, 24; and Miller, *National Rural Letter Carriers' Association*, 30.

48. See John, *Spreading the News*; Kielbowicz, *News in the Mail*; and Henkin, *Postal Age*. See also U.S. Postal Service, *United States Postal Service*, 6–11 (quote on 7).

49. Kielbowicz, "Postal Enterprise," chaps. 2 and 3. I am indebted to Richard Kielbowicz for this comprehensive postal background history.

50. Rubio, *There's Always Work*, chap. 1; and Germano, "Labor Relations," chap. 1.

51. On speedup, the gag order, and the Lloyd–La Follette Act, see Walsh and Mangum, *Labor Struggle*, 75–77. On RMA exclusion, see Tennessee, "NAPFE: A Legacy," 12.

52. Merit Systems Protection Board, http://www.mspb.gov/mspm.htm. See also Mikusko and Miller, *Carriers in a Common Cause*, 21–24.

53. See Wolgemuth, "Woodrow Wilson and Federal Segregation," esp. 162–65; Weiss, "Negro and the New Freedom"; Meier and Rudwick, "The Rise of Segregation," 178–84; Logan, *Betrayal of the Negro*, chap. 17; Lewis, *W. E. B. Du Bois: Biography of a Race*, 423–24; and Litwack, *Trouble in Mind*, 373. See also Du Bois, from his "Another Open Letter to Woodrow Wilson" (from the September 1913 *Crisis*) protesting cages built to segregate black work workers within white areas when work areas could not be separated due to the nature of the work. Reprinted in Lewis, ed., *W. E. B. Du Bois: A Reader*, 446. Henry W. McGee has pointed to the demands by white Southern congressmen for Wilson to declare such an order after they had failed to pass similar legislation, in *The Negro in the Chicago Post Office*, 9–10, 25. See also Fox, *Guardian of Boston*, 168–86; and Marius, *A Short Guide to Writing about History*, 105–28.

54. See Wolgemuth, "Woodrow Wilson and Federal Segregation," esp. 159–61; Weiss, "Negro and the New Freedom"; Meier and Rudwick, "The Rise of Segregation"; and Rubio, *There's Always Work*, chap. 1. Photo applications were abolished in 1940.

55. "Extracts from the Postmaster General's Report for the Fiscal Year Ending June 30, 1919," published in the *Postal Record*, January 1920, 2.

56. *PR*, January 1920.

57. *PR*, January 1920, 5.

58. *PR*, January 1920, 1.

59. *PR*, January 1920, 2.

60. Mikusko and Miller, *Carriers in a Common Cause*, 26–31.

61. See Walsh and Mangum, *Labor Struggle*, 83–85; Germano, "Labor Relations," 34–35; Mikusko and Miller, *Carriers in a Common Cause*, 38–39; Baarslag, *History of the National*

Federation, 182–83; and Office of the USPS Historian, "James A. Farley," https://about.usps
.com/who-we-are/postal-history/pmg-farley.pdf.

62. See APWU, Brooklyn NFPOC Local 251 Minutes, 1918–1977, reel 1. The left-wing
political tone of Local 251 meetings progressively advanced beginning in the early 1930s.
See also Baarslag, *History of the National Federation*, 184–86. Baarslag considered himself
an "expert" on communism.

63. Schrecker, *Many Are the Crimes*, 95, 110, 119, 209, and 284. Quote on 95.

64. See Biondi, *To Stand and Fight*; and Freeman, *Working-Class New York*. See also
author's interview with Bailey, Tilley, Flagler, Wilson, and John.

65. "Staten Island Withdraws; Suspended By Pres. House" *Progressive Fed*, October
1958, 1; Herman Berlowe, "House Suspends 8 Prog-Fed Locals," *Progressive Fed*,
November-December 1958, 1; Herman Berlowe, "Secession Move Spreads; Feds Flock
to New Locals," *Progressive Fed*, January 1959, 1; and "Hail New Union!," *Progressive*,
February 1959, 1; all from Box 81, NYMAPU, TWA. Members of the breakaway union that
became the NPCU and later the NPU kept the "Progressive Fed" name on their interim
newspaper dating from when they had been an insurgent force within the NFPOC.
In February 1959 they dropped the "Fed" and called their new union newspaper the
Progressive.

66. Berlowe, "NPCU Adopts Constitution; 115 Locals Join in 90 Days," *Progressive*, May
1959, 1, NYMAPU, TWA. Under NFPOC rules, no local—even the 10,000-member New
York City local—could have more than ten delegates to a national convention. See Walsh
and Mangum, *Labor Struggle*, 63, 67. See also interview by author with former Detroit
Postal Union president Douglas C. Holbrook, then APWU Director of Retirees.

67. See "Meany Attacks Union Dualism," *Federation Digest*, February 1959, 1; and
"Security Risks Swaying Dual Union Leadership," *Federation Digest*, April 1959, 1; Box
81, NYMAPU. See esp. the *Progressive*, September 1959, including "Full Text of Noreen
Case Debate on Senate Floor," 2, over the post office's removal of Walter Noreen, NPU
first vice-president, who had protested the post office's hiring part-time Christmas help
from among those with full-time jobs elsewhere. Noreen was defended by Sen. Hubert
Humphrey (D-Minn.), but viciously attacked by Sen. Everett Dirksen (R-Ill.), who called
the NPU "a national independent union composed of extreme leftwing elements." Noreen
was later reinstated. See author's telephone interview with Moore.

68. These included the NALC, the NPU, the NPMHU, the NAPFE, the UFPC,
the NAPOGSME, the NASDM, the NRLCA, and the NAPOMVE. See President's
Commission on Postal Organization, *Towards Postal Excellence*, 19.

69. Rubio, *There's Always Work*, chaps. 6–9. See also Gill, "The Future of Executive
Order 11491," 372–78; and W. J. Usery Jr. in an interview conducted by Les Hough, March
15–16, 1990, Washington, D.C. L1985-12_AV0111, SLA. I am indebted to GSU archivist
Traci Drummond for access to this document.

70. Author's interview with Sombrotto, Orapello, and Marino.

71. Rubio, *There's Always Work*, chap. 6.

72. The section quoted was titled "Collective Bargaining." See "Post Office Department
New York Region Orientation of Postmasters to Union Recognition: The Purposes and
Objectives of the Conference," [n.d. but probably late 1962; unsigned, but probably from
New York City Postmaster Robert Christenberry], Box 3, Folder "10988," NYMAPU
collection. See also EO 10988; and Rhodes-Johnston bill. Rhodes-Johnston's "collective

bargaining" powers were also limited by the strike ban on all federal employees. See also the contract language that evokes collective bargaining without ever using the term in the first *Agreement between United States Post Office Department* and the six national "exclusives" during that time (April 1, 1963–March 31, 1964): the NALC, NAPOGSME, NASDM, NAFPOMVE, NRLCA, and UFPC, Folder "Unions: Agreements," USPS Historian. The NPMHU first won national exclusive recognition for its craft in 1964 (previously it had "formal" status). See Rhodes-Johnston bill (U.S. Congress, S. 473, *Recognition of Federal Employee Unions*), 1961.

73. EO 10988, Sec. 6 (b).

74. See Rubio, *There's Always Work*, chaps. 6–9; and a history of the American Federation of Government Employees (AFGE), at their website, http://www.afge.org.

75. One of few labor historians to note this important feature of EO 10988 is Paul Nehru Tennassee, "NAPFE Battles for Union Recognition 1945–1965," *National Alliance*, September 2001, 13.

76. EO 10988, Sec. 2 (3) (italics added).

77. See Rhodes-Johnston bill, esp. Title II, Section 310 (d). Johnston and Humphrey's silence on civil rights during this bill's presentation came during a year where civil rights was frequently debated on the floor of Congress. Emphasis added. Humphrey also noted in his remarks that federal workers did not and should not have the right to strike, and this bill would not alter that fact. See debate in U.S. Congress, Recognition of Federal Employee Unions bill: 863–65.

78. See "Hear Ye! Hear Ye!," *New York Alliance Leader*, Nov.–Dec. 1958, 4.; and "Fed Briefs," *Progressive Fed*, January 1959, 2. According to Herbert Northrup's 1943 study, the constitution of the National Rural Letter Carriers Association (NRLCA) only allowed blacks to belong to segregated locals. See Foner and Lewis, *Black Worker*, 471–72. The NRLCA constitution quoted in Tennassee, "Perspectives on African American History," 34.

79. See APWU website, http://www.apwu.org.

80. "NRLCA Signs First Agreement under Labor-Management Program," *National Rural Letter Carrier*, July 21, 1962, 439.

81. See "Policy on Employee-Management Cooperation," *National Rural Letter Carrier*, February 10, 1962, 90–93; and "Rural Letter Carriers Will Ballot," *National Rural Letter Carrier*, April 7, 1962. See also "NRLCA Signs First Agreement Under Labor-Management Program," *National Rural Letter Carrier*, July 21, 1962, 439. See also Miller, *National Rural Letter Carriers' Association*.

82. "Task Force Says 84% of Postal Employees Are in Unions," *Progressive*, December 1961, 4. This refers to "President Kennedy's Task Force Report." See also figures compiled by the President's Commission on Postal Organization, *Towards Postal Excellence*, 18–19.

83. Rubio, *There's Always Work*, chaps. 6–9, esp. 154, for 1961 congressional criticisms of postal working conditions. See also Brenner, "Striking Against the State."

84. "Editor's Notebook," *Postal Alliance*, December 1963, 4.

85. See Walsh and Mangum, *Labor Struggle*, 69.

86. See author's interview with Moore.

87. "Dictation by David Silvergleid-February 8, 1961," Box 61, Folder "Merger Joint Letter 1961," NYMAPU, TWA. See earlier talks in June 1960 between the NALC and MBPU, and January 1961 as well, with the Alliance observing, as they did in February of that year. In Box 61, Folder "Merger Joint Letter 1961," NYMAPU, TWA.

88. See "New York Postal Workers in Orderly Visual Demonstration for Pay Increase," Metropolitan Postal Council News Release, March 5, 1964, Box 54, Folder "MPC Outdoor Demo," NYMAPU collection. See April 19, 1952, edition of the *Progressive Fed* monthly national newsletter (produced in New York City by NFPOC Local 10). See also "NYC Letter Carriers Win Fight for Assignments," *Progressive*, April 19, 1952, 2.

89. "All PO Unions Rally in Brooklyn," *Progressive*, May 1965, 1.

90. See for example "Case for One Union," *Progressive*, November 1961, 2; and "Merger — One Union a Must," *Washington Area Postal Employees*, 5.

91. See "Editor's Notebook," *Postal Alliance*, June 1963, 4; "3 Promotions in Dallas Texas Causes Stir," in *Postal Alliance*, June 1963, 10; Tennessee, "NAPFE: A Legacy," 14; L. H. Moses Jr., "Report on Hearing," 41, and "Postal Promotions Rescinded," 58, in *Washington Area Postal Employee*, December 1963.

92. See "Alliance Pickets March in Support of Equal Opportunities," *Postal Alliance*, August 1963, 22; and Ashby G. Smith, "Address to Convention," *New York Alliance Leader*, Sept.-Oct. 1963, 1.

93. See "Alliance Pickets 'Fed' Rally," *Washington Reports*, Aug. 2, 1963, Box 71 (A-15), Folder NPU and NPCU misc. bulletins and leaflets, 1959–1963, NYMAPU collection.

94. See Lorraine Huston, "Comments from Cleveland," *Postal Alliance*, December 1963, 15; Joe Wachtman, "Broadside Accuses Postal Union of Bias," *Postal Alliance*, February 1962, 13, reprinted from the *Baltimore News-Post*, February 1, 1962; and Ashby G. Smith, "No Time for Myths," *Postal Alliance*, October 1963, 17.

95. Paul Tennassee, "The Smith Presidency Part IV," *National Alliance*, May 2002, 16–17.

96. President Kennedy's "affirmative action" executive order EO 10925 (1961) first mandated federal agencies to develop studies and recommendations for equal employment opportunities. The Civil Service and Post Office set up affirmative action EEO committees. Title VII of the 1964 Civil Rights Act established the EEOC for private-sector employees only. Federal workers used their respective agencies' EEOs until the 1972 Employment Opportunity Act allowed federal workers to use both the EEOC and the courts for discrimination complaints. See Tennassee, "NAPFE: A Legacy," 14; and EO 10925. See also "Publication 133 — What You Need to Know About EEO," October 2012, USPS, https://about.usps.com/publications/pub133/welcome.htm.

97. See author's interview with Morris.

98. Author's interview with Thomas and Perry. On black caucuses in auto and steel, respectively, see Georgakas and Surkin, *Detroit: I Do Mind Dying*; and Needleman, *Black Freedom Fighters in Steel*.

99. See President's Commission on Postal Organization, *Towards Postal Excellence*. Besides Kappel, the Commission included the dean of the Harvard Graduate School of Business Administration, along with executives from the Ford Foundation, General Electric, Federated Department Stores, Cummin Engine Company, Campbell Soup, Bank of America, and the law office of Ginsburg and Feldman.

100. See President's Commission on Postal Organization, *Towards Postal Excellence*. See also Kielbowicz, "Postal Enterprise"; Rubio, *There's Always Work*, chap. 9; and McGee, *Negro in the Chicago Post Office*.

101. President's Commission on Postal Organization, *Towards Postal Excellence*, quotation taken from 1, italics original.

102. President's Commission on Postal Organization, *Towards Postal Excellence*, vi-vii.

103. President's Commission on Postal Organization, *Towards Postal Excellence*, 33.

104. President's Commission on Postal Organization, *Towards Postal Excellence*, 16.

105. President's Commission on Postal Organization, *Towards Postal Excellence*, 33.

106. President's Commission on Postal Organization, *Towards Postal Excellence*, viii.

107. President's Commission on Postal Organization, *Towards Postal Excellence*, 35.

108. Kielbowicz, "Postal Enterprise," 66.

109. Kielbowicz, "Postal Enterprise, 66.

110. President's Commission on Postal Organization, *Towards Postal Excellence*.

111. Conkey, *Postal Precipice*, 38.

112. Conkey, *Postal Precipice*, 39.

113. Conkey, *Postal Precipice*, 40.

114. Conkey, *Postal Precipice*, 40.

115. Conkey, *Postal Precipice*, 44–45.

116. Conkey, *Postal Precipice*, 44–45.

117. Conkey, *Postal Precipice*, 54.

118. Fleishman, "Postal Policy and Public Accountability," 27. I am indebted to Mark Jamison for this reference.

119. Fleishman, "Postal Policy and Public Accountability," 27.

120. Benda, "State Organization and Policy Formation," 141.

121. Benda, "State Organization and Policy Formation," 136–37.

122. Benda, "State Organization and Policy Formation," 137, fn16.123. Benda, "State Organization and Policy Formation," 137.

124. Benda, "State Organization and Policy Formation," 136.

125. See Rubio, *There's Always Work*, chap. 9.

126. "Summary of Events in Postal Crisis," *PR*, August 1968, 5.

127. John D. Morris, "Postal Cutbacks Delayed a Week," *NYT*, July 27, 1968, 1A; and Marjorie Hunter, "Congress Exempts Postal Employees From Job Cutback [*sic*]," *NYT*, August 2, 1968, 1A.

128. Morris, "Postal Cutbacks Delayed a Week"; and Hunter, "Congress Exempts Postal Employees." Quote from Hunter article.

129. Morris, "Postal Cutbacks Delayed a Week"; and Hunter, "Congress Exempts Postal Employees." Quotes from Hunter article. FBI agents and air traffic controllers also became exempt from job cutbacks with this congressional action.

130. Brenner, "Rank-and-File Teamster Movements in Comparative Perspective," 112. See also Isaac and Christiansen, "How the Civil Rights Movement," 722–46.

131. See Tierney, *Postal Reorganization*, 11, 16–20; and Conkey, *Postal Precipice*, 45–49. Postmaster General O'Brien was replaced in 1968 by W. Marvin Watson, who was in turn replaced in 1969 by Winton M. Blount, appointed by President Nixon.

132. "National Officers, Citizens Committee for Postal Reform, Inc.," in Box 49, folder 16, Charles Colson Collection, NPLM. The vice-chairs who had also served on the Kappel Commission included Fred Kappel, George P. Baker, Rudolph A. Peterson, Ralph Lazarus, David Ginsburg, and Murray Comarow. See also "Postal Reform Proposal Pits Workers Against Users," 789–91.

133. "Postal Disputes Produce Top Lobby Spending in 1969," July 31, 1970, *Congressional Quarterly*, 1964, in Box 49, folder 3, Colson Collection, NPLM.

134. See also Richard J. Levine, "Restive Postal Workers Pose Mounting Threat of Wildcat Walkouts," *National Alliance*, September 1968, 18, reprinted from *Wall Street Journal*, September 9, 1968.

135. Germano, "Labor Relations," 147.

136. Walsh and Mangum, *Labor Struggle*, chap. 7; and Robert McFadden, "Moe Biller, 87, Labor Chief of Postal Workers, Is Dead," *NYT*, September 6, 2003, https://www.nytimes .com/2003/09/06/nyregion/moe-biller-87-labor-chief-of-postal-workers-is-dead.html.

137. See Max Siderman, "Growl of the Wildcat Heard in POs as CSC Proposes Mini-Sized 4.1% Pay Raise," *Union Mail*, March 1969, 4; and "Nixon Exec. Order Implements 4.1% 'Nothing' Increase," in *Union Mail*, June 1969, 1.

CHAPTER 2

1. Robert Horan, "Union Head Predicts Mail Carrier Strike: Postal Unrest Blamed," *Columbus Dispatch*, April 20, 1969, 17B, archived at USPS Historian.

2. "Winton M. Blount Jr.," *Encyclopedia of Alabama*, http://www.encyclopediaofalabama .org/article/h-1637.

3. See "Task Force Says 84% of Postal Employees Are in Unions," *Progressive*, December 1961, 4 (this refers to "President Kennedy's Task Force Report"). See also President's Commission on Postal Organization, *Towards Postal Excellence*, 18–19 (note: the NPU is here in 1968 listed at 70,000 members but they typically self-represented as 80,000 by 1970, e.g. in Walsh and Mangum, *Labor Struggle*, 36–39). Out of 716,000 postal workers, 620,000 were unionized. The NALC represented approximately 190,000 of 195,386 letter carriers. The UFPC and NPU competed for the representation of about 308,000 clerks, with the NPU also competing for representation of 48,000 mail handlers with the NPMHU. NAPFE competed with all unions for all crafts, and the NRLCA was the only union representing 49,000 rural letter carriers. See also Benda, "State Organization and Policy Formation," 132.

4. Benda, "State Organization and Policy Formation," 136.

5. Germano, "Labor Relations," 159, citing the *Postal Record*, May 1970, 32.

6. Mikusko and Miller, *Carriers in a Common Cause*, 70.

7. Author's interview with Sombrotto, Orapello, and Marino. See also Brenner, "Striking Against the State," 7; Mikusko and Miller, *Carriers in a Common Cause*, 62–80; Rubio, *There's Always Work*, chap. 9; and Isaac and Christiansen, "How the Civil Rights Movement," 722–46.

8. Siderman, "Growl of the Wildcat"; and "Nixon Exec. Order Implements 4.1%." 'Nothing' Increase," *Union* Mail (March 1969), 4., June 1969, 1. See also Richard J. Levine, "Restive Postal Workers Pose Mounting Threat of Wildcat Walkouts; Post Office Hopes to Cope with Stoppages; Unions Drop No Strike Pledges," *National Alliance*, September 1968.

9. Germano, "Labor Relations," 135.

10. Germano, "Labor Relations," 136.

11. Germano, "Labor Relations," 137–38.

12. Germano, "Labor Relations," 131–40, quote on 139.

13. Germano, "Labor Relations," 135. See also author's interview with Sombrotto, Orapello, and Marino.

14. Author's telephone conversations with Germano; and Germano, "Labor Relations," 142. See also Mikusko, *Carriers in a Common Cause*, 62–67; author's interview with Sombrotto, Orapello, and Marino; Marino, "Time of Fury"; and Max Siderman, "'Innocent of Concerted Action'; Incident Wiped from All PO Records," *Union Mail*,

July-August 1969, 1, with the main headline reading: " 'KB'ers' Are Cleared . . . They're Back on Job!" The article hailed this as a "smashing win for unionism." See also "Contingency Plan"; and "UFPC Policy Statement Opposes Work Stoppages," *Federation News Service*, July 3, 1969, 1; Box 3, Folder Officer's Files, TWA. The "direct order" that managers were instructed to give to any strikers under the 1969 "contingency plan" may have had in mind management's vague response in the 1967 Newark walkout. On reimbursing strikers, see Dana Schecter interview with Moe Biller, July 15, 1976, APWU-Moe Biller files, TWA.

15. Loraine M. Huston, "Comments from Cleveland," *National Alliance*, September 1969, 9; and Wyatt C. Williams, "Racism, Labor, and the Alliance," *National Alliance*, May 1968, 6.

16. Ned Young, "Union Board OKs Strike," *National Alliance*, December 1969, 6, reprint from *Washington News American*, Nov. 26, 1969, 4-A; and Mike Causey, "Work Stoppage Threatened by Union," *National Alliance*, December 1969, 5–6, reprinted from *WP*, November 26, 1969, B-9. See also David Holmberg, "Alliance Hits Nixon Order," *National Alliance*, December 1969, 5, reprinted from *Washington Evening Star*, November 25, 1969, A-2.

17. Author interview with Sombrotto, Orapello, and Marino; "Pay Raise Rally in New York City," *National Alliance*, May 1967, 22; "Demonstration at the White House, Pay Raise, Equal Employment Opportunity," *National Alliance*, September 1967, 8.

18. See "News Release, Metropolitan Postal Council, March 5, 1964 [and also] May 23, 1965," Box 54, Folder Metro Postal Council Outdoor demo, NYMAPU, TWA; and author's interview with Bailey, Tilley, Flagler, Wilson, and John. See also "NPU says 'Nuts to 4.1%,'" *Progressive*, April 1969, 1; "The Pay-Nut Rally," *Union Mail*, May 1969, 4–5; and APWU-Moe Biller files oral histories, TWA. The "whistle-blowing" rally was in 1967. See "Historic Pay Rally Rouses Capital; Nat'l Pay Demos Week of June 16th," *Progressive*, June 1967, 2.

19. See, for example, Sidney Goodman [NPU President], "The Time Had Come," editorial, and "The Right to Strike," *Progressive*, November 1967, 3. See also "Outlines 1970 Program," *Progressive*, February 1970, 1.

20. Marino, "Time of Fury," 5–6; Brenner, "Striking Against the State," 11, 122–23; and Mikusko and Miller, *Carriers in a Common Cause*, 68.

21. Author's telephone conversations with Germano; and Branch 36 website, http://www.nylcbr36.org/sombrotto_bio.htm.

22. Author's interview with Sombrotto, Orapello, and Marino. See also Germano, "Labor Relations," 146–47; Rubio, *There's Always Work*; and Tennassee, *History of the National Alliance*.

23. Brenner, "Striking Against the State," 12. See also Germano, "Labor Relations," chap. 4; and Rubio, *There's Always Work*, chaps. 4–6.

24. Germano, "Labor Relations," 91–121. The "inter-craft association" quote comes from p. 92.

25. Author's telephone conversations with Germano.

26. Germano, "Labor Relations," 91–121. See also Germano's chap. 4 summary and chap. 5.

27. Brenner, "Striking Against the State," 12.

28. A. Brenner, "Striking Against the State," 12.

29. See Rubio, *There's Always Work*, chaps. 9–10, esp. p. 228.

30. USPOD, "[Draft of] The Postal Strike—March 1970," September 21, 1970, 31, USPS Historian.

31. USPOD, "Postal Strike—March 1970."

32. USPOD, "Postal Strike—March 1970," 32.

33. USPOD, "Postal Strike—March 1970, 31–32.

34. Rademacher editorial in *PR*, May 1968, 6.

35. Thanks to Nancy Dysart, Director, NALC Information Center, for the June 28, 2010, email providing me with the oral history interview transcript by Mike Smith with James Rademacher, WPRL.

36. Rubio, *There's Always Work*, chaps. 10–11 (based on *Postal Record* articles from 1970).

37. Germano, "Labor Relations," 133. See also author's interview with Sombrotto, Orapello, and Marino.

38. *Annual Report of the Postmaster General 1945–1949*, 23. See also USPS Historian's Office: I am indebted to Jennifer Lynch especially for these figures on veterans in the postal workforce.

39. See Rubio, *There's Always Work*.

40. Brenner, "Striking Against the State," 22.

41. Brenner, "Striking Against the State," 22. See also author's interview with Sombrotto, Orapello, and Marino.

42. See Mikusko and Miller, *Carriers in a Common Cause*; Germano, "Labor Relations"; and Walsh and Mangum, *Labor Struggle*. See also Montgomery, *Workers' Control in America*.

43. Author's interview with Thomas and Perry. See also Schecter interview with Biller, July 7, 1976, TWA; and Germano, "Labor Relations," 127–31.

44. Usery, "The Postal Dispute," 361. I am indebted to Jan Edmiston, Reference Librarian for the WWL for sending me a copy of this document from their archives.

45. See Richard J. Levine, "Restive Postal Workers Pose Mounting Threat of Wildcat Walkouts; Post Office Hopes to Cope with Stoppages; Unions Drop No Strike Pledges," *Wall Street Journal*, September 9, 1968; John Cramer, "Postal Unions Revolt Over Strike Law," *Washington Daily News*, August 26, 1968, reprinted in the *Postal Record* (October 1968), 23; "NPU Drops 'No Strike' Provision," National Postal Union *Washington Report*, September 4, 1968, 1; Mikusko and Miller, *Carriers in a Common Cause*, 66; and "Fourth Day, Morning Session, Thursday August 22, 1968," *46th Biennial Convention of the National Association of Letter Carriers*, Boston, Massachusetts, *Postal Record* (September 1968), 63.

46. Mikusko and Miller, *Carriers in a Common Cause*, 133–39, 141–49; and author's interview with Sombrotto, Orapello, and Marino.

47. Brenner, "Striking Against the State," 11. For quote see Murray Seeger, "Pact by Nixon, Union Leader Rebounds to Embarrass Both" [byline *Los Angeles Times*], *WP*, March 24, 1970, A3, which describes that December 5, 1969, meeting. Article found clipped and saved in Box 49, folder 11, Charles W. Colson Collection, NPLM. See also Smith interview with Rademacher on that meeting, 42–46. The December 5, 1969, Nixon-Rademacher "secret" evening meeting does not appear on Nixon's daily diary, available at the Nixon Presidential Library's website: https://www.nixonlibrary.gov/virtuallibrary /documents/PDD/1969/019%20December%201-15%201969.pdf. The 1970 *Post* article, while its original information source was undisclosed and is still unknown, is more contemporaneous and reliable on the first meeting's date than Rademacher's 2009 oral history account. In the latter, Rademacher remembers answering a call from the White House on December 5, 1969. He said that Colson asked him to come the next day after Rademacher had first offered to come right away. Rademacher is not clear on which

date he actually went, but it sounds like he went that very day. December 6, 1969, was a Saturday, and the presidential diary shows Nixon leaving the White House right after a quick 9:20 a.m. breakfast. Nixon went out of town for the rest of the weekend, so it is unlikely they had time to meet Saturday, and Rademacher's name was not included in any breakfast meeting. Rademacher also said nothing about being Nixon's breakfast guest (he said they fed him lunch in the basement cafeteria). It is possible they called him on Thursday and he went on Friday, or he went right away on Friday. But even if he had met with Nixon on Saturday morning, it would still have been a separate meeting from the December 18, 1969, photo-opportunity meeting with Nixon and with more discussion as well at that earlier meeting.

48. Charles W. Colson, "Memorandum For: The President's File," December 18, 1969, Box 49, folder 8, Colson Collection, NPLM. Cashen was deputy counsel, Ehrlichman was counsel, and Colson the special counsel to the president. See also John Ehrlichman, memo prepared for "The President," December 17, 1969, Box 49, folder 6, Colson Collection, NPLM. See also Nixon's December 18, 1969, daily diary at https://www.nixonlibrary.gov/virtuallibrary/documents/PDD/1969/020%20December%2016-31%201969.pdf. See also Smith interview with Rademacher; and Walsh and Mangum, *Labor Struggle*, 15. The photograph of Nixon and Rademacher shaking hands appeared on the cover of the September 1970 *Postal Record* with the headline: "Presidents Richard M. Nixon and James H. Rademacher Express Mutual Pleasure Upon Enactment of Historical Negotiated Agreement." Rademacher originally wanted it on the January 1970 cover.

49. See Ehrlichman, memo prepared for "The President," December 17, 1969, Box 49, folder 6, Colson Collection, NPLM. See also Box 49, folder 3, folder 4, and folder 7; and Box 82, folder 1, Colson Collection, NPLM, for Nixon White House correspondence with Rademacher and Nixon's gratitude for his role in postal reform.

50. See Winton M. Blount memorandum to President Nixon, May 7, 1969; and Draft of President's Postal Reform Message to Congress, May 16, 1969, Box 39, folder 1, Ehrlichman Collection, NPLM. Nixon's address to Congress was May 27, 1969. See "Congress Clears Landmark Postal Reorganization Plan," *CQ Almanac*, 1970, https://library.cqpress.com/cqalmanac/document.php?id=cqal70-1293327. See also Germano, "Labor Relations," 148, for pledges made to postal unions; Smith interview with Rademacher, 42–46; and Germano email to author, May 7, 2019.

51. Baxter, *Labor and Politics*, 86–89, quote on 89.

52. Baxter, *Labor and Politics*, 86–89, quote on 87. See also Brenner, "Striking Against the State," 11; and Tierney, *Postal Reorganization*, 20–23.

53. See "Congress Clears Landmark Postal Reorganization Plan."

54. Baxter, *Labor and Politics*, 88.

55. Author's interview with Sombrotto, Orapello, and Marino; Smith interview with Rademacher; author's telephone conversations with Germano; and Germano, "Labor Relations," 141–51.

56. Germano, "Labor Relations," 152–59, quote on 156; and email to author May 15, 2019.

57. See "Congress Clears Landmark Postal Reorganization Plan," including Dulski's fear that the USPS would turn into a "conglomerate." See also Walsh and Mangum, *Labor Struggle*, 15–16, 32; Germano, "Labor Relations," 143–46, 160–69; Mikusko and Miller, *Carriers in a Common Cause*, 69, 76; Loewenberg, "Post Office Strike of 1970," 196; Rubio, *There's Always Work*, chap. 9; and author's telephone conversations with Germano.

58. Germano, "Labor Relations," 160–69. "Central Park" quote on 166.

59. Correspondence between Moe Biller and Gustave Johnson, February 5, 12, and 20, 1970, Box 6, NYMAPU collection, TWA. Johnson was writing from Branch 36 headquarters at 261 West 43rd Street, Biller from MBPU headquarters at 254 West 31st Street.

60. Germano, "Labor Relations," 160–69.

61. Brenner, "Striking Against the State," 14; and email from Tom Germano, June 19, 2015. Only two of 75 NALC Branch 36 executive board members voted to strike. Germano, "Labor Relations," 174.

62. Author's interview with Roth. See also Germano, "Labor Relations," 127; and Brenner, "Striking Against the State," 7. See also author's interview with Henry.

63. Author's interviews with Roth and with Evenson. See other interviews at 2014 NALC convention for this idea popular among strikers of the post office having violated its *social* contract.

64. Germano, "Labor Relations," 175–79.

65. Author's interview with Roth.

66. Frank Orapello, "Victory Success," part of "1970 Postal Strike," New York Letter Carriers Branch 36 website, http://www.nylcbr36.org/history.htm, posted in 2005.

67. See Germano, "Labor Relations," 175–79. Former president Joseph Henry of NALC Washington, D.C., Branch 142 told me that his branch's votes were incorrectly tabulated, and that based on the actual count they should have struck. See author's interview with Henry.

68. Germano, "Labor Relations," 179–80; and Orapello, "Victory Success."

69. USPOD, "Postal Strike — March 1970," 29.

70. Germano, "Labor Relations," 179–80; and Orapello, "Victory Success." See also USPOD, "Postal Strike — March 1970," 29.

71. See Walsh and Mangum, *Labor Struggle*, chap. 2; President's Commission on Postal Organization, *Towards Postal Excellence*, 1010–104; author's interview with Bailey, Tilley, Flagler, Wilson, and John; and Rubio, *There's Always Work*, chap. 7, esp. 78–79.

72. USPOD, "Postal Strike — March 1970," 30.

73. USPOD, "Postal Strike — March 1970," 31, 44–45.

74. USPOD, "Postal Strike — March 1970," 29.

75. Freeman, *Working-Class New York*, 3–6, 24.

76. Murphy, "Militancy in Many Forms.". See also Freeman, *Working-Class New York*, chaps. 12–14.

77. Lichtenstein, *State of the Union*, 182. "Akron [Ohio] and Flint [Michigan]" refer to groundbreaking CIO rubber and auto strikes, respectively, in 1936.

78. Germano, "Labor Relations," 124.

79. Freeman, *Working-Class New York*, 201.

80. Author's interview with Sombrotto, Orapello, and Marino.

81. See 2014 NALC Philadelphia convention interviews by author.

82. Cowie, *Stayin' Alive*, chap. 3.

83. Germano, "Labor Relations," 182.

84. Brenner, "Striking Against the State," 27n37; and Brenner, "Rank-and-File Rebellion," 140 (for *Economist* reference).

85. Author's interview with Morgan. See also Rubio, *There's Always Work*, chap. 9–conclusion. See also Freeman, *Working-Class New York*; James, *Holding Aloft the Banner*

of Ethiopia; Fink and Greenberg, *Upheaval in the Quiet Zone*; Nelson, *Divided We Stand*, chap. 2; and Biondi, *To Stand and Fight*.

86. See author's interview with Bailey, Tilley, Flagler, Wilson, and John.

87. See author interview with Bailey, Tilley, Flagler, Wilson, and John; and author's interview with Thomas and Perry. See also Roediger, *Working toward Whiteness*, esp. chap. 7, for discussion of what Roediger calls "nonracial syndicalism."

88. See, for example, author's interviews with NALC strike veterans, July 22 and 24, 2014.

89. Germano, "Labor Relations," 190; National Association of Letter Carriers, *Strike at 40*; and APWU Communications Department, *Strike that Couldn't Happen*. Only the NALC and NAPFE refer to their local unions as "branches," while the other postal unions have used the more common labor-union term "local."

CHAPTER 3

1. Damon Stetson, "Mail Carriers Go on Strike in Manhattan and Bronx," *NYT*, March 18, 1970, 1A. See also "Strike Hits Manhattan, Bronx Mail," *New York Daily News*, March 18, 1970, 1A.

2. Germano, "Labor Relations," chap. 5; and Frank Orapello, "Victory Success," part of "1970 Postal Strike," New York Letter Carriers Branch 36 website, http://www.nylcbr36 .org/history.htm, posted in 2005. The GPO, built in 1912, has been known since 1982 as the James A. Farley Post Office. It is being converted into an Amtrak railroad terminal annex called Moynihan Station, part of Penn Station. See Charles Bagli, "Progress Is Made in Plan to Convert Post Office into Penn Station Annex," *NYT*, August 26, 2014, http://www .nytimes.com/2014/08/27/nyregion/progress-is-made-in-plan-to-convert-post-office -into-penn-station-annex.html.

3. Germano, "Labor Relations," 63. Tour I was the midnight shift, Tour II was the day shift, and Tour III was the afternoon or "swing" shift.

4. See USPOD, Status Report, March 24, 1970, noon; and Summary Report, March 24, 1970, 5:00 P.M., USPS Historian.

5. USPOD, "Postal Strike—March 1970," 1, USPS Historian. See also "Mail Service Continues Throughout Washington," *Oregonian*, March 24, 1970, 5.

6. Orapello, "Victory Success."

7. Germano, "Labor Relations," 184; and author's interview with Morgan.

8. Author's interview with Sombrotto, Orapello, and Marino; and author's interview with Morgan. See also Mikusko and Miller, *Carriers in a Common Cause*, 72. See also Dennis Hevesi, "Vincent Sombrotto, Who Led Postal Strike, Dies at 89," *NYT*, January 16, 2013, http://www.nytimes.com/2013/01/17/nyregion/vincent-sombrotto-leader-of-1970 -postal-strike-dies-at-89.html?_r=0. See also Maria Alvarez, "Renamed Grand Central Post Office Honors Labor Leader," *Newsday*, October 16, 2014, http://www.newsday.com /news/new-york/renamed-grand-central-post-office-honors-labor-leader-1.9513380.

9. Author's interview with Morgan.

10. Stetson, "Mail Carriers Go on Strike."

11. Author's interview with Weiner.

12. Germano, "Labor Relations," 185.

13. USPOD, "Postal Strike—March 1970," 30.

14. See USPOD, "Postal Strike — March 1970," 33–34. See also EO 11491, esp. Section 19 (b) 4, which mandates that labor unions "shall not . . . call or engage in a strike, work stoppage, or slowdown; picket an agency in a labor-management dispute; or condone any such activity by failing to take affirmative action to prevent or stop it," http://www .archives.gov/federal-register/codification/executive-order/11491.html.

15. USPOD, "Information Service," March 22, 1970, USPS Historian.

16. USPOD, "Postal Strike — March 1970," 33–34, 63.

17. Phelan letter to author, March 25, 2015.

18. Rodriguez letter to author, forwarded to author by Jenessa Kildall of NALC *Postal Record*.

19. Author's telephone interview with Illicette.

20. Author's telephone interview with Parrotta.

21. Author's telephone interview with Idoyaga.

22. Author's telephone interview with McDonald.

23. Ross email to Jenessa Kildall, forwarded to author.

24. Ross email to author.

25. See "Work Stoppage — March 18–26, 1970: Mail Embargoes," USPS Historian.

26. Author's telephone interviews and emails with Gallardo author, especially telephone interview, February 18, 2016.

27. "The Following Post Offices Are on Strike — March 20, 1970 — 10 A.M.," USPS Historian. The initial "On Strike" USPOD reports can only be found as early as March 19, 1970 — the second day of the strike. See also status and summary reports from March 22 through March 25, 1970, USPS Historian.

28. Chircop email to Sally Davidow and author, July 28, 2016.

29. Germano, "Labor Relations," 187–88.

30. See Rubio, *There's Always Work*, 243–46; author's interview with Bailey, Tilley, Flagler, Wilson, and John; and Schecter's interview with Biller.

31. Damon Stetson, "Letter Carriers Defy Injunction Ordering Them Back to Work," *NYT*, March 19, 1970, 52.

32. Author's interview with Bailey, Tilley, Flagler, Wilson, and John. See also Walsh and Mangum, *Labor Struggle*, 22.

33. Walsh and Mangum, *Labor Struggle*, 21.

34. Walsh and Mangum, *Labor Struggle*, 22.

35. Email from Nowark to Sally Davidow and author.

36. Author's interview with Daniels.

37. See *Temporary Restraining Order and Notice of Hearing on Motion for Preliminary Injunction, United States of America v. Branch 60 National Association of Letter Carriers, AFL-CIO, ET AL, CIVIL NO. B-36, March 20, 1970*, and other documents in possession of author. I am grateful to Paul Daniels, 1970 postal strike veteran and current president of NALC Connecticut Merged Branch 20, for sharing these documents with me, as well as his article, "The Day the Mail Stopped," in that branch's magazine *Union Courier* 29, no. 1 (March 2014), 9.

38. Author's telephone interview with Salamone.

39. Author's interview with Burrus.

40. Mann's emails to author.

41. Author's interviews with Murphy and Enz; and, from the same branch, Wilson and

Thompson (both African American in a city whose post office had long had a large black population). See also J. Joseph Vacca Collection, WPRL. https://reuther.wayne.edu/files/LR001914.pdf.

42. "Workers Defy U.S. Back-to-Work Order—Leadership Helpless," *SFC*, March 21, 1970, 1A.

43. See also USPOD, Status Reports; and "Postal Strike—March 1970." See also author's interview with Sombrotto, Orapello, and Marino; Brenner, "Striking Against the State"; and Germano, "Labor Relations," chap. 5; Rubio *There's Always Work*, chap. 10.

44. See Germano, "Labor Relations," chap. 5; Brenner, "Striking Against the State"; Loewenberg, "Post Office Strike of 1970," 196; and 2014 NALC Convention interviews. See also Department of the Army, Operation Graphic Hand, *Postal Work Stoppage*, http://www.governmentattic.org/2docs/PostalWorkStoppage_GraphicHand_1970.pdf. Thanks to Eric Kutner for providing me the link to this article, which includes the *After Action Report: Operation Graphic Hand*, 1970, http://www.governmentattic.org/2docs/Army-AAR_Op-GraphicHand_1970.pdf. See also memorandum and examples from seventeen cities from Ben Holman (Department of Justice) to Robert J. Brown (White House) and Ronald B. Lee (USPOD) regarding "Minority Community Reaction to Postal Strike," Box 38, Folder 238, part 7, Ehrlichman Collection, NPLM.

45. Author's interview with Lovett and Armstrong; and Abbott, August 12, 2004.

46. Mariposa email to author.

47. Author's interview with Davenport, Booker, and Palmer, all NALC Chicago Branch 11 members; and from the same branch: Bean, Cross, Newsome, and Sanford. All six are African American, in a city where blacks have long made up the majority of postal workers. See also author interview with Abbott.

48. See author interview with Davenport, Booker, Palmer, Bean, Cross, Newsome, and Sanford. See also USPOD "Status Report, March 23, 1970, 9:00 pm," and "Postal Strike—March 1970," 38, USPS Historian. The latter noted that thirty-seven offices struck were in the "largest 100," which included nine of the ten largest, generating almost one-quarter of total mail volume, with New York City alone handling 6 percent of total U.S. mail. See also author's interview with Abbott. See other interviews, 2014 NALC Philadelphia Convention.

49. See author's interview with Holbrook; and author's interview with Burt. See also USPOD Status Report, March 22, 1970, 2 P.M.; and Rubio, *There's Always Work*, 247.

50. Letter to author from Chappellie.

51. Frank van Riper, "U.S. Postal Chief Suspends Pay of Wildcat Strikers," *New York Daily News*, March 19, 1970, 3.

52. Author's interview with Bernstein, May 30, 2015; and by telephone. See also James LaPenta obituary, http://hosting-1611.tributes.com/obituary/show/James-Joseph-Lapenta-80997379. See also Interview with W. J. Usery Jr., March 16, 1990, Tape 22 and transcript, SLA, http://research.library.gsu.edu/c.php?g=115649&p=753011. George Shultz left his Labor cabinet post on July 1, 1970, and subsequently served the Nixon administration as Director of the Office of Management and Budget, and then as Secretary of the Treasury.

53. Haldeman, *Haldeman Diaries*, 140.

54. Haldeman, *Haldeman Diaries*, 139–40. See also Ehrlichman and Colson collections, NPLM.

55. Haldeman, *Haldeman Diaries*, 140.

56. Haldeman, *Haldeman Diaries*, 141.

57. Haldeman, *Haldeman Diaries*, 141.

58. Author's interview with White; and Mikusko and Miller, *Carriers in a Common Cause*, 74. See also Smith's interview with Rademacher, 51.

59. Author's interview with Holbrook; *PR*, May 1970; Brenner, "Striking Against the State"; and author's interview with White. The automatic dues checkoff was first won in a December 13, 1963, agreement signed under terms provided by EO 10988, effective January 1, 1964. See Rubio, *There's Always Work*, 159. See also James Rademacher, writing in the May 2010 *Postal Record*, http://www.nalc.org/news/the-postal-record/2010/may-2010 /document/0510-stand.pdf.

60. Smith's interview with Rademacher.

61. "The Following Post Offices Are on Strike," USPOD memo, March 20, 1970, 10 A.M., USPS Historian.

62. "The Following Post Offices Are on Strike," USPOD memo, March 20, 1970, 11:30 A.M., USPS Historian.

63. Sally Davidow, "Philadelphia Joins the Great Postal Strike," *Philadelphia Postal Worker*," March 1995, 4–5. I am indebted to Sally Davidow for sending me a copy of this newsletter article, based in large part on *Philadelphia Inquirer* coverage. See also Bell, email to Davidow and author; and telephone interview with author.

64. Davidow, "Philadelphia Joins."

65. Author's interview with Reilly.

66. Author's interview with Hanlon.

67. Author's interview with Miller.

68. Author's telephone interview and emails with Trenga.

69. Author's interview with Brandt.

70. Author's telephone interview and emails with Richards. See also 2014 Philadelphia NALC convention interviews by author.

71. "Regional Recap of Situation, as of 4:00pm, 3/21/70," USPOD strike reports, USPS Historian. Pittsburgh was reported by the USPOD to be back to work in their March 23, 1970, "10:00 AM Status Report" in USPS Historian. Detroit, part of the Chicago postal region, had been reported on strike in a USPOD report from "10:00AM, [Friday] March 20, 1970," USPS Historian.

72. Quotes from Robert Voelker, "Decision Follows Union Leader's Recommendation," *Pittsburgh Post-Gazette*, March 23, 1970, 1. See also headline above the fold that day: "Mail Strike Here Ends, Wage Parley May Begin." See also "Mail Strikes Mounting, City Men Go Out Today: Local Postmen Will Ballot On 5-Day Delay," in *Pittsburgh Post-Gazette*, March 21, 1970, 1.

73. Author's interview with Schwarze; and Schwarze's January 19, 2016, letter to author, with clipping from *Elmhurst Press*, March 20, 1970.

74. Author's interview with Weiner.

75. See, for example, Rubio, *There's Always Work*.

76. See author's interview with Schwarze; and telephone interview with Schwarze, January 9, 2016.

77. "Work Stoppage — March 18–26, 1970, Mail Embargoes," USPS Historian.

78. Emails from Mark Schindeldecker to author, January 13, 2016; "nothing to lose" quote from January 12. Strike sign quote from email from Schindeldecker to Jenessa Kildall, NALC *Postal Record*, March 23, 2015, forwarded to author.

79. "Workers Defy U.S. Back-to-Work Order—Leadership Helpless," *SFC*, March 21, 1970, 1A.

80. See, for example, Dale Featherling, "St. Paul Letter Carriers Join U. S. Postal Strike," *Minneapolis Tribune*, March 20, 1970, 1; and "City Postal Clerks Return; Delivery Expected Today," *Minneapolis Tribune*, March 25, 1970, 1. I am indebted to John Wareham of the *Minneapolis Star Tribune*, and Bailey Diers and the Hennepin County Library Special Collections in Minneapolis for sending me clippings from the *Tribune* during the strike period.

81. Walsh and Mangum, *Labor Struggle*, 20–23.

82. Germano, "Labor Relations," 199–200.

83. Germano, "Labor Relations," 199–200.

84. Germano, "Labor Relations," 199–200.

85. Germano, "Labor Relations," 201.

86. Rubio, *There's Always Work*, 148; author's interview with NALC strike veterans, July 22 and 24, 2014, Philadelphia NALC convention. See also Germano, *Delivering the Dream*, 15, on Chicago's role in the strike.

87. Author's interview with Booker and Palmer.

88. Author's interview with Sanford.

89. Malone email to Sally Davidow and author, July 29, 2016.

90. Walsh and Mangum, *Labor Struggle*, 23. See also Rubio, *There's Always Work*, chap. 10; and Brenner, "Rank-and-File Rebellion," 132.

91. See footage in *The Strike that Couldn't Happen*; and *The Strike at 40*.

92. Haldeman, *Haldeman Diaries*, 141.

93. Haldeman, *Haldeman Diaries*, 141.

94. Haldeman, *Haldeman Diaries*, 141.

95. Dick Meister, "Walkout Vote Set Here Today," *SFC*, March 21, 1970, 1A.

96. Larry Dunn, "Total Strike Monday by S.F. Carriers," *SFC*, March 22, 1970, 1A. The full name of the Sunday edition from 1965–2000 was the *San Francisco Examiner and Chronicle*, reflecting a collaboration between the two newspapers.

97. Larry Dunn, "Total Strike Monday by S.F. Carriers," *SFC*, March 22, 1970, 2A.

98. Dick Meiser, "How the S.F. Strike Ended—Full Services Resume Today," *SFC*, March 17, 1970, 1A.

99. "Mailmen Defy Nixon Threat," *SFC*, March 22, 1970, 4A.

100. See, for example, "Portland Mailmen's Local to Vote on Strike Issue," March 20, 1970, *Oregonian*, 12; "[Seattle] Mailmen Call 2nd Meeting," *Oregonian*, March 22, 1970, 23; and "Local Carriers Set Strike Vote," March 23, 1970, 1, including Mallon quote. See also Civil Rights and Labor History Consortium through the University of Washington, http://depts.washington.edu/labhist/.

101. See Mikusko and Miller, *Carriers in a Common Cause*, 73–74. See also Rubio, *There's Always Work*, chap. 10.

102. See Mikusko and Miller, *Carriers in a Common Cause*, 73–74. See also Rubio, *There's Always Work*, chap. 10; author's interview with Sombrotto, Orapello, and Marino; and 2014 interviews with NALC 1970 strike veterans; Germano, *Labor Relations*, 202–4; Germano, *Delivering the Dream*, 8–9; Rudd, *Underground*; and Sale, *SDS*; Linda Charlton, "'Village' Fire Victim Identified as Leader of '68 Columbia Strike," *NYT*, March 9, 1970, 32; Michael T. Kaufman, "Strikers Reject Aid of Young Radicals," *NYT*, March 24, 1970, 36; Brenner, "Rank-and-File Rebellion," 133. Brenner notes in fn45 of that piece that two

months later Rademacher backtracked, claimed he had been misquoted, and proclaimed his pride that strikers had resisted infiltrators. See also Rademacher, "Carriers Not Revolutionists," *PR*, May 1970, 32. But in his 2009 oral history he accused the pro-strike faction at the March 12, 1970 meeting as being "the SDS group." Smith's interview with Rademacher, 45.

103. Ken O. Botwright and Frank Mahoney, "Wildcat Strike Cripples Boston Mail Service," *Boston Globe*, March 22, 1970, 1A. See also "In Boston: Service Near Normal," *Boston Evening Globe*, March 23, 1970, 1A.

104. Stephen Kirkjian, "Carriers Decide to Stay on Job: 2nd Vote Tuesday," *Boston Globe*, March 23, 1970, 1A, for quote. See also Kirkjian, "Boston Staying on Job," *Boston Globe*, March 25, 1970, 1A.

105. Paul Kinnear, "Postal Unions in State Won't Join Walkouts," *Arizona Daily Star*, March 23, 1970, 1A. See also "Phoenix Mailmen to Vote Today," *Arizona Republic*, March 22, 1970, 14A.

106. Author's telephone interview with Mendrick. Mendrick was later elected Denver Metro APWU President in 1976, serving until 2004 (except for 1992–1995).

107. "Regional Recap of Situation as of 4:00 P.M.," USPOD, March 21, 1970, USPS Historian.

108. "USPOD Status Report-2:00 P.M.," March 22, 1970, USPS Historian.

109. See author's interview with Rose, July, 22, 2014; and Rose telephone interview, January 11, 2016. See also Ron Wiggins, "Some Northbound Mail Likely to Pile Up Here," *St. Petersburg Independent*, March 23, 1970, 1A; and "Neither Sun, Nor Sand, Nor Surf Stops Mail—Yet," *St. Petersburg Independent*, March 24, 1970, 2A.

110. See author's interview with Rose, July, 22, 2014; and Rose telephone interview, January 11, 2016. See also Wiggins, "Some Northbound Mail"; and "Neither Sun, Nor Sand."

111. Author's interview with White; and Mikusko and Miller, *Carriers in a Common Cause*, 78.

112. See author's interview with Windham; and Fred Heller, "Firms Adjust to Postal Strike," *Atlanta Constitution*, March 23, 1970, 41. The Heller article alluded to "rumors" that had circulated the previous week "that Atlanta's letter carriers might be among those joining the strike." But those "rumors" were dismissed by NALC Branch 73 vice president Bobby Kelley, who said his branch "would stand behind" NALC president Rademacher. Branch 73 added the following day that they would only join a nationwide strike called by Rademacher (see Joseph E. Murray, "Nixon Sends GIs to Move N.Y. Mail, *Atlanta Constitution*, March 24, 1970, 1). Interestingly, that October, Executive Vice President Jerry C. Slate of UFPC Local 32 warned of a wildcat strike "within three months" in Atlanta by clerks because of deteriorating working conditions (e.g., no stools, not enough clerks). See Gene Stephens, "Union Chief Predicts Atlanta Postal Strike," *Atlanta Constitution*, October 13, 1970, 1.

113. Richmond quote from Frank Walin, "City Carriers Set Saturday Deadline," *Richmond Times-Dispatch*, March 24, 1970, 1. See also "Birmingham, Ala.," *PR*, May 1970, 72; Jose Baltazar, "Houston, Tex.," *PR*, May 1970, 79; and Al Prince, "City Mailmen Sitting Tight, May Vote on Strike Friday," *Houston Post*, March 25, 1970, 3. See also author's interviews with White; and Windham; and USPOD Strike Status Report 12, March 24, 1970 1 P.M., USPS Historian. See also "City Carriers to Vote Tomorrow on Strike," *Richmond Times-Dispatch*, March 22, 1970, A-4; "Post Offices Hold Much N.C. Mail,"

Charlotte Observer, March 20, 1970, 1; "No Strike Likely Here," *Charlotte Observer*, March 21, 1970, 1; and Cheree Briggs, "Mailmen to Talk Work Stoppage," *Charlotte Observer*, March 22, 1970, 1; "No Area Postal Woes Forecast," *New Orleans Times-Picayune*, March 22, 1970, 1; "Postal Force Here Awaits Union Ruling," *Atlanta Constitution*, March 24, 1970, 8C; James Roper, "25 Called Here: Air Reservists Activated; Memphis Carriers Vote to Stay On Job," *Memphis Commercial Appeal*, March 24, 1970, 1. On Washington, D.C., NALC Branch 142, see author's interview with Henry. The Lanham, Maryland, NALC Branch 4819 voted to strike at midnight March 22, according to the 2:00 P.M. USPOD Status Report for that day, but the March 23, 10:00 A.M. Status Report reported no strike activity there. Roger Kennedy, a Charleston, West Virginia, NALC *Postal Record* "branch scribe," proclaimed that the strike had brought local inter-craft unity: "We have agreed in the future to present a united front to local management." See Roger Kennedy, "Charleston, W.Va.," *PR*, May 1970, 72.

114. Author's telephone interview with Robinson. See also author's telephone interview with retired Richmond and national UFPC and APWU official Walter Kenney Sr.

115. Baxter, *Labor and Politics*, 2.

116. "Post Offices Hold Much N.C. Mail," *Charlotte Observer*, March 20, 1970, 1.

117. Rubio, *There's Always Work*, 145, and 358n85. See also chaps. 1–6 on Jim Crow postal union branches and locals. For a listing of which states passed right-to-work laws and when, see the pro-right-to-work-law advocacy group Right to Work Legal Defense Foundation's website, http://www.nrtw.org/.

118. "The Mail Strike: Today May Tell the Story," [Louisville] *Courier-Journal*, March 23, 1970, 1; and Larry Werner, "In Louisville: Strike May Begin Saturday," *Courier-Journal*, March 23, 1970, 1. I am indebted to Mike Mazurkiewicz for sending me these scanned articles that he received from a postal union colleague.

119. *Courier-Journal*, back page.

120. *Courier-Journal*, back page.

121. *Courier-Journal*, 1.

122. "Montreal Mail Strike Creates Cabinet Crisis," *Courier-Journal*, back page.

123. Haldeman, *Haldeman Diaries*, 141.

124. "USPOD Status Report, 10:00 A.M., March 23, 1970," USPS Historian. See also "USPOD Status Report, 7:00 A.M., March 24, 1970"; and Postmaster General Blount press conference, March 24, 1970, 10:30 P.M., both from USPS Historian.

125. Mike Mazurkiewicz, email to Sally Davidow and author, July 25, 2016.

126. Mike Mazurkiewicz, "The 1970 Postal Strike," *Postmark*, March 2005, 7 (*Postmark* is the newsletter of APWU Local 65 St. Paul, Minnesota). Thanks to Mike Mazurkiewicz for this and other resources on the strike in Minnesota.

127. *Postmark*, 7.

128. *Postmark*, 8.

129. *Postmark*, 7–8, quote on 7.

130. *Postmark*, 8.

131. *Postmark*, 9.

CHAPTER 4

1. Department of the Army, Operation Graphic Hand, *After Action Report*, I-5 (Section I Summary); and I-6.

2. "Vet Remembers Filling in for '70 Strikers," *PR*, March 2018, 12–13.

3. Haldeman, *Haldeman Diaries*, 141.

4. Haldeman, *Haldeman Diaries*, 141; and Department of the Army, Operation Graphic Hand, *After Action Report*, I-7 to I-8.

5. Proclamation 3972, March 23, 1970, Declaring a National Emergency by the President of the United States, http://www.presidency.ucsb.edu/ws/?pid=105789.

6. Executive Order 11519, http://www.presidency.ucsb.edu/ws/index.php?pid=105858.

7. Richard Nixon, "Remarks About Work Stoppages in the Postal System," March 23, 1970, http://www.presidency.ucsb.edu/ws/index.php?pid=2920.

8. See Cowie, *Stayin' Alive*, chap. 3; and McCartin, *Collision Course*, chap. 4.

9. "Briefing on the Postal Strike by Secretary of Labor George Shultz, Press Secretary Ronald Ziegler, and Postmaster-General Winton Blount," Series G-Cabinet Officer's Briefings, G-043, March 23, 1970, WHCA Sound Recordings Collection, NPLM. Italics added.

10. Author's interview with Thomas and Perry.

11. See author's interview with Weiner. See also Department of the Army, Operation Graphic Hand. For for television coverage on the Huntley-Brinkley Report of Nixon's speech, see https://www.youtube.com/watch?v=PMydV2wouU4.

12. See Department of the Army, Operation Graphic Hand, *Postal Work Stoppage*, 56. See also USPOD, "Postal Strike-March 1970," 49–50, USPS Historian. On Cazzie Russell and Michael Riordan, see http://www.basketball-reference.com/teams/NYK/1970 _games.html; and Bill Gutman, *Tales from the 1969–1970 New York Knicks*, 112. See also photo and caption of Cazzie Russell during strike, *Chicago Tribune*, March 25, 1970, 57, http://archives.chicagotribune.com/1970/03/25/page/57/article/bulls-face-atlanta-in -playoffs-tonight. The circus reference can be found at McClandish Phillips, "Circus Here, Ever New and Ever Old," *NYT*, March 24, 1970, https://www.nytimes.com/1970/03/24 /archives/circus-here-ever-new-and-ever-old.html. The Madison Square Garden archivist found no box office records of a basketball game or any other events at the Garden the night of March 23, 1970. Email to author from Mark Toepfer, July 17, 2019.

13. Department of the Army, Operation Graphic Hand, *Postal Work Stoppage*, 56. Note the use of the word "deployment" in that passage, despite official efforts to avoid that term and downplay anything that suggested a military occupation, although that very image seems to have been intended to compel strikers to return to work.

14. Department of the Army, Operation Graphic Hand, *Postal Work Stoppage*, 57

15. Department of the Army, *The Postal Work-Stoppage*, 4–6, 31–37.

16. Author's interview with Alversa.

17. Author's interview with Chester. See also Department of the Army, Operation Graphic Hand, *After Action Report*, I-4, which quantifies the amount of mail loaded, unloaded, sorted, cased, transported, and delivered by military personnel. Postal officials were cited as complimenting troops' "overall performance," but there was no mention of their effectiveness.

18. "Vet Remembers," 13.

19. "Vet Remembers," 13; and "On Post," *New York Daily News*, March 25, 1970, 338. I am grateful for emails on scheme training, October 5, 2019, from Dr. Patricia ("Pat") Williams, former APWU National Clerk Craft assistant director who recently received her Ph.D. in psychology with area of concentration in mediation/conflict resolution. The USPS tried to end manual scheme requirements in 2015 and was compelled to cease that unilateral

action during negotiations with the APWU in 2016, but apparently it is still trying to phase them out as of 2019. See "Clerk Craft Resolves Dispute on Scheme Requirements," January 13, 2016, https://apwu.org/news/clerk-craft-resolves-dispute-scheme-requirements. See also USPS, "Schemes: Construction, Assignment, Training, and Proficiency."

20. "Vet Remembers," 13.

21. See interview with Philip Seligman, June 29, 1976, New York City, Box 4, Folder 1976; Elsie Resnick, interviewed by Milt Rosner, November 26, 1976, both in APWU-Moe Biller Files, TWA. See also Marino, "Time of Fury," 9–10; Brenner, "Striking Against the State," 17, 20; and Loewenberg, "Post Office Strike."

22. Barry Blank, email to author, February 27, 2018.

23. Barry Blank, email to author, March 4, 2018.

24. Raymond Smith, email to author, August 2, 2016.

25. Haldeman, *Haldeman Diaries*, 142.

26. This clip can be found on "NBC Evening News for March 23, 1970," Television News Archive, Vanderbilt University, https://tvnews.vanderbilt.edu/programs/450356, and https://tvnews.vanderbilt.edu/broadcasts/450357.

27. Author's telephone interview with Curtan.

28. Author's telephone interview with Turner.

29. Author's telephone interviews with Lindstrom; and Rollen.

30. Author's telephone interview with Harriman Jr.

31. See author's interview with Rubly; and email from Rubly to author, January 14, 2016. See also Ray Merchant, "Huntington Beach, Anaheim Mail Carriers Go on Strike," *Orange County Evening News*, March 23, 1970, 1; and "Postal Strikes in Huntington Beach, Anaheim" and "3,500 LA Mail Clerks Stay Off Job," *Orange County Register*, March 23, 1970, 1.

32. "L.A. Localities Feeling Pinch," *SFC*, March 22, 1970, 7A.

33. "Deadline Today in Walkout," *SFC*, March 23, 1970, 1A.

34. Email from Carl Jensen to Sally Davidow and author, September 3, 2016.

35. "Opening of New Post Office Set: Operation of New Terminal Annex to Begin at 8 a.m. Tomorrow," *Los Angeles Times*, May 26, 1940.

36. USPOD, "Postal Strike—March 1970," 50, USPS Historian. On federal troop intervention in West Virginia, see, for example, Clayton D. Laurie, "The United States Army and the Return to Normalcy in Labor Dispute Interventions: The Case of the West Virginia Coal Mine Wars, 1920–1921," http://www.wvculture.org/history/journal_wvh/wvh50-1.html. On President Cleveland's use of troops in 1894 to suppress the Pullman Strike, see, for example, http://kansasheritage.org/pullman/index.html.

37. Germano, "Labor Relations," 234.

38. "The Strike that Stunned the Country," *Time*, March 30, 1970, http://content.time.com/time/magazine/article/0,9171,942202,00.html.

39. "Strike that Stunned the Country."

40. "The Day the Mail Stopped," *Newsweek*, March 30, 1970, 11–17, archived at USPS Historian.

41. "Strike that Stunned the Country"; and "Day the Mail Stopped." On "Revolt of the Good Guys," see Mikusko and Miller, *Carriers in a Common Cause*, 76. For negative strike editorial coverage, see, for example, "'Survival of Government,'" editorial, *NYT*, March 24, 1970, 46. Contrast this with John Darnton, "Postman's Pay Just $2 a Week Too High for Welfare," *NYT*, March 25, 1970, 31, the very next day.

42. Department of the Army, Operation Graphic Hand, *Postal Work Stoppage*, 57.

43. "Vet Remembers," 13.

44. Haldeman, *Haldeman Diaries*, 142.

45. Colson, "Memorandum for John Ehrlichman," March 24, 1970, in Box 49, folder 4, Colson Collection, NPLM.

46. Colson, "Memorandum for John Ehrlichman," March 24, 1970, in Box 49, folder 4, Colson Collection, NPLM; and John Ehrlichman, "Memorandum for the President" on H.R. 4 in Colson Collection, NPLM. See also James H. Rademacher, "Editorial Protested," *Birmingham News*, March 21, 1970 [stamped date, probably earlier in March], n.p.; Walsh and Mangum, *Labor Struggle*, 15, 32; and Germano, "Labor Relations," 143–45.

47. See USPOD Summary and Status Reports, March 18–25, esp. Summary Report, 9 P.M., March 23, 1970; Status Report, 5 A.M., March 24, 1970; and Status Report, noon, March 24, 1970, USPS Historian.

48. Author's interview with Brandt.

49. Author's interview with Evenson.

50. Author's interviews with White; and Windham.

51. Blount press conference, March 24, 1970, USPS Historian.

52. Blount press conference, March 24, 1970, USPS Historian.

53. Haldeman, *Haldeman Diaries*, 142.

54. Haldeman, *Haldeman Diaries*, 142.

55. Author's interview with Sombrotto, Orapello, and Marino.

56. Walsh and Mangum, *Labor Struggle*, 27.

57. Germano, "Labor Studies," 225. Mario Biaggi and Frank J. Brasco were the two New York congressmen, both Democrats. Thanks to Tom Germano for the reference.

58. Walsh and Mangum, *Labor Struggle*, 27; and Germano, "Labor Studies," 225. For sandbagging reference, see Schecter's oral history interview with Biller, July 15, 1976, APWU Collection TWA.

59. Germano, "Labor Studies," quote on 229. See also Walsh and Mangum, *Labor Struggle*, 27.

60. Germano, "Labor Studies," 230.

61. Author's interview with Holbrook.

62. Department of the Army, Operation Graphic Hand, *After Action Report*, A-5.

63. USPOD, "Postal Strike — March 1970," 1, USPS Historian.

64. Germano, "Labor Relations," 196

65. Jennifer Lynch email to author, April 25, 2016, noted that figure and rationale in the *1970 Annual Report of the Postmaster General*, 35; and USPOD, "Postal Strike," 38, USPS Historian.

66. *1970 Annual Report of the Postmaster General*, 104. See also Walsh and Mangum, *Labor Struggle*, 70: they note that 14 percent of strikers were *not* in clerk or carrier crafts. See also 2014 NALC Philadelphia convention interviews for stories of strikers being allowed to clock in and out while picketing by sympathetic supervisors or calling in sick from bars across the street from the post office. (APWU interviewees told me similar stories.) See also USPS, "Time and Attendance," Handbook F-21.

67. See USPOD, Summary Reports for March 23, 1970, midnight; March 24, 1970, 1:00 P.M. and 5:00 P.M., USPS Historian; and Status Report, March 24, 1970, 7:00 A.M., USPS Historian. Most summary reports were signed by Henry Albert, Deputy Executive Assistant to the Postmaster General.

68. See USPOD, Summary Report, March 23, 1970, midnight, USPS Historian.

69. President's Commission on Postal Organization, *Towards Postal Excellence*, 102.

70. See author's interview with Henry.

71. USPOD, Status Report, March 24, 1970, 1:00 P.M., USPS Historian.

72. USPOD, Status Report, March 22, 1970, 2:00 P.M., USPS Historian, notes that 85 percent of New York region's postal workers had struck. Summary Report for 11:00 A.M., March 24, 1970, notes the total number of New York region strikers over the week.

73. Department of the Army, Operation Graphic Hand, *After Action Report*, A-5.

CHAPTER 5

1. Haldeman, *Haldeman Diaries*, 143.

2. Haldeman, *Haldeman Diaries*, 145. See also Nixon Daily Diary for April 2, 1970, NPLM, https://www.nixonlibrary.gov/sites/default/files/virtuallibrary/documents /PDD/1970/025%20April%201-15%201970.pdf.

3. Haldeman, *Haldeman Diaries*, 145, italics added.

4. David Nelson, "Sanctions," March 26, 1970, Box 38, Folder 238, part 4, Ehrlichman Collection, NPLM.

5. White House meeting notes, March 28, 1970, in Ehrlichman Collection, NPLM.

6. "Base Position for Negotiations," n.d., probably John Ehrlichman after March 28, 28, 1970 meeting, in part 3, Ehrlichman Collection, NPLM.

7. Meeting notes, March 30, 1970, in part 3, Ehrlichman Collection, NPLM.

8. Mikusko and Miller, *Carriers in a Common Cause*, 75. See also author's interview with Sombrotto, Orapello, and Marino.

9. Germano, "Labor Relations," 229; Walsh and Mangum, *Labor Struggle*, 30–32; and Mikusko and Miller, *Carriers in a Common Cause*, 76.

10. "Work Stoppage Settlement: Negotiation and Agreement," 1, n.d., probably April 1970, USPS Historian.

11. "Work Stoppage Settlement," 1, USPS Historian.

12. "Work Stoppage Settlement," 2, USPS Historian.

13. Internal memo (n.d., probably late March 1970) from Brian Gillespie to John M. Remissong, Director, Labor Relations Division, Bureau of Personnel, USPS Historian.

14. Blount, "Second Press Conference," USPS Historian. See also Clyde Young, "The Great 'Sellout,'" *National Alliance*, August 1970, 5. See also Halpern, *Unions, Radicals, and Democratic Presidents*, chap. 5. According to Halpern, the AFL-CIO had historically not demonstrated much interest in winning collective bargaining rights for federal workers before the 1970 postal wildcat strike.

15. For George Meany testimony and question from Representative Frank Brasco (D-N.Y.), see U.S. Congress, *Hearings Before the Committee*, April 23, 1970, 98.

16. Germano, "Labor Relations," 233–35, quote on 233.

17. Germano, email to author, July 13, 2016.

18. Germano email to author, July 13, 2016.

19. Author's interview with Holbrook. On the UAW and ALA, see, for example, the Georgia State University finding aids, http://digitalcollections.library.gsu.edu/cdm/ref /collection/findingaids/id/419.

20. See 2014 NALC Philadelphia Convention interviews with author. See also Rubio, *There's Always Work*, chap. 10. I am indebted to NALC Branch 47, Denver, Colorado,

for making available to me interviews collected with five Branch 47 strike veterans (Ray Grizzard, Stan Stefanski, Stanley Kohtz, Vern Evenson, and Virgil McCune) by NALC Branch 47 in Denver, Colorado, a 2012 film *A History of Mile Hi Branch 47*, and five 2011 audio recordings, in possession of author. See also 1976 oral history interviews, APWU collection, TWA. See also Smith's interview with Rademacher.

21. See author's interview with Abbott.

22. See "confidential memo" from Jeb S. Magruder to H. R. Haldeman, March 26, 1970, USPS Historian.

23. See, for example, Rubio, *There's Always Work*, 145, and n85.

24. See 2014 NALC Philadelphia convention interviews with author; Rubio, *There's Always Work*, chap. 10; Germano, "Labor Relations," chap. 5; and Walsh and Mangum, *Labor Struggle*, 70. See also Johnston, *Success While Others Fail*.

25. Author's interview with Evenson.

26. Author's interviews with Benjamin Lopez; and Juan Medina.

27. Author's interview with Alversa.

28. Author's interview with Thompson.

29. Author's interview with Schwarze.

30. Germano, email to author, March 25, 2017.

31. Department of the Army, Operation Graphic Hand, *Postal Work-Stoppage*, 38.

32. Brenner, "Striking Against the State," 17–21, quotation on p. 20. See also author's interviews at 2014 NALC Philadelphia convention.

33. Smith's interview with Rademacher, quote on p. 69 of transcript. Most of the strike and negotiation narratives in the Rademacher interview appear on pp. 39–71. Rademacher in 1971 placed Branch 36 under NALC national union trusteeship. See Walsh and Mangum, *Labor Struggle*, 39.

34. Germano, "Labor Relations," 185.

35. Shultz quote in Brenner, "Striking Against the State," 17. For George Shultz's influence on handling the strike distinctly from Postmaster General Blount's more aggressive approach, see Timothy Naftali interview transcript with Arnold Weber of the Nixon White House, November 15, 2007, 21, http://www.nixonlibrary.gov/virtuallibrary/documents/histories/weber-2007-11-15.pdf. I am grateful to Jason Schultz of the NPLM for this and other sources.

36. The APWU and NALC in fact were able to use the strike threat periodically during some contract negotiations for another decade. Walsh and Mangum, *Labor Struggle*, 126–27, 178–79.

37. Loewenberg, "Postal Strike of 1970," 196.

38. Damon Stetson, "Union Faces Fines: Johnson, Leader Here, is Found Guilty of Contempt," *NYT*, March 25, 1970, 1, *NYT*, photos by Barton Silverman.

39. Germano, "Labor Relations," 234.

40. Germano, *Delivering the Dream*, 15.

41. Germano, "Labor Relations," 282. See also Fleishman, "Postal Policy and Public Accountability," with thanks to Mark Jamison for this source.

42. See monthly issues from May to December 1970 of the NALC's *Postal Record*.

43. John Susleck, "San Francisco, Ca.," *PR*, May 1970, 92.

44. Ted R. Little, "Winston-Salem, N.C.," *PR*, September 1970, 119. Among the Rademacher loyalists was the Fall River, Massachusetts, branch, while nearby Framingham proudly upheld the strike. See *PR*, September 1970, 76. Dubuque, Iowa, also opposed the

strike, as did Toledo and Columbus, Ohio, although Cleveland and Cincinnati supported it. Also writing were many new Latino scribes, mostly in the West, with most supporting the strike. See, for example, John Mendez of San Fernando in *PR*, September 1970, 92; David F. Ortega, "Oakland, Ca.," *PR*, June 1970, 74–75; Jose Baltazar, "Houston, Tex.," in *Postal Record*, June 1970, 69; and Tony Montanez, "Miami, Fla.," *PR*, August 1970, 53, the latter being a conciliatory column.

45. See "Birmingham, Ala.," *PR*, May 1970, 72; and Jose Baltazar, "Houston, Tex.," *PR*, May 1970, 79.

46. See for example author's NALC 2014 interviews; and author's interviews with Holbrook; and Burrus.

47. Case strips are long paper strips with printed addresses, often protected by a clear plastic strip that are inserted below each shelf of a metal route case where carriers sort ("case") their letter mail by address in delivery sequence.

48. See author's NALC 2014 interviews.

49. See, for example, author's NALC 2014 interviews.

50. See, for example, "The Day the Mail Stopped," *Newsweek*, March 30, 1970, 14: "And never in the 195 years of their history had the docile servants of the world's largest mail service raised so much as a pinky in organized protest."

51. USPOD, "Postal Strike—March 1970," 50.

52. See for example Department of the Army, Operation Graphic Hand, *Postal Work-Stoppage* and the *After Action Report*. In the latter, the Army's positive post-strike assessment of their mail distribution prowess is questionable.

53. Cowie, *Stayin' Alive*, 140–41, as part of a broader discussion of Nixon's attempted inroads in organized labor support seen in chap. 3, "Nixon's Class Struggle."

54. See Germano, "Labor Relations," chap. 5. See also Nixon, "Remarks on Signing."

55. Colson, memorandum for Dwight Chapin, August 10, 1970, Box 49, Folder 14, Colson Collection, NPLM.

56. Nixon's initial confrontational stance is reported by Brenner, "Striking Against the State," 15, citing Nixon aide H. R. Haldeman's notes of March 20, 1970. Nixon's White House taping system was not in effect at that time. See also Arnold Weber (Assistant Secretary of Labor for Manpower in 1970) interview with Timothy Naftali, http://www .nixonlibrary.gov/virtuallibrary/documents/histories/weber-2007-11-15.pdf. See also former secretary of labor George P. Shultz's interview with Naftali, on Shultz's unique attitude within the Nixon administration toward labor-management conflict mediation, http://www.nixonlibrary.gov/virtuallibrary/documents/histories/shultz-2007-05-10. pdf. See also author's interview with labor lawyer Jules Bernstein, who was part of the 1970 postal strike negotiations, May 30, 2015, Washington, D.C.

57. Brenner, "Striking Against the State," 17. See also Postmaster General Winton Blount, "Press Conference on Work Stoppage," Washington, D.C., March, 24, 1970, 11, transcript found in USPS Historian.

58. Brenner, "Striking Against the State," 16.

59. "Confidential memo" from Jeb S. Magruder to H. R. Haldeman, March 26, 1970, USPS Historian.

60. See Usery interview with Hough. See also Usery, "The Postal Dispute and Settlement"; and "Postal Labor Relations and Employee Morale," *Hearings Before the Subcommittee on Postal Operations, April 23, 24, 25, May 22, 1969; Serial No. 91–7,* 227–28.

61. Brenner, "Striking Against the State," 17.

62. See "Post Office Contingency Plan for Work Stoppages, July 15, 1968," Box 3, Folder Officers Files — Presidents — Moe Biller — Kingsbridge — Postal Reform, *New York Metro Area Postal Union Collection*, TWA.

63. Brenner, "Striking Against the State," 11.

64. See Cowie, *Stayin' Alive*, 128 for the quotes; for the postal strike, see 140–41. See also chap. 3 for Cowie's explanation of Nixon's direct appeal to workers and unions as policy to remake Roosevelt's New Deal Democratic coalition with Nixon's Republican "New Majority" based on so-called ethnic whites, and split Democrats (and civil-rights groups) from labor.

65. See author's interviews with Morgan; with Thomas and Perry; and NALC 2014 interviews.

66. Gildea, "Labor Looks at the Postal Negotiations," 371.

67. Postal Reorganization Act, *Statutes at Large* 84, chap. 1, section 101a, 719.

68. Brenner, "Striking Against the State," 22. See also Brenner et al., *Rebel Rank and File*.

69. President's Commission on Postal Organization, *Towards Postal Excellence*, 1 (first quote), and 15 (second quote).

70. Germano, "Labor Relations," 228.

71. Author's interview with Bailey, Tilley, Flagler, Wilson, and John.

72. Germano, "Labor Relations," 237.

73. Germano, "Labor Relations," 239.

74. Germano, "Labor Relations," 240.

75. Germano, "Labor Relations," 239–55; and Mikusko and Miller, *Carriers in a Common Cause*, 76.

76. Germano, "Labor Relations," 241–42.

77. Clyde Young, "The Great 'Sellout,'" *National Alliance*, August 1970, 5; and Germano, "Labor Relations," 239–57.

78. Silvergleid testimony, *Hearings Before the Committee on Post Office and Civil Service*, April 27, 1970, 114, italics added. H.R. 17070 also included the first reference to what became the USPS's official designation as "an independent establishment in the Executive branch." See "Comparative Analysis of Postal Reorganization Proposals," *Hearings Before the Committee on Post Office and Civil Service*, 62.

79. Dulski comments in *Hearings Before the Committee on Post Office and Civil Service*, 62.

80. Author's interview with Bernstein, May 30, 2015.

81. See *Hearings Before the Committee on Post Office and Civil Service*, April 27, 1970. McClure's comment appears on p. 140 and Henderson's and Waldie's comments are on pp. 157–60. The Waldie and Smith quotes are from p. 159, Williams on pp. 159–60. On EO 11491, see https://www.archives.gov/federal-register/codification/executive-order/11491 .html. EO 11491 was superseded by the 1978 Civil Service Reform Act, https://www.dol.gov /olms/regs/compliance/rights_resps.htm.

82. Germano, "Labor Relations," 296.

83. USPS historian Jennifer Lynch emails to author, July 23, 2019.

84. Germano, "Labor Relations," 239–57, and 297–99. See also "Comparative Analysis of Postal Reorganization Proposals," *Hearings Before the Committee on Post Office and Civil Service*, 62–82.

85. Baxter, *Labor and Politics*, 91.

86. Baxter, *Labor and Politics*, 92.

87. Loewenberg, "Post Office Strike of 1970," 200. Nixon also agreed under "political

pressure to reduce his request for an increase in first class postal rates from 67 percent to 33 percent."

88. Tierney, *Postal Reorganization*, 21, 22.

89. Tierney, *Postal Reorganization*, 21.

90. Smith's interview with Rademacher, 57–61.

91. Tierney, *Postal Reorganization*, 21.

92. Tierney, *Postal Reorganization*, 21.

93. See Halpern, *Unions, Radicals, and Democratic Presidents*, chap. 5; Young, "Great 'Sellout,'" 5; and Germano, "Labor Relations," 239–57, 269. See also Resolution No. 41, "Commendation of George Meany," brought by Branch 40, *Official Proceedings of the 47th Biennial Convention of the National Association of Letter Carriers, Honolulu, Hawaii, August 16–22, 1970*, 63. Resolution No. 40 on the King holiday was offered by Branches 36 and 40.

94. See Postal Reorganization Act, part 1, chap. 2, sec. 201, 720; Baxter, *Labor and Politics*, 91–93; Shannon, "Work Stoppage in Government"; and Levine, "The U.S. Postal Service," 232–33. See also "Congress Clears Landmark Postal Reorganization Plan," 1970 *CQ Almanac*, 350, USPS Archives. Nixon's aides then went to work selling the plan to Congress and the public. See "Appendix C: White House Plan to Sell New Postal Reorganization Legislation, Presented at 4/18/70 meeting in Herb Klein's office," USPS Historian.

95. Rubio, *There's Always Work*, chap. 11.

96. See *Hearings Before the Committee on Post Office and Civil Service*, April 27, 1970.

97. Ashby Smith testimony, and Representative Waldie and Representative Henderson comments in *Hearings Before the Committee on Post Office and Civil Service*, April 27, 1970.

98. See for example Manhattan-Bronx *News Flash* 1970–71, Box 53, NYMAPU, TWA. See also USPOD, "Postal Strike," 68, USPS Historian.

99. Germano, "Labor Relations," 239, 276–77.

100. Germano, "Labor Relations," 239, 254–59, quote from 257.

101. Baxter, *Labor and Politics*, 89–93; and Germano, "Labor Relations," 257–58.

102. Loewenberg, "Post Office Strike of 1970," 201.

103. Nixon, "Remarks on Signing."

104. I am grateful to Jennifer Lynch for access to the document "United States Postal Service Headquarters Buildings, Washington, D.C.," issued by USPS Historian, July 1, 1991, in email to author August 15, 2013. See also U.S. Postal Service, *United States Postal Service*, 53.

105. Mitchell was convicted in 1975 of perjury, obstruction of justice, and conspiracy; Agnew of tax evasion in 1973. On Mitchell and Agnew, see http://www.washingtonpost .com/wp-srv/onpolitics/watergate/Johnmitchell.html; and http://www.nytimes.com /1996/09/19/us/spiro-t-agnew-point-man-for-nixon-who-resigned-vice-presidency-dies -at-77.html?pagewanted=1. Nixon resigned in 1974 facing certain impeachment charges of obstruction of justice and lying to Congress, and was pardoned by his successor, Gerald Ford (1974–1977). Senators Hubert Humphrey (D-Minn.) and Olin Johnston (D-S.C.), were examples of labor supporters with different agendas on civil rights, for and against, respectively. See Rubio, *There's Always Work*, 137, 153–56.

106. Richard M. Nixon, "Postal Strike Text," March 23, 1970, in *Nixon: The Second Year of His Presidency*, 130-A to 131-A. Quotes are from 131-A.

107. Nixon, "Remarks on Signing." I am indebted to Jennifer Lynch and the USPS

Historian's Office for allowing me to view copies of photographs of that event. See also author's interview with Holbrook.

108. Nixon, "Remarks on Signing"; Smith's interview with Rademacher, quote from p. 65. See also Brenner, "Striking against the State"; Mikusko and Miller, *Carriers in a Common Cause: A History*, 70–76; and Rubio, *There's Always Work*, chap. 10.

109. Nixon, "Remarks on Signing." See also, for example, United States Senate Committee on Homeland Security & Governmental Affairs email press release sent to author, May 9, 2014.

110. Nixon, "Remarks on Signing." See also George Will, "Deliver the Mail to New Hands," *News and Observer*, November 27, 2011, 25A. For Representative Darrell Issa (R-Ca.), then chair of the House Oversight Committee, see Devin Leonard, *Bloomberg Businessweek*, January 3, 2014, https://www.bloomberg.com/news/articles/2014-01-03/darrell-issas-mischievous-postal-reform-bill; John Nichols, "Darrell Issa's Cruelest Cut: A Seriously Cynical Attack on the Postal Service," *The Nation*, January 4, 2014, http://www.thenation.com/blog/177781/darrell-issas-cruelest-cut-seriously-cynical-attack-postal-service#; and Josh Eidelson, "'Cynical and diabolical': Issa Attracts Allies in Quest to Demolish Postal Service," *Salon*, January 31, 2014, https://www.salon.com/2014/01/31/cynical_and_diabolical_issa_attracts_allies_in_quest_to_demolish_postal_service. See also Klein, *Shock Doctrine*, 165, on Nixon's turn away from Milton Friedman's neoliberal economic teachings with 1971 wage/price controls, arguably Nixon's first abandonment of Friedman's "free market" economics philosophy. Friedman argued that postal monopoly could not be justified; see *Capitalism and Freedom*, 29–30. After reading those pages and the rest of the book, one is tempted to call the USPS and PRA—along with wage and price controls—Nixon's experiment with a mixed economy.

111. Mikusko and Miller, *Carriers in a Common Cause*, 78.

112. Germano, "Labor Relations," v.

113. Baxter, *Labor and Politics*, chap. 6, quote on 102.

114. Baxter, *Labor and Politics*, 115.

115. See An Act to Increase, 195–96.

116. Brecher, *Strike!*, 231. Brecher notes that all government employees, including military, were entitled to this one-time 6 percent raise. See also Gildea, "'Labor Looks at the Postal Negotiations," 370: "Five million people got a one-year raise totaling two and a half billion dollars."

117. McCartin, *Collision Course*, chap. 4.

118. See Isaac and Christiansen, "How the Civil Rights Movement," 722–46; Mikusko and Miller, *Carriers in a Common Cause*, 77–133; Walsh and Mangum, *Labor Struggle*; and Goodwyn, *Democratic Promise*.

119. Germano, "Labor Relations," chaps. 5–8.

CHAPTER 6

1. Tierney, *Postal Reorganization*, 92–102; Walsh and Mangum, *Labor Struggle*, chaps. 6–7. See also Baxter, *Labor and Politics*, chaps. 5–7, esp. 131–32; and "Technological Change and Labor Relations," 109. See also Rubio, *There's Always Work*, chap. 11; and Perry, "Let Us Not Forget!"

2. Germano, "Labor Relations," 285–301.

3. Germano, "Labor Relations," 321–22.

4. Walsh and Mangum, *Labor Struggle*, 106.

5. Walsh and Mangum, *Labor Struggle*, 105–7; and Germano, "Labor Relations," 301.

6. See MBPU and Branch 36 strike votes on July 1, 1971, strike vote, see Germano, "Labor Relations," 306–09. See also "Postal Service's Talks with 7 Unions Recess; New York Locals Balk," *Wall Street Journal*, July 2, 1971, 4.

7. Germano, *Delivering the Dream*, 41.

8. Press Release, MBPU *News Flash*, June 30, 1971, emphasis in original, Box 5, NYMAPU.

9. Germano, "Labor Relations," 308.

10. Weather History for KJFK, July 1971, Weather Underground website, https://www .wunderground.com/history/airport/KJFK/1971/7/1/DailyHistory.html?req_city=&req _state=&req_statename=&reqdb.zip=&reqdb.magic=&reqdb.wmo=.

11. Walsh and Mangum, *Labor Struggle*, 105–7. See also APWU website, http://www .apwu.org/apwu-history; and Rubio, *There's Always Work*, xxiii.

12. Walsh and Mangum, *Labor Struggle*, 107.

13. Germano, "Labor Relations," 307–8, quote on 308. See also Conkey, *Postal Precipice*, 143–49.

14. Germano, "Labor Relations," 309.

15. Walsh and Mangum, *Labor Struggle*, 107.

16. Author's telephone interview with Richards.

17. Walsh and Mangum, *Labor Struggle*, chap. 6.

18. Walsh and Mangum, *Labor Struggle*, 98, 102; and Burrus, *My Journey*, 69–72.

19. Germano, "Labor Relations," 305.

20. Germano, "Labor Relations," 306–9. See also "Postal Service's Talks with 7 Unions Recess; New York Locals Balk," *Wall Street Journal*, July 2, 1971, 4.

21. Germano, *Delivering the Dream*, 41–48. Names of officers and trustees supplied by Tom Germano to author by email, January 3, 2017. See also "NALC Puts New York Unit in Trusteeship," *Federal Times*, December 15, 1971, 2.

22. Germano, "Labor Relations," 303–19.

23. Germano, "Labor Relations," 303–19.

24. Germano, *Delivering the Dream*, 48.

25. Germano, "Labor Relations," 325, 334–35; and Mikusko and Miller, *Carriers in a Common Cause*, 81.

26. Dennis Mullin, "Independent Unions Lose Court Battle," *Federal Times*, January 27, 1971, 11. There would even be various merger discussions and proposals going on from 1971 to 1973 that included the NALC, APWU, NAPFE, NRLCA, and the Communications Workers of America. See also Walsh and Mangum, *Labor Struggle*, 100–101; and Bob Williams, "The Post Office Box," *Federal Times*, January 17, 1973, 4.

27. "World's Largest Postal Union Hinges on Rank-and-File Vote," *Union Postal Clerk*, April 1971, 2.

28. Rubio, *There's Always Work*, chap. 11.

29. "Merger Agreement is Signed: Members Will Vote on Adoption of Constitution for New Union," *Progressive*, March 1971, 1. See also "APWU History"; and Walsh and Mangum, *Labor Struggle*. See also Burrus, *My Journey*, 72, for his account of the 1972 first APWU convention with "a cadre of former UFPC officers" trying to sabotage the merger.

30. See Rubio, *There's Always Work*, chap. 11.

31. Walsh and Mangum, *Labor Struggle*, 123, 126, 134, 177–232.

32. See Conkey, *Postal Precipice*, 143–49, quote on 146.

33. See "Equal Employment Opportunity Act of 1972," *National Alliance*, April 1972, 12; Wesley Young, "What Is Our Public Posture?" *National Alliance*, November 1972, 8. See also Rubio, *There's Always Work*, chap. 11.

34. See author's telephone interview with Moore.

35. See author's interview with Bailey, Tilley, Flagler, Wilson, and John.

36. See author's interview with James "Jimmy" Mainor Sr., January 15, 2004, Durham, North Carolina. The author and Mainor were guests on two NPR radio talk shows on the postal financial crisis and black postal worker history on June 22, 2010, on Frank Stasio's WUNC-FM *The State of Things*; and on August 8, 2011 on *Tell Me More*, with guest host Tony Cox, http://www.npr.org/2011/08/18/139748182/theres-always-work-at-the-post -office-maybe-not. Mainor passed away March 4, 2012 at the age of 61. He worked for thirty-nine years at the post office, and was still an active NALC union official when he died.

37. See Conkey, *Postal Precipice*, 163; Zwerling and Silver, "Race and Job Dismissals," 651–60; Baxter, *Labor and Politics*, chap. 7; and author's conversation with Wendy Kelly-Carter, August 11, 2004, NAPFE national convention, Washington, D.C. See also author's interview with Holbrook.

38. See for example Jeff Perry, "Getting White Workers Involved"; H. H. Hubert [Jeff Perry], "An Open Letter to All Mail Handlers Who Oppose Racism and Mob Control of Our Union: The Mail Handler Struggle for Democracy and Autonomy," 1988 draft pamphlet in possession of author; Tom DiPiazza, "Discrimination cited at mail facility, *Dispatch* [Hudson/Bergen Counties, New Jersey], 1, 18. I am indebted to Jeff Perry for these sources and analysis. See also Jack Anderson, "Mob Dominates Organized Labor, U. S. Report Says," *WP*, Oct. 3, 1981, E51; Ed Barnes and Bob Windrem, "Six Ways to Take Over a Union," *Mother Jones*, August 1980, 34–42, 46–47.

39. Jacobs, *Mobsters, Unions, and Feds*, 220–27, quote on 222.

40. Author's interview with Thomas and Perry.

41. Author's interview with Thomas and Perry.

42. Rubio, *There's Always Work*, 277.

43. See, for example, Georgakas and Surkin, *Detroit: I Do Mind Dying*.

44. Robert L. White, "From the President's Office," *National Alliance*, August 1971, 2.

45. Biller interview by Schecter; and Crane Associates (construction company) website, http://www.cranepc.com/media/BMC%20bypass%20exp.pdf.

46. See Walsh and Mangum, *Labor Struggle*, 114–16; Biller interview by Schecter. See also http://hqdainet.army.mil/mpsa/jmpa_atl_final/history08.html. The New York Bulk, in 1981 called New York International & Bulk Mail Center, subsequently changed in 1987 to the New Jersey International and Bulk Mail Center. In 2009 it was renamed the New Jersey Network Distribution Center.

47. Walsh and Mangum, *Labor Struggle*, 114–16.

48. See Germano, "Labor Relations," 332–34; Biller interview by Schecter; and Walsh and Mangum, *Labor Struggle*, 114–16. For a critical view of Biller, see Braun, "Battles of the Bulk," 19.

49. Braun, "Battles of the Bulk," 20. See also a discussion of the Revolutionary Union, which in 1975 became the Revolutionary Communist Party, its formation of the Outlaw caucus after the 1970 strike, and Outlaw's role in shop floor organizing, leafleting,

"packing" union meetings, and newsletter publication (12–13), its role in the 1974 New York Bulk lockout/walkout (6–9, 19–22), and its role in BMC walkouts in 1978 in New Jersey; Richmond, California (San Francisco Bulk); Philadelphia; and Washington, D.C. (6–9, 22–25). See also Germano, "Labor Relations," 332–34, on the 1974 New York Bulk lockout/wildcat. See also author's interview with Thomas and Perry; and telephone conversation with Perry, February 27, 2017. See also Germano, "Labor Relations," 361–63. Leiner was removed in 1979 from both his post and his union membership by APWU President Emmett Andrews after losing his bid to get his job back at New York Bulk after having been fired following the 1978 wildcat strike. On the "new communist movement," see, for example, Elbaum, *Revolution in the Air*.

50. Walsh and Mangum, *Labor Struggle*, 115; and Biller interview by Schecter.

51. Germano, "Labor Relations," 330–31.

52. Germano, "Labor Relations," 330–33; and Biller interview by Schecter.

53. See for example Braun, "Battles of the Bulk." See also Perry, "Let Us Not Forget!"; and author's interview with Thomas and Perry.

54. Germano, "Labor Relations," 353.

55. Walsh and Mangum, *Labor Struggle*, 113. See also author's interview with Thomas and Perry. Jeff Perry later earned his Ph.D. in history at Columbia University and is a leading scholar of black and labor history.

56. See author's interview with Thomas and Perry; and telephone conversation with Perry, February 27, 2017. On union democracy issues in the NPMHU in the 1980s, see Fletcher and Gapasin, *Solidarity Divided*, 54–58.

57. Germano, "Labor Relations," 354.

58. Walsh and Mangum, *Labor Struggle*, 126–33.

59. Germano, "Labor Relations," 354, emphasis in original.

60. Walsh and Mangum, *Labor Struggle*, 127.

61. Walsh and Mangum, *Labor Struggle*, 128–33.

62. Mikusko and Miller, *Carriers in a Common Cause*, 90.

63. Germano, "Labor Relations," 348–62; and Mikusko and Miller, *Carriers in a Common Cause*, 89–90.

64. Walsh and Mangum, *Labor Struggle*, 126–33.

65. Author's telephone interview with Rose; and Germano, "Labor Relations," chaps. 5–8, esp. 337.

66. See websites of NALC and APWU; along with Mikusko and Miller, *Carriers in a Common Cause*; and Walsh and Mangum, *Labor Struggle*. See also Staggenborg, *Social Movements*, chaps. 1–3.

67. Germano, "Labor Relations," 325, 334–35.

68. Germano, "Labor Relations," 348–56.

69. See author's NALC Philadelphia 2014 convention interviews, esp. interview with Rose; and author's telephone interview with Rose.

70. See Walsh and Mangum, *Labor Struggle*, 121–39.

71. Mikusko and Miller, *Carriers in a Common Cause*, 88–90. See also author interviews 2014 NALC national convention, Philadelphia. See also author's interview with Bill Fletcher and Gene Bruskin, May 20, 2010, Washington, D.C.

72. Mikusko and Miller, *Carriers in a Common Cause*, 83–89.

73. Walsh and Mangum, *Labor Struggle*, 121–39, 161; and Germano, "Labor Relations," 372.

74. Walsh and Mangum, *Labor Struggle*, 121–39.

75. See author's interview with Burrus. See also Pranay Gupte, "Postal Employees in Still More Cities Threaten to Strike," *NYT*, July 24, 1978, A1; Gupte, "City Area Postmen Taking Strike Vote," *NYT*, July 25, 1978, B9; Walsh and Mangum, *Labor Struggle*, 114–16; and author's interview with Perry and Thomas. Subsequent contract negotiations were characterized by frequent NALC and APWU strike threats, USPS stonewalling, and ultimately arbitrated settlements. Walsh and Mangum, *Labor Struggle*, 169–246. See also author's telephone conversation with Perry.

76. See Burrus, *My Journey*, 238–41; and author's interview with Richards.

77. See author's interview with Burrus; and author's interview from NALC Philadelphia 2014 convention. See also "Postal Service Workers," Bureau of Labor Statistics, https://www.bls.gov/ooh/office-and-administrative-support/postal-service-workers.htm (28 July 2018).

78. Mikusko and Miller, *Carriers in a Common Cause*, 77–90.

79. U.S. Postal Service, *United States Postal Service*, 42–49, 76. The number of postal employees dropped only slightly below 548,000 from 1971 to 1983, except for 1972, but in 1984 it jumped to almost 673,000, growing every year until 2000, when it began to gradually decline. See also National Academy of Public Administration, *Evaluation of the United States Postal Service*, 72–73; and USPS, "FY 2017 Annual Report to Congress," esp. 11. Thanks also to Steve Hutkins for email comments and sources to author. "Flats" (large envelopes and magazines), once cased separately, by 2015 were being presorted as well in the "Flat Sequencing System." See USPS website at https://ribbs.usps.gov/flat/documents/FSS_FAQs/FSS_FAQs.pdf.

80. Shaw, *Preserving the People's Post Office*, 79. See also chapter 10.

81. Mikusko and Miller, *Carriers in a Common Cause*, 32–33.

82. Mikusko and Miller, *Carriers in a Common Cause*, 85–89, quotes on 85.

83. Walsh and Mangum, *Labor Struggle*, chap. 6.

84. Walsh and Mangum, *Labor Struggle*, 114; and Germano, "Labor Relations," 340.

CHAPTER 7

1. See Walsh and Mangum, *Labor Struggle*, 172–79. See also Burrus, *My Journey*, 162–63; and Germano, "Labor Relations," chap. 7.

2. See for example Cunningham, *American Politics in the Postwar Sunbelt*, chap. 6.

3. Germano, "Labor Relations," 369–99, quote on 373. Germano points out that the NRLCA was an independent union of rural letter carriers and not subject to the AFL-CIO "no-raid" clause, but LIUNA and the NPMHU were AFL-CIO member unions. The APWU's failed drive to organize mail handlers away from LIUNA/NMHPU made any "no-raid" violation moot. See also Walsh and Mangum, *Labor Struggle*, 161–75.

4. Germano, "Labor Relations," 380–99.

5. Germano, "Labor Relations," 388–90.

6. Ernest Holsendolph, "Postal Leaders Continue Talks as Pact Expires," *NYT*, July 21, 1981.

7. Moe Biller quoted at Smithsonian Postal Museum, Twenty-Fifth Anniversary of the 1970 Strike, with video link http://postalmuseumblog.si.edu/2010/03/the-1970-postal-strike.html.

8. See author's NALC Philadelphia 2014 convention interviews.

9. Germano, "Labor Relations," 387–99. The author was a letter carrier in Denver, Colorado, at the time and remembers voting on that contract.

10. Author's interview with Richards.

11. Germano, "Labor Relations," 390–94, quote on 391.

12. McCartin, *Collision Course*; and K. Schalch, "1981 Strike Leaves Legacy for American Workers," National Public Radio, 2006,
http://www.npr.org/templates/story/story.php?storyId=5604656.

13. Germano, "Labor Relations," 392–98.

14. Walsh and Mangum, *Labor Struggle*, 174–75.

15. Walsh and Mangum, *Labor Struggle*, 175.

16. Germano, "Labor Relations," 399–400, 453–54.

17. Mikusko and Miller, *Carriers in a Common Cause*, 118; 1993 Hatch Act Reform.

18. See, for example, Brett Heinz, "The Politics of Privatization: How Neoliberalism Took Over U. S. Politics," United for a Fair Economy, September 6, 2017, http://www .faireconomy.org/the_politics_of_privatization; and Fletcher and Gapasin, *Solidarity Divided*, 45. Neoliberalism refers to the twentieth-century rebirth of the free trade/free market economic theories of liberalism pioneered by late eighteenth-century Scottish economist Adam Smith, not a reference to modern social liberalism.

19. U.S. Postal Service, *United States Postal Service*, 69. E. T. Klassen, appointed in 1972 under Nixon, was the second USPS postmaster general; followed by Benjamin Bailar (1975) under Gerald Ford; William Bolger (1978) under Jimmy Carter; Paul Carlin (1985), Albert Casey (1986), Preston Tisch (1986) and Anthony Frank (1988) under Ronald Reagan; Marvin Runyon (1992) under George H. W. Bush; William J. Henderson (1998) under Bill Clinton; John Potter (2001) under George W. Bush; and Patrick Donahoe (2010) and Megan Brennan (2014) under Barack Obama.

20. Germano, "Labor Relations," 371–89, quote on 389.

21. Mikusko and Miller, *Carriers in a Common Cause*, 97–98.

22. Bill Keller, "Two Postal Unions Keeping Options on U. S. Strike Open," *NYT*, August 20, 1984, https://www.nytimes.com/1984/08/21/us/two-postal-unions-keeping -option-on-us-strike-open.html.

23. Keller, "Two Postal Unions."

24. Holsendolph, "Postal Leaders."

25. NALC News and Updates, 2017, https://www.nalc.org/news/nalc-updates.

26. See "APWU History"; Walsh and Mangum, *Labor Struggle*, chaps. 6–9; and Burrus, *My Journey*, 87–88, 111, 246–49, 314–15.

27. Mikusko and Miller, *Carriers in a Common Cause*; and Germano, "Labor Relations," 337–53.

28. Morris, *Origins of the Civil Rights Movement*, chap. 11.

29. Staggenborg, *Social Movements*, chaps. 1–3.

30. Germano, "Labor Relations," 349.

31. Germano, "Labor Relations," 385.

32. USPS, *The United States Postal Service*, 40.

33. Baxter, *Labor and Politics*, 157.

34. Rubio, *There's Always Work*, chaps. 10–11. Three additional small unions include the National Postal Professional Nurses (NPPN) and the Information Technology/ Accounting Services (IT/AS), both of whom bargain with the APWU, and the

independent Postal Police Officer's Association (PPOA). Email to author from Jennifer Lynch, September 17, 2019.

35. Walsh and Mangum, *Labor Struggle*, 171.

36. Mikusko and Miller, *Carriers in a Common Cause*, 113–14, quote on 114. These automation issues included the USPS disallowance of carriers being able to case DPS (Delivery Point Sequence) automated mail, and the introduction of a new temporary Transitional Employee (TE) category in the 1990s.

37. Burrus, *My Journey*, 218–19.

38. Walsh and Mangum, *Labor Struggle*, 100–101.

39. Mikusko and Miller, *Carriers in a Common Cause*, 115; and Baxter, *Labor and Politics*, 171.

40. Mikusko and Miller, *Carriers in a Common Cause*, 113–16.

41. Burrus, *My Journey*, 297.

42. Mikusko and Miller, *Carriers in a Common Cause*, 131; "Letter Carrier Pay Schedule 2016–2019," https://www.nalc.org/news/research-and-economics/body/2016–2019-Pay-Table-Aug-2017.pdf; and Office of Inspector General, *Non-Career Employee Turnover*, esp. 1, 5, 8, 17. I am indebted to Raquel Johnson-Holley for sending me a copy of this report.

43. Office of Inspector General, *Non-Career Employee Turnover*, 131; and Burrus, *My Journey*, 299. See also APWU website, http://www.apwu.org/issues/postal-support-employees-0; NALC, "Letter Carrier Pay Schedule," https://www.nalc.org/news/research-and-economics/body/paychart0914.pdf; and Postal Employee Salary, Postal Employee Network, http://www.postalemployeenetwork.com/public_html/postal-employee-salary-history.htm. Note that for PTFs hired after January 12, 2013, it would now take fourteen years to catch up and reach top pay with those hired before that day, starting several dollars an hour lower. See also "Letter Carrier Pay Schedule," *PR* (November 2015), 15, https://www.nalc.org/news/the-postal-record/2015/november-2015/document/11–2015_wage.pdf. See also author's interview with Fletcher and Bruskin.

44. U.S. Postal Service, *United States Postal Service*, 41–51. See also Williams, "Automation in the Postal Service"; and Mahmud, "Automation and the Future."

45. Mikusko and Miller, *Carriers in a Common Cause*; and Walsh and Mangum, *Labor Struggle*.

46. Walsh and Mangum, *Labor Struggle*, 209–10. According to the authors, Bolger wanted to make Employee Involvement (EI) the "centerpiece of his labor relations policy" (210).

47. Baxter, *Labor and Politics*, 219–21, quote from 220.

48. Mikusko and Miller, *Carriers in a Common Cause*, 106–9.

49. Mikusko and Miller, *Carriers in a Common Cause*, 91–92; and *Glossary of Postal Terms*, 107, USPS Publication 32, 1997.

50. Mikusko and Miller, *Carriers in a Common Cause*, 100.

51. Ferguson, "United States Postal Service," 142–51, quote on 150.

52. Mikusko and Miller, *Carriers in a Common Cause*, 98–99. See also the Office of Personnel Management website on the Federal Employees Retirement System (FERS) established January 1, 1987, which replaced the CSRS for civilian government employees hired after that date, https://www.opm.gov/retirement-services/fers-information/.

53. Mikusko and Miller, *Carriers in a Common Cause*, 109–13. See also Office of Inspector

General, United States Postal Service, "Mobile Delivery Devices," April 28, 2017 https://www.uspsoig.gov/document/mobile-delivery-device-program.

54. Shaw, *Preserving the People's Post Office*, chap. 9, esp. 124–27 (quote on 126).

55. Mikusko and Miller, *Carriers in a Common Cause*, 118.

56. Walsh and Mangum, *Labor Struggle*, 205–9; and Joel Brinkley, "Reagan Appoints Privatization Unit," *NYT*, September 4, 1987, https://www.nytimes.com/1987/09/04/us/reagan-appoints-privatization-unit.html. See also Report of the President's Commission on Privatization, "Privatization Toward More Effective Government," March 25, 1988, https://pdf.usaid.gov/pdf_docs/PNABB472.pdf; and Hutkins, "How to Privatize the Post Office."

57. Ryan, "Understanding Postal Privatization," 8.

58. Ryan, "Understanding Postal Privatization," 21, 41. McHugh in 2006 was also a PAEA cosponsor. See also H.R. 22 — Postal Reform Act of 1997, https://www.congress.gov/bill/105th-congress/house-bill/22/all-actions?overview=closed (8 September 2019).

59. Ryan, "Understanding Postal Privatization," 92 and chap. 4; and Miller and Mikusko, *Carriers in a Common Cause*, 117–19.

60. Ryan, "Understanding Postal Privatization," 64, 89.

61. Mikusko and Miller, *Carriers in a Common Cause*, 119.

62. Burrus, *My Journey*, 252–60; Robert D. McFadden, "Moe Biller, 87, Labor Chief of Postal Workers, is Dead," *NYT*, September 6, 2003, http://www.nytimes.com/2003/09/06/nyregion/moe-biller-87-labor-chief-of-postal-workers-is-dead.html; and Dennis Hevesi, "Vincent Sombrotto, Who Led Postal Strike, Dies at 89," *NYT*, January 16, 2013, http://www.nytimes.com/2013/01/17/nyregion/vincent-sombrotto-leader-of-1970-postal-strike-dies-at-89.html; and author's interview with Burrus.

63. Mikusko and Miller, *Carriers in a Common Cause*, 97–98, 105–23, and 124–32. See also Stiglitz, *Free Fall*; and USPS, "A Decade of Facts and Figures" http://about.usps.com/who-we-are/postal-facts/decade-of-facts-and-figures.htm.

CHAPTER 8

1. Phillip Herr testimony, http://www.gao.gov/assets/130/124292.pdf.

2. See PAEA, esp. Title VIII, http://www.gpo.gov/fdsys/pkg/BILLS-109hr6407enr/pdf/BILLS-109hr6407enr.pdf. See also Jamison, "By Default or Design"; USPS, "U. S. Postal Service Records Second Quarter Loss of $1.9 Billion," May 9, 2014, http://about.usps.com/news/national-releases/2014/pr14_031.htm, which notes also a $379 million revenue gain, and an inability to pay the September 2014 retiree health benefit prefunding annual installment. See also USPS, "Fiscal Year 2018 Integrated Financial Plan" https://about.usps.com/who-we-are/financials/integrated-financial-plans/fy2018.pdf, 3–5.

3. See the Cato Institute website, for example Tad DeHaven, "Why the USPS Should Be Privatized," July 28, 2011, http://www.cato.org/publications/commentary/why-usps-should-be-privatized. See also American Enterprise Institute (AEI), article published online October 11, 2010, by resident AEI scholar Kevin A. Hassett, "Post Office Shows Where United States Is Headed," http://www.aei.org/article/economics/fiscal-policy/labor/post-office-shows-where-united-states-is-headed/; James L. Gattuso, "Does the Postal Service Have a Future?" http://www.heritage.org/research/reports/2013/10/can-the-postal-service-have-a-future. Leading the Public Service Research Center and its publications *Government Union Review* and *Government Union Critique*. See, for example,

Denholm, "Case Against Public Sector Unionism"; and Savas, "It's Time to Privatize." See also National Right to Work Committee's efforts against public sector unionism. See also William F. Buckley Jr., "On the Right," *National Review*, December 14, 1992, 62–63; Kevin D. Williamson, "USPS, R.I.P.: We Never Needed a Postal Monopoly," *National Review*, March 11, 2013, 36–37. For critiques of privatization forces, see Shaw, *Preserving the People's Post Office*, 20–23. See also James Brebard, "The Last Dinosaur: The U.S. Postal Service," http://www.cato.org/pubs/pas/pa047.html. The Cato Institute has also published book length studies such as: Hudgins, *Mail at the Millennium*; Ferrara, *Free the Mail*; and, on their website, promote Adie, *Monopoly Mail*. See also Steve Hutkins, "Who's Behind the Government Shutdown? Some of the Same People Trying to Privatize the Postal Service," October 6, 2013, http://www.savethepostoffice.com/who%E2%80%99s-behind-government-shutdown-some-same-people-trying-privatize-postal-service. An excellent rebuttal of privatization literature and arguments in the 1980s-1990s can be found in Ryan, "Understanding Postal Privatization."

4. Ryan, "Understanding Postal Privatization," 20.

5. USPS, *United States Postal Service Transformation Plan*, April 2002, https://about.usps.com/strategic-planning/2002transformationplan.pdf, vii-ix, quotes on viii. See also President's Commission on the United States Postal Service, *Embracing the Future*, http://govinfo.library.unt.edu/usps/offices/domestic-finance/usps/pdf/freport.pdf.

6. President's Commission, *Embracing the Future*, xiv; Mikusko and Miller, *Carriers in a Common Cause*, 120.

7. President's Commission, *Embracing the Future*, chap. 6.

8. See USPS, *United States Postal Service Transformation Plan*; President's Commission, *Embracing the Future*; and U.S. Postal Service, *United States Postal Service*, 58. See also Mikusko and Miller, *Carriers in a Common Cause*, 120–23.

9. Hutkins, "How the Postal Service Began Prefunding"; Hutkins, "How Prefunding Retiree Health Benefits."

10. Kosar, "The Postal Accountability and Enhancement Act," https://www.fas.org/sgp/crs/misc/R40983.pdf.

11. See also "Message from President Young: Regarding Testimony by PMG Potter to Congress on Impact of the Economic Crisis on USPS and Possible Cutback of Six-Day Mail Delivery," *NALC Bulletin*, January 30, 2009, No. 09–02.

12. Office of Inspector General, "The Postal Service's Financial Crisis," February 2, 2009, https://www.uspsoig.gov/blog/postal-service%E2%80%99s-financial-crisis.

13. "Call for Help: Postal Chief Says Agency Crashing," *HeraldNet*, March 25, 2009, https://www.heraldnet.com/news/call-for-help-postal-chief-says-agency-crashing/.

14. Randolph Schmid, "Postal Service Will Cut Costs and Offices," *News and Observer*, August 9, 2000, 5A.

15. See, for example, Jeff Spross, "How George Bush Broke the Post Office" in Theweek.com, April 16, 2018, http://theweek.com/articles/767184/how-george-bush-broke-post-office.

16. Mark Jamison, email to author, June 9, 2018. See also Hutkins, "Thumb on the Scale." "Market-dominant products" are those such as first-class mail, standard mail, periodicals, where the USPS faces little competition.

17. Jamison, "Masquerade Continues."

18. Brown, "Congress Ties Postal Service into Knots." Thanks to Steve Hutkins for this reference.

19. Brown, "Congress Ties Postal Service into Knots." See also Office of Inspector General, "Be Careful What You Assume."

20. Mikusko and Miller, *Carriers in a Common Cause* (2006 ed.), 121–27, quote on 126. The narrative here is essentially the same as found in the most recent 2014 edition used in this book, although the content was updated. On p. 127 of the 2014 edition, the authors pointed to how the "fatal flaw in the 2006 reform law became apparent" as both the recession and the USPS financial situation worsened.

21. Mikusko and Miller, *Carriers in a Common Cause* (2006 ed.), 127. This is the last citation in this book using the 2006 edition.

22. Mikusko and Miller, *Carriers in a Common Cause* (2014 ed.), 127.

23. Mikusko and Miller, *Carriers in a Common Cause*, 122.

24. Mikusko and Miller, *Carriers in a Common Cause*, 127.

25. See for example Jamison, "By Default or Design." See also President's Commission, *Embracing the Future*; and USPS, *United States Postal Service Transformation Plan*.

26. See, for example, "Burrus Addresses Letter Carriers Convention," July 24, 2008, http://www.apwu.org/news/web-news-article/burrus-addresses-letter-carriers-convention. See also Steven Greenhouse, "A.F.L.-C.I.O. Endorses Obama," *NYT*, Junes 26, 2008, https://thecaucus.blogs.nytimes.com/2008/06/26/afl-cio-endorses-obama/; and author's interview with Burrus.

27. "Not a Done Deal: NALC vows to oppose 5-day delivery in Obama plan," September 18, 2011, news article on NALC website, https://www.nalc.org/news/nalc-updates/not-a-done-deal-nalc-vows-to-oppose-5-day-delivery-in-obama-plan. See also Hutkins, "Who's Behind the Government Shutdown?"

28. See, for example, this APWU bulletin from August 9, 2009, http://www.apwu.org/news/news-bulletin?field_terms_topics=387&year=2010. See also NALC bulletin from February 2, 2009, http://search.nalc.org/?index=312403&calln=18&lastq=&sortsel=date&opt=ANY&doc0=270&query=crisis; USPS bulletin "Postal Service Ends 2009 with $3.8 Billion Loss," November 16, 2009, http://about.usps.com/news/national-releases/2009/pr09_098.htm.

29. "Postmaster General John E. Potter to Retire," October 25, 2010, http://about.usps.com/news/national-releases/2010/pr10_pm096.htm. Potter retired December 3, 2010, and was replaced by Patrick Donahoe. For a comparison of both postmasters general proposing essentially the same semi-privatizing programs for the USPS, see Hutkins, "Who's Who in the Great Postal Debate."

30. See Fredric Rolando, "Licking the Postal Service's Money Problem," *News and Observer*, July 1, 2011, 13A. See also news article on September 2011 protest called by the NALC to Save America's Postal Service, http://www.postalemployeenetwork.com/sept2011-news.htm.

31. See Leonard, *Neither Snow nor Rain*, 235–36; and Leonard, "The U.S. Postal Service Nears Collapse," *Bloomberg Businessweek*, May 26, 2011, http://www.bloomberg.com/news/articles/2011-05-26/the-u-dot-s-dot-postal-service-nears-collapse. See also Kosar, "Postal Accountability."

32. See Gallagher, *How the Post Office Created America*.

33. See Todisco and Dicken, "U.S. Postal Service Health and Pension." See also Richardson, "U.S. Postal Service's Financial Condition: A Primer." For a rebuttal, see Sheehan, former financial analyst, http://postalnews.com/blog/2015/08/18/what-do-those-four-charts-really-explain/. See also "Postal Service Proposes Breaking Union

Deal to Cut Jobs," August 12, 2011, *News and Observer*, 3A; Jennifer Levitz, "Postal Service Eyes Closing Thousands of Post Offices," *Wall Street Journal*, January 25, 2011, http:// online.wsj.com/news/articles/SB10001424052748704881304576094000352599050; and "Postal Service to cut 35K jobs, close plants," *News and Observer*, February 24, 2012, 5B. See also Jamison, "Betrayal Without Remedy." See also "Committee OKs End to Door-slot Delivery for Millions," on 18–13 vote on a bill that would tell the USPS to cut door-to-door delivery for about 15 million Americans by the House Oversight and Government Reform Committee, chaired by a leading proponent of postal privatization, Representative Darryl Issa (R-Calif.), in *WP*, May 21, 2014, http://www.washingtonpost.com/politics/congress /proposal-would-stop-door-to-door-mail-for-millions/2014/05/21/c2c06c26-e105–11e3 –9442–54189bf1a809_story.html.

34. Leonard, "U.S. Postal Service Nears Collapse."

35. See Jamison, "Disappearing Postal Workforce."

36. See, for example, Brian Naylor, "Post Office Could Rack Up Billions By Offering Money Services," *National Public Radio*, February 7, 2014, http://www.npr.org/2014/02 /07/272652648/post-office-could-rack-up-billions-by-offering-money-services; and Joshua Brustein, "Would the U.S. Postal Service Make a Better Banker for the Poor?," *Bloomberg Businessweek*, February 3, 2014, http://www.businessweek.com/articles/2014 –02–03/would-u-dot-s-dot-post-office-make-a-better-banker-for-the-poor. See also Baradaran, *How the Other Half Banks*, esp. chap. 7; and USPS Postal Facts, 6 August 2019.

37. Carten Cordell, "USPS Reform Is Long Overdue, Stakeholders Say," *Federal Times*, January 21, 2016, http://www.federaltimes.com/story/government/management/agency /2016/01/21/usps-past-need-reform-stakeholders-say/79124844/. See also Postal Regulatory Commission, "Financial Analysis of United States Postal Service Financial Health and 10-K Statement," FY 2015, March 29, 2016, http://www.prc.gov/sites/default /files/reports/FY%202015%20Financial%20Analysis%20Report.pdf.

38. USPS, "A Decade of Facts and Figures." See also USPS, "U.S. Postal Service Reports End of Fiscal Year Results," https://about.usps.com/news/national-releases/2015/pr15 _060.htm; and National Association of Letter Carriers website, "What's in a Name? Controllable Income Is Operating Profit," https://www.nalc.org/news/research-and -economics/economics/whats-in-a-name-controllable-income-is-operating-profit; and USPS, "FY 2018 Integrated Financial Plan," https://about.usps.com/who-we-are /financials/integrated-financial-plans/fy2018.pdf, 3–5; and USPS, "U.S. Postal Service Reports Fiscal Year 2018."

39. Hutkins, "USPS Reviews 5,000 More Post Offices." For more on the POStPlan to cut hours at 13,000 small offices and eliminate their postmasters, see Hutkins, "GAO questions USPS cost savings."

40. See for example APWU, "Our Postal Service is Under Attack," http://www.apwu .org/sites/apwu/files/resource-files/Our%20U.S.%20Postal%20Service%20Is%20Under %20Attack.pdf; and Paul Courson and Jennifer Liberto, "Nearly 3,700 Post Offices Slated to Close," CNN, July 26, 2011, http://money.cnn.com/2011/07/26/news/economy/post _office_closings/.

41. Hutkins, "Emergency Suspensions of Post Offices." See for example the Facebook page of Save Our Roanoke Processing and Distribution Center, https://www.facebook .com/roanokepdc/. The Roanoke, Virginia, facility had originally been slated to close in April 2015 and moved to Greensboro, North Carolina, over two hours away. See also Hutkins, "Post Office Discontinuances and Suspensions."

42. Rubio, *There's Always Work*, 185.

43. Rubio, *There's Always Work*, chap. 7, and postal union women's auxiliaries' support work.

44. Boustan and Margo, "Race, Segregation, and Postal Employment," 1–10.

45. Timothy Williams, "As Public Sector Sheds Jobs, Blacks are Hit Hardest," *NYT*, November 28, 2011, https://www.nytimes.com/2011/11/29/us/as-public-sector-sheds-jobs-black-americans-are-hit-hard.html.

46. See, for example, Mary Wisniewski, "U.S. Post Office Job Cuts Threaten Black Middle Class," *Huffington Post*, January 20, 2013, http://www.huffingtonpost.com/2013/01/20/us-post-office-job-cuts-black-middle-class_n_2514917.html.

47. President's Commission on Postal Organization, *Towards Postal Excellence*, 104.

48. See Walsh and Mangum, *Labor Struggle*, 117–18, and 214–15, including quote on 118. See also Burrus, *My Journey*, 129–30; Mikusko and Miller, *Carriers in a Common Cause*, 64–65; Rubio, *There's Always Work*, esp. chap. 7. On labor feminists, see Cobble, *Other Women's Movement*, chap. 6.

49. Drew DeSilver, "Job Shifts Under Obama: Fewer Government Workers, More Caregivers, Servers, and Temps," Pew Research Center, http://www.pewresearch.org/fact-tank/2015/01/14/job-shifts-under-obama-fewer-government-workers-more-caregivers-servers-and-temps/, italics added.

50. Note the USPS figures are based on full-time "career" positions: https://about.usps.com/who-we-are/postal-history/employees-since-1926.pdf. See also author quoted in Wisniewski, "U.S. Post Office Job Cuts." See also USPS, "Size and Scope," http://about.usps.com/who-we-are/postal-facts/size-scope.htm; and Jamison, "What It's All About."

51. See page 104 of the *1970 Annual Report of the Postmaster General*: there were a total of 739,002 employees as of June 30, 1969, which included 192,821 "substitute employees" alongside 546,181 "regular employees." The following year at the same time (three months after the strike) there were 741,216 employees: 548,572 full-time and 192,644 part-time. See also USPS, *FY 2017 Annual Report to Congress*, esp. 7, 11; "2016 Postal Facts"; USPS, *United States Postal Service*, 70; and USPS, *FY 2018 Annual Report to Congress*, esp. 2–13.

52. Jake Bittle, "In Rural America, the Postal Service is Already Collapsing," *Nation*, May 3, 2018. Rural letter carriers work at an "evaluated pay" or flat rate salary system.

53. See Slater, *Public Workers*. See also Mikusko and Miller, *Carriers in a Common Cause*, 130; email to author from Michael Shea, NALC *Postal Record*, June 4, 2019; and email to author from Ashley See, APWU national office.

54. Shaw, *Preserving the People's Post Office*, 144.

55. For 2019 Gallup Poll results, see Lydia Saad, "Postal Service Still Americans' Favorites Agency," May 13, 2019, https://news.gallup.com/poll/257510/postal-service-americans-favorite-federal-agency.aspx. See also 2014 Gallup Poll results, http://www.gallup.com/poll/179519/americans-rate-postal-service-highest-major-agencies.aspx.

56. For references to labor costs, see, for example, Leonard, *Neither Snow nor Rain*, 143, and for reference to 80 percent of postal volume being business mail in 1963. See also Adie, "Why Marginal Reform of the U. S. Postal Service Won't Succeed," in Ferrara, *Free the Mail*, 83: "The most glaring example of inefficiency may be the level of postal wages. Postal labor costs are approximately 83 percent of total costs." On household-to-household mail, see USPS, "The Household Diary Study: Mail Use and Attitudes in FY 2014," March 2015, Table A1–1, http://www.prc.gov/docs/93/93171/2014%20USPS%20HDS%20Annual%20Report_Final_V3.pdf. See also HDS for FY 2013, http://www.prc.gov/docs/90/90246/USPS_HDS_FY13.pdf; and the HDS study for FY 2007, http://about.usps.com

/studying-americans-mail-use/household-diary/usps-hds-fy07.pdf. See also Shaw, *Preserving the People's Post Office*, 101.

57. Office of Inspector General, "One Small Step for First-Class Mail," December 21, 2015, https://www.uspsoig.gov/blog/one-small-step-first-class-mail; italics added.

58. Mikusko and Miller, *Carriers in a Common Cause*, 131; Hutkins, "Multiplier Effect"; and author's telephone conversations with Germano.

59. Office of Inspector General, "Postal Strike of 1970," June 23, 2016, https://www .uspsoig.gov/blog/postal-strike-1970.

60. Hutkins, "How the Postal Service"; and Hutkins, "USPS Releases May 2015 Financial Statement"; and *Testimony of Fredric V. Rolando*.

61. McCartin, *Collision Course*, 344–51. See also Joe Nocera, "Scott Walker's Wisconsin Audition," *NYT*, June 12, 2015, http://www.nytimes.com/2015/06/13/opinion/joe-nocera -scott-walkers-wisconsin-audition.html?emc=eta1. See also Robert Reich (secretary of labor under President Bill Clinton), "Just in Time Scheduling," SFGate, April 23, 2015, https://www.sfgate.com/opinion/reich/article/Just-in-time-scheduling-means-no-life -for-workers-6219861.php; and Noam Scheiber, "Growth in the 'Gig Economy' Fuels Work Force Anxieties," *NYT*, July 12, 2015, http://www.nytimes.com/2015/07/13/business /rising-economic-insecurity-tied-to-decades-long-trend-in-employment-practices.html ?_r=0.

62. Baxter, *Labor and Politics*, 229.

63. Jamison, "What It's Really All About."

64. "President Trump Criticizes USPS-Amazon Relationship on Twitter," Robert Siegel interview with Devin Leonard, National Public Radio, December 29, 2017, https://www .npr.org/2017/12/29/574693607/president-trump-criticizes-usps-amazon-relationship -on-twitter. See also Julie Creswell, "Amazon Has a Business Proposition for You: Deliver Its Packages," *NYT*, June 29, 2018, https://www.nytimes.com/2018/06/28/technology /amazon-start-up-delivery-services.html; Heather Kelly, "Amazon Is 20,000 Vans Closer to Its Own Fleet," CNN, September 6, 2018, https://money.cnn.com/2018/09/06 /technology/amazon-van-mercedes/index.html; and coverage in Save the Post Office, at savethepostoffice.com.

65. Mikusko and Miller, *Carriers in a Common Cause*, 131.

66. Jake Bittle, "Postal-Service Workers are Shouldering the Burden for Amazon," *Nation*, February 22, 2018, https://www.thenation.com/article/postal-service-workers-are -shouldering-the-burden-for-amazon/.

67. Bittle, "Postal-Service Workers." See also Hutkins, "Trucks on Fire." At 211,000 postal vehicles, this is the largest civilian fleet in the world, and three times as old as other U.S. civilian federal agencies.

68. Mikusko and Miller, *Carriers in a Common Cause*, 131.

69. Hutkins, "'We Deliver for Amazon.'"

70. Mikusko and Miller, *Carriers in a Common Cause*, 131.

71. Jen Kirby, "Is Amazon Really Ripping Off the US Postal Service?," Vox.com, December 29, 2017, https://www.vox.com/2017/12/29/16830128/amazon-trump-twitter -postal-service-feud.

72. Lisa Rein, "Postal Service Backs Down from Five-Day Delivery Plan," *WP*, April 10, 2013, https://www.washingtonpost.com/politics/postal-service-backs-down-from-five -day-delivery-plan/2013/04/10/c2617640-a21c-11e2-82bc-511538ae90a4_story.html?no redirect=on&utm_term=.69023cb70c47.

73. Brian Fung, "Cheap Amazon Shipping Leaves the Postal Service 'Dumber and Poorer,' Trump Says," *WP*, December 29, 2017, https://www.washingtonpost.com/news/the-switch/wp/2017/12/29/trump-calls-for-u-s-postal-service-to-raise-amazons-shipping-rates/?utm_term=.533b9ba4139 f.

74. Damian Paletta and Josh Dawsey, "Trump Personally Pushed Postmaster General to Double Rates on Amazon, Other Firms," *WP*, May 10, 2018, https://www.washingtonpost.com/business/economy/trump-personally-pushed-postmaster-general-to-double-rates-on-amazon-other-firms/2018/05/18/2b6438d2-5931-11e8-858f-12becb4d6067_story.html?utm_term=.5a4c6ac69b7d.

75. Saheli Roy Choudhury, "Trump Orders an Evaluation of the Postal Service Following His Criticism of Amazon," CNBC, April 12, 2018, https://www.cnbc.com/2018/04/12/trump-issues-executive-order-to-reform-usps.html.

76. Choudhury, "Trump Orders an Evaluation of the Postal Service." Much of Trump's attacks on the USPS and Amazon apparently stem from a personal animus toward Amazon's owner Jeff Bezos, who also owns the *Washington Post*, which has often been critical of Trump. See also Wright, "Privatization, the State, and Public Interest."

77. See "Trump's Fixes for Post Office's Deep Losses: Cut Back Saturday Delivery," MSN, May 26, 2017, https://www.msn.com/en-us/money/markets/trumps-fix-for-post-offices-deep-losses-cut-back-saturday-delivery/ar-BBByVAe.

78. See for example Eric Katz, "Trump's Postal Privatization Plan Met with Bipartisan Rebuke in Congress," *Government Executive*, June 26, 2018, https://www.govexec.com/management/2018/06/trumps-postal-privatization-plan-met-bipartisan-rebuke-congress/149306/.

79. "United States Postal Service: A Sustainable Path Forward: Report from the Task Force on the United States Postal System," December 4, 2018, prefunding quote on 63, collective bargaining quote on 60, https://home.treasury.gov/system/files/136/USPS_A_Sustainable_Path_Forward_report_12-04-2018.pdf. Thanks to Nathan Abse for connecting me to this source, and Steve Hutkins for providing some background and context. See also Rachel Siegel, "Treasury Suggests Review of Postal Rates—But Not Just Amazon," *WP*, December 4, 2018, https://www.washingtonpost.com/business/2018/12/04/treasury-suggests-review-postal-rates-not-just-amazon/?utm_term=.e513e2e88bf2.

80. "USPS Posts $610M operating profit in FY '16," *PR*, December 2016, 5, https://www.nalc.org/news/the-postal-record/2016/december-2016/document/2016-12_fy2016.pdf. See also "The United States Postal Service Delivers the Facts," https://about.usps.com/news/delivers-facts/usps-delivers-the-facts.pdf, with thanks to Jennifer Lynch, USPS historian.

81. Shaw, *Preserving the People's Postal Service*, chap. 8, quote on 112–13.

82. Wayne Risher, "FedEx, USPS Extend Air Express Contract through 2024," *Commercial Appeal*, February 23, 2017, https://www.commercialappeal.com/story/money/2017/02/23/fedex-usps-extend-air-express-contract-through-2024/98313700/; and Shaw, *Preserving the People's Post Office*, 132.

83. See for example Hutkins, "How to Privatize the Post Office"; Shaw, *Preserving the People's Post Office*; Gallagher, *How the Post Office Created America*; and Leonard, *Neither Snow nor Rain*.

84. See "In Stinging Rebuke, NLRB Rules USPS-Staples Deal Violated Federal Law," APWU website, November 17, 2016, http://www.apwu.org/news/web-news-article/stinging-rebuke-nlrb-rules-usps-staples-deal-violated-federal-law; and Joe Davidson,

"U.S. Postal Service to Halt Retail Sales at Staples Stores after Union Complaints," *WP*, January 5, 2017, https://www.washingtonpost.com/news/powerpost/wp/2017/01/05/usps-to-halt-retail-sales-at-staples-stores-after-union-complaints/?utm_term=.d26559c8d4 ff. In *Neither Snow nor Rain*, Devin Leonard curiously writes that in early 2014 Staples "canceled its plan for the in-store post offices" because of APWU opposition (248).

85. See "Next in Postal Privatization: Goin' Postal Counters in 2,000 Wal-Marts," October 15, 2014, http://www.savethepostoffice.com/next-postal-privatization-goin-postal-counters-2000-walmarts.

86. See for example Baxter, *Labor and Politics*, chap. 10; Braverman, *Preventing Workplace Violence*; and Neuman and Baron, "Workplace Violence and Workplace Aggression," 391–419.

87. USPS, *FY2018 Annual Report to Congress*, 2–11. See also Rolando, "Licking"; and "Like It or Not, the US Postal Service Isn't Going Away Anytime Soon," *Forbes*, March 20, 2013, http://www.forbes.com/sites/tarunwadhwa/2013/03/20/like-it-or-not-the-us-postal-service-isnt-going-away-anytime-soon/.

88. Grand Alliance to Save our Public Postal Service, "Field Hearings 2016: The Future of the U. S. Postal Service: A Report from a Grand Alliance to Save Our Public Postal Service," Washington, D.C., 2016. Field hearings were held in Baltimore, San Jose, New York, Cleveland, and Greensboro. The author testified in Greensboro.

89. Grand Alliance proclamation, http://www.nalc.org/news/latest/03112014_alliance.html, italics in original. See also the Grand Alliance website, http://agrandalliance.org/. For the 2011 campaign, see the APWU website, http://www.apwu.org/news/nsb/2011/nsb20–110908-sept27rallies.htm.

90. See *Communities and Postal Workers United*, Summer 2018 newsletter, on their website, https://www.cpwunited.com/. See also the winter 2019 newsletter that announced the Rank and File Bargaining Advisory Committee's rejection of the 2018 tentative agreement, sending the contract not to membership by referendum but arbitration. See also https://usmailnotforsale.org, the website of "The U.S. Mail Is Not for Sale" coalition; and "Message Delivered: U.S. Mail Is Not for Sale," *Postal Record*, November 2018, 6–10 (I am indebted to Michael Shea for this background and source). Copies of the *Voice* and the *Postmark* in possession of author. See also nalc.org (NALC) and apwu.org (APWU). For NALC Branch 36, see nylcbr36.org, and for APWU New York Metro, see nymetro.org. I am grateful to Florence Summergrad, New York Metro APWU, for notifying me of the December 2018 passing of veteran strike activist Eleanor Bailey, and providing me with a copy of *Union Mail* 62, no. 2 (February 2019), which published a tribute to Bailey, including a contribution from me.

91. Emails to author from Pat Williams, June 6, 2019. See also author's interview with Bailey, Tilley, Flagler, Wilson, and John; and Rubio, *There's Always Work*.

92. "Economic News Release: Union Members Summary," Bureau of Labor Statistics, United States Department of Labor, https://www.bls.gov/news.release/union2.nro.htm.

93. See Lichtenstein, *State of the Union*; Thomas B. Edsall, "Republicans Sure Love to Hate Unions," *NYT*, November 19, 2014, http://www.nytimes.com/2014/11/19/opinion/republicans-sure-love-to-hate-unions.html?hp&action=click&pgtype=Homepage&module=c-column-top-span-region&region=c-column-top-span-region&WT.nav=c-column-top-span-region&_r=0; and Kay McSpadden, "Teacher Walkouts Could Be Next #MeToo Movement," *News and Observer*, May 4, 2018, 8A. Of the six states that

saw teacher walkouts in 2018, only Colorado is *not* a "right to work" state. See also Adam Liptak, "Supreme Court Delivers a Sharp Blow to Labor Unions," *NYT*, June 27, 2018, https://www.nytimes.com/2018/06/27/us/politics/supreme-court-unions-organized -labor.html. See also Alexia Elejalde-Ruiz, "Workers at the forefront of minimum wage victory press on for union rights," *News and Observer*, February 26, 2019, 5A; and Joel Shannon, "'When We Strike, We Win': Tentative Agreement Reached in Oakland Teacher Strike," *USA Today*, March 1, 2019,

https://www.usatoday.com/story/news/education/2019/03/01/oakland-teacher -strike-tentative-agreement-reached-union-says/3033892002/. On ALEC and SPN, see Mary Bottari, "ALEC's New Union-Busting Toolkit Illustrates the Goal Is to Bankrupt Unions Not Protect Workers," *PR Watch*, January 22, 2019, https://www.prwatch.org /news/2019/01/13438/alecs-new-union-busting-toolkit.

94. See Patrick McGeehan, "T.S.A. Agents Refuse to Work During Shutdown, Raising Fears of Airport Turmoil," *NYT*, January 11, 2019, https://www.nytimes.com/2019/01 /11/nyregion/tsa-shutdown.html?action=click&module=Top%20Stories&pgtype= Homepage; Frederick Kunkle, "Air Traffic Controllers, Pilots and Flight Attendants Rally at Capitol, Urging End to Government Shutdown," *WP*, January 10, 2019, https://www .washingtonpost.com/transportation/2019/01/10/air-traffic-controllers-pilots-flight -attendants-rally-capitol-urging-end-government-shutdown/?utm_term=.7bc171a 5884a; Marissa J. Lang, "'Pay the Workers, Furlough Trump.' Federal Workers Rally at White House for End to Shutdown," *WP*, January 10, 2019, https://www.washingtonpost .com/local/federal-workers-to-demand-end-to-government-shutdown-at-white-house -protest/2019/01/10/330d1c4e-144c-11e9-803c-4ef28312c8b9_story.html?noredirect=on &utm_term=.fdf012bcde58; David Koenig, "TSA Screener Sick-Outs Hit 10 Percent over Holiday Weekend," AP News, January 21, 2019, https://www.apnews.com/ff9ced23db82 44bfb4e23d44cffab217; Jill Colvin, Lisa Mascaro, and Zeke Miller, "Deal Without Wall Money Will Reopen Government," *News and Observer*, January 26, 2019, 1A; Patrick McGeehan, "Short on Controllers, Airports Delay Flights," in *News and Observer*, January 26, 2019, 10A; and Ellie Kaufman and Rene March, "The Government Shutdown Ended After Only 10 Air Traffic Controllers Stayed Home," CNN, February 6, 2019, https://www .cnn.com/2019/02/06/politics/ten-air-traffic-controllers-shutdown/index.html.

95. Hutkins, "How Prefunding Retiree Health Benefits."

96. Josh Hicks and Lisa Rein, "Postmaster General to Retire in February; First Woman Poised to Take the Reins," *WP*, November 14, 2014, http://www.washingtonpost.com /blogs/federal-eye/wp/2014/11/14/postmaster-general-to-retire-in-february-postal -service-to-have-first-female-head/. Donahoe had been a postal clerk who began his career in Pittsburgh and was reportedly once an APWU member. See also "U.S. Postal Service Selects First Female Postmaster General," *Time*, https://time.com/3585604/usps -megan-brennan-mail-patrick-donahoe/.

97. HSGAC Press Release, November 11, 2014, sent to author by email; and "First Female Postmaster."

98. See USPS, "About the Board of Governors." The 2006 PAEA shortened BOG terms from nine years to seven. No more than five members of one political party can serve at one time. See also Alina Selyukh, "As Trump Attacks Amazon–Postal Service Ties, He Fails to Fill Postal Governing Board," *NPR*, April 3, 2018, https://www.npr.org/2018 /04/03/598854059/as-trump-attacks-amazon-postal-service-ties-he-fails-to-fill-postal -governing-bo, 16 July 2019.

99. See USPS, "Top Twelve Things You Should Know About the U.S. Postal Service," https://facts.usps.com/top-facts/. See also Shaw, *Preserving the People's Post Office*, 35–43; and Ryan, "Understanding Postal Privatization," 35–38, on the experiences of other countries with the rise in costs and cuts in service with privatized mail.

100. Mark Jamison email to author, July 1, 2019.

101. Arthur Delaney and Dave Jamieson, "The Postal Service Wants to Make Deep Cuts to Worker Benefits, Internal Plan Shows," *HuffPost.com*, June 18, 2019, https://www .huffpost.com/entry/the-postal-service-wants-to-make-deep-cuts-to-worker-benefits -internal-plan-shows_n_5d092020e4b0e560b70a12d4, 29 July 2019. Thanks to Steve Hutkins for this link.

102. Baxter, *Labor and Politics*, 243.

103. Author's telephone conversations with Germano; and Germano, "Labor Relations," chap. 5. Thanks also to Jennifer Lynch, USPS historian, email December 18, 2018, for USPS statistics from their website.

104. Office of Inspector General, *Non-Career Employee Turnover*, 17. The total of "career" postal employees in 2016 was 508,908. See Historian, United States Postal Service, "Number of Postal Employees Since 1926," https://about.usps.com/who-we-are/postal -history/employees-since-1926.pdf.

105. See for example Kielbowicz, "Postal Enterprise"; Henkin, *Postal Age*; Gallagher, *How the Post Office Created America*; and U.S. Postal Service, *United States Postal Service*.

106. Jamison email to author, July 1, 2019.

107. USPS OIG, "Peeling the Onion," 1.

108. John, *Spreading the News*; and Gallagher, *How the Post Office Created America*.

109. Neoliberalism and conservatism are discrete ideologies, but exponents of both share many philosophical and policy assumptions. See, for example Friedman, *Capitalism and Freedom*; and Will, "Deliver the Mail."

110. See, for example, Johnston, *Success While Others Fail*.

BIBLIOGRAPHY

ARCHIVES

American Postal Workers Union. Tamiment Library and Robert F. Wagner Labor
  Archives, Bobst Library, New York University.
———. Brooklyn National Federation of Post Office Clerks Local 251 Minutes, 1918–
  1977, microfilm, Tamiment/Wagner Archives.
National Association of Letter Carriers. NALC Headquarters, Washington, D.C.; and
  Walter P.
Reuther Library, Wayne State University Archives, Detroit, Michigan.
Philip F. Rubio Papers, 2004–2006, 2009. David M. Rubenstein Rare Book & Manuscript
  Library, Duke University, Durham, North Carolina.
Richard M. Nixon Presidential Library and Museum, Yorba Linda, California.
Smithsonian Institution National Postal Museum, Washington, D.C.
Southern Labor Archives, Georgia State University, Atlanta, Georgia.
USPS Historian, Files of the. United States Postal Service Historian's Office, Archives,
  and Library, Washington, D.C.
Walter P. Reuther Library, Wayne State University, Detroit, Michigan.
Willard Wirtz Labor Library, Department of Labor, Washington, D.C.

GOVERNMENT DOCUMENTS

An Act to Increase the Pay of Federal Employees. Public Law 91–231, April 15, 1970.
Annual Report of the Postmaster General 1945–1949. Washington: USGPO, 1946–1950.
Annual Report of the Postmaster General 1966–1970. Washington: USGPO, 1967–1971.
*A Brief Review of Strikes, Work Stoppages, Demonstrations, and Related Incidents in the
  Federal Service.* U.S. Office of Personnel Management, Office of Labor-Management
  Relations. February 1982.
Bureau of Labor Statistics. "Postal Service Worker." https://www.bls.gov/ooh/office
  -and-administrative-support/postal-service-workers.htm.
Civil Service Reform Act, ch. 27, 22 Stat. 403, also known as the Pendleton Act.
Civil Service Reform Act of 1978, PL 95–454 (S 2640).
Congressional Quarterly
Department of the Army. Operation Graphic Hand, 1970. *After Action Report* and *The
  Postal Work Stoppage, March 17–26, 1970.* http://www.governmentattic.org/2docs
  /Army-AAR_Op-GraphicHand_1970.pdf, and https://www.governmentattic.org
  /2docs/PostalWorkStoppage_GraphicHand_1970.pdf.

Department of Commerce and Labor Bureau of the Census. S. N. D. North, Director. Bulletin 94.

Executive Order 163 (1902)

Executive Order 402 (1906)

Executive Order 1142 (1909)

Executive Order 8802 (1941)

Executive Order 9346 (1943)

Executive Order 9835 (1947)

Executive Order 9980 (1948)

Executive Order 9981 (1948)

Executive Order 10590 (1955)

Executive Order 10926 (1961)

Executive Order 10980 (1961)

Executive Order 10988 (1962)

Executive Order 11126 (1963)

Executive Order 11246 (1965)

Executive Order 11397 (1968)

Executive Order 11491 (1970)

Executive Order 11521 (1970)

Gill, W. V. "The Future of Executive Order 11491." In *Collective Bargaining Today, Proceedings of the Collective Bargaining Forum—1970, a Conference Sponsored by the Institute of Collective Bargaining and Group Relations, May 18–20, 1970, New York City*, 372–78. Washington, D.C.: Bureau of National Affairs, 1971.

Labor Management Relations Act [Taft-Hartley Act], Title 29, Chapter 7, U.S.C. (1947)

Labor-Management Representative Disclosure Act of 1959

National Labor Relations Act (1935)

Nixon, Richard M. *Richard M. Nixon: The Second Year of His Presidency.* Washington, D.C.: Congressional Quarterly, 1971.

———. XXXVII President of the United States: 1969–1974, "Remarks on Signing the Postal Reorganization Act, August 12, 1970," from *The American Presidency Project*, available at http://www.presidency.ucsb.edu/ws/?pid=2623.

Office of Inspector General, United States Postal Service. *Non-Career Employee Turnover, Audit Report, December 20, 2016.* https://www.uspsoig.gov/document/non-career-employee-turnover.

———. "Peeling the Onion: The Real Cost of Mail." April 18, 2016. https://www.uspsoig.gov/document/peeling-onion-real-cost-mail.

Postal Accountability and Enhancement Act (2006)

"Postal Reform Proposal Pits Workers Against Users." In *CQ Almanac 1969*, 25th ed., 789–91. Washington, D.C.: Congressional Quarterly, 1970. http://library.cqpress.com/cqalmanac/cqal69-1246883.

Postal Reorganization Act, *Statutes at Large* 84, 1970.

President's Commission on Postal Organization. *Towards Postal Excellence: The Report of the President's Commission on Postal Organization.* Washington, D.C.: USGPO, 1968. (Also known as the Kappel Commission report.)

President's Commission on the United States Postal Service. *Embracing the Future: Making the Tough Choices to Preserve Universal Mail Service.* Washington, D.C., 2003. https://www.treasury.gov/press-center/press-releases/documents/pcusps_report.pdf.

President's Commission on Privatization, Report of. "Privatization Toward More Effective Government." March 25, 1988. https://pdf.usaid.gov/pdf_docs/PNABB472.pdf.

Statistics of Employees. Executive Civil Service of the United States 1907. Washington, D.C.: GPO, 1908.

Statutes at Large 1, 232, 1792.

Statutes at Large 1, 354, 1794.

Statutes at Large 1, chap. 48, sec. 4, 1802.

Statutes at Large 2, chap. 592, sect. 4, 594, 1810.

Statutes at Large 4, chap. 64, sect. 7, 104, 1825.

Statutes at Large 12, Sec. 71, 701–709, 1863.

Statutes at Large 13, chap. 96, 515, 1865.

Testimony of Fredric V. Rolando, President, National Association of Letter Carriers to a hearing titled "Outside the Box: Reforming and Renewing the Postal Service, Part II — Promoting a 21st century Workforce" by the Senate Committee on Homeland Security and Governmental Affairs, September 26, 2013, http://www.hsgac.senate.gov/hearings/outside-the-box-reforming-and-renewing-the-postal-service-part-ii_-promoting-a-21st-century-workforce.

Todisco, Frank, and John E. Dicken. *Testimony Before the Committee on Homeland Security and Governmental Affairs, U. S. Senate,* "U.S. Postal Service Health and Pension Benefits Proposals Involve Trade-offs," September 26, 2013. https://www.gao.gov/assets/660/658176.pdf.

U.S. Congress. Senate. *Senator Johnston of South Carolina and Senator Humphrey of Minnesota, speaking for the Recognition of Federal Employee Unions, S.473,* 87th Cong., 1st sess., 1961. Washington, D.C.: USGPO, 1961. (Also known as the Rhodes-Johnston bill.)

U.S. Congress. *Hearings Before the Committee on Post Office and Civil Service House of Representatives, Ninety-First Congress, Second Session on H. R. 17070 and similar bills, Bills to Improve and Modernize the Postal Service, to Reorganize the Post Office Department, and for Other Purposes, April 22, 23, and 27, 1970.* Washington, D.C.: USGPO, 1970.

United States Postal Service. "About the Board of Governors." https://about.usps.com/who/leadership/board-governors/, 16 July 2019.

———. *FY 2017 Annual Report to Congress.* http://about.usps.com/who-we-are/financials/annual-reports/fy2017/fy2017.pdf.

———. *FY 2018 Annual Report to Congress.* https://about.usps.com/who-we-are/financials/annual-reports/fy2018.pdf.

———. *Postal Facts.* https://facts.usps.com/ [Regularly updated, last accessed 27 September 2019].

———. "Schemes: Construction, Assignment, Training, and Proficiency." *Handbook M-5* — August 1980, https://apwu.org/sites/apwu/files/resource-files/M-05%20Scheme%20Training%208-80%20(2.77%20MB).pdf.

———. "Time and Attendance." Handbook F-21, August 2009. https://nalc.org/workplace-issues/resources/manuals/F-21-August-2009-Time-and-Attendence.pdf.

———. "United States Postal Service: A Sustainable Path Forward: Report from the Task Force on the United States Postal System." December 4, 2018. https://home.treasury.gov/system/files/136/USPS_A_Sustainable_Path_Forward_report_12-04-2018.pdf.

———. *United States Postal Service Transformation Plan, April 2002.* https://about.usps.com/strategic-planning/transform.htm.

———. "U.S. Postal Service Reports Fiscal Year 2018 Results." *Postal News.* November 14, 2018. https://about.usps.com/news/national-releases/2018/pr18_093.htm.

Usery, William J., Jr., "The Postal Dispute and Settlement As Seen By Government." In *Collective Bargaining Today, Proceedings of the Collective Bargaining Forum—1970, a Conference Sponsored by the Institute of Collective Bargaining and Group Relations, May 18–20, 1970, New York City.* Washington, D.C.: Bureau of National Affairs, Inc., 1971.

NEWSPAPERS, NEWSLETTERS, MAGAZINES, AND NEWS OUTLETS

American Postal Worker (APWU)
AP (Associated Press) News
Arizona Daily Star (Tucson)
Arizona Republic (Phoenix)
Atlanta Constitution
Bloomberg BusinessWeek
Boston Globe
Cable News Network (CNN)
Charlotte Observer
Chicago Tribune
Columbus Dispatch
Commercial Appeal (Memphis, Tenn.)
Communities and Postal Workers United
Courier-Journal (Louisville, Ky.)
Dispatch (New Jersey)
Economist
Federal Times
Federation Digest
Federation News Service
Government Executive
HeraldNet (Everett, Wash.)
Houston Post
Huffington Post (online)
Mail Handler
Mother Jones
MSN (website)
The Nation
National Alliance
National Review
National Rural Letter Carrier
New Orleans Times-Picayune
New York Alliance Leader
New York Daily News

New York Times
News and Observer (Raleigh, N.C.)
Newsday (Long Island, N.Y.)
Newsweek
Orange County Daily Pilot (Calif.)
Orange County Evening News (Calif.)
Orange County Independent (Calif.)
Orange County Register (Calif.)
Oregonian (Portland)
Postal Alliance (later *National Alliance*)
Postal Record
Postmark
Progressive
Progressive Fed
PR Watch (online)
Richmond Times-Dispatch
San Francisco Chronicle
San Francisco Examiner
SFGate (San Francisco, Calif.)
St. Petersburg Independent (Fla.)
Time
Union Courier (Meriden, Conn.)
Union Mail (New York, N.Y.)
Union Postal Clerk
USA Today
Voice of the Golden Gate Letter Carriers Branch 214 (San Francisco, Calif.)
Wall Street Journal
Washington Evening Star
Washington News American
Washington Post
Washington Reports

Braun, Michael. "Battles of the Bulk: The Conflict Between Management, Unions, and Workers of the U.S. Postal Service Bulk Mailing Center, Jersey City, New Jersey (1973–1980)." MA thesis, State University of New York-Empire State College, 2006.

Brenner, Aaron. "Rank-and-File Rebellion, 1966–1975." PhD diss., Columbia University, 1996.

Brodie, Jeffrey L. "A Revolution by Mail: A New Postal System for a New Nation." PhD diss., George Washington University, 2005.

DeLancey, Toni G. "The Challenges of the United States Postal Service in Adapting in the Information Age." PhD diss., Regent University, 2010.

Ferguson, Dale L. "The United States Postal Service: A Case Study of Large Scale Government Transformation." PhD diss., Indiana University of Pennsylvania, 2008.

Germano, Thomas J. "Labor Relations in the United States Postal Service: A Sociological Perspective." PhD diss., City University of New York Graduate Center, 1983.

Harris, Mahmud. "Automation and the Future of the United States Postal Service." MS thesis, California State University–Long Beach, 2000.

Marino, Al. "A Time of Fury: The Postal Strike of 1970." 2001 Research Paper Workshop, Empire State College, May 15, 1982, in author's possession.

Olds, Kelly Barton. "Public Service and Privatization in Antebellum America." PhD diss., University of Rochester, 1993.

Ryan, Sarah F. "Understanding Postal Privatization: Corporations, Unions and 'the Public Interest.'" MA thesis, Rutgers University, 1999.

Williams, Patricia Ann. "Automation in the Postal Service from the Perspective of the Workers." MA thesis, California State University–Dominguez Hills, 1997.

Wright, Michael D. "Privatization, the State, and Public Interest Trade Unionism: A Comparison of Canadian and American Postal Services." JSD diss., Stanford University, 1993.

BOOKS

Adie, Douglas K. *Monopoly Mail: Privatizing the United States Postal Service.* New Brunswick, N.J.: Transaction Books, 1989.

Baarslag, Karl. *History of the National Federation of Post Office Clerks.* Washington, D.C.: National Federation of Post Office Clerks, 1945.

Baradaran, Mehrsa. *How the Other Half Banks: Exclusion, Exploitation, and the Threat to Democracy.* Cambridge, Mass.: Harvard University Press, 2015.

Baxter, Vern K. *Labor and Politics in the U. S. Postal Service.* New York: Plenum, 1994.

Bennett, Lerone, Jr. *The Shaping of Black America.* New York: Penguin, 1993; 1974.

Biondi, Martha. *To Stand and Fight: The Struggle for Civil Rights in Postwar New York City* Cambridge, Mass.: Harvard University Press, 2003.

Braverman, Mark. *Preventing Workplace Violence: A Guide for Employers and Practitioners.* Thousand Oaks, Calif.: Sage Publishers, 1999.

Brecher, Jeremy. *Strike!* 1972. Revised and updated ed., Boston: South End Press, 1997.

Brenner, Aaron, Robert Brenner, and Cal Winslow, eds. *Rebel Rank and File: Labor Militancy and Revolt from Below during the Long 1970s.* London: Verso, 2010.

Burrus, Bill. *My Journey: A Postal and Unique American Experience*. Dallas: Brown Books, 2013.

Cobble, Dorothy Sue. *The Other Women's Movement: Workplace Justice and Social Rights in Modern America*. Princeton, N.J.: Princeton University Press, 2004.

Conkey, Kathleen. *The Postal Precipice: Can the U.S. Postal Service be Saved?* Washington, D.C.: Center for the Study of Responsive Law, 1983.

Cowie, Jefferson. *Stayin' Alive: The 1970s and the Last Days of the Working Class*. New York: New Press, 2010.

Cunningham, Sean P. *American Politics in the Postwar Sunbelt: Conservative Growth in a Battleground Region*. New York: Cambridge University Press, 2014.

Cushing, Marshall. *The Story of Our Post Office: The Greatest Government Department in All Its Phases*. Boston: A.M. Thayer, 1893.

Dearing, Mary R. *Veterans in Politics: The Story of the G.A.R.* Baton Rouge, La., 1952.

Dittmer, John. *Local People: The Struggle for Civil Rights in Mississippi*. Urbana: University of Illinois Press, 1994.

Elbaum, Max. *Revolution in the Air: Sixties Radicals Turn to Lenin, Mao, and Che*. London: Verso, 2002.

Ferrara, Peter J. *Free the Mail: Ending the Postal Monopoly*. Washington, D.C.: Cato Institute, 1990.

Fine, Sidney. *Sit Down: The General Motors Strike of 1936–1937*. Ann Arbor: University of Michigan Press, 1969.

Fink, Leon, and Brian Greenberg. *Upheaval in the Quiet Zone: A History of Hospital Workers' Union, Local 1199*. Urbana: University of Illinois Press, 1989.

Fletcher, Bill, Jr., and Fernando Gapasin. *Solidarity Divided: The Crisis in Organized Labor and a New Path toward Social Justice*. Berkeley: University of California Press, 2008.

Litwack, Leon F. *North of Slavery: The Negro in the Free States, 1790–1860*. Chicago: University of Chicago Press, 1969; 1961.

———. *Trouble in Mind: Black Southerners in the Age of Jim Crow*. New York: Knopf, 1998.

Foner, Philip S., and Ronald L. Lewis, eds. *The Black Worker: A Documentary History from Colonial Times to the Present*, vol. 7, *The Black Worker from the Founding of the CIO to the AFL-CIO Merger, 1936–1955*. Philadelphia: Temple University Press, 1983.

Fox, Stephen R. *The Guardian of Boston: William Monroe Trotter*. New York: Atheneum, 1970.

Franklin, John Hope, and Alfred A. Moss Jr. *From Slavery to Freedom: A History of African Americans*. 1947. 8th ed. Boston: McGraw-Hill, 2000.

Freeman, Joshua B. *Working-Class New York: Life and Labor Since World War II*. New York: New Press, 2000.

Friedman, Milton. *Capitalism and Freedom*. 1962. 40th anniv. ed. Chicago: University of Chicago Press, 2002.

Fuller, Wayne E. *The American Mail: Enlarger of the Common Life*. Chicago: University of Chicago Press, 1975.

Gallagher, Winifred. *How the Post Office Created America*. New York: Penguin Press, 2016.

Gannon, Barbara A. *The Won Cause: Black and White Comradeship in The Grand Army of the Republic*. Chapel Hill: University of North Carolina Press, 2011.

Garcia, Matt. *From the Jaws of Victory: The Triumph and Tragedy of Cesar Chavez and the Farm Worker Movement*. Berkeley: University of California Press, 2012.

Georgakas, Dan, and Marvin Surkin. *Detroit: I Do Mind Dying: A Study in Urban Revolution*. 1975. Updated ed. Cambridge, Mass.: South End Press, 1998.

Glenn, A. L. *History of the National Alliance of Postal Employees 1913–1955*. Washington, D.C.: National Alliance of Postal Employees, 1956.

Goodwyn, Lawrence C. *Democratic Promise: The Populist Moment in America*, 1st ed. New York: Oxford University Press, 1976.

Gottfried, Frances. *The Merit System and Municipal Civil Service: A Fostering of Social Inequality*. New York: Greenwood, 1988.

Gutman, Bill. *Tales from the 1969–1970 New York Knicks*. Champaign, Ill.: Sports Publishing, 2005.

Haldeman, Harry R. *The Haldeman Diaries: Inside the Nixon White House*. New York: G. P. Putnam's, 1994.

Halpern, Martin. *Unions, Radicals, and Democratic Presidents: Seeking Social Change in the Twentieth Century*. Westport, Conn.: Praeger, 2003.

Harris, William H. *The Harder We Run: Black Workers since the Civil War*. New York: Oxford University Press, 1982.

Henkin, David M. *The Postal Age: The Emergence of Modern Communications in Nineteenth-Century America*. Chicago, Ill.: University of Chicago Press, 2006.

Hill, Herbert. *Black Labor and the American Legal System: Race, Work, and the Law*. 1977; Madison: University of Wisconsin Press, 1985.

Honey, Michael Keith. *Black Workers Remember: An Oral History of Segregation, Unionism, and the Freedom Struggle*. Berkeley: University of California Press, 1999.

Hudgins, Edward L., ed. *Mail at the Millennium: Will the Postal Service Go Private?* Washington, D.C.: Cato Institute, 2001.

Jacobs, James B. *Mobsters, Unions, and Feds: The Mafia and the American Labor Movement* New York: New York University Press, 2006.

James, Winston. *Holding Aloft the Banner of Ethiopia: Caribbean Radicalism in Early Twentieth-Century America*. London: Verso, 2000.

John, Richard R. *Spreading the News: The American Postal System from Franklin to Morse*. Cambridge, Mass.: Harvard University Press, 1995.

Johnston, Paul. *Success While Others Fail: Social Movement Unionism and the Public Workplace*. Ithaca, N.Y.: ILR Press, 1994.

Kielbowicz, Richard B. *News in the Mail: The Press, Post Office, and Public Information, 1700–1860s*. New York: Greenwood Press, 1989.

Klein, Naomi. *The Shock Doctrine: The Rise of Disaster Capitalism*. New York: Henry Holt, 2008.

Leonard, Devin. *Neither Snow nor Rain: A History of the United States Postal Service*. New York: Grove Press, 2016.

Lewis, David Levering, ed. *W. E. B. Du Bois: A Reader*. New York: Henry Holt, 1995.

——— . *W. E. B. Du Bois: Biography of a Race 1868–1919*. New York: Henry Holt, 1993.

Lewis, Penny W. *Hard Hats, Hippies, and Hawks: The Vietnam Antiwar Movement*. Ithaca, NY: ILR Press, 2013.

Lichtenstein, Nelson. *State of the Union: A Century of American Labor*. Princeton: Princeton University Press, 2002.

Litwack, Leon F. *North of Slavery: The Negro in the Free States, 1790–1860*. Chicago: University of Chicago Press, 1961.

Logan, Rayford W. *The Betrayal of the Negro: From Rutherford B. Hayes to Woodrow Wilson.* 1954. New enlarged ed. New York: Collier, 1965.

————. *The Negro in American Life and Thought: The Nadir 1877–1901.* New York: Dial, 1954.

Marius, Richard. *A Short Guide to Writing about History.* New York: HarperCollins, 1995.

McCartin, Joseph A. *Collision Course: Ronald Reagan, the Air Traffic Controllers, and the Strike That Changed America.* New York: Oxford University Press, 2011.

McConnell, Stuart. *Glorious Contention: The Grand Army of the Republic, 1865–1900.* Chapel Hill: University of North Carolina Press, 1992.

McGee, Henry W. *The Negro in the Chicago Post Office: Henry W. McGee Autobiography and Dissertation.* Chicago: VolumeOne Press, 1999.

Mikusko, M. Brady, and F. John Miller. *Carriers in a Common Cause: A History of Letter Carriers and the NALC.* Washington, D.C.: National Association of Letter Carriers, 2014.

Miller, Lester F. *The National Rural Letter Carriers' Association: A Centennial Portrait.* Encino, Calif.: Cherbo Publishing, 2003.

Montgomery, David. *Workers' Control in America: Studies in the History of Work, Technology, and Labor Struggles.* Cambridge, UK: Cambridge University Press, 1986; 1979.

Morris, Aldon D. *The Origins of the Civil Rights Movement: Black Communities Organizing for Change.* New York: Free Press, 1986.

Murphy, Marjorie. *Blackboard Unions: The AFT and the NEA, 1900–1980.* Ithaca: Cornell University Press, 1992.

National Academy of Public Administration. *Evaluation of the United States Postal Service.* Washington, D.C.: National Academy of Public Administration, 1982.

National Postal Mail Handlers Union. *We're the Hidden Heroes of the Postal Service.* Washington, D.C.: NPMHU, 1990.

National Urban League. *Negro Membership in American Labor Unions.* New York: Alexander Press, 1930.

Needleman, Ruth. *Black Freedom Fighters in Steel: The Struggle for Democratic Unionism.* Ithaca: Cornell University Press, 2003.

Nelson, Bruce. *Divided We Stand: American Workers and the Struggle for Black Equality.* Princeton: Princeton University Press, 2001.

Ortiz, Paul. *Emancipation Betrayed: The Hidden History of Black Organizing and White Violence in Florida from Reconstruction to the Bloody Election of 1920.* Berkeley: University of California Press, 2005.

Rich, Wesley Everett. *The History of the United States Post Office to the Year 1829.* Cambridge, Mass.: Harvard University Press, 1924.

Roediger, David R. *Working toward Whiteness: How America's Immigrants Became White.* New York: Basic Books, 2005.

Rubio, Philip F. *A History of Affirmative Action, 1619–2000.* Jackson: University Press of Mississippi, 2001.

————. *There's Always Work at the Post Office: African American Postal Workers and the Fight for Jobs, Justice, and Equality.* Chapel Hill: University of North Carolina Press, 2010.

Rudd, Mark. *Underground: My Life with SDS and the Weathermen.* New York: HarperCollins, 2009.

Sale, Kirkpatrick. *SDS.* New York: Vintage Books, 1974.

Schrecker, Ellen. *Many are the Crimes: McCarthyism in America.* Princeton, N.J.: Princeton University Press, 1998.

Shaw, Christopher W. *Preserving the People's Post Office.* Washington, D.C.: Essential Books, 2006.

Slater, Joseph. *Public Workers: Government Employee Unions, the Law, and the State.* Ithaca, N.Y.: ILR Press, 2004.

Spero, Sterling D. *Government as Employer.* Carbondale: Southern Illinois University Press, 1972; 1948.

Spero, Sterling D., and Abram L. Harris. *The Black Worker: The Negro and the Labor Movement.* New York: Atheneum, 1969.

Staggenborg, Suzanne. *Social Movements.* 2nd ed. New York: Oxford University Press, 2016.

Stiglitz, Joseph E. *Free Fall: America, Free Markets, and the Sinking of the World Economy.* New York: W.W. Norton, 2010.

Tennassee, Paul Nehru. *History of the National Alliance of Postal and Federal Employees, 1913–1945: Treat Us Right Not White.* Bloomington, Ind.: iEssentials, 2011.

Tierney, John T. *Postal Reorganization: Managing the Public's Business.* Boston: Auburn House, 1981.

U.S. Postal Service. *The United States Postal Service: An American History, 1775–2006.* Washington, D.C.: USPS, 2006.

Van Riper, Paul P. *History of the United States Civil Service.* Evanston, Ill.: Row, Peterson, and Co., 1958.

Walsh, John, and Garth Mangum. *Labor Struggle in the Post Office: From Selective Lobbying to Collective Bargaining.* Armonk, N.Y.: M.E. Sharpe, 1992.

Windham, Lane. *Knocking on Labor's Door: Union Organizing in the 1970s and the Roots of a New Economic Divide.* Chapel Hill: University of North Carolina Press, 2017.

Yellin, Eric. *Racism in the Nation's Service: Government Workers and the Color Line in Woodrow Wilson's America.* Chapel Hill: University of North Carolina Press, 2013.

Zieger, Robert H., and Gilbert J. Gall. *American Workers, American Unions.* 1986. 3rd ed. Baltimore: Johns Hopkins University Press, 2002.

ARTICLES, PAMPHLETS, BOOKLETS, REPORTS, AND CHAPTERS IN BOOKS

Acemoglu, Daron, Jacob Moscona, and James A. Robinson. "State Capacity and American Technology: Evidence from the 19th Century." National Bureau of Economic Research Working Paper 21932, available at http://www.nber.org/papers/w21932.

"APWU History." American Postal Workers Union. http://www.apwu.org/apwu-history.

Aronowitz, Stanley, and Jeremy Brecher. "Notes on the Postal Strike." *Root and Branch* 1 (1970): 1–5.

Baxter, Vern. "Technological Change and Labor Relations in the United States Postal Service." In *Workers, Managers, and Technological Change: Emerging Patterns of Labor Relations,* edited by Daniel B. Cornfield, 91–110. New York: Plenum, 1987.

Benda, Charles G. "State Organization and Policy Formation: The 1970 Reorganization of the Post Office Department." *Politics and Society* 9, no. 2 (May 1980): 123–51.

Boustan, Leah Platt, and Robert A. Margo. "Race, Segregation, and Postal Employment:

New Evidence on Spatial Mismatch." *Journal of Urban Economics* 65 (2009): 1–10. Revised version of NBER Working Paper 13462.

Boyd, Deanna, and Kendra Chen. "The History and Experience of African Americans in America's Postal Service." Smithsonian National Postal Museum, Washington, D.C. https://postalmuseum.si.edu/AfricanAmericanHistory/index.html.

Brenner, Aaron. "Rank-and-File Teamster Movements in Comparative Perspective." In *Trade Union Politics: American Unions and Economic Change, 1960s-1990s,* edited by Glenn Perusek and Kent Worcester, 110–39. Atlantic Highlands, N.J.: Humanities Press, 1995.

———. "Striking Against the State: The Postal Wildcat of 1970." *Labor's Heritage* 7, no. 4, (Spring 1996): 4–27.

Brown, Kevin C. "Congress Ties Postal Service into Knots." *Remapping Debate,* November 1, 2012. http://www.remappingdebate.org/article/congress-ties-postal -service-knots.

Campbell, James I. "Legislative History of the Postal Accountability and Enhancement Act Public Law 109–435." September 2007. Produced by committee staff of the Postal Regulatory Commission.

Denholm, David. "The Case Against Public Sector Unionism and Collective Bargaining." *Government Union Review* 18, no. 1 (1998): 31–52.

Devins, Neal. "Tempest in an Envelope: Reflections on the Bush White House's Failed Takeover of the U.S. Postal Service" (1994). *Faculty Publications.* Paper 435. Available at http://scholarship.law.wm.edu/facpubs.

Fleishman, Joel C. "Postal Policy and Public Accountability: Is the 1970 Bargain Coming Unglued?" Harvard University Program on Information Resources Policy, 1982.

Frick, Walter. "How the Rise of the Post Office Explains American Innovation." *Harvard Business Review,* February 3, 2016, https://hbr.org/2016/02/how-the-rise-of-the-post -office-explains-american-innovation.

Germano, Thomas J. *Delivering the Dream: The Struggle of America's Letter Carriers 1969– 1974.* New York: Letter Carrier Committee to Elect Vincent R. Sombrotto National President, 1974.

Germano, Thomas, III. "The 1970 Postal Strike: An Artist's Interpretation." *Labor's Heritage* 7, no. 4 (Spring 1996): 18–19.

Gildea, James. "Labor Looks at the Postal Negotiations." In *Collective Bargaining Today, Proceedings of the Collective Bargaining Forum—1970, a Conference Sponsored by the Institute of Collective Bargaining and Group Relations, May 18–20, 1970, New York City.* Washington, D.C.: Bureau of National Affairs, 1971.

Hutkins, Steve. "Emergency Suspensions of Post Offices." February 2, 2016. https://www.savethepostoffice.com/?s=emergency+suspensions+of+post+offices.

———. "GAO Questions USPS Cost Savings." May 3, 2016. https://www.savethepostoffice.com/?s=GAO+questions+USPS+cost+savings.

———. "How Prefunding Retiree Health Benefits Impacts the Postal Service's Bottom Line—and How Brookings Got It Wrong." *Save the Post Office,* October 8, 2015, https:// savethepostoffice.com/how-prefunding-retiree-health-benefits-impacts-postal-services -bottom-line-how-brookings-got-it-wrong/.

———. "How the Postal Service Began Prefunding Retiree Health Care and Fell into a Deep Hole." *Save the Post Office,* http://www.savethepostoffice.com/how-postal-service -began-prefunding-retiree-health-care-and-fell-deep-hole.

———. "How to Privatize the Post Office: Piece by Piece, Step by Step." *Save the Post Office*, June 24, 2018, https://savethepostoffice.com/how-to-privatize-the-post-office-piece-by-piece-step-by-step/.

———. "Post Office Discontinuances and Suspensions: A Decade in Review." *Save the Post Office*, February 26, 2018, https://savethepostoffice.com/post-office-discontinuances-and-suspensions-a-decade-in-review/.

———. "The Multiplier Effect: How Consolidating Mail Processing Plants Hurts the Economy." *Save the Post Office*, January 26, 2015, http://savethepostoffice.com/multiplier-effect-how-consolidating-mail-processing-plants-hurts-economy/.

———. "Thumb on the Scale: OIG Reports on Postal Service Share of CSRS Pension Responsibility." *Save the Post Office*, May 10, 2018, https://savethepostoffice.com/oig-reports-on-postal-service-share-of-csrs-pension-responsibility/.

———. "Trucks on Fire: USPS Long Life Vehicles Outlive Their Lifespan." *Save the Post Office*, January 10, 2016, https://savethepostoffice.com/trucks-fire-usps-long-life-vehicles-outlive-their-lifespan/.

———. "USPS Releases May 2015 Financial Statement." *Save the Post Office*, June 24, 2015, http://www.savethepostoffice.com/usps-releases-may-2015-financial-statement.

———. "USPS Reviews 5,000 More Post Offices." *Save the Post Office*, August 20, 2015, https://www.savethepostoffice.com/usps-reviews-5000-more-post-offices-reduced-hours/.

———. "We Deliver for Amazon." *Save the Post Office*, March 15, 2015. https://www.savethepostoffice.com/?s=we+deliver+for+amazon.

———. "Who's Behind the Government Shutdown? Some of the Same People Trying to Privatize the Postal Service." *Save the Post Office*, October 6, 2013, http://www.savethepostoffice.com/who%E2%80%99s-behind-government-shutdown-some-same-people-trying-privatize-postal-service.

———. "Who's Who in the Great Postal Debate." *Save the Post Office*, June 30, 2011. https://www.savethepostoffice.com/whos-who-great-postal-service-debate/, 26 September 2019.

Isaac, Larry, and Lars Christiansen. "How the Civil Rights Movement Revitalized Labor Militancy." *American Sociological Review* 67, no. 5 (Oct. 2002): 722–746.

Jamison, Mark. "Betrayal Without Remedy: The Unwinding of the Postal Service." *Save the Post Office*, June 17, 2013, https://savethepostoffice.com/betrayal-without-remedy-unwinding-postal-service/.

———. "By Default or Design: The Demise of the Postal Service." *Save the Post Office*, August 3, 2012, http://www.savethepostoffice.com/default-or-design-demise-postal-service.

———. "The Disappearing Postal Workforce: Counting Up the Losses." *Save the Post Office*, January 27, 2014, http://www.savethepostoffice.com/disappearing-postal-workforce-counting-losses.

———. "The Masquerade Continues: Playing Politics with the Postal Service's Unfunded Liabilities." *Save the Post Office*, March 17, 2014, https://savethepostoffice.com/masquerade-continues-playing-politics-postal-services-unfunded-liabilities/.

———. "We Don't Care, We Don't Have To, We're the Postal Service." *Save the Post Office*, May 8, 2014, http://www.savethepostoffice.com/we-dont-care-we-dont-have-to-we-are-postal-service.

―――. "What It's All About: The War on Workers Goes to the Post Office." *Save the Post Office*, August 14, 2013, http://savethepostoffice.com/what-its-all-about-war-workers -goes-post-office/.

Kielbowicz, Richard B. "Postal Enterprise: Postal Innovations with Congressional Constraints, 1789–1970. Prepared for the Postal Rate Commission," May 30, 2000. https://www.prc.gov/sites/default/files/papers/enterprise.pdf.

Kosar, Kevin R. "The Postal Accountability and Enhancement Act: Overview and Issues for Congress." *Congressional Research Service*, December 14, 2009, https://www.fas.org /sgp/crs/misc/R40983.pdf.

Levine, Marvin J. "The U.S. Postal Service: A Labor Relations Hybrid." *Employee Relations Law Journal* 4, no. 2 (1978): 220–40.

Loewenberg, J. Joseph. "The Post Office Strike of 1970." In *Collective Bargaining in Government: Readings and Cases*, edited by J. Joseph Loewenberg and Michael H. Moskow, 192–215. Englewood Cliffs, N.J.: Prentice-Hall, 1972.

McCartin, Joseph A. "'A Wagner Act for Public Employees': Labor's Deferred Dream and the Rise of Conservatism, 1970–1976." *Journal of American History* 95, no. 1 (June 2008): 123–48.

McConnell, Stuart. *Glorious Contention: The Grand Army of the Republic, 1865–1900*. Chapel Hill: University of North Carolina Press, 1992.

Meier, August, and Elliott Rudwick. "The Rise of Segregation in the Federal Bureaucracy, 1900–1930." *Phylon* 28, no. 2 (2nd quarter, 1967): 178–84.

Murphy, Marjorie. "Militancy in Many Forms: Teachers' Strikes and Urban Insurrection, 1967–74." In Brenner et al., *Rebel Rank and File*, 229–50.

Neuman, Joel H., and Robert A. Baron. "Workplace Violence and Workplace Aggression: Evidence Concerning Specific Forms, Potential Causes, and Preferred Targets." *Journal of Management* 24, no. 3 (1998): 391–419.

Office of the Historian, U.S. Postal Service. "African-American Postal Workers in the 20th Century," https://about.usps.com/who-we-are/postal-history/african-american -workers-20thc.htm.

Office of the Inspector General, United States Postal Service. "Be Careful What You Assume." February 15, 2016, https://www.uspsoig.gov/blog/be-careful-what-you -assume.

Perry, Jeff. "Getting White Workers Involved." In *A Troublemaker's Handbook 2: How to Fight Back Where You Work—and Win!*, edited by Jane Slaughter, 170–72. 1991; Detroit: Labor Notes, 2005.

―――. "Let Us Not Forget! Postal Workers Wildcat Strike of 1978," July 21, 2014, http:// www.jeffreybperry.net/blog.htm?post=964257.

Richardson, Daniel J. "The U.S. Postal Service's Financial Condition: A Primer." Originally written by Kevin R. Kosar. *Congressional Research Service*, September 22, 2014, https:// www.fas.org/sgp/crs/misc/R43162.pdf.

Rubio, Philip F. "After the Storm: Postal Politics and Labor Relations Following the 1970 U.S. Postal Wildcat Strike, 1970–1981." *Employee Responsibilities and Rights* 30, no. 1 (March 2018): 65–80.

―――. "Organizing a Wildcat: The United States Postal Strike of 1970." *Labor History* 57, no. 6 (Oct. 2016): 565–87.

Savas, E. S. "It's Time to Privatize." *Government Union Review* 14, no. 1 (Winter 1993): 37–52.

Shannon, Stephen. "Work Stoppage in Government: the postal strike of 1970." *Monthly Labor Review* 101, no. 7 (July 1978): 14–22.

Tennassee, Paul Nehru. "Perspectives on African American History: 12th and 13th Compromise, Part V." *Guyana Journal* (October 2000): 34–40.

Weiss, Nancy J. "The Negro and the New Freedom: Fighting Wilsonian Segregation." *Political Science Quarterly* 84, no. 1 (March 1969): 63–67.

Windham, Lane. "Author's Response." *Labor: Studies in Working-Class History* 15, no. 3 (Sept. 2018): 102.

Winslow, Cal. "Overview: The Rebellion from Below, 1965–81." In Brenner et al., *Rebel Rank and File*, 1–36.

Wolgemuth, Kathleen L. "Woodrow Wilson and Federal Segregation." *Journal of Negro History* 44, no. 2 (April 1959): 158–73.

Zwerling, Craig, and Hilary Silver. "Race and Job Dismissals in a Federal Bureaucracy." *American Sociological Review* 57, no. 5 (October 1992): 651–60.

VIDEOS AND DVDS

APWU Communications Department. *The Strike That Couldn't Happen: The Great Postal Strike of 1970*. 1994. http://apwumembers.apwu.org/about/history-strikevideo.htm.

A History of Mile Hi Branch 47. 2012 video copy in possession of author.

National Association of Letter Carriers. *The Strike at 40: Celebrating the Letter Carriers Who Shaped the Future* and *125 Years of Delivering for America*. NALC DVD, 2014, dir. Ann D. Sutherland.

ORAL HISTORIES

Author Interviews at *Philip F. Rubio Papers, 2004–2006, 2009,* Rubenstein Rare Books, Manuscripts, and Special Collections, Duke University Library, Durham, N.C.

Abbott, Countee. August 12, 2004, Washington, D.C.

Armstrong, Sam. August 11, 2004, Washington, D.C.

Bailey, Eleanor. October 14, 2004, New York City.

Bruskin, Gene. May 20, 2010, Washington, D.C.

Burrus, William, Jr. January 16, 2009, Washington, D.C.

Flagler, Joann. October 14, 2004, New York City.

Fletcher, Bill, Jr. May 20, 2010, Washington, D.C.

Henry, Joseph. August 15, 2005, Washington, D.C.

Holbrook, Douglas. August 16, 2005, Washington, D.C.

John, Frederick. October 14, 2004, New York City.

Lovett, Samuel. August 11, 2004, Washington, D.C.

Mainor, James "Jimmy," Sr. January 15, 2004, Durham, N.C.

Marino, Al. October 15, 2004, New York City.

Moore, Raydell. By telephone, January 13, 2006, from Pahrump, Nev.

Morgan, Cleveland. July 18, 2005, New York City.

Morris, James. August 11, 2004, Washington, D.C.

Orapello, Frank. October 15, 2004, New York City.

Perry, Jeff. July 18, 2005, New York City.
Smith, George Booth. August 27, 2004, Durham, N.C.
Sombrotto, Vincent. October 15, 2004, New York City.
Thomas, Richard. July 18, 2005, New York City.
Tilley, Carlton. October 14, 2004, New York City.
Wilson, Gregory. October 14, 2004, New York City.

Oral History Interviews by Author to Be Deposited at
Duke University after Publication of This Book

Part I: NALC National Convention Oral Histories, Philadelphia, Pa., July 22, 2014

Alversa, John P.
Askew, Roger
Attea, Frank J.
Barnett, Thomas J.
Brandt, Howard, Jr.
Booker, Cornell
Breslin, Michael
Burr, Willie
Burt, Stephen W.
Davenport, James
DeSorbo, Joseph C., Sr.
Enz, Robert R.
Evenson, Vernon H.

Kelly, Edward
Lopez, Benjamin D., Sr.
Martone, Anthony
Medina, Juan
Murphy, Robert
Palmer, Booker T.
Roach, Stanley
Rose, Matty
Rubly, Kathleen
Sauer, James C.
Shaw, Fred
Williams, Willie L.

Part II: NALC National Convention Oral Histories, Philadelphia, Pa., July 24, 2014

Bean, William, Jr.
Boone, Laurence S.
Bush, Michael
Chester, Jeffrey C.
Connors, Carol
Connors, Robert
Craven, Verle G.
Cross, Mildred
Daniels, Paul
Ferranto, Alan
Griggs, Raymond
Hanlon, Joseph A.
Herrera, Steve G.
Kirby, James M.
Litka, Terrence L., Sr.

McGowan, Joseph A.
Miller, Samuel W.
Newsome, Juanita
Padulo, Wally
Poole, Tom
Reilly, James
Roth, William
Sanford, Pearline
Schwarze, Richard
Thompson, Leroy
Weiner, Barry
Wessinger, William A.
White, Wayne E.
Wilson, Alfonzo T.
Windham, Charles, Jr.

Other Interviews by Author (in Possession of Author from Telephone Recordings, Emails, or Letters)

Bell, Greg. September 2, 2016.

Bernstein, Jules. May 30, 2015, and July 20, 2016.

Chapellie, Joe. August 6, 2016.

Curtan, Martin. April 17, 2015.

Gallardo, Hector. February 18, 2016.

Germano, Thomas J. 2014–2019.

Harriman, Sidney, Jr. April 9, 2015.

Idoyaga, Thomas. March 19, 2015.

Illicette, Matthew. April 7, 2015.

Jensen, Carl. September 3, 2016.

Kenney, Walter, Sr. January 24, 2009.

Lindstrom, Alice. March 10, 2019.

Malone, James W. July 29, 2016.

Mariposa, Ann. August 27, 2016.

McDonald, Dave. April 14, 2015.

Mendrick, Paul. March 27, 2019.

Nowark, Ron. August 3, 2016.

Parrotta, Anthony. April 13, 2015.

Phelan, John. March 25, 2015.

Richards, John P. July 5, 2017.

Robinson, Joyce. July 1, 2005.

Rodriguez, Jaime. May 15, 2015, and February 18, 2016.

Rollen, Sidney. March 17, 2019.

Rose, Matty. January 11, 2016.

Ross, Murray. March 31, 2015.

Salamone, Ernest. April 1, 2015.

Schindeldecker, Mark. January 13, 2016.

Smith, Raymond. August 2, 2016.

Trenga, Joe. March 25, 2015.

Turner, Lowell. August 26, 2017.

Williams, Patricia. June 6, 2019.

Oral Histories by Other Authors

Biller, Morris "Moe," Elsie Resnick, Milt Rosner, and Philip Seligman. Interviewed by Dana Schecter and Milt Rosner, July 7, 15, 21, and September 21, 1976, at Tamiment/Wagner Archives, New York University.

Rademacher, James. Interviewed by Mike Smith, Roanoke, Virginia, November 16, 2009, transcript at NALC Collection, Walter P. Reuther Library, Wayne State University Archives.

Usery, William, Jr. Interviewed by Leslie S. Hough, March 16, 1990, at Southern Labor Archives, Georgia State University, http://research.library.gsu.edu/c.php?g=115649&p=753011.

Weber, Arnold. Interviewed by Timothy Naftali, November 15, 2007, at Nixon Presidential Library and Museum, http://www.nixonlibrary.gov/virtuallibrary/documents/histories/weber-2007-11-15.pdf.

INDEX

Morris Heights Station (Bronx), 63
Murphy, Bob, 71
Murphy, George, 74
Murphy, Marjorie, 7
Murray Hill Station (Manhattan), 60

Nashville, Tenn., 93
National Alliance (1966–), 31. See also *Postal Alliance* (1914–1965)
National Alliance of Postal and Federal Employees (NAPFE, 1965–), 25, 27, 31, 39, 42, 44, 58, 60, 72, 111, 120–24, 135, 137–40, 142, 147, 149, 153–55, 157
National Alliance of Postal Employees (NAPE, 1913–1965), 18–20, 26–31, 44
National Association for the Advancement of Colored People (NAACP, 1909), 19–20, 203
National Association of Government Employees (NAGE), 145
National Association of Letter Carriers (NALC, 1889–), 1–2, 5–7, 9, 15–16, 18–20, 23, 25–26, 28–30, 34–35, 37–46, 48–55, 58, 60–64, 66–73, 75–76, 78–84, 86–95, 102, 104–6, 110, 112–13, 117, 120–21, 125–30, 132, 135, 137, 139, 142–43, 146–52, 154–55, 159–65, 168–87, 189–90, 195–97, 199, 202–4, 209, 212
National Association of Post Office and General Services Maintenance Employees (NAPOGSME, 1947–1971), 150, 153
National Association of Post Office Clerks (NAPOC, 1884), 18
National Association of Special Delivery Messengers (NASDM, 1937 AFL charter; merged with APWU, 1971), 150, 153
National Democratic Fair Play Association, 22
National Education Association (NEA), 202
National Federation of Federal Employees (NFFE), 145
National Federation of Post Office Clerks (NFPOC, 1906–1961; merged into UFPC, 1961; merged into APWU, 1971), 18, 20, 23–24, 27, 30, 37

National Grange, 18
National Guard, 89, 97–98, 100–104, 212
National Labor Union, 17
National Postal Clerks Union (NPCU, 1959–1960; changed name to National Postal Union), 24. *See also* National Postal Union
National Postal Mail Handlers Union (NPMHU, 1912–), 6, 73, 147, 151, 154–56, 160–61, 164, 170, 173, 175, 180, 202–3
National Postal Transport Association (NPTA; merged into UFPC, 1961), 18, 27–28. *See also* Railway Mail Association
National Postal Union (NPU, 1959–1971), 24, 30, 35, 37, 39–40, 42, 45, 48, 52, 60, 63, 71–73, 77, 80, 90, 92, 95, 103, 106–7, 111, 114, 116, 120–24, 130, 135, 137–39, 142, 147, 149–55, 165, 177
National Rank and File Movement, 152–53, 174
National Right to Work Committee, 140. *See also* "right to work" laws
National Rural Letter Carriers Association (NRLCA, 1903–), 6, 21, 27–28, 39, 60, 123, 139, 142, 147, 151, 170, 173, 175, 196, 202
Nelson, David, 46, 120
Network Distribution Centers (NDCs, formerly BMCs), 156
Newark, N.J., 157, 159–60
New Bedford, Mass., 15
New Deal, 8, 33
New Orleans, La., 15, 93, 194
News and Observer (Raleigh, N.C.), 188
Newsweek, 108–9
New York, N.Y., 7, 11, 14–15, 18, 23–24, 26, 29, 37, 39, 41–47, 50, 155–62, 165, 169, 171, 175, 178, 191, 194, 196, 203–4, 209; role in the 1970 strike, 1–2, 4, 9, 52, 54–69, 71–74, 77, 79–82, 84–90, 94, 96–109, 111–18, 121–23, 126–29, 131, 133–35, 137–38, 142–43, 147, 149–50, 152, 211–13
New York Bulk and Foreign Mail Center (now known as New Jersey Network Distribution Center), 147, 157–62
New York Daily News, 60, 103, 212
New York Letter Carriers Branch 36 (NALC), 1, 7, 15, 29–30, 37, 39–48, 51–58,

Wagner Act (National Labor Relations Act, 1935), 8
Waldie, Jerome, 138–39
Wall Street Journal, 48
Wal-Mart, 202
Walsh, John, 6, 68, 148, 157, 173
Wanamaker, John, 21
Washington, D.C., 22, 30, 39, 43, 52, 62, 71, 76–77, 87, 91, 93–94, 111, 113, 116–17, 124, 127, 138, 143, 147, 149, 153, 160–61, 170–71, 178, 194, 203, 205
Washington Post, 48, 206
Washington Star, 63
Watson, Marvin, 36
Weiner, Barry, 62, 81, 100
Whipple, Lawrence, 159
White, Robert, 154, 157
White, Wayne, 76
Williams, Patricia, 203

Williams, Timothy, 194
Williams, Wyatt, 139
Williamson, Jeffrey, 188
Wilson, Woodrow, 22
Windham, Charles, Jr., 92–93
Windham, Lane, 7
Winslow, Cal, 4
Winston-Salem, N.C., 93, 129
women's auxiliaries, 258n43
Worcester, Mass., 90
World War I, 22, 194
World War II, 4, 20, 37, 44, 57, 61, 73, 100

Young, Jack, 19
Young, William, 186–87, 189

Zeredy, Debbie, 203
Ziegler, Ronald, 98–99
Zych, Henry S., 72, 84